THE GUINNESS
CHRONICLE
OF THE
20th Century
in
Quotations

THE GUINNESS
CHRONICLE
OF THE

20th Century
in
Quotations

**DAVID
MILSTED**

For Sheila,
with love and faith reciprocated

Editor: Anne Marshall
Design: Vox Inc, Steeple Ashton, Wiltshire

First published in 1996 by Guinness Publishing Ltd
Reprint 10 9 8 7 6 5 4 3 2 1 0

Printed and bound in Great Britain by The Bath Press

A catalogue record for this book is available from the British Library
ISBN 0-85112-606-5

Cover Design; Ad Vantage, London
Front cover illustrations (*clockwise from left*): Indira Gandhi (Popperfoto), Neil Armstrong (NASA),
Franklin D. Roosevelt (Hulton Deutsch), Bob Dylan (Eatwell/Hulton Deutsch)

The Author
David Milsted was born in 1954 in Balcombe, Sussex and was educated at Haywards Heath
Grammar School and the University of Newcastle upon Tyne. After a period as the Liberal parliamentary candidate for Carlisle he moved to the Orkney Islands, where he taught at Stromness
Academy before becoming a full-time writer (and part-time postman) in the Isle of Islay; he subsequently lived in Skye before moving back to England in 1993. His novels include *Market Forces*
(1989) and *Telling Stories* (1992) and he has also contributed to the *Bluffer's Guide* series with
Weather Forecasting, World Affairs, Whisky, and *The Green Bluffer's Guide.* Following the death of
his wife, the writer Jan Holt, he completed the manuscript of her novel, *Web of Innocence,* which
was published under her name by Warner paperbacks in 1995. His latest book for Guinness
Publishing is *They Got it Wrong: The Guinness Dictionary of Regrettable Quotations,* also published
in 1995. He lives in Dorset with his four sons.

Contents

How to Use this Book

The basic organization of the book is chronological, in decades from 1900–1996, but within this format there are exceptions. The First and Second World Wars are each accorded a separate chapter, as are the years, up to the end of that decade, that followed each conflict. Within each chapter, significant individual events or topics –such as the Falklands War of 1982 – are accorded separate 'boxed sections'. At several points within the main body of the text, certain sequences of events – such as the Abdication Crisis of 1936, and the British General Election of 1945 – are followed through, with linked quotations and commentary, from the point at which they arise to their conclusion. Although this has the effect of slightly disrupting the basic chronological plan (since the quotation that follows such a sequence is frequently dated a little earlier) it is thought preferable to the splitting-up of narrative that naturally exists as a coherent whole. A glance at the examples cited above should be enough to familiarize the reader with the consistent pattern of the book.

The Guinness Chronicle of the 20th Century in Quotations is essentially a narrative of events as they unfold, told in the context of the words of the people who were involved in them. While the quotations themselves form the framework of the book, it is first and foremost a *chronicle*, and not just another dictionary of quotations with unusually long footnotes; it is this that makes it unique and, I hope, usefully entertaining and informative. The inclusion of songs, slogans, catchphrases, lines from films and plays, extracts from radio and television shows, and quotations from novels and poems will help to evoke and enhance the flavour of the times.

As the book's 'only begetter' I have had the power to select, discard, arrange and comment as I have seen fit; with that comes full responsibility for all sins of commission and omission, and for any contentious personal observations – as well, of course, as for anything that is incorrect. As a chronicler born a small way into the second half of the century, I have begun to see the strange wisdom of an utterance, hitherto received in derision, of Vice-President T. Danforth Quayle: 'We all lived in this century; I didn't live in this century, but in this century's history.' In my case, however, the buck stops with me.

David Milsted
July 1996

An Era Suspended
1900-1914

Our civilization is still in the middle stage; scarcely beast, in that
it is no longer wholly guided by instinct; scarcely human,
in that it is not yet wholly guided by reason

~ *Theodore Dreiser*, Sister Carrie, *1900*

Viewed at this perspective, the early years of the century seem to be characterized by a sort of golden inertia, like a long sunny afternoon in late summer. New centuries, still less new decades, do not bring change with them as a matter of course, and there is no inherent reason for things to become suddenly and greatly different simply because two or three digits have altered on the calendar, yet there is a feeling that this ought to be so. It is as if a symbolic opportunity has presented itself to improve the way we live, and there was a feeling in 1900 – as there certainly will be in 2000 – that things ought, somehow, to be changed for the better; and, just as certainly, there was and will be a resistance to change.

In Britain, the turn of the century saw the birth of the Labour Party and its rapid growth towards significant parliamentary representation, while a reinvented Liberal Party in government set about the implementation of social and economic reforms against stubborn resistance. In Tsarist Russia, an essentially feudal polity tried to suppress and abolish an increasingly militant reform movement whose grievances and demands it simply could not comprehend; in China, a decaying empire teetered on the brink of collapse in the face of a modernist movement for democracy. In the US, Theodore Roosevelt lost patience with his own Republican colleagues and formed the Progressive Party, while Eugene Debs gained nearly a million votes for his Socialist Party in the 1912 presidential election, which was won by the self-proclaimed 'progressive', Woodrow Wilson. No sooner had reformists triumphed over conservatives than they themselves were assailed by self-styled Modernists.

Germany, however, was a different matter. Recently unified under Bismarck, the new nation had typically 'nineteenth-century' ambitions for expansion and empire, and it pursued them with a vigour and determination for which the older states of Europe were unprepared. While the first 14 years of the century saw the development of the social and ideological concerns that were significantly to shape events in the century to come, they were not the cause of its first cataclysm. The shattering of Europe, and its most catastrophic loss of life since the medieval Black Death, was brought about by 20th-century warfare: but it was an essentially 19th-century war.

1900

It has come. Poor little child of danger, nursling of the storm. May it be blessed.
James Keir Hardie hails the birth of the Labour Representation Committee, 2 February 1900. Formed to establish 'a distinct Labour Group in Parliament', its first organizing secretary was the future Prime Minister James Ramsay MacDonald.

Thank God for news you have telegraphed to me. Congratulate you and all under you with all my heart. VRI.
A telegram from Queen Victoria for General Sir Redvers Buller after the relief of the British garrison at Ladysmith, South Africa, 28 February 1900.

Though cowards flinch and traitors sneer,
We'll keep the Red Flag flying here.
Until recently, the British Labour Party's conference anthem: The Red Flag, *attributed to James Connell, 1900.*

1901

We shall not pretend that there is nothing in his long career which those who respect and admire him would wish otherwise.
The Times marks the accession of the 59-year-old Prince of Wales as Edward VII in a leader of 23 January 1901. The new monarch had made no particular secret of his fondness for good living and extra-marital affairs, but had at times sailed very close to disastrous public scandal.

The wars of the peoples will be more terrible than those of kings … A European war can only end in the ruin of the vanquished and the hardly less fatal commercial dislocation and exhaustion of the conquerors.
Sitting in his first Parliament, the young Conservative MP Winston Churchill looks forward in 1901 to the conflicts of the new century.

There is no power but knows that if it defies the might of England it defies one of the most formidable enemies it could possibly encounter.
Prime Minister Lord Salisbury sets his face against Home Rule for Ireland and sends a warning to Irish Nationalist rebels, 13 May 1901.

When was a war not a war? When it was carried on by methods of barbarism.
Liberal MP and Leader of the Opposition Henry Campbell-Bannerman in a speech to the National Reform Union Dinner on 14 June 1901. During the second Boer War of 1899–1902, c.20,000 Boer women and children died in 'concentration camps' set up by the British to confine the rebellious populace. Campbell-Bannerman's words were used by the South African politician Louis Botha after the Boers' defeat: Three words made peace and union in South Africa: 'methods of barbarism'.

Everything can be a subject for Picasso. He is capable of using any idiom and is in such a feverish hurry that he is capable of doing three canvases a day, which could easily lead to facile virtuosity.
La Revue Blanche on the first exhibition of a 19-year-old Spanish artist, 24 June 1901.

1902

Perhaps it is God's will to lead the people of South Africa through defeat and humiliation to a better future and a brighter day.
General Jan Smuts addresses Boer delegates at the Peace Conference, 31 May 1902. But for South Africa's majority population, a better future still lay many years and many humiliations ahead.

Heart of Darkness
Novel title: Joseph Conrad, 1902.

1903

The airplane stays up because it doesn't have the time to fall.
Orville Wright's interpretation of the principles of avionics after the first successful flight of the plane he built with his brother Wilbur: 17 December 1903.

1904

The Admiral of the Atlantic salutes the Admiral of the Pacific.
Kaiser Wilhelm II of Germany sends a telegram to Tsar

Nicholas II as Russian warships exercise prior to the declaration of war against a modernizing Japan in 1904. After many defeats, and an abortive revolution in 1905, a weakened and demoralized Russia settled peace terms. German ambitions continued to grow.

The day of small nations has long passed away. The day of Empires has come.
The British elder statesman Joseph Chamberlain, speech, 12 May 1904.

You cannot feed the hungry on statistics.
Liberal politician David Lloyd George anticipates his party's future social legislation in a speech advocating Tariff Reform in 1904.

The principles for which we stand are the principles of fair play and a square deal for every man and every woman in the United States.
Having succeeded to the Presidency after William McKinley's assassination in 1901, Theodore Roosevelt successfully campaigns for re-election in 1904. The Square Deal Policy led to a vigorous enforcement of Anti-Trust legislation aimed at large monopolistic corporations.

In the Western hemisphere the adherence of the United States to the Monroe Doctrine may force the United States, however reluctantly, in flagrant cases of wrongdoing or impotence, to the exercise of an international police power.
Paving the way for intervention in foreign wars: President Theodore Roosevelt's message to Congress on 6 December 1904, since known as the 'Roosevelt Corollary', signals an end to a long-established isolationism in US government. The Monroe Doctrine, promulgated in 1823 and reinterpreted since, proclaimed non-intervention in the affairs of European states except when they were perceived by the US to threaten American interests. Designed at first to signal the USA's intention to repel European interference in South America, the Doctrine's scope was extended as the US developed widening trade and political relations elsewhere. It is still appealed to by both 'interventionists' and 'isolationists' in US politics.

. . . .

Those who cannot remember the past are condemned to repeat it.
George Santayana, The Life of Reason, *1905.*

. . . .

One Step Forwards, Two Steps Back.
Vladimir Ilyich Lenin: book title, 1904.

1905

But how can that be? Everything is so quiet – the strikes are ceasing. The excitement is subsiding. Whatever do they want?
Tsar Nicholas II receives the news of the death of his uncle and counsellor, Grand Duke Sergei, killed by a bomb as his carriage drove through the Kremlin Gate, 17 February 1905.

$E = mc^2$
Albert Einstein publishes the Special Theory of Relativity, *1905.*

1906

Lenin's method leads to this: the Party organization at first substitutes itself for the Party as a whole. Then the Central Committee substitutes itself for the Party organization, and finally a single dictator substitutes himself for the Central Committee.
A neat definition of what was to become the political system in the future USSR: Leon Trotsky, 1906, on the man who split the Russian Social Democratic Labour Party and became leader of the Bolshevik faction. Lenin himself spent 12 years in voluntary exile after the failure of the 1905 revolution.

1907

A mastiff? It is the Right Honourable Gentleman's Poodle. It fetches and carries for him. It barks for him. It bites anybody that he sets it on to.
David Lloyd George considers the House of Lords, speech, House of Commons, 26 June 1907. The 'Rt Hon Gentleman' was Arthur Balfour, the Conservative leader (see below).

1909

There are no credentials. They do not even need a medical certificate. They need not be sound either in body or mind. They only require a certificate of birth –

Civil Rights: The Suffragettes

The campaign for women's rights, including the right to vote, had been gathering pace during the last quarter of the 19th century. In 1870, as British women won back, after a gap of over 800 years, the right to own and inherit property, Queen Victoria felt moved to write of the 'mad, wicked folly of "Woman's Rights", with all its attendant horrors', which she believed made women forget 'every sense of womanly feeling and propriety'. In the US, Elizabeth Stanton adapted the US Constitution to a Declaration of Sentiments: 'We hold these truths to be self-evident: that all men and women are created equal.'

In Britain, campaigners for female suffrage – dubbed 'Suffragettes' by the press – formed themselves, under the leadership of Mrs Emmeline Pankhurst, into the Women's Social and Political Union in 1905. To a campaign of meetings, rallies and marches was added what would later be called 'direct action' designed to gain sensational publicity for the cause. Pictures in the National Gallery were slashed, windows – particularly in the houses of politicians opposed to votes for women – were broken, and women chained themselves to railings. Many women were arrested, including Mrs Pankhurst and her daughters, Christabel and Sylvia; women who refused food in prison were force-fed. A game of 'cat and mouse' began in which women protesters were regularly gaoled, released, and then immediately rearrested. In 1913 the Suffragette Emily Wilding Davidson was killed when she threw herself in front of the King's horse at the Epsom Derby.

The campaign was suspended when war broke out in 1914, and Mrs Pankhurst threw her energies into the mobilization of women for munitions work in the factories. In 1918 Parliament granted the vote to women aged over 30 but it was not until 1928, the year of Emmeline Pankhurst's death, that women won the vote on equal terms with men.

In the US the campaign began in earnest in 1890, with the union of the American Woman Suffrage Association and the more aggressive and radical National Woman Suffrage Association, whose leader, Susan B. Anthony, was admired by Emmeline Pankhurst. Eleven States had granted women the vote by 1914, and in 1920 the 19th Amendment to the Constitution – the 'Susan Anthony Amendment' – made victory complete.

Finland was the first European country to grant women the vote, in 1906; the first women members of the Finnish parliament were elected the following year.

Men their rights and nothing more; women their rights and nothing less.
Susan B. Anthony, the motto of the US Women's Suffrage journal, The Revolution.

The emancipation of women is practically the greatest egotistic movement of the nineteenth century and the most intense affirmation of the right of the self that history has yet seen.
The Swedish writer Ellen Key, The Century of the Child, c.1900.

Let us by all means throw open to them all employments in which their health, their purity and their womanliness do not suffer; but let this be regarded, not as a special privilege and an indication of social progress, but as a necessary evil to be cured in as many cases as possible by marriage or some other way of bringing the workers back to their deserted homes ... Doctors tell us, too, that thousands of children would be harmed or killed before birth by the injurious effect of untimely political excitement on their mothers ... One of the most important problems to be solved in the new century is this: shall women be flowers or vegetables, ornamental or useful?
US commentator Henry T. Finck, The Independent, *30 January 1901.*

The whole aim of the woman movement has been to destroy the idea that obedience is necessary to women; to train women to such self-respect that they would not grant obedience and to train men to such comprehension of equity that they would not exact it.
Carrie Chapman Catt, National American Woman Suffrage Association, February 1902.

Sensible and responsible women do not want to vote. The relative positions to be assumed by man and woman in the working out of our civilization were assigned long ago by a higher intelligence than ours.
The judgment of Eve is invoked by former President Grover Cleveland in the Ladies' Home Journal, *April 1905.*

We are not ashamed of what we have done, because, when you have a great cause to fight for, the moment of greatest humiliation is the moment when our spirit is proudest.
Christabel Pankhurst speaks at the Albert Hall, 19 March 1908.

We have taken this action, because as women … we realise that the condition of our sex is so deplorable that it is our duty even to break the law in order to call attention to the reasons why we do so.
Emmeline Pankhurst, speech in court, 21 October 1908.

You cannot trust the interests of any class entirely to another class; and you cannot trust the interests of any sex entirely to another sex.
David Lloyd George, speech on Women's Suffrage, 1911. When Suffragettes interrupted one of his election meetings in 1909 he is alleged to have said: 'I see some rats have got in; let them squeal; it doesn't matter.'

So greatly did she care for freedom that she died for it. So dearly did she love women that she offered her life as its ransom. That is the verdict given at the great Inquest of the Nation on the death of Emily Wilding Davidson.
Christabel Pankhurst, The Suffragette, *3 June 1913.*

Looking back …

It didn't take me long to realise that the vote was only just one thing, and not very much. There were other things that were more worth fighting for. A vote – well, that was nothing.
Elizabeth Dean (b. 1886): broadcast on BBC radio in 1995. (As an example of the other things to be fought for, official figures for 1994 show that women's earnings in Britain are 70 per cent of those for men in work of equal value.)

just to prove that they are the first of the litter. You would not choose a spaniel on these principles.
David Lloyd George, Chancellor of the Exchequer, Budget speech, 1909. Lloyd George's Budget set in place the mechanism for providing a state-funded old-age pension; Conservative hereditary peers, who formed a majority in the House of Lords, viewed the prospect with horror; one of them said the scheme would 'rot the moral fibre of the labouring class'. The Liberal government threat-

ened to create 400 Liberal peers to overturn the majority, and Lloyd George conducted a vigorous campaign against hereditary privilege. Eventually the House of Lords assented to the Budget, and the 1911 Parliament Act deprived it of the right to vote on Budget Bills and reduced its powers to amend other Bills passed in the House of Commons.

A fully equipped Duke costs as much to keep up as two Dreadnoughts, and Dukes are just as great a terror, and they last longer.

In a speech in Limehouse on 30 July 1909, Lloyd George addresses two themes with one epithet: popular demand for the building of Dreadnought battleships was a response to the armament race in continental Europe (see box below).

1910

HAVE STRONG SUSPICIONS THAT CRIPPEN LONDON CELLAR MURDERER AND ACCOMPLICE ARE AMONGST SALOON PASSENGERS MOUSTACHE TAKEN OFF GROWING BEARD ACCOMPLICE DRESSED AS BOY VOICE MANNER AND BUILD UNDOUBTEDLY A GIRL BOTH TRAVELLING AS MR AND MASTER ROBINSON

A cable to Scotland Yard from the Captain of a liner bound from Amsterdam to New York on 22 July 1910 leads to the capture of Dr Hawley Harvey Crippen and Ethel le Neve: the

• •

Only connect.

E. M. Forster, Howards End 1910.

• •

first use of radiotelegraphy for the purposes of criminal detection. Crippen was executed later that year.

Four spectres haunt the poor: old age, accidents, sickness and unemployment. We are going to exorcise them.

Anticipating Beveridge's 'four giants', Lloyd George, 1910.

Land of Hope and Glory, Mother of the Free,
How shall we extol thee, who are born of thee?

A. C. Benson, 'Land of Hope and Glory', 1910.

1911

I would make great sacrifices to preserve peace ... But if a situation were to be forced upon us, in which peace could only be preserved by the surrender of the great and beneficial position Britain has won by centuries of heroism and achievement ... I say emphatically that peace at that price would be a humiliation intolerable for a great country like ours to endure.

David Lloyd George reflects on the aggressive foreign policies of the continental powers in 1911.

SAYINGS and SLOGANS

I married beneath me - all women do.
Nancy Astor, 1900.

Speak softly and carry a big stick.
US President Theodore Roosevelt interprets the Monroe Doctrine and makes an old saying memorable, 1901.

All progress is based upon a universal innate desire on the part of every organism to live beyond its means.
Samuel Butler, Notebook, 1902.

Remember that you are an Englishman, and have consequently won first prize in the lottery of life.
Cecil Rhodes, 1902.

We want eight and we won't wait.
Crowd chant in UK, demanding the building of more Dreadnought battleships: 1908.

Get on the Raft with Taft.
US Republican Party campaign slogan: W. H. Taft, 1908.

Ninepence for fourpence.
Slogan used by Chancellor of the Exchequer David Lloyd George (and others) to promote contributory National Insurance in the UK: 1909.

Nothing over sixpence.
UK slogan for Woolworth stores, from 1909.

Wait and see.
Henry Herbert Asquith, British Prime Minister, in speeches from 1910.

Walk? Not bloody likely! I took a taxi.

Eliza in George Bernard Shaw's Pygmalion,
1911.

The foundation of the government of a nation must be built on the rights of the people, but the administration must be entrusted to experts: not grand ministers and presidents, but chauffeurs, guards at the gate, cooks, physicians, carpenters and tailors.

The Chinese revolutionary leader Dr Sun Yat-sen, speaking after the Wuhan rising of 1911.

If, therefore, war should ever come between these two countries, which Heaven forbid! it will not, I think, be due to irresistible natural laws, it will be due to the want of human wisdom.

The Unionist Leader Andrew Bonar Law on the increasingly strained relations between Britain and Germany, speech, House of Commons, 27 November 1911.

I hope to see the day when the American flag will float over every square foot of the British North American possessions clear to the North Pole.

Territorial ambition is not confined to Germany and Austria-Hungary, James Beauchamp Clark, Speaker of the US House of Representatives, June 1911.

America, America!
God shed his grace on thee...

Katharine Lee Bates, America the Beautiful. *final revision, 1911.*

1912

Great God! This is an awful place.

Captain Robert Falcon Scott on reaching the South Pole, Journal, *17 January 1912.*

~

I am just going outside and may be some time.

Captain Lawrence Oates, one of Scott's polar expedition party, fears that his lameness is holding back his companions on their return journey from the South Pole, and leaves the shelter of the tent

on 17 March 1912; recorded in Scott's Journal. *His body was never found.*

~

Had we lived, I should have had a tale to tell of the hardihood, endurance, and courage of my companions which would have stirred the heart of every Englishman. These rough notes and our dead bodies must tell the tale.

Captain Robert Falcon Scott leaves a Message to the Public *at the end of his* Journal. *Although Scott's party reached the Pole it was beaten there by Amundsen's better equipped and better organized Norwegian expedition.*

~

For God's sake look after our people.

The last entry in Scott's Journal. *Hungry, exhausted and beset by ferocious blizzards, the expedition survivors perished at the end of March only a few miles from shelter and safety.*

The band was still playing. I guess all of them went down.

Harold Bride, wireless operator on board the SS Titanic, *which struck an iceberg on her maiden voyage from Southampton to New York and sank with huge casualties on 15 April 1912; more than 1500 people perished, including Captain Edward J. Smith, found guilty of negligence by a Board of Trade enquiry in July.*

The British people, just and generous by nature, are not going to be frightened out of doing a just thing by the language of intimidation.

Prime Minister Herbert Asquith, speaking after the House of Commons gave a 94-vote majority for his Irish Home Rule Bill despite threats of civil war by Ulster Unionists, 9 May 1912.

... Stands the Church clock at ten to
    three
And is there honey still for tea?

Rupert Brooke: The Old Vicarage, Grantchester, *1912.*

1913

We must abolish everything that bears even the semblance of privilege.

US President Woodrow Wilson, speech to Congress urging the reduction of tariff levels, 4 April 1913.

1914

We come to Sarajevo, Herr Burger-meister, and have a bomb thrown at us.
Archduke Franz Ferdinand of Austria-Hungary. His last public utterance before his assassination by a Serb nationalist gunman, an act that was to provoke world war, 26 June 1914.

We Americans can't seem to get it that you can't commit rape a little.
Lincoln Steffens (1931) on the US military inter-vention in Mexico, 1914.

The rich are the scum of the earth in every country.
G. K. Chesterton,The Flying Inn, 1914.

Civil Rights: Racism

The problem of the twentieth century is the problem of the colour line.
W. E. B. Du Bois, Pan African Conference, London, January 1900.

Mr President, the times call for candour. The Philippines are ours for ever … We will not renounce our part in the mission of our race, trustee, under God, of the civilization of the world … It has been charged that our conduct of the war has been cruel … Senators must remember that we are not dealing with Americans or Europeans. We are dealing with Orientals.
Senator Abert Beveridge, speech in Congress, 9 January 1900, on the conduct of US forces in crushing the Filipino Rebellion. The marriage of white Americans with Filipinos was, as with blacks, forbidden by law.

You tie us and then taunt us for a lack of bravery, but one day we will break the bonds. You may use our labour for two and a half centuries and then taunt us for our poverty, but let me remind you we will not always remain poor. You may withhold even the knowledge of how to read God's word and learn the way from earth to glory and then taunt us for our ignorance, but we would remind you that there is plenty of room at the top, and we are climbing.
George Henry White, speech to US Congress, 29 January 1901.

Any discrimination based on race or colour is barbarous, we care not how hallowed it may be by custom, expedience or prejudice … We repudiate the monstrous doc-trine that the oppressor should be the sole authority as to the rights of the oppressed.
W. E. B. Du Bois, The Niagara Movement Declaration of Principles, *Niagara Fall, NY, 1905.*

It is impossible for any white person in the United States, no matter how sym-pathetic and broad, to realise what life would mean to him if his incentive to effort were suddenly snatched away. To the lack of incentive to effort, which is the awful shadow under which we live, may be traced the wreck and ruin of scores of coloured people.
Mary Church Terrell, What it Means to Be Colored in the Capital of the United States, *1907.*

Looking back …

Negroes in many places could not go to the polls to vote although the law said they'd got the right to do so … They'd be lynched, Negro men trying to vote.
Remembering US democracy at the turn of the century: John Morton-Finney (b. 1887) interviewed in The People's Century, BBC (1995).

The Shattering of Europe
1914~1920

Dead battles, like dead generals, hold the
military mind in their dead grip

~ *Barbara W. Tuchman*, August 1914

1914

On 28 June 1914 Gavrilo Princip, a 19-year-old Serb nationalist student, shot dead Archduke Franz Ferdinand of Austria-Hungary in Sarajevo, capital of the Austro-Hungarian province of Bosnia-Herzegovina, and triggered a war which the aggressive foreign policies of Russia, Austria-Hungary and, most of all, Germany had been pursuing during the preceding decade. Austria-Hungary gave Serbia 48 hours to reply to an ultimatum demanding that Austrian officials be allowed to investigate Serbian complicity in the assassination, and to enforce the suppression of 'subversive movements' in Serbia itself; to no one's surprise, Serbia rejected these demands. An offer from the British government to mediate was curtly rejected by Germany as 'insolence' and Austria-Hungary, at Germany's prompting, declared war on Serbia on 31 July. Russia immediately mobilized in support of Serbia, Germany in support of Austria-Hungary and France – which, together with Britain, was a member of the 'Triple Alliance' – in support of Russia. After a last effort to salvage an agreement without recourse to war had failed, Britain joined the hostilities on 4 August after the German invasion of Belgium; 80,000 members of the British Expeditionary Force (BEF) were sent across the Channel within a few days. Within a month, 16 million had been mobilized across Europe. France recruited from its colonies in Africa and Indo-China, Britain from Australia, Canada, India and New Zealand.

After swift territorial gains by the Central Powers – Germany, Austria-Hungary and Turkey – in the second half of 1914, the 'Balance of Power' engineered by years of diplomatic alliance in Europe soon translated into a bloody stalemate in the various theatres of war. Russia and Germany became locked in confrontation in Poland, while the French Army thwarted the 'Schlieffen Plan' to encircle Paris and, together with the BEF, blocked the German advance at the First Battle of Ypres. A naval action off the Falklands in December, in which four German cruisers were sunk with no British casualties, largely ensured that Allied shipping was safe from surface attack in the Atlantic. As winter settled over Europe, soldiers on all sides 'dug in' and a long, deadly period of attritional 'trench warfare' began. By the year's end, British casualties alone exceeded 100,000.

A 'shining angel' was seen during the Battle of Mons in August, and credited with holding up a German cavalry advance during the BEF's retreat. By September, Field Marshal Lord Kitchener was calling for 500,000 new recruits. Generals on both sides condemned the many unofficial 'truces' between front line troops on Christmas Day, during which rations were exchanged, carols sung, and impromptu football matches played.

No sorrow is spared me.
A weeping Emperor Franz Josef of Austria-Hungary mourns the death of his heir on 30 June 1914.

The lamps are going out all over Europe; we shall not see them lit again in our lifetime.
British Foreign Secretary Sir Edward Grey, 3 August 1914.

God heard the embattled nations sing and
   shout:
'Gott strafe England,' 'God save the King,'
God this, God that, and God the other
   thing.
'My God,' said God, 'I've got my work cut
   out.'
The British journalist John Collings Squire, 1914.

SONGS and SLOGANS of 1914

The Hun is at the gate! ...
What stands if Freedom fail?
Who dies if England live?
Rudyard Kipling, For All We Have and Are.

Your country needs YOU
British recruiting poster featuring Lord Kitchener's pointing finger.

Remember Scarborough!
A recruiting campaign was mounted after the Yorkshire town, along with Whitby, Hartlepool and West Hartlepool, suffered the first British civilian casualties in a German naval bombardment on 16 December; over 100 people were killed and 200 injured.

Keep the Home Fires Burning
Song: words by Lena Guilbert Ford, music by Ivor Novello.

We draw the sword with a clear conscience and with clean hands.
The German Kaiser Wilhelm II, Berlin, 4 August 1914.

You will be home before the leaves have fallen from the trees.
Wilhelm II addresses German troops leaving for the Front in early August 1914.

When you march into France, let the last man on the right brush the Channel with his sleeve.
German Admiral Graf von Schlieffen addresses the troops, August 1914.

Our gallant fellows at the Front are carrying their football training into practice on the battlefield. They are 'playing the game' in all conscience.
Lord Baden-Powell, founder of the Boy Scout movement, Headquarters Gazette, August 1914.

The United States must be neutral in fact as well as in name during these days that are to try men's souls. We must be impartial in thought as well as in action.
Conscious of America's large and growing European immigrant population, President Woodrow Wilson campaigns on a platform of strict neutrality on 19 August 1914.

I have the honour to inform you that Togoland surrendered unconditionally today.
A signal from Lieutenant F. C. Bryant to the British Colonial Office announces the first conclusive defeat of Germany in its West African colony, 26 August 1914.

It is my Royal and Imperial command that you exterminate first the treacherous English and walk over General French's contemptible little army.
A decree of Wilhelm II, 1 October 1914. Veterans

of French's BEF afterwards adopted the nickname of the 'Old Contemptibles'.

We shall never sheathe the sword which we have not lightly drawn until Belgium receives in full measure all and more than all she has sacrificed, until France is adequately secured against the menace of aggression, until the rights of the smaller nationalities of Europe are placed upon an unassailable foundation, and until the military domination of Prussia is wholly and finally destroyed.
British Prime Minister H. H. Asquith, speech at the Guildhall, 9 November 1914.

I am bound to assume the war will be long.
Chancellor of the Exchequer David Lloyd George

announces a doubling of income tax to one shilling and sixpence in the pound, or 7 per cent, on 17 November 1914. Tax on unearned income was increased to 12 per cent.

I don't mind your being killed, but I object to your being taken prisoner.
Field Marshal Lord Kitchener refuses the Prince of Wales (afterwards Edward VIII) permission to go to the Front, 18 December 1914.

Bullets have little stopping power against the horse.
General Sir Douglas Haig pins his hopes on the cavalry in France and Belgium.
     He restructured the supply of machine guns to three per battallion, saying, 'this should be more than enough'.

1915

In January, Britain experienced the first Zeppelin raids, as the hydrogen-filled airships bombed Great Yarmouth and King's Lynn. The most powerful battle-cruiser in the world, the *Blucher*, was sunk by the Royal Navy on the Dogger Bank. German High Command announced that all shipping in UK territorial waters would be regarded as hostile; the sinking of two American vessels by German 'U-boats' in the North Sea was condemned in Washington as 'a threat to the world'. On 8 May, some 1400 lives were lost, 128 of them American, when a German submarine sank the Cunard liner, SS *Lusitania*, 8 miles (13 km) off the Irish coast.

British women were recruited for factory work as more men volunteered for the armed forces and production began to fall; production at many factories doubled in consequence. Delays and shortfalls in arms production were blamed on drunkenness, and it was made a criminal offence to 'stand a round' in public houses; in the munitions-producing Carlisle area, breweries were nationalized. Income tax was increased by 40 per cent, to 2/11d in the pound, and a war profits tax was introduced.

A major Allied offensive was launched at Ypres in April, with huge losses on all sides; 69,000 French troops were killed or taken prisoner and 164,000 wounded in an action that resulted in the gain of one-quarter of an acre of woodland. The Germans used gas for the first time, and British troops were advised to hold wet cloths to their faces.

Allied forces, including many from Australia and New Zealand, attempted an invasion of the Gallipoli peninsula in the Dardanelles, an effort to resupply the flagging Russian Empire and knock Turkey out of the war, and were repelled with very heavy losses in the disease-ridden heat by well-armed and well-forewarned Turkish forces. Allied troops withdrew in December with known losses of 25,000, 13,000 missing, 76,000 wounded and 96,000 ill in hospital.

Under mounting pressure to change sides, including a campaign by a newspaper owned and edited by a young radical politician named Benito Mussolini, the Italian government signed a treaty with Britain, France and Russia and its armies opened up an offensive against Austria; by the end of the year, 250,000 Italian soldiers were dead.

In a series of autumn offences, the Central Powers occupied Russian Poland and most of Lithuania, overran Serbia and pushed on into Albania. On the Western Front, where Sir Douglas Haig replaced Sir John French as commander of British forces, there was a bloody stalemate.

SONGS and SLOGANS of 1915

What's the use of worrying?
It never was worthwhile –
So, pack up your troubles in your
old kit bag and smile, smile, smile.
Anon.

I Didn't Raise My Boy To Be A Soldier
*Popular American song: words by Alfred
Bryan, music by Al Piantadosi. For the English
edition, Bryan changed the words to, 'I'm Glad
I Raised My Boy To Be A Soldier'.*

Women of Britain say – Go!
Recruiting poster.

Daddy, what did you do in the Great
War?
Recruiting poster.

Well, if you knows of a better 'ole,
go to it.
*Said by 'Old Bill', up to his waist in mud on
the Somme: cartoon by Bill Bairnsfather in
Sketches From France. It rapidly became a
catchphrase.*

Our whole duty, for the present, at any rate, is summed up in this motto: 'America first'.
US President Woodrow Wilson, speech in New York City, 20 April 1915.

The example of America must be the example not merely of peace because it will not fight, but of peace because peace is the healing and elevating influence of the world and strife is not. There is such a thing as a man too proud to fight.
Woodrow Wilson speaks in Philadelphia, three days

after the sinking of the Lusitania, 11 May 1915.

Do not talk to me of naval tradition. It is nothing but rum, buggery and the lash.
First Lord of the Admiralty Winston Churchill overrides objections from naval staff before launching the Gallipoli campaign. Afterwards, he complained of being badly briefed.

Casualties? What do I care for casualties?
Major-General A. G. Hunter-Weston was nicknamed 'The Butcher of Hellas' after losing three divisions in daylight frontal attacks on the cliffs of the Gallipoli peninsula in May 1915.

They were never in better heart, and are longing for a fight. With the enthusiasm of ignorance they will tear their way through the German line.
General Sir Douglas Haig assesses the readiness of British troops before the Battle of Loos, diary entry, 12 September 1915.

LUDENDORFF: The English soldiers fight like lions.
HOFFMANN: True. But don't we know that they are lions led by donkeys.
German General Max Hoffmann, in the aftermath of the Battle of Loos.

Patriotism is not enough. I must have no hatred or bitterness toward anyone.
The last words of British nurse, Edith Cavell, shot by the German authorities in Brussels on 12 October 1915 for helping Allied soldiers to escape.

I am an officer and I place myself unreservedly at the disposal of the military authorities, observing that my regiment is in France. With much respect and unaltered friendship, I bid you goodbye.
Sacked from the Admiralty in May, Winston Churchill resigns from the government after being excluded from the newly formed War Cabinet, 11 November 1915.

1916

The year began with Allied victories over the Turks at Tigris and Erzerum, and the Germans in the Cameroons and Togoland. The House of Commons voted on 6 January in favour of conscription; the miners' unions voted overwhelmingly against it, and some Cabinet ministers resigned. Around half a million single men of military age were said to be 'shirking their duty', and military commanders insisted that voluntary effort would not be enough to break the stalemate. In March, anti-conscription leaders of a munitions workers' strike on the Clyde were arrested and charged with sedition.

On 21 February the German army began a massive assault on the French stronghold of Verdun, a key point in Allied defences on the Western Front. This continued until July, when the Allies under General Douglas Haig launched a 'big push' along a 15-mile (25-km) front on the River Somme, in Picardy; 26 British divisions, all volunteers, took part in the initial assault which followed; the French contingent was reduced to 18 from the promised 40 divisions following the five-month battle of Verdun. The attempt proved disastrous in terms of casualties and the gains were minimal; at the point of deepest penetration a mere 5 miles (8 km) of territory was gained, while the shattered remnants of many divisions withdrew to their original positions. In the first half hour 1000 British troops were killed, and total casualties on both sides were one million men, of whom 380,000 died. British military casualties for August to October totalled 350,000, 40 per cent of the total on both sides.

The German and British fleets met at Jutland, off the coast of Denmark, on 31 May and a full-scale naval battle ensued in which nearly 10,000 sailors, three-quarters of them British, lost their lives. Both sides claimed victory; henceforward Germany's surface fleet remained in port, and the U-boat campaign began in earnest. On 7 June the British War Minister, Lord Kitchener, was lost at sea when an explosion sank the cruiser HMS *Hampshire* off Marwick Head in the Orkney Islands; he had been on his way to Russia from Scapa Flow, despite a forecast of severe stormy weather. Orcadian civilians who hurried to the coast to rescue survisors were turned back at gunpoint by military police. Kitchener was succeeded in office by his long-time opponent David Lloyd George.

On 24 April, Irish nationalists Patrick Pearse of the Irish Republican Brotherhood and James Connolly of Sinn Féin led an armed rebellion in Dublin and declared the country a republic. They were defeated after five days of fighting and both leaders, along with 12 others, were executed by firing squad. In August, Sir Roger Casement, a former British diplomat who had attempted to smuggle arms to the rebels, was hanged in London. The British government proposed partition as a solution to the 'Irish Question'.

In the US, President Woodrow Wilson was re-elected by a narrow majority over his Republican rival Charles Evans Hughes, whom Democrats had accused of being a warmonger, although Wilson himself said he would be prepared to declare war for a 'just cause'. On 7 December, following three days of bitter in-fighting among the coalition Cabinet, David Lloyd George succeeded Herbert Asquith as British Prime Minister.

During 1916 the British government took control of wheat distribution and vacant agricultural land, and ordered an inquiry into allegations of profiteering in food supplies. Imports of tobacco, spirits, motor cars and pianos were banned. Urgent measures were announced to combat the spread of venereal diseases after 50,000 cases were reported among British servicemen. In October the cost of a standard loaf reached a record 10d (4p), while in Germany there were frequent food riots as the Allied blockade was tightened.

This war, like the next war, is the war to end war.
David Lloyd George, alluding to H.G. Wells's 1914 book, The War That Will End War. *In 1917 Woodrow Wilson popularized the slogan, 'A war to end all wars'. Lloyd George is frequently misquoted, minus the ironic codicil.*

The spirit of the Lord has descended upon me. Because I am the Emperor of the Germans, I am the instrument of the Most High. I am His sword and His right hand.
Kaiser Wilhelm II begins the year with a speech in Berlin.

The Republic guarantees religious and civil liberty, equal rights and equal opportunities to all its citizens, and declares its resolve to pursue the happiness of the whole nation.
Schoolteacher Patrick Pearse reads a proclamation from the portico of the Dublin post office, captured by rebels on 24 April 1916. The death toll for the rebellion: 794 civilians, 521 police and troops.

Where all your rights become only an accumulated wrong; where men must beg with bated breath for leave to subsist in their

own land … then surely it is a braver, a saner and a truer thing to be a rebel than tamely to accept it as the natural lot of men.
Sir Roger Casement speaks in his defence during his trial for treason.

The grass grows green on the battlefield, but never on the scaffold.
Attributed to Winston Churchill, May 1916.

I write it out in verse –
MacDonagh and MacBride
And Connolly and Pearse
Now and in time to be,
Wherever green is worn,
Are changed, changed utterly:
A terrible beauty is born.
W. B. Yeats, 'Easter 1916'.

Ireland is an old sow that eats her farrow.
James Joyce, A Portrait of the Artist as a Young Man *(1916).*

Things fall apart; the centre cannot hold;
    Mere anarchy is loosed upon the world [...]
And what rough beast, its hour come round at last,
Slouches towards Bethlehem to be born?
W. B. Yeats, 'The Second Coming'.

I had always to remember that I could have lost the war in an afternoon.
Admiral Lord Jellicoe, on the Battle of Jutland. On

13 February 1927, the Observer's *'Sayings of the Week' reported Winston Churchill's 'Jellicoe was the only man on either side who could lose the war in an afternoon'; he is also supposed to have said: 'Jellicoe contrived to snatch defeat from the jaws of victory'.*

The general who never spared himself cared little for others. He treated all men like machines, from private soldiers, whose salutes he disdained, to the superior officers he rigidly controlled.
Winston Churchill's 1902 assessment of Kitchener republished in the Daily Mirror, *7 June 1916.*

Ils ne passeront pas! ['They shall not pass!'].
Order to French troops defending Verdun: attributed to Marshal Pétain, but in fact more likely to be a corruption of the Order of the Day issued by General Robert Nivelle in June 1916: 'Vous ne les laisserez pas passer' ['You will not let them pass'].

We had to jump from corpse to corpse. If we stepped in the mud on either side, we'd get stuck. We had to use the dead face-down because if we stepped on their stomachs our feet would sink in. It was disgusting. It was terrible. We were surrounded by death.
Marcel Batreau, interviewed for The People's Century *(BBC, 1995).*

The men are in splendid spirits … The wire has never been so well cut, nor the artillery preparations so thorough.
Field Marshal Earl Haig, Diary, 1 July 1916.

You will be able to go over the top with a walking stick, you will not need rifles. When you get to Thiepval you will find the Germans all dead, not even a rat will have survived.
A Brigadier-General addresses the Newcastle Regiment, 1 July 1916.

They advanced in line after line, dressed as if on parade, and not a man shirked going through the extremely heavy barrage, or facing machine-gun fire that finally wiped them out … hardly a man of ours got to the German front line.
Brigadier-General Rees, GOC 94th Infantry Brigade of 31 Division, diary entry, 1 July 1916 (evening).

I kept going, I got to the German barbed wire, I got through that all right, and jumped into a German trench. We stayed there all that day and the following night, with no food, no water, dead short of ammunition. One of our chaps contacted headquarters, then came forward to us and said, 'I've got orders for you. You've to retire to the trenches you left as best you can, get back as best you can.' So I finished up there, where I left.
Walter Hare, interviewed for The People's Century *(BBC, 1995).*

How can we ever win if this plea is allowed?
Private Arthur Earp had been found, crouched and shivering from shell-shock in his dug-out after the order to attack. His court martial recommended mercy on the grounds of 'the intense bombardment he had been subjected to, and on account of his good character' but Haig overturned the decision on 19 July 1916, and Earp was shot.

America cannot be an ostrich with its head in the sand.
Woodrow Wilson, speech, Des Moines, 1 February 1916.

~

He kept us out of war!
Martin H. Glynn, Governor of New York State, coins an election slogan for Wilson in a speech to the Democratic National Convention in St Louis, 15 July 1916.

What should I do? I think the best thing is to order a new stamp to be made with my face on it.
Charles, Emperor of Austria-Hungary following the death of Franz Josef on 21 November 1916.

Madam, I am the civilization they are fighting to defend.
The classical scholar Heathcote William Garrod's reply to a critic who berated him for not joining up to 'defend civilization'.

1917

In Britain and Germany the year began with a shocked assessment of the financial cost of war. Total German expenditure to date was estimated at £5000 million while British costs were running at £5.7 million a day; the government issued War Loan stock and the Prudential Assurance Company invested £20 million at 5 per cent, payable in 1947. By the end of the month £1000 million of War Loan stock had been bought. In July it was announced that Britain's daily war expenditure stood at £7 million. Winston Churchill rejoined the government in July, as Minister of Munitions. In Ireland the East Clare by-election was won by the Sinn Féin candidate, Eamon de Valera. Britain released the remaining prisoners of the 1916 Easter Rising.

In February, the US severed diplomatic relations with Germany and Austria, and Congress approved the arming of US ships, as the *Housatonic* became the 134th neutral vessel to be sunk by German U-boats that month. The following month, three more US ships were sunk and President Wilson called a special session of Congress to discuss relations with Germany. On 6 April, as 91 German ships were seized in New York harbour, Congress approved President Wilson's declaration of war on Germany; a $7000 million War Loan was also voted through and at the end of the month Wilson signed a War Finance Act under which Britain was lent $200 million. The USS *Mongolia* fired the first American shots of the war on 19 April, sinking a German submarine; the first US combat troops landed in France on 27 June under the command of Major General Pershing. Colonel Douglas MacArthur's 'Rainbow Division', comprising men from every US State, arrived on 30 November. On 7 December, the USA declared war on Austria-Hungary.

As Russia launched a new offensive on the Baltic Front there were widespread food shortages at home and strikes in munitions factories as ministerial resignations weakened the Tsar's government; the Tsar himself abdicated in March and the way was cleared for revolution (see p. 24). On 22 December, the new Bolshevik government opened peace negotiations with Germany at Brest-Litovsk.

On 2 May, King George V issued a Royal proclamation, to be read from pulpits on four successive Sundays, exhorting the British to consume 25 per cent less bread; it was revealed that the Royal household had been on 'strict rations' since February. Calls for general rationing, on grounds of fairness, were resisted. German aircraft carried out their first bombing raid on London on 14 June, killing over 100 people in the East End; one bomb fell on a school. In September, 108 people died in a raid on the Isles of Sheppey and Thanet, while a Zeppelin raid in October killed another 27. The German potato harvest failed, leading to the 'turnip winter'.

There was success for British, Canadian and Australian forces on the Hindenburg Line at Arras, but a French assault at Chemin des Dames gained 600 yards at the cost of 120,000 casualties. The Third Battle of Ypres, also known as the Battle of Passchendaele, began on 31 July and ended on 10 November with the capture of the village of Passchendaele itself by Canadian troops. The avowed objective of breaking through to the Belgian ports could never be realized in the appallingly muddy conditions, which account-ed for many of the deaths among the 300,000-plus British and Empire casualties. On 31 October the Italian army collapsed at the Battle of Caporetto; 10,000 members of the Second Army were killed, 30,000 wounded, half a million threw away their arms and fled in the face of a massive German-Austrian advance from the mountains, and 293,000 were taken prisoner; Italy's Commander-in-Chief withdrew to within 15 miles (24 km) of Venice. In December, British forces advancing from Bethlehem captured Jerusalem from the Turks; Islamic shrines were put under the protection of Indian Moslem troops. Tanks were used successfully by Allied forces at Cambrai.

Greece's pro-German King Constantine was forced by the Allies to abdicate in June, but in December there was a pro-German military coup in Portugal. Mutiny broke out in sections of the French army in May and spread to two-thirds of French units; of 3000 men convicted, 600 were sentenced to death, although only 50 executions were car-ried out. Following the rout at Riga in September, thousands of Russian troops laid down their arms and headed home as the government in Petrograd began to collapse. There were hunger strikes and mutinies in the German fleet at Wilhelmshaven, and defections among Austro-Hungarian infantry. Britain recruited more Military Police to hunt deserters. The latest peace plan of Pope Benedict XV was accepted by Germany but rejected by the Allies, including the USA.

King George V changed the Royal Family's titles from Saxe-Coburg-Gotha to Windsor and from Battenberg to Mountbatten. On 7 March the Victor Company of America issued the first jazz recording, 'The Dixieland Jazz Band One-Step'. On 17 July three peasant children claimed to have held a conversation with the Virgin Mary at Fatima in Portugal. On 18 December the US Senate voted for Prohibition.

Though victory is difficult, defeat is impossible.
Prime Minister Lloyd George launches five shilling (25p) War Loan bonds at the Guildhall, 11 January 1917.

It must be a peace without victory ... Victory would mean peace forced upon the loser, a victor's terms imposed upon the vanquished ... and would leave a sting, a resentment, a bitter memory upon which terms of peace would rest, not permanently, but only as upon quick-sand. Only peace between equals can last.
President Wilson's fears were to be realized by the

Treaty of Versailles: speech to US Senate, 22 January 1917.

_____

Since it has unhappily proved impossi-ble to safeguard our neutral rights by diplomatic means ... there may be no recourse but to armed neutrality.
President Wilson informs Congress of his deci-sion to arm US ships, 26 February 1917.

~

The world must be made safe for democracy. Its peace must be planted upon the tested foundations of politi-cal liberty. We have no selfish ends to serve. We desire no conquest, no dominion. We seek no indemnities for ourselves, no material compensation for the sacrifices we shall freely make ...

There are, it may be, many months of fiery trial and sacrifice ahead of us. It is a fearful thing to lead this great peaceful people into war, into the most terrible and disastrous of all wars, civilization itself seeming to be in the balance. But the right is more precious than peace ...

To such a task we can dedicate our lives and our fortunes, everything that we are and everything that we have, with the pride of those who know that the day has come when America is privileged to spend her blood and her might for the principles that gave her birth and happiness and the peace which she has treasured. God helping her, she can do no other.
President Wilson, message to Congress, 2 April 1917.

~

I want to stand by my country, but I cannot vote for war.
A tearful Senator Jeanette Rankin, the only woman member of the US Congress, was one of six to vote against the Declaration of War.

_____

My message was one of death for young men. How odd it seems to applaud that.
After the rapturous reception for his speech, President Wilson also weeps.

The first casualty when war comes is truth.
Senator Hiram Warren Johnson, 4 April 1917.

We are about to do the bidding of wealth's terrible mandate.
Senator George Norris, 4 April 1917.

America has at one bound become a world power.
David Lloyd George, press conference, 6 April 1917.

Lafayette, we are here!
US Colonel C. E. Stanton at the grave of the Marquis de Lafayette, who aided the colonists in the US War of Independence, 4 July 1917.

SONGS and SLOGANS of 1917

Goodbye-ee, goodbye-ee,
Wipe a tear, baby dear,
From your eye-ee.
Anonymous (?).

America – Here's My Boy!
'The Sentiment of Every American Mother' according to Andrew B. Sterling (words) and Arthur Lange (music).

The Yanks are coming!
Battle cry.

Deleted By French Censor.
The American newspaper owner and editor James Gordon Bennett used this mantra to fill empty spaces in his papers when news was thin; it became synonymous with 'Nothing to say'.

I never knew what the hell I was fighting for. I'd never heard of democracy before.
Black US soldier Tela Burt, interviewed for The People's Century *(BBC, 1995). On 9 October 1917 the US Congress had approved the formation of a Negro Division, but many blacks were not trusted to fight; instead they dug trenches and graves.*

The Church should no longer be satisfied to represent only the Conservative Party at prayer.
Congregationalist Minister Agnes Maude Royden, speech, London, 16 July 1917.

Peace with Germany will only be achieved with the German people and not with its authoritarian regime.
Lloyd George, speech, 23 July 1917.

Nothing in art must be accidental, not even movement.
Edgar Degas, who died in September 1917.

He is the only man in whose presence I feel really humble.
George Bernard Shaw on Auguste Rodin, who died in November 1917.

The Russian Revolution

The third year of war brought Russia to the crisis to which long years of authoritarian and inefficient Imperial rule had been leading it. There was mass starvation and privation; protest was put down with great brutality. Factories closed for lack of coal, bakeries for lack of flour; bureaucratic corruption and ineptitude ensured that what few resources there were usually failed to reach those who needed them. The catastrophic conduct of the war – Russian casualties totalled nine million, three-quarters of the total mobilized – brought widespread demands for peace, to which Tsar Nicholas II responded by taking personal command of the armed forces and ordering fresh offensives.

On 16 March the Tsar left the capital, Petrograd (afterwards Leningrad, now St Petersburg, its pre-First World War Germanic name), under the command of General Khabalov. There followed a series of largely spontaneous protests and riots; people in bread queues broke into bakeries and workers went on strike and took to the streets, where they were joined by students, soldiers and sailors. Khabalov responded by sending in the Cossack Guard, renowned for its savagery in putting down protest; on this occasion, however, the Cossacks fraternized with the protesters, whose numbers were swelled by deserters from the front. On 12 March the Tsar dissolved the Duma (parliament) but its members ignored the edict, and were joined by a Bolshevist 'Soviet' (collective committee) of workers and soldiers; at this stage however, the Bolsheviks took little part in the unfolding revolution, their leaders (principally Lenin and Trotsky) being either in exile or in hiding. As Nicholas's generals forced him to abdicate in favour of his brother, the Grand Duke Michael, on the 16th, a new government emerged under the leadership of Alexander Kerensky, a Social Democrat deputy. The Tsar, with his wife and family, was arrested.

In April the German authorities returned Vladimir Ilyich Lenin to Russia from Zürich in a sealed train, after securing an agreement that any administration led by his Bolsheviks would declare an immediate armistice. Lenin began to prepare for an organized 'Soviet Revolution' but in July there was a spontaneous uprising against the new government, demanding immediate peace and 'all power to the Soviets'; this was put down by force and Lenin fled again, this time to Finland, disguised as a fireman on a train. Trotsky surrendered to the police, but the Petrograd Soviet continued to work in an uneasy 'dual power' alliance with Kerensky's government.

By the autumn, this 'dual power' arrangement broke down when the Bolsheviks walked out. On 25 October (7 November under the new calendar) the Military Revolutionary Committee of the Petrograd Soviet led a largely bloodless revolution; the Winter Palace was taken over. Members of Kerensky's Provisional Government were placed under arrest and replaced by a Soviet of People's Commissars under the chairmanship of Lenin, by now returned to Petrograd.

Lenin swiftly sued for peace, though this was initially opposed by Trotsky; he also formed a Red Army under Trotsky's leadership, and a security police force, the Cheka, whose task was to 'combat counter-revolution, speculation and sabotage'; he used both to dissolve the Duma, which had voted down his proposal to govern Russia through a pyramid of Soviet Councils. The Cheka moved swiftly to arrest and imprison dissidents. Tsar Nicholas II and his family were shot and bayonetted to death on 16 July 1918 in the cellar of a house in Ekaterinburg.

Lenin signed a peace treaty with Germany at Brest-Litovsk in March 1918, handing Poland, Lithuania, Courland, Riga, and part of Belorussia to Germany and large areas of the Caucasus to Turkey; he also agreed to pay 3000 million roubles in reparation, and recognized Ukraine as a German protectorate. Trotsky's task now was to organize the Red Army to fight a civil war against pro-Tsarist and anti-Bolshevik 'White' forces who had the support of Britain, France, the USA and Japan; victory for the Red Army was finally gained in 1922 at the cost of great suffering; millions died of starvation, and a revolt at the Kronstadt naval base was violently crushed.

Following a period of rigid and often ruthless 'War Communism', Lenin moved away from total central control of what was still an overwhelmingly agricultural economy with the introduction of a 'New Economic Policy' designed principally to give more market freedom to peasant farmers and traders, and so avert further famine; his critics saw this a retreat from Socialism. Lenin died in 1924 and was succeeded by Joseph Stalin, General Secretary of the Central Committee of the Communist Party, despite Lenin's previously stated disapproval. Stalin scrapped the New Economic Plan, sent Trotsky into exile and embarked on a policy of enforced centralized planning and collectivization of all areas of economic, social and cultural life under his personal and absolute authority.

To the Emperor of all the Russias belongs the supreme and unlimited power. Not only fear, but also conscience commanded by God Himself, is the basis of obedience to this power.
A definition of feudal authority: extract from the Fundamental Laws of Imperial Russia.

In a state worthy of the name there is no liberty. The people want to exercise power but what on earth would they do with it if it were given to them?
Vladimir Ilyich Lenin, The State and the Revolution.

Be the Emperor, be Peter the Great, John the Terrible, the Emperor Paul – crush them all under you – Now don't you laugh, naughty one – but I long to see you so with those men who try to govern you and it must be the contrary.
Letter (in English) from the Czarina Alexandra to Tsar Nicholas II, 27 December 1916.

Peace, Bread and Land.
Slogan of the Petrograd streets, February 1917.

I order that the disorders in the capital shall be ended by tomorrow; they are quite inadmissible.
Cable from Tsar Nicholas II to General Khabalov, 10 March 1917.

May the Lord God help Russia.
The final sentence of the Instrument of Abdication; 12 March 1917.

Dear comrades, soldiers, sailors and workers! I am happy to greet in your persons the victorious Russian Revolution, and greet you as the vanguard of the world-wide proletarian army ... The piratical imperialist war is the beginning of civil war throughout Europe ... Any day now the whole of European capitalism may crash ... Long live the world-wide socialist revolution!
Lenin hails the 'Bourgeois Revolution' at Petrograd's Finland Station, 16 April 1917.

The dictatorship of the proletariat.
Slogan of the Petrograd streets, October 1917.

When the *Aurora* fired everyone rushed forward shouting 'hurrah'. I was at the front; I ran up the stairs and stumbled into a big hall where there was a detachment of officer cadets

→

with their rifles at the ready. I shouted to the defenders, 'Throw down your rifles!' and they threw down their weapons as if to order.
A blank shell fired from the cruiser Aurora, *which had (like the railway stations, banks, post offices and telephone exchanges) been occupied by Bolshevik forces signalled what one eye-witness described as 'little more than a changing of the guard' at the Winter Palace; six people were killed in the takeover. Alexander Briansky recalls the scene for* The People's Century (BBC, 1995).

We shall now proceed to construct the Socialist order.
The opening words of Lenin's address to the Congress of Soviets, 26 October 1917.

Ten Days That Shook The World
Title of what may well be the first 'instant book': US journalist John Reed's account of the Bolshevik Revolution, November 1917.

Russia is a collapse, not a revolution.
The verdict of D. H. Lawrence in Phoenix *(1917).*

We did not overthrow the Czar and the bourgeoisie in order to fall on our knees before the German Kaiser and beg for peace ... We invoke all to a holy war against Imperialism in all countries.
Leon Trotsky, 22 December 1917.

I have seen the future and it works.
US journalist Lincoln Steffens, 1919.

Communism is Soviet power plus the electrification of the whole country.
Lenin, Report to the 8th Congress of Soviets, 1920.

A good man fallen among Fabians.
Lenin's reported verdict on George Bernard Shaw, who visited Russia after the Revolution.

Who, whom? We or they?
The two great categories of 'Dialectical Materialism' – those who act, and those on whom action is performed. Lenin quoted by F. MacLean in Disputed Barricade.

You must learn to be businessmen, not revolutionaries.
Lenin addresses the Party in 1922: recalled by the founder of the Socialist Party of Great Britain, Gerry Healy, who died in 1996.

Stalin's rudeness is becoming unbearable in the office of the General Secretary. Therefore, I propose the comrades should think about ways of removing him from that post.
A dictated memo from Lenin after his second and massive stroke, 4 January 1923.

Socialism in one country.
Slogan coined by Joseph Stalin after his assumption of power, 1924.

The state is an instrument in the hands of the ruling class for suppressing the resistance of its class enemies.
Joseph Stalin on 'proletarian democracy', quoted in M. R. Warner (ed): Stalin's Kampf.

It was the supreme expression of the mediocrity of the apparatus that Stalin himself rose to his position.
Leon Trotsky, My Life, *chapter 40.*

The Germans turned upon Russia the most grisly of all weapons. They transported Lenin in a sealed truck like a plague bacillus from Switzerland to Russia ... He alone could have led Russia into the enchanted quagmire; he alone could have found the way back to the causeway. He saw; he turned; he perished ... The Russian people were left floundering in the bog. Their worst misfortune was his birth, their next worst – his death.
Winston S. Churchill, The World Crisis *(1923–29).*

His Majesty's Government view with favour the establishment in Palestine of a national home for the Jewish people, and will use their best endeavours to facilitate the achievement of this object, it being clearly understood that nothing shall be done which may prejudice the civil and religious rights of existing non-Jewish communities in Palestine, or the rights and political status enjoyed in any other country.
A Declaration of Intent given by British Foreign Secretary Arthur Balfour to Zionist representative Baron Rothschild, 9 November 1917.

Who knows that today's thrilling victory may form as glorious a landmark as any in the history of mankind?
Dr Hertz, Chief Rabbi in Britain, after the occupation of Jerusalem, 9 December 1917.

I am making this statement as a wilful defiance of military authority because I believe that the War is being deliberately prolonged by those who have the power to end it [and by] the callous complacence with which the majority of those at home regard the continuance of agonies which they do not share, and which they have not sufficient imagination to realise.
Siegfried Sassoon, Counterattack. *(Quoted again in* Memoirs of an Infantry Officer *(1936)).*

1918

German troops, freed from the Eastern Front following the collapse of the Russian army and the peace talks at Brest-Litovsk, were drafted to the Western Front to meet the new challenge of American forces in what was to become the decisive phase of the war; meanwhile, the German people endured severe shortages of staple foods. General rationing was at last introduced in Britain in June; food rationing had been introduced for London and the Home Counties in February. As the year wore on the war-weariness of forces on all sides became more and more apparent; two whole troops of Bavarian cavalry were hanged in May for refusing to go to the Western Front. On 9 January, US President Wilson announced a 14-point peace plan largely derived from a report drawn up by 'The Inquiry', a New York policy group headed by a young journalist, Walter Lippmann. Under Wilson's proposals, conquered territory was, by and large, to be returned while the peoples of the Austro-Hungarian and Ottoman empires were to be granted autonomy, and an 'association of nations' would be formed to guarantee national integrity. There was no mention of reparations.

Using new tactics – specific assaults by 'shock troops' at weak points following artillery bombardment, instead of a blanket infantry assault – the German General Erich von Ludendorff smashed through the Allied lines in the Arras sector in March and threatened to push British forces back to the Channel before American troops could arrive in significant numbers; in a 40-mile (68-km) advance, 80,000 prisoners were taken in an offensive involving over three million men. In April, Ludendorff broke through the lines at Ypres; Marshal Foch, chief of the French General Staff, took over as head of Allied operations. The Royal Air Force was formed on 1 April from a merger of the Royal Flying Corps and the Royal Navy Air Service; on 22 April Manfred von Richthofen, the 'Red Baron', was shot down by a British pilot and killed.

On 9 March a new Military Service Act raised the conscription age to 50 and extended the call-up to Ireland. Following widespread rioting and the arrest of Sinn Féin MP Eamon de Valera, Irish conscription was abandoned and Home Rule postponed. The Commons granted a fresh War Loan of £600 million, followed by £500 million in June, while £138 million in public donations was raised from 'Tank Week'. Further £700 million loans were granted in August and November, bringing the total war debt to £7100 million. Parliament passed legislation awarding the vote to married women over 30, and allowing women to be elected as MPs. On 26 February a special conference of the Labour Party approved a new constitution; it was announced that over 300 candidates would be fielded at the next General Election.

There were strikes in Britain, particularly over the issue of equal pay for women. Cases of Spanish influenza began to be reported from around the world; the disease hit the Western Front in late spring, and Britain in the autumn. A looming timber crisis prompted the creation of the Forestry Commission in January and the planting of two million acres of state-owned woodland.

The high point of the German offensive, in which half a million Allied soldiers died, was reached in June as Soissons was taken, Rheims threatened and Amiens destroyed, and 'Big Bertha', a 420-mm gun named after the wife of the arms manufacturer Gustav Krupp, pounded Paris with 1764 lb shells from a range of 65 miles (105 km). The Allied counter-offensive began on 22 June as German troops were halted 45 miles (72 km) from Paris, and slowly turned back. After a four-week lull, caused by the influenza epidemic, a 'Big Push' began at the end of July. In a change of Allied tactics, the Germans had found Allied front lines lightly defended, and had pushed on; now, with German supply lines fully extended and American troops arriving at the rate of 300,000 a month, the Allies hit back. Twenty divisions, spearheaded by 400 tanks and supported by low-flying planes, went into action at Amiens and German forces were pushed back to the Hindenburg Line. Bulgaria surrendered on 30 September, by which time the German Army was in full retreat across the whole Western Front and taking civilian prisoners to work as slave labourers to defend the borders of Germany itself; a state of siege was declared in Berlin and the province of Brandenberg, while in German cities rioters tore up portraits of the Kaiser and burned him in effigy. There was a series of crushing defeats of often numerically superior Turkish forces in Palestine. Major T. E. Lawrence led his Arab army into Damascus on 1 October; Turkey surrendered on the 31st, by which time Germany's Central Power allies were also suing for peace; independent republics had already been declared in Czechoslovakia and Hungary.

Its armies in full retreat and its people in a state of insurrection, Germany surrendered on 11 November, the Armistice being signed at 11 a.m. in a railway carriage in the forest of Compiègne. Its terms dictated a surrender of the entire surface and U-boat fleet (which had been in action right to the end; the passenger ship *Leinster* was sunk on the 9th with the loss of 600 lives) and the handing over of 5000 heavy guns, 30,000 machine guns, 2000 warplanes, 5000 railway locomotives, 5000 lorries and 150,000 wagons; Alsace-Lorraine, seized in 1871, was returned to France; the Rhineland was to be occupied by Allied troops at Germany's expense, and the Allied blockade of German ports was to continue. 15 November was declared Victory Day and the whole of Britain, it seemed, was given over to celebration; blackout curtains were burned, licensing laws ignored, streets thronged with people. The Mayor of Blackburn, it was reported, gave his 2000 cotton workers £1 each and two days' holiday.

Kaiser Wilhelm II fled to Holland and Germany was declared a Republic by Friedrich Ebert, the 47-year-old trade unionist and President of the Social Democratic Party, who at once organized militia forces to put down any attempts at a 'Bolshevist' revolution. All over Germany, Dukes, Kings and Princes were chased out of their castles. The Hapsburg Emperor Charles abdicated on 11 November and Austria became, like Hungary and Czechoslovakia, a republic. A confederation of Serbs, Slovenes, Croats, Montenegrins and Muslims of Bosnia-Herzegovina was formed under the rule of the Serbian King Peter; it was afterwards known as Yugoslavia.

The coalition government of David Lloyd George won 478 seats in the General Election, in which 11 million people voted, twice as many as in 1910; Tories made gains at the expense of both pro- and anti-coalition Liberals; Asquith lost his seat, as did Labour's Ramsay MacDonald and Arthur Henderson, although 63 anti-coalition Labour MPs were returned. Countess Markievicz was elected as a Sinn Féin MP in Dublin but refused to take her seat as she did not recognize British sovereignty. President Woodrow Wilson visited London and was greeted by cheering crowds.

The total cost of the war was estimated at £60,643,160 for the Central Powers (£37,775,000 for Germany) and £125,690,477 for the Allies (Britain £35,334,012; France £24,265,583; USA £22,625,950).

Total Central Powers military casualties were 15,404,477; 3,386,200 died including 1,773,700 Germans and 1,200,000 from Austria-Hungary. Total Allied military casualties were 22,064,427 of whom 5,142,631 died: 1,700,000 Russian, 1,357,800 French, 908,371 British and Empire, 650,000 Italian and 116,516 American.

The influenza epidemic that swept the world in 1918–19 claimed twenty million lives, roughly the same as the combined military and civilian toll after four years and three months of war.

The moral climax of this, the culminating and final war for liberty, has come ... What we demand in this war is nothing peculiar to ourselves. It is that the world be made fit and safe to live in.
Woodrow Wilson's preamble to the Fourteen Points, speech to Congress, 8 January 1918.

Hell, Heaven or Hoboken by Christmas.
Attributed to the US General John J. Pershing, 1918.

Common ownership of the means of production and the best obtainable system of popular administration and control of each industry and service.
The stated aim of Clause Four of the Labour Party Constitution, adopted on 26 February 1918. Delegates from several Socialist societies complained that it was too ambiguous. It was later altered to 'common ownership of the means of production, distribution and control'.

My home policy? I wage war. My foreign policy? I wage war. Always, everywhere, I wage war ... And I shall continue to wage war until the last quarter of an hour.
The French premier Georges Clemençeau, speech to the Chamber of Deputies, 8 March 1918.

There is ... but one response possible from us: force, force to the utmost, force without stint or limit. The righteous and triumphant force shall make right the law of the world and cast every selfish dominion down in the dust.
Woodrow Wilson responds to German successes on the Western Front, 6 April 1918.

Everyone out here staking everything; everyone knows and trusts we shall win everything.
Kaiser Wilhelm II issues a rallying call to troops from his Headquarters at Spa, 11 April 1918.

Every position must be held to the last man: there must be no retirement. With our backs to the wall and believing in the justice of our cause, each one of us must fight on to the end.
Sir Douglas (afterwards Earl) Haig delivers a personal message to all ranks after a three-week period in which 400,000 Allied troops died, 13 April 1918.

If we can hold on until July we can resume the offensive; after that victory will be ours.
Marshal Pétain, May 1918.

The purpose of the Allies is exactly the purpose of the Central Powers, and that is the conquest and spoliation of the weaker nations that has always been the purpose of war.
The American Socialist leader Eugene V. Debs, speech at Canton, Ohio, 16 June 1918.

SONGS and SLOGANS of 1918

A mademoiselle from Armenteers
She hasn't been kissed for forty
 years
Hinky, dinky, par-lee-voo.
Edward Rowland: much plagiarized, more or less obscenely, since 1918.

Oh, Oh, Oh What A Lovely War!
Anonymous parody of a military march.

Per Ardua Ad Astra [Through endeavour to the stars]
The motto of the Royal Air Force, founded on 1 April (Anon).

The Poetry of War

They shall not grow old, as we that are left grow old:
Age shall not weary them, nor the years condemn.
At the going down of the sun and in the morning
We will remember them.

Laurence Binyon: 'For The Fallen', September 1914. Afterwards set to music by Edward Elgar. This extract is read aloud at Remembrance Day services and is found on War Memorials around the world.

If I should die, think only this of me:
That there's some corner of a foreign field
That is for ever England.

Rupert Brooke, 'The Soldier', 1914. Brooke died on service on the island of Skyros, on his way to the Dardanelles, and was buried there.

Yes. I remember Adelstrop –
The name, because one afternoon
Of heat the express-train drew up there
Unwontedly. It was late June.

Edward Thomas: 'Adelstrop': a moment of an English summer nostalgically recalled in the trenches on the Western Front. Thomas was killed in action at Arras in April 1917.

'Good morning, good morning,' the General said,
When we met him last week on our way to line.
Now the soldiers he smiled at are most of them dead,
And we're cursing his staff for incompetent swine.

Siegfried Sassoon, 'The General'.

I died in Hell
(They called it
Passchendaele).

Siegfried Sassoon, 'Memorial Tablet'.

My centre is giving way, my right is in retreat; situation excellent; I shall attack.
Marshal Foch, dispatch during the Second Battle of the Marne.

Come on, you sons of bitches! Do you want to live forever?
Attributed to US Marine Sergeant Dan Daly, Belleau Wood, 6 June 1918.

This has been the black day of the German Army.
General Ludendorff after the collapse of German forces at Amiens, 8 August 1918.

Sire, you no longer have an army ... If you won't abdicate, then the best thing for you to do is to shoot yourself.
German Chief of Staff General Wilhelm Groener speaks to the Kaiser on the telephone, 9 November 1918.

As an English General has very truly said, 'The German army was stabbed in the back.'
General – and future President – Paul von Hindenburg, statement to a Reichstag Committee, 18 November 1918. The 'English General' was never identified.

It is the soul that has faltered while the body is still strong.
An anonymous eye-witness to the surrender of the German fleet, 21 November 1918.

Here was the world's worst wound. And here with pride
'Their name liveth for evermore,' the Gateway claims.
Was ever an immolation so belied
As these intolerably nameless names?
Siegfried Sassoon, 'On Passing the New Menin Gate'.

Known as 'Mad Jack' and awarded the Military Cross for his solitary exploits in no-man's land, Sassoon risked court-martial and perhaps execution in 1917 by declaring his refusal to fight on, and his belief in the necessity of an immediate negotiated peace (see 1917). His friend and fellow writer Robert Graves arranged his discharge to Craiglockhart Hospital in Scotland (known to soldiers as 'Dottyville') where, among the men being treated for mental breakdown, he met and encouraged a young soldier-poet called Wilfred Owen. Some of his, and Owen's, bitterest anti-war poems were first published in the hospital magazine.

I have seen a green country, useful to the race,
Knocked silly with guns and mines, its villages vanished,
Even the last rat and last kestrel banished
God bless us all, this was peculiar grace.
Edmund Blunden, 'Report on Experience'. Blunden, like Sassoon, was awarded the Military Cross on the Western Front. He published a prose work, Undertones of War, *in 1928.*

… The old Lie: Dulce et decorum est
Pro patria mori.
Wilfred Owen, 'Dulce Et Decorum Est'.

What passing-bells for these who die as cattle?
Only the monstrous anger of the guns.
Only the stuttering rifles' rapid rattle
Can patter out their hasty orisons.
Wilfred Owen, 'Anthem for Doomed Youth'. Also awarded the Military Cross after leaving Craiglockhart to return to France, Owen was killed by a sniper's bullet a week before the Armistice. His poems were first collected and published by Sassoon in 1920.

The war we have just been through, though it was shot through with terror, is not to be compared with the war we would have to face next time.
Woodrow Wilson, quoted in John Dos Passos, Mr Wilson's War *(1930).*

The British flag has never flown over a more powerful or a more united Empire … Never did our voice count for more in the councils of nations; or in determining the future destinies of mankind.
Lord Carson, speech, House of Lords, 18 November 1918.

What is our task? To make Britain a fit country for heroes to live in.
David Lloyd George, speech, 24 November 1918.

The Germans, if this Government is returned, are going to pay every penny; they are going to be squeezed, as a lemon is squeezed – until the pips squeak. My only doubt is not whether we can squeeze hard enough, but whether there is enough juice.
Eric Geddes MP, campaign speech, Cambridge, 10 December 1918.

I saw Major Johnstone, who is here to lay the bases of an American History. We discussed the right name of the war. I said that we called it now *The War*, but

that this could not last. The Napoleonic War was *The Great War*. To call it *The German War* was too much flattery for the Boche. I suggested *The World War* as a shade better title, and finally we mutually agreed to call it *The First World War* in order to prevent the millennium folk from forgetting that the history of the world was the history of war.
Lieutenant-Colonel Charles A'Court Repington, diary entry, 10 September. Repington's book, The First World War 1914–18, was published in 1920.

That's what you are. That's what you all are. All of you young people who served in the war. You are a lost generation.
The American writer Gertrude Stein, quoted in Ernest Hemingway's A Moveable Feast (1926). The last sentence is also attributed to a garage proprietor, addressing a young mechanic who had failed to repair Ms Stein's car.

WAR'S AFTERMATH

1919-1920

A lot of hard-faced men who look as if they had done very well out of the war.
The Conservative statesman Stanley Baldwin views the new House of Commons, January 1919.

We are fighting for the gates of heaven.
Former Reichstag deputy and self-styled 'Spartacist' Karl Liebknecht who, with Rosa Luxembourg, led an abortive 'workers' coup' against the German state in January 1919. Their call to arms was largely ignored, and an attempted occupation of the War Ministry failed when the Under-Secretary of State told the leader of the raiding party that he lacked the proper written authority. There was fighting in the streets, and several hundred fatalities before the two leaders were arrested and murdered by Freikorps officers escorting them to prison.

Famine spread throughout Germany as the year progressed; food aid from the former Allied countries was granted on condition that it was paid for by appropriations from Germany's frozen credit abroad.

I believe the conscience of the world has long been prepared to express itself in some such way.
US President Woodrow Wilson outlines his proposals for the League of Nations – one of his Fourteen Points of 1917 – at the Paris Peace Conference, where sharp divisions emerged between France, who wished to 'make Germany pay', and America, who favoured a 'just peace'; Britain inclined to the American view. Twenty-seven countries agreed to Wilson's proposals for the League of Nations, although when it was formed the US did not join. The first meeting of the League took place at St James's Palace, London, on 11 February 1920.

We are all Home Rulers today.
The Times, 25 March 1919. Twenty-five Sinn Féin MPs elected at the end of 1918 had refused to attend Parliament in Westminster and instead set up their own assembly, the Dáil Éireann, in Dublin. The Irish Republican Army (IRA) was created as the 'military wing' of Sinn Féin to resist British rule, or any attempt to partition Ireland and grant Home Rule to the South, under British sovereignty. In October the Dáil was declared a 'seditious assembly' and surrounded by troops and police; most of its members were arrested but Michael Collins, the 'Minister of Finance', escaped through a skylight.

I never met anyone in Ireland who understood the Irish question, except one Englishman who had only been there a week.
Keith Fraser MP, speech, House of Commons, May 1919.

No party in Ireland is prepared to accept anything except the impossible. But that is no excuse for British government inaction.
Prime Minister Lloyd George announces plans for partition, 22 December 1919. As the IRA began a terror campaign in Ireland, the government dispached 800 'special constables' in March 1920. Known by their uniform as the 'Black and Tans', they were noted for their ruthlessness. The death toll accelerated after the assassination of Thomas MacCurtain, Lord Mayor of Cork, and the death on hunger strike of his Sinn Féin successor, Terence MacSwiney.

I want to make it possible for the humblest woman who may be elected to follow the precedent I set.
Nancy Astor, elected Member of Parliament for Plymouth on 28 November 1919; her husband, Waldorf Astor, had previously held it. Parliament lifted restrictions on women entering the professions, and the first female Bar student was admitted to Lincoln's Inn on 30 December 1919.

The demand is made that we shall acknowledge that we alone are guilty of having caused the war. Such a confession in my mouth would be a lie.
Count Ulrich Brockdorff-Rantzau, German Foreign Minister, protests at the conditions insisted on by France at the Paris talks, in particular Article 231 of the proposed Treaty, assigning to Germany and her allies responsibility for causing the war, and ordering heavy reparation payments. Other clauses stripped Germany of her overseas colonies, and assigned large territories in the East to Poland. The Rhineland was to be demilitarized and occupied by Allied troops for up to 15 years, and German armed forces were limited to keeping civil order in Germany. Faced with a choice between acceptance or military occupation, Germany signed the Treaty at the Palace of Versailles on 28 June 1919.

We shall have to fight another war all over again in 25 years at three times the cost.
Lloyd George's verdict on the Treaty of Versailles.

'Curious, I seem to hear a child weeping.'
Caption to a cartoon by Will Dyson, Daily Herald, 29 June 1919. The speaker is Clemençeau; he stands outside the Palace of Versailles while in the background a child is seen bearing a placard that reads: 'Class of 1940'.

Verdicts

Man, it seemed, had been created to jab the life out of Germans.
Siegfried Sassoon, Memoirs of an Infantry Officer.

There is nothing that war has ever achieved that we could not better achieve without it.
Havelock Ellis, The Philosophy of Conflict, 1919.

It is far easier to make war than to make peace.
Georges Clemençeau, speech, 14 July 1919.

A man may build himself a throne of bayonets, but he cannot sit on it.
Dean Inge, 1920.

We want to get rid of the militarist not simply because he hurts and kills, but because he is an intolerable thick-voiced blockhead who stands hectoring and blustering in our way of achievement.
H. G. Wells, The Outline of History, 1920.

Haig was devoid of the gift of intelligible and coherent expression. ...Brilliant to the top of his boots.
David Lloyd George on Douglas Haig.

Only a frantic pair of moustaches.
T. E. Lawrence on Marshal Foch.

The only time he ever put up a fight in his life was when we asked him for his resignation.
Georges Clemençeau on Marshal Joffre.

One to mislead the public, another to mislead the Cabinet, and the third to mislead itself.
H. H. Asquith on why the War Office kept three sets of figures: in Price of Glory, 1920.

The Twenties: You Ain't Heard Nothin' Yet
1920~1929

My candle burns at both ends;
It will not last the night;
But ah, my foes, and oh my friends -
It gives a lovely light!

~ *Edna St Vincent Millay*, A Few Figs from Thistles, *1920*

The devastation wrought by the First World War was measured not only in terms of the destruction of life, property and trade but also in the shattering of the political and cultural certainties that had sustained pre-war Europe. Imperial Russia had already crumbled and vanished, to be replaced by an entirely new order which held nothing in common with what had gone before – and which, moreover, proclaimed its intention to help foster similar revolutions throughout a continent brought to the brink of bankruptcy by four years of ruinous conflict and, in Germany's case, its crippling burden of 'reparation'. Governments sought to meet this threat with measures which, in some cases, paralleled in their draconian rigour the reaction of British governments of the late 18th century to revolutionary fervour in France.

In Britain itself, the growing Labour movement brought about the country's first general strike and produced a Labour government whose leaders were at pains to avoid any charge of 'Bolshevism'. In the USA where Socialist Party leader Eugene V. Debs was jailed for his activities, the demands of organized labour for a greater share of the prosperity it helped create were met with often vicious brutality.

There was a widespread feeling of anger and betrayal: living conditions in the post-war world were, for very many people, harsher and more uncertain than they had ever been, and the old establishment, which had led its peoples into disaster and carnage, was still (albeit feebly) intact; this made fertile ground for the growth of populist authoritarian movements claiming ready-made 'modern' solutions and appealing to sentiments of national pride, unity and strength. Italy became the first country to be governed by such a movement; its example was admired elsewhere as providing a 'containable' check to Bolshevism – but it was not to be successfully imitated until the next decade.

The ethos of the 1920s – the 'Jazz Age' – may be defined as one of desparate gaiety produced by an uneasy and volatile mixture of aspiraton and cynicism; a demoralization that found its expression, amongst those who could afford it, in the pursuit of instant personal gratification. Elsewhere it was expressed in an equally febrile resentment and discontent.

A decade born out of the ruin of war ended with stock market crashes that heralded devastating economic depression. The 1920s was a decade that burned its candle at both ends.

- -

One thing I know. If living isn't a seeking for the grail it may be a damned amusing game.

F. Scott Fitzgerald, the chronicler of the 'Jazz Age', This Side of Paradise, 1920.

- -

1920

Pray for me. Old Lloyd George with all his faults is the best we've got.

Nancy Astor, Conservative MP, speech to voters after her election, November 1919. The new decade began with a Liberal-Conservative coalition government in Britain.

America's present need is not heroics but healing; not nostrums but normalcy; not revolution but restoration; not surgery but serenity.

The Republican presidential candidate Warren G. Harding campaigning in 1920. He and his running mate, Calvin Coolidge, won a convincing victory over the Democrats' James M. Cox and Franklin D. Roosevelt; disabling illness had forced Woodrow Wilson's retirement from politics.

Labour is not fit to govern.

Winston S. Churchill, speech, 1920.

1922

Count not his broken pledges as a crime; He MEANT them. HOW he meant them – at the time.

Kensal Green, 1922, on Lloyd George; quoted in The Faber Book of English History in Verse

(1989) (ed. Kenneth Baker). In 1922 Lloyd George was ousted by the Conservative majority in the coalition Cabinet, and replaced by Andrew Bonar Law.

Poor Bonar can't bear being called a liar. Now, I don't mind.

David Lloyd George, 1922, quoted in Baldwin by G. M. Young.

I must follow them; I am their leader.

Andrew Bonar Law, 1922, quoted by E. T. Raymond in Mr Balfour.

1923

Baldwin's outlook is very close to ours.

A remark that startled his colleagues: Labour Party leader Ramsay MacDonald after the Conservative Stanley Baldwin succeeded Bonar Law as Prime Minister, 21 May 1923.

'Sewing, Bottomley?'
-'No – reaping.'

A prison visitor sees a convict sewing mailbags. On 29 May 1922 the Independent MP and founding editor of John Bull, Horatio Bottomley, was sentenced to seven years' penal servitude for selling fraudulent 'Victory Bonds'.

- -

Drum on your drums, batter on your banjos,
sob on the long cool winding saxophones.
Go to it, O jazzmen.

Carl Sandburg, 'Jazz Fantasia', Smoke and Steel, 1920.

- -

Prohibition

There will not be any violations to speak of.
16 January 1920: Colonel Daniel Porter, the supervising revenue agent charged with enforcing the Volstead Act, the 18th Amendment to the US Constitution, which prohibited the sale, consumption and distribution of alcoholic liquor. The Mayor of New York forecast that he would need 250,000 extra police as a result.

Puritanism: the haunting fear that someone, somewhere, may be happy.
The US writer H. L. Mencken's reaction to Prohibition, 1920.

In a generation, those who are now children will have lost their taste for alcohol.
John Fuller, Atlantis: America and the Future (1925).

Communism is like Prohibition – it's a good idea but it won't work.
American comedian Will Rogers, Autobiography, November 1927.

A great social and economic experiment, noble in motive and far-reaching in purpose.
Presidential candidate Herbert Hoover on Prohibition: 28 February 1928; but four years later, as President, he called for its repeal. Organized crime thrived on 'bootlegging' – smuggling illegal liquor – and in 'speakeasys' – illegal drinking clubs.

The Prohibition law, written for weaklings and derelicts, has divided the nation, like Gaul, into three parts – wets, drys and hypocrites.
Florence Sabin, speech, 9 February 1931. Congress passed the 21st Amendment, repealing Prohibition, in 1933.

Destruction is also Construction!
Slogan of the Dadaists

The League exists as a foreign agency. We hope it will be helpful. But the United States sees no reason to limit its own freedom and independence of action by joining it.
6 December 1923: US President Calvin Coolidge, who succeeded to the presidency after Harding's sudden death on 2 August, keeps the USA out of the recently formed League of Nations which had been the brainchild of President Woodrow Wilson. America's absence greatly inhibited The League's ability to act effectively in any 'policing' role.

It is fitting that we should have buried the Unknown Prime Minister by the side of the Unknown Soldier.
Attributed to Herbert Henry Asquith, attending

SLOGANS and CATCHPHRASES
of
THE TWENTIES

It beats... as it sweeps... as it cleans.
Still going strong: the Hoover vacuum cleaner slogan was coined in 1919.

Say It With Flowers.
Slogan of American florists from 1917; and afterwards in Britain.

Hell Is The Well Of Whisky!
O Death Where Is Thy Sting?
Rival banners in Aberdeen, as Scots vote in a referendum on Prohibition, January 1920. The 'Wets' won.

Back to Normalcy.
US presidential campaign slogan: Harding, Republican, 1920.

Convict No. 6953 for President.
US presidential campaign slogan: Debs, Socialist, 1920.

Bonar Law's funeral at Westminster Abbey, 5 November 1923, after being restored as Liberal Party leader.

Of all the politicians I ever saw
The least significant was Bonar Law.
Unless it was MacDonald, by the way –
Or Baldwin – it's impossible to say.
Hilaire Belloc, 1923.

1924

I am a broken piece of machinery.
Woodrow Wilson, weeks before his death on 3 February 1924.

The business of America is business.
President Coolidge, 1924.

Today 23 years ago dear Grandmama died. I wonder what she would have thought of a Labour Government.
Presumably Queen Victoria would have found it unamusing: entry for 22 January 1924 in the diary of King George V. Baldwin had called a General Election in December 1923 with the result that the Tories had 258 seats to Labour's 191 and the Liberals' 159; Labour leader Ramsay MacDonald formed a minority administration with Liberal support.

Well, what are you Socialists going to do about me?
King George V grants an audience in January 1924 to his new Prime Minister, whose cabinet included two Tories and a Liberal, owing to lack of talent in Labour's ranks; MacDonald acted as his own Foreign Secretary.

The paradox of British politics: the moment one appropriates power one becomes impotent.
Ramsay MacDonald, on being Prime Minister for ten months; the Conservatives won a massive victory in the General Election on 29 October 1924. Baldwin became Prime Minister, Winston Churchill Chancellor of the Exchequer.

Desperation, Pacification, Expectation, Acclamation, Realisation.
UK slogan for Fry's chocolate, 1920s.

From the Sahara to the Ritz.
...That'll do nicely: American Travelers Cheques, 1922.

Il Duce ha sempre ragione [The Duce is always right].
Italian Fascist slogan, 1922.

Never knowingly undersold.
The John Lewis Partnership first issued this pledge in 1923.

Stop me and buy one.
Walls Ice Cream vans, from 1923. Vulgarized to 'Buy me and stop one' for contraceptives.

If They Tax Them We Can't Buy Them.
Liberal Party election slogan, capitalizing on the above, 1923.

The customer is always right.
Slogan adopted at the stores of H. Gordon Selfridge, USA, 1924.

Keep Cool With Coolidge.
US presidential campaign slogan, Coolidge, Republican, 1924.

Not a penny off the pay, not a minute on the day.
Miners' union leader A. J. Cook, 1925–26.

Blow some my way.
Chesterfield cigarettes, USA, 1926.

Snap... Crackle... Pop!
US slogan for Kellogg's Rice Crispies, 1928, and afterwards in Britain.

A chicken in Every Pot.
US presidential campaign slogan, Hoover, Republican, 1928.

Safety First.
Conservative Party slogan, UK, 1929; it had earlier been used to promote road safety.

Guinness Is Good For You.
Guinness Extra Stout: UK slogan from 1929.

Ireland:
Partition, Home Rule and Civil War

I am signing my own death warrant.
7 December 1921: the IRA leader Michael Collins, having led a bitter fight against British forces in which many atrocities were committed on both sides, signs the Treaty accepting the partition of Ireland. The 'Six Counties' of Ulster, which had already been granted their own assembly, were, with their Protestant majority, to remain part of the UK and send MPs to Westminster. The remaining 26 counties became the Irish Free State, a self-governing Dominion like Canada, with its own revenue-raising parliament. Privately, British ministers believed that Ireland would be best governed as a whole, from Dublin; Collins, knowing of the IRA's fierce allegiance to a united Ireland, signed the agreement on the understanding, given him by Lloyd George, that areas of Ulster with a large nationalist majority would be able to join the South.

The Dáil Éireann approved Collins's deal by 64 votes to 57 but Eamon de Valera refused the offer of the presidency and vowed to continue the fight for a united republican Ireland. The IRA split into pro- and anti-Treaty factions. Collins was shot dead in an ambush at Beal-na-mBlath, in County Cork, on 22 August 1922. The Council of Ireland, a provision of the Treaty designed to facilitate cooperation between North and South, was subsequently abandoned after threats of armed insurrection from Ulster Unionists.

Stand calmly by your posts. Bend bravely and undaunted to your work, let no cruel act of reprisal blemish your bright honour.
General Richard Mulcahy, Chief of Staff of the Irish Free State Army, issues an order following the assassination of its Commander-in-Chief Michael Collins on 22 August 1922. Mulcahy led the Free State forces in a bitter civil war against the anti-Treaty republican forces of Eamon de Valera ('the Irregulars'), who finally surrendered in May 1923.

We preferred to burn our homes, blow up our bridges, rob our banks and saddle ourselves with millions of debt … and now we wonder why the Orangemen are not hopping over the border like fleas to come under our jurisdiction.
Kevin O'Higgins, Vice-President of the Irish Free State, who was gunned down on 10 July 1927 by the IRA. The following month legislation was passed, on the casting vote of the Speaker, obliging de Valéra to bring his Fianna Fáil deputies into the Dáil, which they had been boycotting. Fears of renewed civil war were not realized.

The Liberals were reduced to a rump of 40.
The Tory landslide was assisted by the Daily Mail*'s publication of the 'Zinoviev Letter' – instructions for revolution from the Communist International to British Socialists. It was a forgery.*

A sheep in sheep's clothing.
Winston Churchill: frequently quoted as referring

● ●

A house is a machine for living in.
'Le Corbusier', Towards a New Architecture, 1923.

● ●

to Clement Attlee, but Churchill himself insisted it referred to Ramsay MacDonald.

I want to see the spirit of service to the whole nation the birthright of every member of the Unionist Party – Unionist in the sense that we stand for the union of those two nations of which Disraeli spoke two generations ago; union among our own people to make one nation of our own people at home which, if secured, nothing else matters in the world.
Prime Minister Stanley Baldwin, speech, Albert Hall, 4 December 1924. The Conservatives pre-

ferred to be known as 'Unionists' between the wars.

We did it to show our intellectual superiority.
Chicago 'thrill murderer' Nathan Leopold, 31 May 1924. Leopold and his friend Richard Loeb, both 19-year-old university students and millionaires' sons, kidnapped and strangled a 14-year-old boy because they 'wanted to murder someone' and believed they could not be caught by detectives with 'inferior minds'. Their attorney, Clarence Darrow, successfully pleaded for a sentence of life imprisonment rather than execution.

You stand forth as the leader of the forces of progress in their assault upon the powers of reaction. I ask leave to range myself beneath your standard.
The ex-Tory MP and future leader of the British Union of Fascists, Sir Edward Mosley, makes a successful application to join the Labour Party. Letter to Ramsay MacDonald, 31 March 1924.

Because it's there.
George Leigh Mallory's reply when asked why he wanted to climb Mount Everest. He and Andrew Irvine died, having ascended without oxygen, on 19 June 1924; they were last seen less than 1000 ft (300 m) from the summit, then disappeared in a snowstorm. They may have succeeded, but this is improvable.

The Negro is not a menace to Americanism in the sense that the Jew or the Roman Catholic is a menace. He is not actually hostile to it. He is simply racially incapable of understanding, sharing, or contributing to Americanism.
Imperial Wizard Hiram W. Evans, Ku Klux Klan leader, 1924. The Democratic National Convention in July 1924 defeated a motion condemning the Klan's activities, which included the flogging and lynching of black Americans.

Nothing I say or write can bring the two communities together ... It is an expression of my unbearable hopelessness ... It is both a penance and a prayer.
Mohandas (Mahatma) Gandhi, leader of India's Congress Party, begins a 21-day fast in an attempt to bring to an end the conflict between India's Hindus and Muslims, 18 September 1924.

• •

This is the way the world ends
Not with a bang but a whimper.
T. S. Eliot, 'The Hollow Men', 1925.

• •

"Clear out, you fellows, double quick I say. We may hate one another but we hate you most. If it's fifty or five hundred years we shall get rid of you, yes, we shall drive every blasted Englishman into the sea. And then you and I shall be friends."
The controversial words of Dr Aziz to Fielding in A Passage to India *by E. M. Forster, 1924.*

How can what an Englishman believes be heresy? It is a contradiction in terms.
G. B. Shaw: St. Joan, 1924. In 1925 Shaw was awarded the Nobel Prize for Literature.

It's a musical kaleidoscope of America, our pep, our blues, our metropolitan madness.
George Gershwin on his Rhapsody in Blue, *orchestrated by Ferde Grofe, 1924.*

1925

It shall be unlawful for any teacher ... to teach any theory that denies the story of the divine creation of man as taught in the Bible, and to teach instead that man has descended from a lower state of animals.
Statute of the State of Tennessee, 1925. On 25 May the trial began of John Scopes, a teacher in Dayton who taught his classes the facts of evolution, and the world's press descended on the small town. The judge ruled scientific evidence inadmissible; after a spirited defence led by Clarence Darrow, Scopes was found guilty as charged and fined $100. It was a Pyrrhic victory for the 'creationists', however.

To think is to differ.
Clarence Darrow, Scopes Trial, Dayton, Tennessee, 13 July 1925.

They hired the money, didn't they?
President Coolidge, on being told of Britain's war debt, 1925.

Labour Unrest

There is no right to strike against the public safety by anybody, anywhere, any time.
Calvin Coolidge on the Boston Police Strike, 14 September 1919.

The nation must and will resist such an attack with all its strength.
Prime Minister Lloyd George on the miners' strike, 18 October 1920. It was called off on 3 November; the miners' union had demanded a minimum wage of 2 shillings (10p) per shift for men, 1 shilling for youths and 9d (c. 4p) for boys under 16. A further strike, from March to April 1921, collapsed after rail and transport unions in the 'Triple Alliance' ended their support for it. A degree of nationalization had been added to the miners' union demands. Mine owners subsequently cut wages and set wage rates locally.

The most pressing problem which confronts you is that of unemployment, consequent upon a world-wide restriction of trade.
In a speech written by his Prime Minister, King George V opens Parliament on 16 February 1921, the month UK unemployment rose above one million, including 368,000 ex-servicemen.

The country cannot continue to support a burden of this magnitude.
Preparing to wield 'Geddes' Axe': the Committee on National Expenditure, chaired by Sir Eric Geddes, is aghast at the public sector wage bill of £297 million per annum, and proposes cuts in pay for civil servants, the armed forces, police and teachers, 25 February 1922. Wages in industry were already falling.

England is at last ripe for revolution.
Leon Trotsky, 1923.

I think we ought to have as great a regard for religion as we can, so as to keep it out of as many things as possible.
Sean O'Casey, 'The Plough and the Stars', 1926. The play, which deals with the Easter Rising, aroused passionate feelings in Dublin, where the stage was stormed and fighting broke out. It was warmly received in London.

Do you realise, young woman, that you're the first American writer ever to poke fun at sex?
A publisher's reaction to Anita Loos's Gentlemen Prefer Blondes, 1925.

It is the government that should ask me for a pardon.
American Socialist leader Eugene V. Debs, 1921.

He was jailed for sedition in 1918 and released under an amnesty ordered by President Harding.

1927

Nation shall speak peace unto nation.
Schoolteacher Montague John Rendall's motto for the British Broadcasting Corporation, 1927. Regular broadcasts from the British Broadcasting Company had begun on 15 November 1922; 2 May 1923 saw the first broadcast of Woman's Hour – *a talk by Princess Alice on adoption.*

Who the hell wants to hear actors talk?
Studio mogul Harry M. Warner of Warner Bros Pictures, 1927.

~

If I were an actor with a squeaky voice I would worry.
The *Film Spectator, October 1927.*

The general strike is a challenge to Parliament, and it is the road to anarchy and ruin.
Prime Minister Stanley Baldwin, 5 May 1926. After the Samuels Commission recommended a 'temporary reduction' in miners' pay, an all out-strike was called, supported by the 'Triple Alliance' and the Trades Union Congress (TUC). Baldwin's statement appeared in The British Gazette, *a government propaganda news-sheet edited by Winston Churchill; newspaper workers, too, were on strike. Trains, buses and trams were run by middle-class volunteers; some 6000 people signed up on the first day at London's Organization for the Maintenance of Supplies.*

As far as we can see, we have no intention to allow cricket to be interrupted.
Displaying a stiff upper lip made of finest willow, the Secretary of the MCC, 10 May 1926. The strike began to crumble after a week, as workers desperate for pay and uncertain of their jobs began to return to work. The TUC called off its support but the miners, bitter at what they considered an act of betrayal, carried on until 12 November when, after six months, They conceded almost all the mine owners' demands: working hours were increased from seven to eight while in the north-east of England and North Wales wages were reduced below April levels.

Neither the common law nor the Fourteenth Amendment confers the absolute right to strike.
Supreme Court Judge Louis D. Brandeis, Dorchy v. Kansas, *1926. Henry Ford paid $5 for an eight-hour shift, but this was exceptional; America's post-war boom was substantially financed by poorly-paid labour with little or no job security; unions were, more often then not, unrecognized and strikes were frequently broken by brute force, using bullets rather than the rolled-up mackintoshes employed by police at Tonypandy in Wales during the miners' strike.*

Unless the government faces the situation, a revolutionary situation will be created in this country which no leader will be able to withstand.
Miners' leader Arthur Cook adresses 200 unemployed Welsh miners who marched 180 miles (290 km) from Rhondda to London; the Prime Minister refused to meet them: 23 November 1927.

Gentlemen, it was necessary to abolish the fez, which sat on the heads of our nation as an emblem of ignorance, negligence, fanaticism and hatred of progress and civilization, to accept in its place the hat, the headgear worn by the whole civilized world.
Kemal Atatürk, founder of the Turkish Republic, attempts a throroughgoing secularization and westernization of his country, speech to the Turkish Assembly, October 1927.

Defeat in the Great War no doubt rankles in the German mind and will continue to do so.
Lieutenant-General Sir A. Montgomery-Massingberd predicts another war 'within twenty years', 3 November 1927.

Every man has a House of Lords in his own head. Fears, prejudices, misconceptions – those are the peers, and they are hereditary.
David Lloyd George, speech, Cambridge, 1927.

It is impossible to imagine its having happened in any fully civilized country – in any country, that is to say, in which civilization is more than skin deep.
The London New Statesman *on the execution of Sacco and Vanzetti, two immigrant Italian anarchist sympathizers convicted – wrongly, it was widely believed – in Massachusetts for murder and executed in 1927 after seven years of appeals. The case aroused extraordinary*

. . . .

Wait a minute, wait a minute, you ain't heard nothin' yet!
The first soundtrack, the first words: one of four segments in the film The Jazz Singer *(1927).*

. . . .

interest throughout Europe; a crowd of 200,000 demonstrated in London's Hyde Park on 22 August and listened to speeches from Labour, Liberal, Communist and trade union leaders. President Coolidge rejected the final appeal on 23 August.

1928

We shall soon be in sight of the day when poverty will be banished from this nation.
Herbert Hoover, Republican candidate for the US presidency, campaign speech, 1928. Hoover defeated his opponent, Al Smith, by 444 College votes to 87 although Smith's popular vote of 15 million was the highest ever polled by a Democrat.

I put forth this novel as an honest, healthy book.

D. H. Lawrence on Lady Chatterley's Lover *(1928), which was banned in the UK.*

1929

Holding the balance is a very responsible position.
Liberal leader Lloyd George, 31 May 1929, after Britain's General Election produced 288 seats for Labour, 260 for the Conservatives and

Fascism's First Light

We allow ourselves the luxury of being aristocratic and democratic, reactionary and revolutionary.
The political philosopher speaks: Benito Mussolini styles himself 'Il Duce' as 35 members of his National Fascist Party take their seats in the Italian Parliament, 7 November 1921. Italy's Fascists received support from business to break up strikes and attack Socialist groups. After successful marches on Fiume and Milan, 24,000 of Mussolini's armed supporters – the Blackshirts – took control of Rome in November 1924. Mussolini and King Victor Emmanuel appeared on the Palace balcony, waving to a large cheering crowd. The following month the Chamber of Deputies, threatened with dissolution, granted him absolute power for one year. He began by arresting known Socialists. In April 1924 the Fascists won a huge majority in the General Election; Mussolini set about suppressing all opposition.

And now get ready for my funeral.
The prophetic last words of Socialist Deputy Giacomo Matteoti, speaking in the Italian Parliament on 1 June 1924. On 10 June he was abducted in broad daylight on a Rome street by a Blackshirt gang; he was never seen again.

This is a new sign that Mussolini has God's full protection.
Pope Pius XII hails Divine intervention as Il Duce survives his fourth assassination attempt on 2 November 1926. At the March 1929 General Election, by which time all opposition activity was banned by law, the Fascists won 99 per cent of the votes cast. The 'fasces' were incorporated into Italy's national coat of arms, symbolic of the merging of State and Party in the person of the Leader.

I could not help being charmed, like so many other people have been, by Signor Mussolini's gentle and simple bearing and by his calm detached poise in spite of so many burdens and dangers.
Winston S. Churchill, The Times, 21 January 1927.

59 for the Liberals. Labour's Ramsay MacDonald became Prime Minister with Liberal support; Margaret Bondfield (Minister of Labour) became the first female cabinet member. Also appointed was Labour's 'rising star', Sir Oswald Mosley.

A federal tie must exist between peoples grouped geographically like the peoples of Europe.
French Prime Minister Aristide Briand, 5 September 1929 (see 1946, p. 100).

Any lack of confidence in the economic future or the basic strength of business in the United States is foolish.
President Herbert Hoover, inaugural address, 4 March 1929.

All Quiet on the Western Front.
Erich Maria Remarque: title of his anti-war novel, published 1929.

Goodbye To All That.
Robert Graves: title of autobiography, published 1929.

• •

They lounge at corners of the street
And greet friends with a shrug of the shoulder
And turn their empty pockets out.
The cynical gestures of the poor.

Stephen Spender, 'Unemployed', 1929.

• •

The national revolution has begun.
A nondescript ex Lance-Corporal called Adolf Hitler fires a shot into the ceiling of the Burgerbraukeller in Munich on 12 November 1923. Despite the support of Field Marshal Erich von Ludendorff, the coup fizzled out in farce and the Bavarian authorities arrested Hitler, who was sentenced to five years' imprisonment with parole after six months. Ludendorff was acquitted.
In 1921 Germany's war reparations had been set at £10 billion payable over 42 years, with a 12.5 per cent tax on exports. As the economy collapsed, hyper-inflation took hold; at its height in November 1923 a loaf of bread cost 201 billion marks. Conditions were ripe for demagogues.

Four and a Half Years of Struggle against Lies, Stupidity and Cowardice.
The provisional title of a book dictated by Hitler while in prison; the title was altered to My Struggle [Mein Kampf]. Hitler was released on 20 December 1924.

To this struggle of ours there are only two possible issues. Either the enemy pass over our bodies or we pass over theirs.
Adolf Hitler, speech, Munich, 27 February 1925, immediately after pledging himself and his followers to good behaviour and renouncing the use of force.

All those who are not racially pure are mere chaff. [...] The broad mass of an nation ... will more easily fall victim to a big lie than to a small one. [...] Germany will be either a world power or will not be at all.
Adolf Hitler, Mein Kampf, published on 18 July 1925.

The story of Hitler's struggle cannot be read without admiration for the courage, the perseverance, and the vital force which enabled him to challenge, defy, conciliate and overcome all the authorities and resistance in his path.
Winston S. Churchill, Great Contemporaries.

In Britain, a special edition of Mein Kampf was sold in aid of the Red Cross.

The Wall Street Crash

Stocks have reached what looks like a permanently high plateau.
Irving Fisher, Professor of Economics at Yale University, 17 October 1929.

EXPERTS PREDICT RISING MARKET
Headline in the New York Journal, 25 October 1929.

WALL ST. LAYS AN EGG
Headline, Variety, October 1929.

The US stock market boomed in the second half of the decade as millions of investors made paper profits on their deals. By buying and reselling within the period prescribed for settlement, millions of citizens – as well as banks and businesses – were able to reap profits without apparent risk, although the subsequent purchasers were, of course, doing the same. A few prescient corporations and large shareholders began quietly unloading stock at the beginning of the month, sensing that the bubble was about to burst. Panic hit Wall Street on 24 October, when $6 billion was wiped off share values; by 11.30 a.m. the system of recording transactions collapsed and traders began marking prices down by huge amounts. Crowds assembled in Wall Street and the riot police were called. New York's leading bankers held a crisis meeting at midday.

There has been a little distress selling on the Stock Exchange ... the situation is a technical one.
Thomas W. Lamont, senior partner in the firm of J. P. Morgan, makes a statement at 1 p.m. on 24 October 1929. Prices rallied in the afternoon, thanks largely to the banks' concerted buying policy, and some stocks showed a gain on the day; others, however, were wiped out and whatever the big banks undertook to buy would have to be paid for or resold.

Hysteria has now disappeared from Wall Street.
The Times, London, 2 November 1929. Shares had begun to fall sharply in London.

This doesn't mean that there will be any general or serious business depression ... For six years American business has been diverting a substantial part of its attention, its energies and its resources to the speculative game ... Now that irrelevant, alien and hazardous adventure is over. Business has come home again, back to its job, providentially unscathed, sound in wind and limb, financially stronger than ever before.
Reassuring words in Business Week, 2 November 1929. On 29 October, shares on Wall Street fell a further $10 billion – more than twice the amount of currency then in US circulation. Prices continued to fall; by December 1932, $50 billion had been wiped out.

Gentlemen, you have come sixty days too late. The depression is over.
June 1930: President Hoover rejects calls for reflation. But the depression was to last ten years.

The Thirties: The Years the Locust Ate
1930~1939

What a decade! A riot of appalling folly that suddenly becomes a nightmare, a scenic railway ending in a torture-chamber. It starts off in the hangover of the 'enlightened' post-war age, with Ramsay MacDonald soft-soaping into the microphone and the League of Nations flapping vague wings in the background, and it ends up with twenty thousand bombing planes darkening the sky and Himmler's masked executioner whacking women's heads off on a block borrowed from the Nuremberg museum. In between are the politics of the umbrella and the hand-grenade.

~ *George Orwell on* The Thirties, *by Malcolm Muggeridge,*
New English Weekly, *April 1940*

The depression that began with the Wall Street Crash of 1929 affected the whole of the Western world: while the Fascist dictatorship consolidated itself in Italy, economic conditions helped to bring Adolf Hitler to power in Germany, and in both countries the militaristic nationalism inherent in Fascism was to lead to the pursuit of more territory. In the US where 'Bolshevist' bombs exploded at the beginning of the decade, the hungry and the unemployed turned in their millions to what was in effect (though never proclaimed as such) the Social Democratic programme of Franklin D. Roosevelt, much of which was inspired by the 'Yellow Book' of the British Liberal Party. In Britain, the piecemeal attempts of coalition governments, notionally led by a Labour Prime Minister, to ameliorate the effects of the depression led to the defection of the Labour politician Oswald Mosley and the formation of the British Union of Fascists. Britain's political leaders largely viewed the ascendancy of Fascist dictatorship in Europe with approval, or at least complacency: it was regarded as a bulwark against Communism and the saviour of trade. The overthrow in civil war of Spain's elected government by the Fascist General Francisco Franco, with German Nazi help, was applauded in Parliament, with few vocal dissenters. Of those who did view these developments with alarm, many saw Communism as the only available refuge and hope. Those who rejected and opposed both ideologies were few: Winston Churchill, on the political right, and George Orwell on the left made strange and lonely allies, until the events that both had foreseen overtook a world plunged once more into war.

The three themes that dominated the decade – Depression, Dictatorship, and War, with their concomitant themes of Poverty, Oppression and Appeasement – are dealt with separately from the chronology of its other significant events; each self-contained sequence of events is grouped together within the text.

THE HUNGRY THIRTIES – DEPRESSION and DUST BOWL

I KNOW 3 TRADES
I SPEAK 3 LANGUAGES
FOUGHT FOR 3 YEARS
HAVE 3 CHILDREN
AND NO WORK FOR 3 MONTHS
BUT I ONLY WANT
ONE JOB

Placard worn by unemployed man, London, 1930

UK unemployment doubled to 2 million between 1929 and 1930; it hit a peak of 3.1 million (18 per cent of the workforce) at the end of 1932. In Germany it peaked at 30 per cent, in the US at 11.6 million (25 per cent), in Norway 35 per cent. Italy and Japan (8 per cent) escaped relatively unscathed.

In America, the aftershocks of the Wall Street Crash proved more damaging than the crash itself, as hundreds of thousands of 'small investors' rushed to draw money from the banks to cover their obligations on the stock market; hundreds of small banks collapsed, having first called in all their secured loans, because the money demanded simply wasn't there, and they brought some of the big banks down with them. A financial crisis thus became a social and economic catastrophe. Millions of people found themselves ruined and thrown out of work.

The British banking system was protected from this sort of disaster by the federation of nearly all small banks into the 'Big Five'; nonetheless unemployment rose steeply as American export orders fell away, the US suspended all foreign loans, world trade slumped and the Australian government banned immigration, a traditional British working-class standby in times of hardship; unemployment in Australia reached 30 per cent. As Britain was obliged to pay its foreign debts in gold, UK Treasury reserves were dangerously depleted and there was a run on the pound. In September 1931, the newly formed National Government, led by Ramsay MacDonald but dominated by Conservatives, took sterling off the gold standard and devalued the pound by 30 per cent. A 'global' cut of 10 per cent was ordered in the UK government's wages and welfare bill.

A banking collapse in Austria led to financial problems in Central Europe; Germany's reparation burdens were first eased, then quietly written off altogether after Britain, France and Belgium had agreed to extend credit to Germany in order to prevent the total collapse of its finances.

When a great many people are unable to find work, unemployment results.
Ex-President Calvin Coolidge, City Editor, *1930*.

[The Crash] turned out to be the first outbreak of a wasting economic fever which, through long years of depression, debilitated an entire nation, deprived it of the use of its productive strength, and created want in the midst of plenty. The public discovered that 'sound' business thinking had been mostly superstition.

Respectable theories of the function of the state had to be abandoned. A hesitant Federal Government was forced, step by step, into a dominant role in the operation of our economy, against every American habit and tradition.
Thurman Arnold, The Aspiring Age: 1919–1941.

This year, when we all needed something to take our minds off our troubles, miniature golf did it ... It we cannot find bread, we are satisfied with the circus.
Elmer Davis, Harper's, 1930.

A descent from respectability ... must be numbered in the millions. This is what we have accomplished with our bread lines and soup kitchens ... defeated, discouraged, hopeless men and women cringing and bowing as they come to ask for public aid ... It is a spectacle of national degradation. This is the fundamental tragedy for America.
Joseph L. Heffernan, Atlantic Monthly, 1932.

It is quite likely that fish-and-chips, art-silk stockings, tinned salmon, cut-price chocolate (five two-ounce bars for sixpence), the movies, the radio, strong tea, and the Football Pools have between them averted revolution. Therefore we are sometimes told that the whole thing is an astute manouevre by the governing classes – a sort of 'bread and circuses' business to hold the unemployed down. What I have seen of our governing class does not convince me that they have that much intelligence.
George Orwell, The Road to Wigan Pier (1937).

Industrial Depression

These really are good times, but only a few know it. If this period of convalescence through which we have been passing must be spoken of as a depression, it is far and away the finest depression that we have ever had,
Henry Ford, c. 1930.

I don't know anything about any depression.
US banker J. P. Morgan Jr, c. 1930.

• •

Twentieth Century Blues.
Noel Coward, song in Cavalcade, 1931.

• •

The majority of people just stood and stood, and waited and waited. You had a bunch of strangers, expressionless, looking down at the ground. They looked like they were half dead, hopeless. And when you looked into their eyes you thought maybe that is what you looked like, too.
Paul Boatin recalls waiting outside the Ford factory at River Rouge, Dearborn, Michigan, in 1930, The People's Century (BBC, 1995).

They are playing politics at the expense of human misery.
President Hoover condemns Congressmen sponsoring bills for the relief of the unemployed, 9 December 1930.

We have magneto trouble. How, then, can we start it up again?
British economist John Maynard Keynes, December 1930.

The British Navy at Jutland in 1916 beat the ex-Kaiser, and at Invergordon in 1931 it beat Mr Montague Norman.
Labour Party posters at the October 1931 General Election: in response to the cuts in public spending, the Royal Navy tried to dock a flat shilling a day from the pay of all ranks, from the lowliest seaman to the grandest Admiral; in a well-managed 'mutiny', sailors at the Invergordon base in north-east Scotland refused to put to sea, and the Admiralty instead cut pay on a percentage basis. Montague Norman was the Governor of the Bank of England, whose financial report had shocked the National Government into action.

There was always a queue of people outside the gate, waiting to come in. You were paid by the hour, but you were dismissed by the minute.
Les Holder, on life at the Ford factory in Dagenham, Essex, 1931, The People's Century (BBC, 1995).

She was sitting on the stoop. When I walked by, she crossed her legs showing

her thighs and winked. I walked over to her. She said: 'How about it, hon?' I said: 'Christ, kid, if I had any dough I'd rather eat.'
M. Shulimson, in Albert Maltz, New Masses (1932).

In a complicated industrial and commercial state constant employment at regular wages is impossible; while dole-supported unemployment, at anything like the wages of employment, is demoralizing to begin with and ruinous at its more or less quickly arriving end.
Professor George Saintsbury, Last Scrap-Book (1932).

This is the way in which civil strife begins, and civil strife may not end until it is civil war.
Prime Minister Stanley Baldwin refuses to meet the hunger marchers of the 'Jarrow Crusade', who had walked down from the north-east of England to present a petition. Labour Party leaders also distanced themselves; the marchers' rally in Hyde Park was organized by the Communist Party in November 1936. Following the closure of the shipyard, unemployment in Jarrow stood at 75 per cent.

I see an America where the workers are really free and through their great unions, undominated by any outside force or any dictator within, can take their proper place in the council tables with the owners and managers of business.
President Franklin D. Roosevelt, speech at the Democratic National Convention, 27 June 1936.

We'll never recognize the United Auto Workers Union or any other union.
Henry Ford, 1937.

• •

Once I built a railroad, made it run,
Made it race against time.
Once I built a railroad, now it's done:
Brother, can you spare a dime?

E. Y. 'Yip' Harburg, song, 'Brother, Can You Spare A Dime?' in New Americana, 1932.

• •

No tin hat brigade of goose-stepping vigilantes or Bible-babbling mob of blackguarding and corporation-paid scoundrels will prevent the onward march of labor.
John L. Lewis of the Committee for Industrial Organisation, Time, 9 September 1937.

You can imagine 80,000 people marching down a road, and for no reason at all on a cold day in March, six below zero, the water hoses are turned on you. And to see your friend being shot … .
David Moore remembers the day Ford shut down the River Rouge plant; four workers were shot dead. From The People's Century (BBC, 1995).

When a quarter of million miners are unemployed, it is part of the order of things that Alf Smith, a miner living in the back streets of Newcastle, should be out of work. … So long as Bert Jones across the street is still at work, Alf Smith is bound to feel himself dishonoured and a failure. Hence that frightful feeling of impotence and despair which is almost the worst evil of unemployment...

But, I think not again – or at least, not so often. That is the real point: people are ceasing to kick against the pricks. … It is not only Alf Smith who is out of work now; Bert Jones is out of work as well, and both of them have been 'out' for years. It makes a great deal of difference when things are the same for everybody.
George Orwell, The Road to Wigan Pier (1937).

I'm the only person of distinction who's ever had a depression named for him.
Herbert Hoover, quoted by Richard Norton Smith in An Uncommon Man (1984).

Agricultural Disaster

In the last quarter of the 19th century the mid-Western grassland States of the USA, opened up to settlers by the railroad, had been ploughed under for wheat and turned into the 'breadbasket of America'; 50 years of ploughing, single-cropping, and increased mechanization exhausted the soil, and three years of drought and heatwave in the early

1930s turned them, literally, into a dust bowl. Crops failed, and successive windstorms scoured off the topsoil and swept it thousands of miles. Banks, already panicked by the Wall Street Crash, foreclosed on farm mortgages and the population began to starve. By the mid-Thirties a mass exodus was underway; around half a million people – nicknamed 'Okies' whether they came from Oklahoma or not – piled their belongings into trucks, carts or cars and headed out, 300,000 of them to California where, crowded into fruit-picking camps, they lived lives of appalling degradation.

....

Oh God, send me some work!

Walter Greenwood, Love on the Dole, *1932.*

....

But it's our land. We measured it and broke it up. We were born on it, and we got killed on it, died on it. Even if it's no good, it's still ours. That's what makes it ours – being born on it, working on it, dying on it. That makes ownership, not a paper with numbers on it.

...

And all their love was thinned with money, and all their fierceness dribbled away in interest until they were no longer farmers at all, but little shopkeepers of crops, little manufacturers who must sell before they can make.

...

[Route] 66 is the path of a people in flight, refugees from dust and shrinking land, from the thunder of tractors and shrinking ownership, from the desert's slow northward invasion, from the twisting winds that howl up out of Texas, from the floods that bring no richnes to the land and steal what little richness is there. From all of these the people are in flight, and they come into 66 from the tributary side roads, from the wagon tracks and the rutted country roads. 66 is the mother road, the road of flight.

...

Okie use' to mean you was from Oklahoma. Now it means you're scum. Don't mean nothing itself, it's just the way they say it.

John Steinbeck, The Grapes of Wrath *(1939).*

Steps Towards Recovery

In England we have come to rely upon a comfortable time lag of fifty years or a century intervening between the perception that something ought to be done and a serious attempt to do it.

H. G. Wells, The Work, Wealth and Happiness of Mankind *(1932).*

I pledge to you, I pledge myself, to a New Deal for the American people.

Franklin D. Roosevelt, who had proclaimed himself the candidate of 'the forgotten man at the bottom of the economic pyramid', accepts the nomination of the Democratic Party on the fourth ballot, 2 July 1932.

The country needs, the country demands, bold, persistent experimentation.

Roosevelt, victory speech, 8 November 1932. After a campaign in which he travelled over 12,500 miles (20,850 km) by train, he defeated Herbert Hoover by 472 electoral college votes to 59.

First of all, let me assert my firm belief that the only thing we have to fear is fear itself – nameless, unreasoning, unjustified terror which paralyses needed efforts to convert retreat into advance. ... Plenty is at our doorstep, but a generous use of it languishes in the very sight of the supply ... When there is no vision the people perish. ... The money changers have fled from their high seats in the temple of our civilization. We may now restore that temple to the ancient truths.

Roosevelt, inaugural speech as President, 4 March 1933. In its first hundred days, Roosevelt's administration enacted the National Recovery Act, the Tennessee Valley Authority and the Agricultural Adjustment Act, all of which had the effect of putting unemployed people to work on public projects and reviving the commercial economy; a 'Second New Deal' encacted such social legislation as the National Labor Relations Act and the Social Security Act, both 1935.

Everybody understands him – even the bankers.
US comedian Will Rogers on President Roosevelt, 1933.

This may be the last Presidential election America will have. The New Deal is to America what the early phase of Nazism was to Germany and the early phase of fascism to Italy.
Mark Sullivan, Buffalo Evening News, *1935.*

The hand of Moscow backs the Communist leaders in America ... I ask you to purge the man who claims to be a Democrat from the Democratic Party, and I mean Franklin Double-Crossing Roosevelt.
Father Charles Coughlin, appeal to registered Democrats, 1936.

I murdered my grandmother this morning.
Roosevelt's standard conversational gambit whenever he thought someone wasn't listening to him.

• •

A man got to do what he got to do.
John Steinbeck, The Grapes of Wrath, *1939: the first published use of the phrase.*

• •

Something must be done.
Edward VIII visits the closed steelworks at Dowlais, South Wales, designated a Special Area under government measures for public works, on 18 November 1936. Partial recovery in Britain, aided by reduced labour costs, owed most to the the recovery in the US and the subsequent boost for world trade.

Democratic government has the innate capacity to protect its people against disasters once considered inevitable, to solve problems once considered unsolvable. ... We refused to leave the problems of our current welfare to be solved by the winds of chance and the hurricane of disaster.
President Roosevelt, second inaugural address, 20 January 1937.

DICTATORSHIP

Fascism is a religion; the twentieth century will be known as the century of Fascism.

Benito Mussolini, February 1933.

With us the Leader and the Idea are one. Every party member has to do what the Leader orders.
Adolf Hitler in conversation with Otto Strasser, 21 May 1930.
   In October's elections Hitler's National Socialist Party finished narrowly behind the Socialists, increasing its votes from 800,000 in 1928 to 6,409,000; voters returned 107 Nazi deputies, up from 12. There was uproar in the Reichstag when they took their seats dressed in the Party uniform. Nazi supporters in the streets smashed the windows of Jewish-owned shops. On 10 April 1932 Hitler narrowly failed to be elected President, with 36.8 per cent of the vote to Hindenburg's 53 per cent; Thälmann, the Communist candidate, received 10 per cent.
   ~

The keystone of the Fascist doctrine is its conception of the State, of its essence, its functions, its aims. For Fascism the State is absolute, individuals and groups relative.
Benito Mussolini, Fascism, Doctrine and Institutions *(1935).*

A creed entirely given over to hate, to irreverence and to violence.
Pope Pius XI has second thoughts about Fascism, two years after praising Mussolini, 31 May 1930. In February 1932 he granted the Italian dictator a private audience.

Fascism is not an article for export.
Mussolini, speech reported in the German press,

1932, as an example of his contempt for 'the little Bavarian corporal'.

The essential thing is the formation of the political will of the nation: that is the starting point for political action.
Adolf Hitler, speech, Düsseldorf, 27 January 1932. In elections that July, the National Socialists became the largest party in the Reichstag, with 230 seats out of 608. The Nazi Hermann Goering was elected President of the Reichstag but Hitler was thwarted in his attempt to become Chancellor by Hindenburg and von Papen, the incumbent right-wing Chancellor. When Hitler, declaring himself 'chosen by Providence for a great mission', promised to combine with the 89 Communist deputies to bring him down, von Papen threatened to dissolve the Reichstag by decree. In further elections that November, von Papen's Nationalists took 52 seats from the Nazis after bankers and businessmen, alarmed by Hitler's collaboration with the Communists, switched their allegiance. Kurt von Schleicher was appointed Chancellor; Nazis and Communists engaged in hand-to-hand fighting in the Reichstag and there was armed gang warfare in the streets.

Once we decide to go to Berlin we shall never leave it. My aim is a complete victory for the movement.
Adolf Hitler rallies his supporters in December 1932. Von Papen, believing he could use the National Socialists to his own advantage, took Hitler into talks with bankers, big business and the army, and forced von Schleicher's resignation, and on 30 January 1933 Hindenburg appointed Hitler as Chancellor with von Papen as his deputy; two Nazis, Hermann Goering and Wilhelm Frick, were appointed to a cabinet otherwise dominated by von Papen's Nationalists. One of Hitler's first acts was to authorize Nazi paramilitaries to act as police in Prussia, which comprised two-thirds of the country.

By then, a state of emergency will exist which will authorise the government to remain in office.
A self-fulfilling prophecy: Interior Minister Wilhelm Frick, 24 February 1933, on the impending Reichstag elections.

The Communist Party is the culprit. This is a Communist crime against the new government. We will show no mercy. Every Communist must be shot on the spot.
Hermann Goering, 28 February 1933.

This is a God-given signal. There is nothing that shall stop us now crushing out this murder pest with an iron fist.
Adolf Hitler, 28 February 1933. On the night of 27/28 February the Reichstag – connected by a tunnel to the home of Hermann Goering – was destroyed by fire; a simple-minded Dutch Communist, Marinus van der Lubbe, was arrested, and executed by guillotine the following year after confessing to starting the fire, on his own, in 20 minutes, using only firelighters and his shirt.

For the Protection of the People and the State.
Decree signed by President von Hindenburg, 28 February 1933 suspending all legal guarantees for personal liberty, freedom of speech, freedom of the Press and the right of assembly. Nazi Storm Troopers, now enrolled as special police, began a terror campaign against all forms of opposition to the regime. Nazis occupied the Bavarian Parliament on 12 March and expelled opposition deputies; the following day, Hindenburg banned the German republican flag and ordered the Imperial flag and the Nazi swastika to be flown side by side. Hitler proclaimed the Third German Reich on 15 March; on 20 March a concentration camp 'for the containment of subversive and dangerous elements' was opened at Dachau, near Munich.

Germans! Defend yourselves against Jewish atrocity propaganda! Buy only at German shops!
Posters plastered over the windows of Jewish-owned shops, April 1933. The practice of smashing the windows was officially frowned on as 'the real sufferers are not the Jewish firms but the German insurance companies'.

Thousands of bank accounts belonging to German Jews – including that of Albert Einstein – were seized by the Nazis on 1 April; on the 8th, all 'non-Aryan' government officials were ordered to retire. All Jewish teachers in Prussia were sacked on 13 April. Trade unions were banned on 2 May, and on the 5th Hitler announced legislation to prohibit marriages between Jews and 'Aryans', and to sterilize 'imperfect' human breeding stock.

As you watch the fire burn these un-German books, let it also burn into your hearts love of the Fatherland.
Exhortation to schoolchildren, 10 May 1933, as bonfires of blacklisted titles are lit in Berlin and Munich.

What progress we are making. In the Middle Ages they would have burned me. Now they are content with burning my books.
Austrian psychoanalyst Sigmund Freud, letter, May 1933.

Stronghold after stronghold we have taken. There are gigantic tasks before us, but we shall master them. No one can resist us.
Hitler addresses 70,000 Stormtroopers on 9 July 1933 as Germany signs a concordat with the Vatican: the decree banning Roman Catholic institutions in Germany was withdrawn as the German Catholic Party, in return, dissolved itself. Nazi Party membership was then made a prerequisite of German citizenship. Towards the end of August it was confirmed that Jews were being sent to Dachau. In September, Field Marshal von Ludendorff, First World War hero and Hitler's former colleague, was outlawed as a Communist.

The German people and their government are deeply humiliated by the deliberate refusal of a real, moral and actual equality to Germany.
Hitler takes Germany out of the League of Nations and the Geneva disarmament talks, 14 October 1933, and announces a referendum on the issue to be held on the same day as the Reichstag elections, for which only National Socialist candidates were permitted to stand. In the referendum 95 per cent voted 'Yes'; 92 per cent voted Nazi, the remaining 8 per cent spoiling their ballot papers. It was reported that 2154 of Dachau's 2242 inmates had voted for Hitler. The new Reichstag met for 12 minutes on 12 December and then adjourned indefinitely, as the government announced plans to abolish women's suffrage.

Before the world we protest against this regime, which has no majority behind it and which, for over a year, has ruled unconstitutionally, supported by bayonets. We protest against the restriction of liberty, against the mass persecutions of innocent men, women and children, against the system of hostages and concentration camps, and of spies and informers who are undermining the morality of the nation.
Two Austrian deputies, Drs Kaempel and Foppa of the Pan-German League, protest as the rump Austrian Parliament, already stripped of all its Social Democrats and Communists, appoints Engelbert Dollfuss dictator, and votes to dissolve itself, 30 April 1934.

Dollfuss became Chancellor in 1932 at the head of a 'Patriotic' coalition. Dollfuss, a Fascist who modelled himself on Mussolini, banned all Nazi Party activity; in 1933 an alleged German Nazi plot to invade Austria was revealed.

It is my will, and the indomitable will of the German people, that Austria become an integral part of the Reich!
Hitler rages at Mussolini as the two dictators meet in a former royal palace at Strà, near Padua, on 15 June 1934. Mussolini, who afterwards described the German Chancellor as 'a mad little clown', insisted on Austria's independence.

On 25 July 1934 a gang of Austrian Nazis assassinated Chancellor Dollfuss; Hitler's elation was brief, as Austrian Heimwehr forces – the equivalent of Germany's Stormtroopers – arrested the assassins and over 150 others, including a group who briefly took over the radio station. Mussolini ordered 40,000 troops to the Italian-Austrian border, and joined with France and Britain in reaffirming support for Austrian independence.

He throws his anger into their pale faces and tears off their identification lapels.
On 30 June 1934 a hysterical-sounding Propaganda Minister, Josef Goebbels, informs listeners to Nazi radio of the 'liquidation' of the leadership of the Stormtroopers, the SA. Thousands were murdered between the 29 June and 2 July, including many ex- and non-Nazis such as former Chancellor von Schleicher and his wife. Hitler had feared the SA, particularly its leader Ernst Roehm, as a threat to his security, and the army had become uneasy about its 'Socialist' leanings.

It was no secret that this time the revolution would have to be bloody … When we spoke of it, we called it 'The Night of the Long Knives'.

Adolf Hitler, speech, 13 July 1934 – the day he appointed the SS leader, Heinrich Himmler, to overall control of the Concentration Camp programme.

By the National Socialist Revolution, the German form of life has been definitely settled for the next thousand years.

Adolf Hitler, speech to 750,000 Nazis at Nuremberg, 5 September 1934. On 2 August, President Hindenburg died, aged 87. Hitler immediately abolished the office of President and proclaimed himself Führer – literally 'Leader' – Reich Chancellor, and Supreme Commander of the Armed Forces, whose members would henceforth be required to swear 'a sacred oath of unconditional obedience' to him. In a plebiscite, 90 per cent of Germans approved these arrangements.

I should be pleased, I suppose, that Hitler has carried out a revolution on our lines. But they are Germans. So they will end by ruining our idea.

Benito Mussolini, 1935: quoted in Benito Mussolini *by C. Hibbert.*

I go the way that Providence dictates with the assurance of a sleepwalker.

Adolf Hitler, speech, Munich, 15 March 1936, after the reoccupation of the Rhineland in defiance of the Treaty of Versailles. A plebiscite showed 99 per cent support for the Führer; in April, those who did not vote lost their jobs.

A decadent by-product of Bolshevik Jewish corruption ... We had Futurism, Expressionism, Realism, Cubism, even Dadaism. Could insanity go further? There were pictures with green skies and purple seas. There were paintings which could only be due to abnormal eyesight.

Hitler opens an exhibition of 'Degenerate Art', banned work whose creators were threatened with compulsory treatment in asylums, at the Haus der Kunst *in Munich, 19 July 1937.*

The law as a racial and national instrument entrusts German parents with the education of their children only on condition that they educate them in the fashion that the nation and the state expect.

A judge in Waldenberg, Silesia, orders the children of a Christian pacifist family to be made wards of the state, after the parents had refused to teach Nazi ideology, 29 November 1937. The Catholic Youth Association had, meanwhile, been outlawed.

The Great Spring Cleaning Has Begun!

On 14 March 1938 German troops marched into Vienna at the 'request' of Austria's puppet Chancellor, Arthur Seyss-Inquart, to complete the process of Anschluss *– annexation. A thoroughgoing pogrom and a programme of 'Nazification' of all areas of Austrian life were begun. The process was, on the whole, warmly welcomed by Austrians; 99.75 per cent of voters in a 'pan-German' plebiscite, in which 'non-Aryans' were not allowed to vote, approved the merger. On 6 April the first Austrian Jews were transported to Dachau.*

It is an obvious duty for we Bishops to declare ourselves as Germans for the German Empire, and we expect that all faithful Christians will also know what they owe to their people.

The Austrian Cardinal Innitzec welcomes the Anschluss, *March 1938.*

They should have killed more Jews and broken less glass.

Hermann Goering's verdict on Kristallnacht – *Crystal Night – 8/9 November 1938, when thousands of windows in Jewish shops and businesses were smashed as premises were looted and set on fire; synagogues were also burned and many Jews beaten up and murdered, thousands of 'respectable' people joining in. The authorities announced that any insurance money paid out would be confiscated and returned to the insurers.*

The USSR: Workers and Peasants

We are fifty or a hundred years behind the advanced countries. We must make good this distance within ten years. Either we do it, or they crush us.

Joseph Stalin launches the first Five Year Plan, 1928.

The kulaks are to be liquidated as a class.

Joseph Stalin, March 1930.

If Stalin decided to start dekulakization to start creating collective farms then it was what we needed. I thought it should be done, so I didn't think about my feelings towards these people. If Stalin said 'Do it,' then it was necessary.

Izrail Chernitsky, Komsomol (Communist Youth Movement) member in the 1930s, The People's Century (BBC, 1995).

The corpses were piled up like bales of straw. They threw on my mother. Then they threw on my father. My father gestured to me, but the man said, 'He's almost ready, he's almost dead.' When my father gestured to me I knew I must go and hide. I crawled away on my hands and knees, that's why I survived. The men took the cart to big hole and tipped the bodies in, regardless of whether they were dead or alive.

Pelagaya Ovcharenko, a child in 1931, The People's Century (BBC, 1995).

Stalin's successful policy to industrialize the Soviet Union was carried out largely at the expense of peasant farmers (kulaks) who had been allowed to believe that they would own their land, and who had begun to prosper under Lenin's New Economic Policy. Their farms were forcibly 'collectivized'; those who objected were sent away to labour camps or else shot. Farm production fell as government demand for food in towns and cities rose by half; grain was also required for export, to bring in foreign currency. Breeding stock and seed corn was taken; famine resulted. By 1935 at least 7 million people, and perhaps 10 million, had died as the result of a policy of deliberate starvation. The labour camp population itself undertook much of the work of implementing Stalin's economic policies; swelled by his many mass purges of 'traitors and counter-revolutionaries', it constituted a massive slave labour force.

The party has succeeded in routing the kulaks as a class.

Joseph Stalin, 7 January 1933.

The USSR: The Purges

Of course I sacrificed general human values, as well as my conscience, to class and proletarian values. Soviet power demanded this; I did it. If the party asked me to say that I was an English spy, I would agree to it. If the party wanted to take my life away, fine. If it wanted to take my honesty, well, that was fine too.

Valentin Astrov, a journalist on Pravda, who gave 'evidence' in the show trial of Nikolai Bukharin, an old Bolshevik and senior colleague of Stalin, dubbed by Lenin 'the darling of the party', who was shot in 1937. Interview in The People's Century (BBC, 1995).

They are contemptible, base, vile, despicable murderous scoundrels, not tigers or lions but merely mad Fascist police dogs, humanity's dregs, the scum of the underworld, traitors and bandits. Shoot these mad curs, every one of them.

Andrei Vishinsky, State Prosecutor at the trial of Grigori Zinoviev, Leon Kamenev and 14 others, 20–25 August 1936; no defence lawyers were permitted. The first purges began in 1934, when Sergei Kirov, head of the party in Leningrad, was shot on Stalin's orders in the Smolny Institute; like Hitler after the Reichstag fire, Stalin blamed a conspiracy to terrorize and overthrow the State, and ordered Genrikh Yagoda, head of the secret police, to round up influential survivors of the Revolution and the Lenin years, many of whom were critical of his regime. In the next wave, Yagoda himself was executed and succeeded by Nikolai Yezhov; the 'Great Purge' of 1936–38 was known as the Yezhovshchina; he, too, disappeared in 1939 to be succeeded by Lavrenti Beria.

When finally the doorbell rang one night there was a feeling of relief. When I was taken into the cell the elder of the cell said to me, 'Sit down. Breathe in the freedom. You don't have to fear any more. Your arrest is over.' He expressed what we all felt.

Lev Razgon, survivor of the labour camps, The People's Century (BBC, 1995). Stalin's purges, which removed the upper echelons of the Communist Party and the Army (thus leaving the USSR vulnerable four years later) were also directed against doctors, scientists and engineers, but were not confined to those classes: a Great Terror had begun.

Stalin set quotas for every town and region: so many thousand to be shot, so many thousand to be sent to the camps. In a climate of fear and obedience, most people confessed to anything that was suggested to them without the necessity for beatings or torture. By the end of the decade a million people were in prison, many awaiting death, and ten million were in the camps, where the annual death rate varied between 10 and 20 per cent.

Gaiety is the outstanding feature of the Soviet Union.
Joseph Stalin, after enjoying an exhibition of folk dancing by collectivized farm workers to celebrate his 55th birthday, 1934.

CHRONOLOGY OF EVENTS

We shall not make Britain's mistake. Too wise to try to govern the world, we shall merely own it. Nothing can stop us.

Ludwell Denny, America Conquers Britain *(1930)*

I repudiate this law and regard it as my sacred duty to break the mournful monotony of compulsory peace that is choking the heart of the nation for want of a free vent.
Mahatma Gandhi, leader of the Indian Congress Party, sets out on a 300-mile (480-km) walk to defy a British law establishing a government monopoly in the production of salt. On 6 April 1930 he reached the Gulf of Cambay and courted arrest by picking up a salt crystal which was afterwards auctioned for 1600 rupees. He was arrested on 5 May.

~

Victory gained by violence is tantamount to a defeat.
Gandhi launches his campaign of 'civil disobedience', 1930. In 1931 he came to London for 'round table' talks and demanded independence for India; on his return he was arrested, imprisoned, and released after a hunger strike in August 1933.

~

The loss of India would mark and consummate the downfall of the British Empire.
Winston Churchill addresses the Indian Empire Society, 12 December 1930. The following month, he resigned from the Cabinet over its plans for a federally governed India with Dominion status.

Gladstone ... spent his declining years trying to guess the answer to the Irish Question; unfortunately, whenever he was getting warm, the Irish secretly changed the Question...
W.C. Sellar and R.J. Yeatman, 1066 And All That, *1930.*

We will harness modern machinery and ask for a mobilisation of energy, vitality and manhood to save the nation ... We shall rely on the good old English fist.
Sir Oswald Mosley leaves the Labour government after it rejects his reflationary investment policy, and founds the New Party, 28 February 1931. After making no headway, the New Party fell apart; some members joined Labour while others, led by Mosley, formed the British Union of Fascists.

I believe I have conscientiously served my country. Such has been my intention. At this moment I feel more a Spaniard than ever.
King Alfonso XIII of Spain on his abdication, 14 April 1931. Following the collapse of the government led by the King's ally, the military dictator Primo de Rivera, the Republican Party won an overwhelming majority in the Spanish Parliament, the Cortes.

~

They would not be brutally sincere, but sincerely brutal.
Niceto Alcala Zamora, elected republican President of Spain, 10 December 1931, on the followers of his predecessor.

They can't collect legal taxes from illegal money.
Al Capone, Chicago gang leader, after his arrest for tax evasion in June 1931. He was sentenced to 11 years' imprisonment.

Time ... marches on! As it must to all men, death came this week to [...].
Announcer, The March of Time *(US), 1931*

55

What the proprietorship of these papers is aiming at is power, and power without responsibility – the prerogative of the harlot through the ages.
Stanley Baldwin employs a Rudyard Kipling expression to attack the press barons Lords Rothermere and Beaverbrook, election speech, 18 March 1931.

~

Good God, that's done it; he's lost us the tarts' vote.
The Duke of Devonshire, on being told of Baldwin's speech.

I have changed none of my ideals. I have a national duty.
Ramsay MacDonald, Labour Prime Minister of the new National Government, 24 August 1931. Earlier in the year, Lloyd George's Liberals had withdrawn their support for the Labour government on the issue of electoral reform, then MacDonald's Labour cabinet had refused to endorse spending cuts of £96 million a year; he tendered his government's resignation to the King and advised him to invite the other party leaders to head a joint government. The Labour Party expelled MacDonald and elected Arthur Henderson to succeed him. An election followed in October, in which the coalition parties asked for a 'doctor's mandate' to do whatever they considered necessary for revival. The National Coalition won 554 of the 610 seats; 473 were held by Tories. MacDonald continued as Prime Minister. In September 1932 four cabinet minsters, three of them Liberal, left the government after it negotiated preferential Empire tariff agreements; this left MacDonald effectively the titular head of a Tory government.

~

Tomorrow every Duchess in London will be wanting to kiss me!
Ramsay MacDonald, August 1931; quoted in Viscount Snowdon, Autobiography.

~

••••••••••••••••••••••••••••••••••

Goodbye, children … everywhere.
Derek MacCulloch ('Uncle Mac'), Children's Hour, (BBC), 1935.

••••••••••••••••••••••••••••••••••

When they circumcised Herbert Samuel they threw away the wrong bit.
Lloyd George, his influence gone, on the new National Liberal Home Secretary and party leader, November 1931.

~

Sit down, man. You're a bloody tragedy.
The Labour MP James Maxton intervenes during MacDonald's last Commons speech, June 1935. MacDonald resigned for health reasons, and was succeeded by Stanley Baldwin, whose National – effectively Tory – government won 432 seats at the subsequent election in November.

This is only the beginning.
Paul Gorguloff, a White Russian emigré afterwards pronounced insane, assassinates President Paul Doumer of France, 10 May 1932.

Good evening, Mr and Mrs America, and all the ships at sea.
Walter Winchell opens US radio news broadcasts from 1932.

The Fascist government will be armed with powers to overcome the problems the people want overcome.
Sir Oswald Mosley addresses a rally of uniformed members of the British Union of Fascists in Birmingham, 21 January 1934, and promises a 'modern dictatorship'.

~

Certain movements in the country might very well shake parliamentary government in the future.
Government minister Sir Kingsley Wood, after violence at a rally of the BUF at Olympia, 9 June 1934.

~

We fought Germany before in a British quarrel; we are not going to fight them now in a Jewish one.
Sir Oswald Mosley addresses an 'easily bamboozled' audience in Barnsley Public Hall, 15 March 1936; recorded in the diary George Orwell kept for The Road to Wigan Pier *(1937).*

~

The blame for everything was put upon mysterious international gangs of Jews who are said to be financing, among other things, the British Labour Party … M kept extolling Italy and Germany, but

when questioned about concentration camps etc. always replied, 'We have no foreign models; what happens in Germany need not happen here.'
George Orwell, The Road to Wigan Pier (Diary), 16 March 1936.

~

Before the organisation of the Blackshirt movement free speech did not exist in this country … We shall reach the helm within five years.
Sir Oswald Mosley, speech, 1938. The BUF attracted no significant electoral support; when Mosley attempted to lead 7000 Blackshirts through the East End of London on 11 October 1936, 100,000 people built barricades and filled the streets to keep them out and a pitched battle ensued. In January 1937 a Public Order Act banned political uniforms.

How could they tell?
Dorothy Parker (or it may have been H. L. Mencken) reacts to the news that Calvin Coolidge has died, 5 January 1933.

I think now would be a good time for a beer.
President Roosevelt announces the end of Prohibition, March 1933.

It is certain as the day that a Labour town council, a Socialist or Communist government, would not for a day tolerate strikes in social or other services necessary for the life of the nation.
George Lansbury, leader of the Labour Party, 1934: on 8 March, Labour won the London County Council elections by 69 seats to 55. The new LCC leader was Herbert Morrison.

Consumption seems to have been contracting, like the ladies.
The chairman of the Fruit and Potato Trades Association explains a dramatic slump in the potato market, 21 March 1934; the word 'slimming' had been added to the Oxford English Dictionary the previous year.

If cars continue to be made at the same rate as now and with increasing cheapness, there will soon be no pedestrians left.
The Minister of Transport, Sir Leslie Hore-Belisha, introduces a Road Traffic Bill, 28 March 1934,

What's up, doc?
Bugs Bunny makes his debut for Warner Brothers, 1937.

imposing driving tests, speed limits and pedestrian crossings – the Belisha Beacon was named after him. Deaths on Britain's roads were running at an average of 22 a day.

The government burns down whole cities while the people are forbidden to light lamps.
October 1934: the rebel Communist forces of Mao Tse-Tung, encircled by General Chiang Kai-Shek's Nationalist army, break out and begin a long march to Yenan, 6000 miles (9645 km) to the north; they arrived a year later.

Like Shelley and like Baudelaire, it may be said of him that he suffered, in his own person, the neurotic ills of an entire generation.
British novelist Christopher Isherwood on the death of T. E. Lawrence ('Lawrence of Arabia') on 19 May 1935; following what appeared to be a motorcycle accident he lay unconscious for five days. Speculation still persists that his death was not accidental.

The man who pulls the plow gets the plunder in politics.
Lousiana Senator Huey Long, speech, 30 January 1934. On 8 September 1935 he was shot by the son-in-law of a judge whom Long was attempting to gerrymander out of office; he died two days later, and was succeeded by his widow.

After I am dead the boy will ruin himself in twelve months.
According to Stanley Baldwin, this was said to him by King George V in 1935. He is supposed to have once said: 'My father was frightened of his mother. I was frightened of my father, and I'm damned well going to make sure my children are frightened of me'.

~

The King's life is drawing peacefully to a close.
Bulletin posted on the gates of Buckingham Palace by the King's doctors on 20 January

• •

Ladies and gentlemen, I have a grave announcement to make. Incredible as it may seem, strange beings who landed in New Jersey tonight are the vanguard of an invading army from Mars. ... I'm speaking from the roof of the Broadcasting Building, New York City. The bells you hear are ringing to warn people to evacuate the city as the Martians approach.

Orson Welles causes panic on the streets as he introduces the Mercury Radio Theatre production of H. G. Wells' The War of the Worlds, 31 October 1938.

• •

1936; it has since become apparent that the King's death was 'managed' for him to accord with the press deadline for the next day's Times.

~

How is the Empire?
The last words of King George V, according to The Times, 21 January 1936.

~

Bugger Bognor.
The unofficial last words of King George V, allegedly uttered when he was told he might shortly be well enough to go there. He once said, 'I don't like abroad, I've been there.'

~

Some of us wish that he gave more positive signs of awareness of his Christian duty.
A sermon by the Bishop of Bradford in November 1936, reported by the Yorkshire Post as 'plainly having a foundation in fact'. Britain's press had known for some time of the intention of the King, Edward VIII, to marry an American divorcée, Mrs Wallis Simpson, who had recently obtained her second divorce at Ipswich Assizes, but had agreed to keep silent; the reporting of the Bishop's words opened the floodgates.

~

Well, Mr Baldwin! This is a pretty kettle of fish!
The Queen Dowager grants an audience to the Prime Minister in early December. The King's suggestion that his marriage be a morganatic one – his wife would not be Queen and any children would have no right of succession – was rejected by the Cabinet. Cosmo Lang, the Archbishop of Canterbury, was firm in his insistence that the

government should 'stand firm in defence of public morality'.

~

The spectacle of the National Government laying down a code of morals and behaviour for the King is indeed a sight ... There is no crisis in all this business for the working class.
Harry Pollitt, British Communist leader, speech, Cambridge, 8 December 1936.

The public mood was mostly for the King, the Establishment mostly against, on the grounds that the marriage would be unconstitutional and incompatible with the status of the Monarch as head of the Established Church and 'Defender of the Faith'.

~

Our cock won't fight.
The press baron Lord Beaverbrook, to Winston Churchill, 9 December 1936. The two men had led the 'pro-Edward' campaign, Beaverbrook through the Daily Express and Churchill by lobbying MPs and speaking at the Albert Hall. But the King had decided on abdication, the first English monarch to do so since 1399, and became instead the Duke of Windsor. He went into exile and his brother the Duke of York became King George VI.

~

I have found it impossible to carry the heavy burden of responsibility and to discharge my duties as King as I would wish to do, without the help and support of the woman I love. ... God bless you all. God Save the King.
The Duke of Windsor, radio broadcast, 11 December 1936.

~

My Lord Archbishop, what a scold you are,
And when a man is down, how bold you are,
Of Christian charity how scant you are,
You auld Lang Swine, how full of cant you are!
Anonymous jingle: Archbishop Lang continued to censure the Duke of Windsor after his departure from Britain in the belief that such a 'moral' campaign would revive church-going. It did not.

~

God grant him peace and happiness but never understanding of what he has lost.
Stanley Baldwin, December 1936.

~

SLOGANS, SAYINGS and CATCHPHRASES of THE THIRTIES

Don't tell my mother I'm in politics – she thinks I play piano in a whorehouse.
A US saying of the Depression years.

Buy British
Government campaign, 1931; in November the Prince of Wales made a 'Buy British' broadcast.

B.O.
The invention of a worry, Body Odour, in advertisements for Lifebuoy Soap from 1933.

Five o'clock shadow.
Another worry, in advertisments for Gem Razors and Blades (US); early 1930s.

Who But Hoover?
Republican slogan for the losing candidate, Herbert Hoover, 1932.

Today […], tomorrow the world!
A catchprase, originating in a German National Socialist Party slogan of c.1930, Heute Presse der Nationalsozialisten, Morgan Presse der Nation ('Today the press of the Nazis, tomorrow the press of the nation').

Kraft durch Freude (Strength through joy)
German Labour Front slogan, coined in 1933 by Robert Ley; it became the name of the Nazi organization providing regimented leisure.

Ein Reich, ein Volk, ein Führer (One realm, one people, one leader).
German Nazi slogan from 1934.

Learner driver
Britain introduced driving tests in 1934, and the 30mph speed limit in built-up areas.

Forward with the people
Masthead slogan of the Daily Mirror, 1935-59.

Lousy but loyal
London's East End salutes the Silver Jubilee of George V in 1935.

Keep Fit
A serious fad of the Thirties: The Times in November 1936 urged the undertaking of 'a great national effort to improve the physique of the nation'.

Television won't matter in your lifetime or mine.
Rex Lambert, editor of Radio Times, 1936.

Life, Liberty and Landon
Republican campaign slogan for the losing candidate, Landon, in 1936.

Hark the herald angels sing,
Mrs Simpson's pinched our King.
Playground song, overheard by Clement Attlee in December 1936.

This generation has a rendezvous with destiny.
Franklin D. Roosevelt, speech at the 1936 Democratic convention.

Frankly, my dear, I don't give a damn!

Clark Gable, Gone With The Wind *(1939)*.

After the trying times we have been through we now look forward to a happy and useful private life.

Statement issued by the Duke of Windsor after his marriage to Wallis Simpson, 3 June 1937. They spent their honeymoon in Austria.

~

The Duke and Duchess of Windsor will study social conditions and housing problems.

German government press release, on 22 October 1937 the Duke and Duchess were received by Adolf Hitler in Berlin and toured a National Socialist model factory.

~

The Windsors, bearing up well under their hereditary burden of chinlessless and a tendency to run to twits, managed nonetheless to turn the saga of the stunningly unbright Duke and Duchess of Windsor into one of the century's great love stories.

Lance Morrow, Time, *22 July 1996.*

She was one of the thousands of women who are suffering suburban neurosis. Out-patients departments are full of them.

Depression stalks Metro-land in the days before Valium: a coroner's verdict on a Barnet houswife who gassed herself, 8 June 1938. Four million houses were built in Britain between the wars, most of them in newly created suburbs on the extremities of the London Underground; 60,000 acres a year disappeared under building, and a 'Green Belt' was established round London to preserve some semblance of a rural environment.

Toto, I have a feeling we're not in Kansas anymore.

Judy Garland, The Wizard of Oz *(1939).*

One of the most priceless possessions is the liberty of the subject. If once we show any signs of giving way to the abominable doctrine that because things are done by officials therefore some immunity must be extended towards them, what is to become of our country?

The Lord Chief Justice, Lord Howard, finds in favour of actor Patrick Ludlow in a private prosecution for wrongful imprisonment against the Metropolitan Police, who had arrested him at a bus-stop on suspicion of being a race-course tout; he was awarded £300.

There is no ideal scheme. It is a conflict between right and right.

UK Colonial Secretary Malcolm MacDonald on the problem of Palestine, governed by Britain under a League of Nations mandate, 10 February 1939. Britain planned to limit Jewish immigration to 75,000 a year for five years; Jews were to form no more than one-third of Palestine's population, and an independent Arab-Jewish state was to be established in 1949, governed by representatives of both communities.

~

We can never acquiesce in this British breach of faith.

The wife of the Chief Rabbi of Jerusalem leads a march of 10,000 women on the British headquarters at the King David Hotel, Jerusalem, 22 May 1939. The British were accused of reneging on the Balfour Declaration; the British replied that 'a Jewish homeland in Palestine' had not been intended to mean the whole of Palestine.

Why pick on us? It's not as if Coventry's got anything to do with it.

Survivor of an IRA bomb in Coventry, 25 August 1939. Five were killed, 50 injured.

There can hardly be a town in the South of England where you could throw a brick without hitting the niece of a bishop.

George Orwell, The Road to Wigan Pier, *1937.*

WAR and APPEASEMENT

Fascism means war.

The ex-Labour MP John St Loe Strachey, The Menace of Fascism (1933).
After leaving Labour, Strachey was briefly a member of Mosley's New Party,
then joined the Communists. He rejoined Labour as Air Minister
during the Second World War.

Let them especially put their demands in such a way that Great Britain could say that she supported both sides.
Prime Minister Ramsay MacDonald, on reparation negotiations between France and Germany, 1930.

I think it is well also for the man in the street to realise that there is no power on earth that can protect him from being bombed. ... The only defence is in offence, which means that you have to kill more women and children more quickly than the enemy if you want to save yourselves.
Stanley Baldwin, speech, House of Commons, November 1932; the government followed a disarmament policy in the expectation that other European powers would follow suit. Support for pacifism was widespread, as organizations like the Peace Pledge Union attracted members by the tens of thousands.

War alone brings up to their highest tension all human energies and imposes the stamp of nobility upon the peoples who have the courage to make it.
Benito Mussolini, Encyclopedia Italiane (1932).

That this house will in no circumstances fight for its King and Country.
Motion for debate in the Oxford Union, 9 February 1933: it was carried by 275 votes to 153.

~

I renounce war and never again will I support or sanction another.
The Peace Pledge: by 1936, 130,000 people had signed it. The previous year, 75,000 people demonstrated for peace in New York's Central Park.

His actions have brought us nearer to war and made us weaker, poorer and more defenceless.
Winston Churchill, 23 March 1933, criticizes Ramsay MacDonald's disarmament talks with Mussolini, designed in MacDonald's words to 'remove the causes of war in Europe'. The Under-Secretary of State for Foreign Affairs, the Tory Anthony Eden, described Churchill's criticism as 'mischievous absurdity'.

~

We cannot continue in our present inferiority. Our air force must be as strong as any other nation.
Lord Londonderry, UK Air Minister, speech, House of Lords, 29 November 1933. The Admiralty also announced that the policy of building small ships in the hope that other countries would follow suit, had failed; a naval building programme was announced. But Baldwin told the Commons that the government was still working towards international controls on armaments, and warned that a 'sudden and quick' increase in air force spending 'would threaten Anglo-German relations'.

~

When you think about the defence of England you no longer think of the chalk cliffs of Dover. You think of the Rhine. That is where our frontier lies today.
Stanley Baldwin, speech, House of Commons, 30 July 1934.

~

••••••••••••••••••••••••••••••••••••••

It is a good thing for an uneducated man to read books of quotations.

Winston Churchill, My Early Life (1930).

••••••••••••••••••••••••••••••••••••••

Our attempt to lead the world towards disarmament by unilateral example has failed.

Stanley Baldwin, speech, House of Commons, 4 March 1935. On 16 March, Germany introduced conscription and announced its intention to form a 500,000-strong conscript army; the Versailles Treaty allowed for 100,000. On 31 March Hitler demanded the abolition of the 'Polish Corridor' and reunification with East Prussia, and the annexation of the Sudetenland, a part of Czechoslovakia with a significant German population. On 22 May the UK government announced that the RAF was to be trebled in size to 1500 aircraft, the same number announced by Hitler as the German target.

The Pope! How many divisions has he got?

Stalin's reply to Pierre Laval, who urged him to tolerate Catholicism in order to appease the Pope, 13 May 1935.

The Empire of Japan, in the name of righteousness and justice, assisted in the establishment of this state. Armed hostilities have ceased. The country is bathed in the radiance of the sun and the moon.

The former 'boy emperor' of China, Pu Yi, installed by Japan as the puppet dictator of Manchuria after Japanese invasion, 1 March 1934. Pu Yi became Kang Teh, and Manchuria was renamed Manchukuo. Japanese aggression against China continued by coercion, subversion and, in August 1937, full-scale invasion; Peking was occupied, and tens of thousands died in the carpet bombing of Shanghai; in 1938, tens of thousands died in the aerial bombardment of Canton. The Chinese president, Chiang Kai-shek, was obliged to join forces with his Communist enemy, Mao Tse-tung. In Japan, a right-wing polit-

• •

TRENTINO: I'm willing to do anything to prevent this war.
FIREFLY: It's too late, I've already paid a month's rent on the battlefield.

Zeppo Marx and Groucho Marx, Duck Soup (1933).

• •

ical and military movement formed on the lines of Hitler's National Socialism was gaining power despite the failure of an attempted coup in February 1936, and organizing itself behind the figure of the god-emperor, Hirohito.

~

Every Communist must grasp the truth, that political power grows out of the barrel of a gun.

Mao Tse-tung, 6 November 1938; from The Thoughts of Chairman Mao Tse-tung.

~

She tried to resist the men and bit one of them in his arm. She was then taken to the courtyard and in front of all of us, her head was cut off with a sword and her body was cut into small pieces.

February 1996: Hwang So Gyun gives evidence to a United Nations investigation into the fate of thousands of Korean women forced, in the Thirties and Forties, to provide 'comfort' to Japanese soldiers in army brothels – a practice officially denied by Japan until the 1990s.

The First Fascist Invasion

For 40 years, Italy has desired to conquer our country, but Abyssinia knows how to fight to the last man to preserve the country's independence. Italians, fortified though they may be by all modern weapons, will yet see how a poor but united people will defend their country and their emperor.

Haile Selassie, Emperor of Abyssinia (Ethiopia), addresses Parliament in Addis Ababa, 18 July 1935, after a prolonged build-up of Italian forces on his border with the Italian colony of Eritrea in response to a stage-managed dispute. Italy had attempted to invade Ethiopia in 1896, and had been defeated. On 25 July, Britain banned arms sales to both countries. In September the League of Nations proposed a peace plan, granting Italy some territory; it was rejected by both sides, and Mussolini demanded the disarmament of the Ethiopian army.

A solemn hour is about to break in the history of our fatherland. … We will answer with our discipline and our abstemiousness and our spirit of sacrifice.

Benito Mussolini launches the invasion of Ethiopia, 3 October 1935.

The Spanish Civil War

The Spanish Restoration Movement will triumph very shortly and we will demand explanations of your conduct. The energy which we will employ will be in proportion to the resistance which you may put up. We urge you especially to avoid useless shedding of blood.

A message from the Spanish Foreign Legion General and leader of the Phalange Party, General Francisco Franco, Morocco, 31 July 1936. The Spanish Republic had been in turmoil for most of the decade as various factions, ranging from Anarchist to Monarchist, fought for regional and national power; Catalonia, whose regional capital was Barcelona, had declared independence in October 1934, but its Marxist and Anarcho-Syndicalist revolt was crushed by government forces. When a left-wing government under Mañuel Azana came to power in February 1936 it excluded the Communists, who began an uprising against it. Franco, aided by General Mola in the north, began a civil war to establish military rule and a Fascist policy.

It is better to be the widow of a hero than the wife of a coward. ... It is better to die on your feet than live on your knees.

Dolores Ibarruri, 'La Pasionaria', founder of the Spanish Communist Party: speeches in Valencia and Paris, 1936. The various factions of Republican Spain formed a loose alliance to fight Franco's Nationalist forces; both sides recruited abroad, with over 60,000 volunteering to fight on the Republican side. The Nationalists attracted about 5000 – including the American novelist Ernest Hemingway – but were assisted by 25,000 German and 30,000 Italian troops sent to aid a Fascist ally.

Fire – without hatred.

The Nationalist commander Antonio Rivera, during the first, unsuccessful attack on Madrid, October 1936; he was executed by a Republican firing squad in Alicante on 20 November.

Georges Kopp, on his periodical tours of inspection, was quite frank with us. 'This is not a war,' he used to say, 'it is a comic opera with an occasional death.' ... In this war everyone always did miss everyone else, when it was humanly possible.

George Orwell, Homage to Catalonia (1938). In December 1936 Orwell went to Spain under the ægis of the Independent Labour Party and joined the militia of the Workers' Party of Marxist Unification, the POUM, in Barcelona. At the end of April he tried to join the larger, Soviet-backed International Brigade in order to help in its defence of Madrid, but found himself denounced, with other POUM people, as a 'Trotsky-Fascist' by the Communists, who began rounding up and killing their left-wing rivals after they had been excluded from the Republican government. Orwell was wounded in the throat by a Fascist sniper on 18 May; in June he and his wife found themselves on the run from Communist police. They slipped over the French border on 23 June, and returned to England.

I had a most amusing time with the *New Statesman* ... As soon as I got out of Spain I wired from France asking if they would like an article and of course they said yes, but when they saw my article was on the suppression of the POUM they said they couldn't print it. ... I am also having to change

→

➤

my publisher ... Gollancz is of course part of the Communism-racket, and as soon as he heard I had been associated with the POUM and the Anarchists ... he said he did not think he would be able to publish my book, though not a word of it was written yet.

George Orwell, letter to Frank Jellinek, 20 December 1938. In Britain, the Labour Party had adopted a position of neutrality over the Spanish Civil War; the Conservative Party and its supporters were, more or less openly, pro-Franco, as were nearly all the mainstream newspapers. The left-wing press, dominated by Kingsley Martin of the New Statesman *and the publisher Victor Gollancz, took its line from Moscow. Orwell's book was eventually published by Secker and Warburg.*

It was impossible to go down many of the streets, because they were walls of flame. Debris was piled high. The shocked survivors all had the same story to tell: aeroplanes, bullets, bombs, fire.

Market day, 26 April 1937: the German Air Force, sent by Hitler to assist the Nationalists, bombs and strafes the Basque town of Guernica and then drops incendiaries. An anonymous reporter visited the next day and spoke to survivors; thousands died, and the town was destroyed. Picasso exhibited his Guernica *at that year's Paris Exhibition, and the town's name became synonymous with Franco's regime.*

We bear no hostile sentiments towards other nations. We do not believe in a democratic liberal regime for the damage it has done to Spain is very great.

General Franco, 19 April 1938, after capturing much of Catalonia and cutting in two the remaining territory of Republican Spain. Despite occasional setbacks, the advance of his forces had been a steady one, albeit much slower than he had anticipated; following the death of General Mola in a plane crash, Franco was poised to assume undisputed dictatorship. Barcelona was the last city to be taken, after a long blockade, on 26 January 1939. President Azana fled to Paris, where he disclaimed the presidency on 26 February. Two days later, amid Opposition cries of 'Heil Chamberlain', the British government recognized Franco's regime. The Civil War was declared officially over on 1 April; the following month, Spain left the League of Nations.

In 1936 it was clear to everyone that if Britain would only help the Spanish Government ... Franco would collapse and German strategy would be severely dislocated. By that time one did not need to be a clairvoyant to foresee that war between Britain and Germany was coming; one could even foretell within a year or two when it would come. Yet in the most mean, cowardly, hypocritical way the British ruling class did all they could to hand Spain over to Franco and the Nazis. ... It is still very uncertain what plan they acted on in backing Franco, and they may have had no clear plan at all. Whether the British ruling class are wicked or merely stupid is one of the most difficult questions of our time, and at certain moments a very important question.

George Orwell, Looking Back on the Spanish War, *published posthumously in 1953.*

To protect European culture and civilization and world peace from the Bolshevik menace.

The aims of the pact signed between Germany, Italy and Japan, November 1936. It was called the 'Axis'.

....

Come, friendly bombs, and fall on
Slough
It isn't fit for humans now,
There isn't grass to graze a cow
Swarm over, Death!

John Betjeman, 'Slough', 1937.

....

Can we not use this time to make it
unnecessary to proceed further along the
unattractive road of economic action
against a fellow League member, an old
friend and a former ally?

*The British Foreign Secretary, Sir Samuel Hoare,
resists a League of Nations proposal for economic
sanctions against Italy; speech, House of
Commons, 22 October 1935. Economic sanctions were applied – and widely broken – in
November, but a proposed oil embargo was never
put into effect.*

I have seldom spoken with greater regret,
for my lips are not yet unsealed. Were
these troubles over I would make a case,
and I guarantee that not a man would go
into the Lobby against us.

*Britain's Prime Minister, Stanley Baldwin, in a
Commons debate on Abyssinia, 10 December
1935. Eight days later he forced the resignation
of Sir Samuel Hoare, for signing the 'Hoare-Laval
Pact' with the French Prime Minister, recognizing
Italy's right to keep its spoils in Ethiopia. Hoare's
friends complained that he had been made a
scapegoat for carrying out government policy, only
after it had proved unexpectedly unpopular. The
policy was then dropped – officially.*

I dropped an aerial torpedo right in the
centre, and the group opened up like a
flowering rose. It was most amusing.

*The dictator's son Vittorio Mussolini, a pilot in
the Italian Air Force, on the joys of bombing
Ethiopians, February 1936. Poison gas was
used, in contravention of the Geneva Convention
of 1925; the Red Cross was one of the 'targets'.*

Italy has her Empire. It is a Fascist empire
because it bears the indestructible sign of
the will and power of Rome.

*Mussolini, Rome, 9 May 1936, a few days after
Italian troops entered Addis Ababa. Italy had to
commit over 650,000 troops to secure victory*

*over a medieval army; Haile Selassie went into
exile. The following month, Britain and France
unilaterally abandoned sanctions against Italy;
the League of Nations afterwards abandoned the
policy, and admitted the puppet Fascist state of
Abyssinia as a member.*

The clouds of mistrust and suspicion
have been cleared away.

*Britain's new Prime Minister, Neville
Chamberlain, signs the Anglo-Italian Agreement,
2 May 1938, and praises Mussolini's 'vigour and
efficiency'; Britain recognized the annexation of
Ethiopia in return for a promise to withdraw
Italian troops from Spain. The Foreign Secretary,
Anthony Eden, resigned in protest at this and
other acts of appeasement of the European dictators; his successor, Lord Halifax, went with
Chamberlain to Rome in January 1939, where
they toasted Victor Emmanuel as 'Emperor of
Abyssinia'. On 8 April 1939 Italy invaded and
occupied Albania.*

Concerning the Abyssinian episode, the
less said now the better. When old friends
are reconciled after a quarrel, it is always
dangerous for them to discuss its original
causes.

*Sir Alfred Duff Cooper, First Lord of the
Admiralty, May 1938; he resigned in October, in
protest at the Munich Agreement.*

Lebensraum

Where peace and war are concerned legal
obligations are not alone involved and, if
war broke out, it would be unlikely to be
confined to those who have assumed
such obligations. This is especially true
in the case of two countries like Great
Britain and France, devoted to the ideals
of democratic liberty and determined to
uphold them.

*UK Prime Minister Neville Chamberlain, 24
March 1938; Britain and France had agreed that,
in the event of France going to war to protect
Czechoslovakia from invasion, Britain would be
obliged to support France. But Chamberlain was
at pains to give no direct guarantee of British protection to Czechoslovakia itself, as the Nazis, led
by Konrad Henlein, organized rioting and terrorism among the ethnic German population in the
south of that country – the 'Sudetenland'.*

*In June, the Sudeten German Party made big
gains in national elections after much of the non-*

German population had been terrorized into abstention.

Without colonies Germany's space is too small to guarantee that our people can be fed safely and continuously. The attitude of other Powers to our demand is simply incomprehensible.
Hitler demands more 'living space' – Lebensraum – for Germany at the annual Nazi rally in Nuremberg, 5 September 1937.

I can only tell the representatives of the democracies that, if these tormented creatures cannot by their own exertions come to their rights, they will demand both their rights and assistance from us.
Adolf Hitler, speech, Berlin, 16 September 1938, referring to the Sudeten Germans.

Before us stands the last problem that must be solved and will be solved. It is the last territorial claim which I have to make in Europe, but it is the claim from which I will not recede.
Adolf Hitler, speech, Berlin, 26 September 1938.

Armed conflict between nations is a nightmare to me, but if I were convinced that any nation had made up its mind to dominate the world by fear of its force I should feel it should be resisted.
Neville Chamberlain announces the mobilization of the British Fleet, 26 September 1938.

How horrible, fantastic, incredible it is that we should be digging trenches and trying on gas masks here because of a quarrel in a faraway country between people of whom we know nothing.
Neville Chamberlain, radio broadcast, 27 September 1938. On the 29th he flew to Munich for talks on the Sudeten Crisis with Hitler, Mussolini, and the French premier, Daladier. The Czechoslovak government was not permitted to send a representative.

The occupation by stages of the predominantly German territories by German troops will begin on October 1st. ... The evacuation of the region shall be completed by October 10th, without destruction of any of the existing installations.
Terms of the four-power Munich Agreement, signed on 30 September 1938.

This is the second time in our history that there has come back from Germany to Downing Street peace with honour. I believe it is peace for our time. Go home and get a nice quiet sleep.
Neville Chamberlain addresses cheering crowds in Downing Street on his return from Munich, 30 September 1938.

Forget the crisis but remember to put your clocks back tonight.
Advice to readers of the Daily Express, 1 October 1938.

We have sustained a defeat without a war.
Winston Churchill, speech on the Munich Agreement, House of Commons, 5 October 1938.

Thus we begin our march into the great German future, and in this hour we wish to thank the Almighty for giving us His blessing on our way in the past and ask Him to accompany our way in the future.
Adolf Hitler addresses occupying troops and Sudeten German crowds, Eger, 5 October 1938. Polish troops occupied Teschen-Silesia, while Hungary moved to occupy territory inside its border with Slovakia and Ruthenia; the state of Czechoslovakia, created by the victorious allies after the First World War, was effectively dismembered.

A vote for Hogg is a vote for Hitler.
Dissident student Tories, led by future PM Edward Heath, campaign against the government candidate, Quintin Hogg, at the 27 October Oxford by-election; Winston Churchill, Anthony Eden and Harold Macmillan were among those Tories to support the Independent candidacy of the Master of Balliol, who halved the official Conservative majority.

• •

And we who have been brought up to
think of 'Gallant Belgium'
As so much blague
Are now prepared again to essay good
through evil
For the sake of Prague.
Louis MacNeice, Autumn Journal VII, 1939.

• •

P.S. I suppose the Quintin Hogg who won the Oxford election was the little squirt who was a fag when I left school.
George Orwell (Eric Blair), letter to Cyril Connolly, 14 December 1938.

Bloody Terror of the Czechs against Germans and Slovaks creates an Intolerable Situation.
Nazi newspaper headline, March 1939. Following the pattern of the Sudetenland, riots had been fomented in Bohemia; on 15 March, Hitler entered Prague with an army of occupation following a Blitzkrieg – a 'lightning attack'. Czechs were forced at gunpoint to give the Nazi salute as he processed through the streets. A round-up of Jews then began.

I believe we are very foolish in this House sometimes, those of us who refuse to believe there is any good in National Socialism, or that there is no unselfishness in men like Hitler and Goering.
A. Beverley Baxter, Conservative MP for Wood Green, speech, 26 July 1938.

What has Hitler done of which we can reasonably complain? Let us try to forget his misdeeds of the past, and the methods which, no doubt, we all of us deplore, but which I suggest have been very largely forced upon him.
C. T. Culverwell, Conservative MP for Bristol West, 6 October 1938.

Why can we not make friends with Italy and Germany? There are people saying that Herr Hitler has broken his word. I tell you there is one bargain he has made – that is that the German Navy shall be only one-third of the British Navy – which he has kept, and kept loyally.
The Rt Hon. R.A. Butler, Conservative MP for Saffron Walden, speech, 15 November 1938. The following month, the German Navy began doubling its U-Boat forces.

When one thinks of the lies and betrayals of those years, the cynical abandonment of one ally after another, the imbecile optimism of the Tory press, the flat refusal to believe that the dictators meant war, even when they shouted it from the house-tops, the inability of the moneyed class to see anything wrong whatever in

I am a camera with its shutter open, quite passive, recording, not thinking.
Christopher Isherwood, Goodbye to Berlin, 1939.

concentration camps, ghettoes, massacres and undeclared wars, one is driven to feel that moral decadence played its part as well as mere stupidity.
George Orwell, 'Who Are the War Criminals?', essay in Tribune, 22 October 1943.

It might be worthwhile for the Czechoslovak Government to consider whether they should altogether exclude the project, which has found favour in some quarters, of making Czechoslovakia a more homogeneous state.
Reflecting the mood of the Establishment, The Times editorializes, 7 September 1938.

If we are involved in war our contribution will not be half-hearted nor based on any theory of limited liability.
Lesie Hore-Belisha, UK Secretary for War, speech, House of Commons, 31 March 1939, following a Prime Minsterial statement that Poland would be defended against attack; an Anglo-French-Polish military treaty was signed the following week.
In February 1939 the government began a free distribution of air-raid shelters to poor families in areas most likely to be bombed; the process was widened and accelerated in April, when a Bill was passed enabling up to 2,500,000 children to be evacuated from areas vulnerable to air attack. Opposition MPs, particularly the Liberal Megan Lloyd George, deplored the lack of planning for communal 'deep shelters'.

A very little weight one way or the other may decide whether war is going to come or not.
Neville Chamberlain, House of Commons, 24 April 1939, announcing that all men of 20 and over will be liable for military conscription.

If we are going in without the help of Russia we are walking into a trap.
David Lloyd George, House of Commons, 3 April 1939. But Stalin's Foreign Minister, Vyacheslav

Molotov, was negotiating with his Nazi opposite, Joachim von Ribbentrop.

The Third Reich and the Italian Empire are resolved to act side by side and with united forces to secure their living space.
A clause of the 'Pact of Steel' signed by Hitler and Mussolini, 22 May 1939.

War today is not only not inevitable, but it is unlikely. The Government have good reason for saying that.
Sir Thomas Inskip, UK Minister for Co-ordination of Defence, 3 August 1939.

That bastard of the Versailles Treaty.
Vyacheslav Molotov, Foreign Minister of the USSR, on Poland, during negotiations in Berlin, July 1939; in Danzig (Gdansk), a Free City established by the Treaty, the Nazis were behaving as though they were already the occupying force, arresting Polish shipyard workers and sending them to concentration camps. Chamberlain told the Commons that if Poland chose to defend the status of Danzig, Britain would support the action.

I know how much the German people love their Führer. I should therefore like to drink to his health.
A salute from one Great Father of the People to another: Stalin proposes a toast after signing a Non-Aggression Pact with Hitler, 23 August 1939.

The whispered lies to the effect that the Soviet Union will enter into a treaty of understanding with Nazi Germany are nothing but poison spread by the enemies of peace and democracy, the appeasement mongers, the Munichmen of Fascism.
Before the Pact: the Communist Daily Worker, 26 May 1939.

By compelling Germany to sign a non-aggression pact, the Soviet Union has tremendously limited the direction of Nazi war aims.
After the Pact: Daily Worker, 24 August 1939. A similar U-turn was shortly to be executed by the pro-Fascist British press.

The machine is running away with him as it ran away with me.
The ex-Kaiser Wilhelm II, remark, 27 August 1939.

To execute the orders in time, heavy withdrawals were made from stores in the United Kingdom. A third of our stocks of rubber and a quarter of our supplies of nickel have gone and are on their way to Germany. All deliveries had to be made before September 1st 1939.
Business as usual, as reported in the Evening Standard, *21 August 1939. The Minister of Supply, the Rt Hon. Leslie Burgin, had the power to ban exports of war materials to Germany, but refused to do so. After Britain declared war on Germany on 3 September, exports continued to Italy, theoretically neutral but bound to Germany by the 'Pact of Steel'.*

Sir,
May I, through your columns, appeal to caricaturists and humorous writers to suspend during the present crisis the practice of making the dachshund a symbol of Nazidom or of the German nation? Absurd as it may seem, the prevalence of this idea in the popular imagination has produced a real risk of thoughtless acts of cruelty being committed against harmless little animals which are English by birth and often by generations of breeding.
I am, Sir, yours faithfully,
D.L. MURRAY
Letter to The Times, *29 August 1939; taken from* The First Cuckoo *(1976).*

Speak for England, Arthur.
The Conservative MP Leopold Amery, a Munich rebel, encourages the Labour leader Arthur Henderson as he rises to reply to the Prime Minister, 2 September 1939.
Germany invaded Poland on 1 September 1939; when Hitler failed to answer to an Anglo-French ultimatum by midnight on 2 September, Britain and France declared war on Germany.

• •

There'll Always Be An England.
Song: Ross Parker & Charlie Hughes, 1939.

• •

The Second World War 1939~1945

What they could do with round here is a good war.

~ *Bertolt Brecht*, Mother Courage, *1941*

1939

After the German invasion of Bohemia-Moravia in March 1939, Britain and France pledged support for Poland, which feared it was to be next in line. Germany's invasion of Poland on 1 September led to a declaration of war by the two countries two days later, but this did not prevent Poland being completely overrun in four weeks. A six-month period of general inactivity – the 'Phoney War' – then followed, during which appeasers (and Nazi sympathizers) in both Britain and France actively hoped to reach an 'understanding' with the Nazi regime.

The Second World War began on 3 September 1939 after the British Government had issued an ultimatum to the German Government to withdraw from Polish territory invaded on 1 September.

I have to tell you that no such undertaking has been received and that consequently this country is at war with Germany.
UK Prime Minister Neville Chamberlain's radio broadcast at 11.15 a.m., 3 September 1939.

We can only do the right as we see the right, and reverently commit our cause to God.
King George VI, BBC broadcast, 3 September 1939.

This is the people's war. It is our war. We are the fighters. Fight it with all that is in us. And may God defend the right.
Jan Struther speaks to the 'Home Front' in her Times *column, writing as 'Mrs Miniver', from September 1939 onwards.*

When peace has been broken anywhere, the peace of all countries everywhere is in danger.
US President F. D. Roosevelt, radio broadcast, 3 September 1939.

Winston's back.
Radio message from the Admiralty to all ships, 3 September 1939. Churchill was reappointed First Lord of the Admiralty in Chamberlain's first War Cabinet; the Labour and Liberal Parties promised their full support but declined to join a coalition.

69

●●●●●●●●●●●●●●●●●●●●●●●●●●●●●●●●

We're going to hang out the washing on
the Siegfried Line,
Have you any dirty washing, mother
dear?

Bud Flanagan (with Chesney Allen), song, 1939.

●●●●●●●●●●●●●●●●●●●●●●●●●●●●●●●●

No enemy bomber can reach the Ruhr. If
one reaches the Ruhr, my name is not
Goering. You can call me Meyer.
*Reichsmarschall Hermann Goering addresses the
Luftwaffe in September 1939.*

———————————

The aim is to restore peace and order in
Poland … The friendly Soviet Peoples
will help the Polish people establish new
conditions for its political life.
*Pravda report of Red Army invasion of Poland, 17
September 1939.*

~

A wheel always turns. This one will.
*Polish officer to German captors after the surren-
der of Warsaw, 27 September 1939.*

~

The people living in the former Polish
State will have a peaceful life in keeping
with their national character.
*German-Soviet Boundary and Friendship
Treaty, signed in Moscow 29 September 1939.
Approximately 60,000 Polish troops were
killed in the invasion; 200,000 were wounded
and 700,000 taken prisoner. Poland was parti-
tioned, the USSR taking 76,000 square miles,
with a population of 13 million, in the East, and
Germany taking the rest, including Warsaw. The
Polish government fled to Romania.*

———————————

To Joseph Stalin: Best wishes for your
personal well-being as well as for the
prosperous future of the friendly Soviet
Union. Adolf Hitler.
60th birthday greetings, 21 September 1939.

Are you aware that it is private property?
Why, you will be asking me to bomb
Essen next!
*Sir Kingsley Wood, UK Minister for Air, rejects an
RAF plan to bomb the Black Forest, 30 September
1939.*

I cannot forecast to you the action of
Russia. It is a riddle wrapped in a mystery
inside an enigma; but perhaps there is a
key. That key is Russian national interest.
Winston Churchill, speech, London, 1 October 1939.

Germany's Will for Peace – No War Aims
against France and England.
Headline in the Nazi Party newspaper, the
Völkischer Beobachter, *24 October 1939. Britain
had by then landed over 150,000 troops in France;
on 12 October, the battleship HMS* Royal Oak *was
sunk at her moorings in Scapa Flow by a German U-
Boat; over 800 seamen died, and Churchill ordered
that the South Isles of Orkney be joined by cause-
ways to the main island to deter future raids.*

C'est une drôle de guerre. ('It is a phoney
war'.)
*Edouard Daladier, Prime Minister of France,
speech, 22 December 1939.*

I said to the man who stood at the gate of the
year: 'Give me light that I may tread safely
into the unknown.' And he replied: 'Go out
into the darkness and put your hand into
the hand of God. That shall be to you better
than a light and safer than a known way.'
US writer Minnie Louise Haskins, introduction to
The Desert; *quoted by King George VI in his
Christmas Day BBC broadcast.*

We shall only talk of peace when we have
won the war. The Jewish-capitalistic world
will not survive the twentieth century.
*Adolf Hitler, New Year message to Germany, 31
December 1939.*

●●●●●●●●●●●●●●●●●●●●●●●●●●●●●●●●

In my experience, I have always found
that you cannot have an efficient ship
unless you have a happy ship, and you
cannot have a happy ship unless you
have an efficient ship ….
*The opening words of Captain Mountbatten's –
afterwards Admiral Earl Mountbatten of Burma
– address to the officers and crew of HMS* Kelly
in 1939: used verbatim by Noël Coward in In
Which We Serve, *1942 – a year that also saw
the Hollywood realization of* Mrs Miniver, *which
won six Oscars and was, according to Churchill,
'worth 100 warships' as propaganda.*

●●●●●●●●●●●●●●●●●●●●●●●●●●●●●●●●

1940

The German invasion of Norway and Denmark in April, and of Belgium and Holland in May, were followed by the invasion of France and the retreat of the British Expeditionary Force, and its subsequent evacuation from Dunkirk; Italy then declared war on Britain and France. There followed the Battle of Britain, in which the Royal Air Force repelled the Luftwaffe's campaign to disable British defences prior to an invasion; Hitler then attempted to negotiate a separate peace with Britain but Churchill, now Prime Minister, would have none of it. There then followed the first 'Blitz', and a U-boat campaign against British merchant shipping.

The service rendered by Finland to mankind is magnificent. They have exposed for all the world to see the military incapacity of the Red Army and of the Red Air Force.
Winston Churchill, BBC broadcast, 20 January 1940, after Soviet setbacks in the Finnish campaign; the numerically superior but poorly led and chaotically indisciplined Red Army sustained huge casualties. Although Finland finally surrendered on 13 March, Stalin's position as an ally of Hitler was much weakened.

The Navy's here!
Ecstatic greeting for Royal Navy liberators of some 300 British prisoners of war held on the German prison ship Altmark *in a Norwegian fjord, 26 February 1940; an earlier 'search' by neutral Norwegian authorities had failed to locate them.*

One thing is certain: he has missed the bus.
Prime Minister Neville Chamberlain, speech, House of Commons, 2 April 1940. Soon afterwards, Germany overran Denmark and on 9 April invaded Norway, which soon surrendered; a puppet Nazi government was established under Vidkun Quisling. There followed a bungled British attempt to invade Norway; the troops were poorly armed, lacked air support, and were not equipped for the arctic conditions. Discontent with Chamberlain's leadership grew as the extent of the débâcle became clear.

You have sat too long for any good that you have been doing. Depart, I say, and let us have done with you. In the name of God, go!
Conservative MP Leo Amery quoting Oliver Cromwell to demand Chamberlain's resignation as Prime Minister in a House of Commons debate on 8 May 1940, the day Germany launched a Blitzkrieg against Belgium and Holland. On a vote of confidence in his government, Chamberlain won

by 281 to 200, with 41 Conservative MPs voting against him and some 60 abstaining. The Tory rebels refused to support the government unless Labour and the Liberals were brought in; Labour refused to serve under Chamberlain and rejected the alternative proposal of Lord Halifax. The First Lord of the Admiralty, Winston Churchill, was sworn in as Prime Minister on 10 May.

I felt as if I were walking with destiny, and that all my past life had been but a preparation for this hour and this trial.
Winston Churchill, The Gathering Storm (part of The Second World War, 6 vols, 1948–54), on his appointment as Prime Minister.

~

They are the only people who like to be told how bad things are – who like to be told the worst.
Winston Churchill on the British: a prophetic speech in 1921.

~

I have nothing to offer but blood, toil, tears and sweat. [...]

You ask: 'What is our aim?' I can answer you in one word: 'Victory!' Victory at all costs, victory in spite of all terror, victory however long and hard the road may be: for without victory there is no survival. [...]

Come then, let us go forward together, with our united strength.
Winston Churchill, first House of Commons speech as Prime Minister, 13 May 1940.

Most of you know your policeman and your ARP warden by sight. If you keep your heads you can also tell whether a

● ●

This … is … London.
Goodnight … and good luck.

Ed Murrow reports for CBS on the British Home Front. Churchill often said that Murrow's reports did more than anything else to persuade the US to aid Britain's war effort.

● ●

military officer is really British or only pretending to be so.

Government pamphlet issued on 17 May 1940. BBC news bulletins urged listeners to be on the look-out for parachutists.

Everybody should continue at their jobs until ordered to do otherwise.

The Labour politician Ernest Bevin, who as Minister of Labour assumed dictatorial powers under the Emergency Powers Act passed through Parliament in three hours on 22 May 1940. Aircraft factory workers were ordered to work ten hours a day, seven days a week, and strikes were banned. The government reserved the right to impose a 100 per cent tax on company profits.

We are not Poles. It could not happen here.

French General Gamelin, responding to reports that Germany might use blitzkrieg tactics, 13 May 1940. Paris fell on 14 June; France surrendered a week later.

Nothing but a miracle can save the British Expeditionary Force now, and the end cannot be far off. The German armoured divisions have penetrated to the coast.

The diary of Field Marshal Lord Alanbrooke, 27 May 1940.

We must be careful not to assign to this deliverance the attributes of a victory. Wars are not won by evacuations.

Winston Churchill, Their Finest Hour. On 4 June 1940, at the end of a week-long evacuation from Dunkirk, the last of the 338,226 rescued British troops arrived in England after sustaining a massive bombardment from a German force of over 750,000, and strafing by the Luftwaffe.

Oh, my dear fellow, the noise – and the people!

An anonymous wit describes the Dunkirk beaches; it has also been attributed to a Captain Strahan at the Battle of Bastogne, 1944.

No bunching, no pushing – much more orderly than a theatre queue.

Morale-boosting quote from an anonymous Tommy, one of the last to be evacuated.

We shall not flag or fail … we shall defend our island, whatever the cost may be, we shall fight on the beaches, we shall fight on the landing grounds, we shall fight in the fields and the streets, we shall fight in the hills; we shall never surrender.

Winston Churchill, speech, House of Commons, 4 June 1940.

Our great-grandchildren, when they learn how we began this war by snatching glory out of defeat … may also learn how the little holiday steamers made an excursion to hell and came back glorious.

The author and playwright turned BBC commentator J. B. Priestley, 5 June 1940. The Dunkirk evacuation could not have been carried out without the help of a fleet of requisitioned private vessels, including fishing boats, ferries and river steamers.

Deutschland siegt auf allen Fronten. ('Germany conquers on all fronts'.)

Sign fixed to the Chamber of Deputies after the surrender of Paris, 14 June 1940.

The Italians will laugh at me; every time Hitler occupies a country he sends me a message.

Benito Mussolini, who declared war on Britain and France on 10 June 1940.

In three weeks Britain will have her neck wrung like a chicken.

French General Maxime Weygard, 5 June 1940.

To make a union with Great Britain would be fusion with a corpse.

First World War hero Marshal Pétain, 16 June

● ●

Run, Adolf, run, Adolf, run, run, run,
Look what you've bin gorn an' done,
done, done.

Bud Flanagan (with Chesney Allen) from their own song, Run, Rabbit, Run, 1940.

● ●

1940, after Churchill proposed a Franco-British Union with joint citizenship. Pétain became the titular head of a puppet Nazi regime in Vichy.

Let us brace ourselves to our duty and so bear ourselves that if the British Commonwealth and Empire lasts for a thousand years, men will still say: 'This was their finest hour.'
Winston Churchill, speech, House of Commons, 18 June 1940.

We hope that Germany will be guided by a spirit which will permit the two great neighbouring peoples to live and work in peace.
French General Charles Huntziger after signing surrender treaty, 22 June 1940. France surrendered to Germany in the same railway carriage used to take the German surrender in 1918; Hitler sat in the chair occupied on that occasion by General Foch.

To all Frenchmen: France has lost a battle but France has not lost the war. […] The war is not lost, the country is not dead, hope is not extinct. Vive la France!
General Charles de Gaulle, broadcast to France from London, 23 June 1940. Shortly afterwards, the Vichy government sentenced him to death.

The battle for France is over, for the time being. The Battle of Britain is about to begin.
Winston Churchill, speech, House of Commons, 1 July 1940 – the day German forces occupied the Channel Islands. Two days later, the Royal Navy sank the French fleet at anchor at Mers-el-Kebir, Algeria, to prevent it falling into German hands; 1000 French sailors died.

As England, in spite of the hopelessness of her military position, has so far shown herself unwilling to come to any compromise, I have decided to begin to prepare for, and if necessary to carry out, an invasion of England.
Adolf Hitler, secret directive signed on 16 July 1940.

I have often wondered what would have happened if two hundred thousand German storm troops had actually established themselves ashore … I intended to use the slogan, 'You can always take one with you.'
Winston Churchill, Their Finest Hour.

Constantly, as I walk down the street, I find myself looking up at the windows to see which of them would make good machine-gun nests.
George Orwell, Diary, 25 July 1940. Orwell had joined the civilian militia originally known as the Parashots, then as the Local Defence Volunteers, and finally as the Home Guard – 'Dad's Army'. At first lacking uniforms, the Home Guard began its existence desperately ill-equipped, with such weapons of national defence as pikes, pitchforks, scythes, and antique fowling-pieces 'liberated' from local museums; 250,000 men volunteered in the first week.

••••••••••••••••••••••••••••••••••••••

Here is the News and this is [—] reading it.
For the first time, and as a security measure, BBC newsreaders like Frank Philips and Alvar Liddell identified themselves at the start of the bulletin.

••••••••••••••••••••••••••••••••••••••

I am sure of victory of the Fourth International. Go forward.
Last words of Leon Trotsky, assassinated in Mexico on Stalin's orders, 21 August 1940.

———————————

The universe is so vast and so ageless that the life of one man can only be justified by the measure of his sacrifice.
RAF pilot V. A. Roswarne, who died during the Battle of Britain, aged 24, letter to his mother, August 1940. Goering's Luftwaffe first targeted Channel shipping, then RAF airfields in the south of England, then began a 'blitz' of London itself, with 300 bombers and 600 fighters sent on the evening of 7 September, of which 99 – according to the Air Ministry – were shot down.

~

Never in the field of human conflict was so much owed by so many to so few.
Winston Churchill, speech, House of Commons, on the RAF as the Battle of Britain began in earnest, 20 August 1940. Goering's attempt to destroy the RAF and gain air supremacy failed, and the planned invasion of Britain was postponed indefinitely; instead, bombing of British cities was intensified, as much to destroy morale as to hit militarily significant targets.

Send all the pumps you can, the whole bloody world's on fire.
Fire officer during London docklands blitz, 7 September 1940.

~

As I lay there looking where the windows had been blown out, I heard the air raid warden calling my mother's name: 'Nance, come on, you've copped it girl, come out of there, you've got five incendiary bombs!' All this time my mum's shouting, 'come out, come out you silly'. Then she grabbed me. 'Let it burn', she said. And I just went to get away from her when the whole of the house caved in. I would have been in there, picking up the clock and the ornaments off the mantelpiece.
Kitty Murphy, aged 16, of North Woolwich, 14 September 1940.

~

Oh, that Hitler! He is a fidget.
'Little old lady' overheard by BBC radio commentator in a Tube station shelter, September 1940.

~

It was like a shuttle service, the way the German planes came up the Thames, the fires acting as a flare path. Often they were above the smoke. The searchlights bored into that black roof but couldn't penetrate it. They looked like long pillars supporting a black canopy. The shrapnel clicked on the road, and still the German bombers came.
Ed Murrow reports for CBS on the first London blitz.

~

Now we can look the East End in the face.
Remark by Queen Elizabeth, wife of George VI, to a policeman after Buckingham Palace was bombed; over 7000 civilians died during

SAYINGS and SLOGANS of WAR

Don't you know there's a war on?
In Britain, the catch-all response to complaints of delay and inefficiency.

Put that light out!
The merry cry of the Air-Raid Warden, from September 1939.

YOUR Effort
YOUR Sacrifice
Will Bring OUR Victory
UK poster slogan, abandoned because of its 'Them and Us' overtones.

Let Us Go Forward Together
Replacement for the above, based on a speech of Churchill.

Is Your Journey Really Necessary?
Question expecting the answer, 'No': from 1939.

A bayonet is a weapon with a worker at each end
British pacifist slogan, 1940. As the British pacifist movement was largely Communist-inspired, the slogan disappeared after Hitler's invasion of the USSR.

Dig for Victory
Dig On for Victory
The Need is Growing – Dig for Victory Still
UK poster campaign to encourage self-sufficiency.

Be Like Dad – Keep Mum
UK poster to combat 'loose talk' – hastily abandoned, in view of the need to attract women into the factories, and replaced by
Careless Talk Costs Lives
and
Walls Have Ears
and
Keep Mum – She's Not So Dumb
– a poster depicting a slimly stunning blonde nightclub hostess surrounded by male Army, Navy and Air Force admirers.

Better an end with horror than a horror without end
Nazi slogan. 'Now that we are fighting the man who coined it,' wrote Orwell in March 1940, 'we ought not to underrate its emotional appeal.'

Jarmany calling, Jarmany calling...
The call-sign of William Joyce, 'Lord Haw-Haw', in English-language Nazi broadcasts beamed to Britain.

September 1940; thereafter the figure averaged 3000 a week for the rest of 1940; Churchill claimed in November that 'it takes a ton of German bombs to kill three-quarters of a person.'

~

Be good – we're still open.
Sign pasted on the wall of a bomb-damaged police station, London, September 1940. Provincial cities such as Birmingham, Sheffield, Manchester, Glasgow, Cardiff, Bristol, South-ampton and Coventry – where the cathedral was destroyed and over 1000 people killed in one night – were also targeted. On 29 December, 10,000 incendiary bombs fell on the City of London. Over 24,000 British civilians died in air raids by year's end. An emergency budget raised the basic rate of income tax to 42 per cent.

The marshalling yards at Hamm
The frequent target of unspecifiable – and sometimes non-existent – RAF bombing raids, according to BBC news bulletins.

London Can Take It
Also 'Britain Can Take It' – a morale-booster during the Blitz; title of a propaganda film produced by the Ministry of Information, 1940.

Two Good Terms Deserve a Rest
No Man Is Good Three Times
Republican Party slogans, Presidential election, 1940; the Democrats used 'New Deal'.

Gone for a Burton
In the 1930s, a slogan promoting Burton Ale; adopted by RAF personnel to mean 'Missing, presumed dead.'

Gung-ho
Chinese for 'Work together'; adopted by US Marines under General Carlson.

Make Do And Mend
US 'Domestic Front' slogan, adopted from Royal Navy expression for off-duty time devoted to running repairs.

Français, c'est moi – Churchill – qui vous parle. ('French people, it is I – Churchill – who speaks to you.') [...] We are waiting for the long-promised invasion. So are the fishes.
Winston Churchill, broadcast to France, 21 October 1940.

He acted in perfect sincerity according to his lights.
Winston Churchill on the death of Neville Chamberlain, 9 November 1940.

I have said this before but I say it again and again and again: your boys are not going to be sent to any foreign wars.
US President Franklin D Roosevelt, election speech, November 1940.

~

The best immediate defence of the United States is the success of Great Britain defending itself.
US President Franklin D. Roosevelt, press conference, 17 December 1940.

The German Armed Forces must be prepared, even before the conclusion of the war against England, to crush Soviet Russia in a rapid campaign.
Adolf Hitler, War Directive number 21, 18 December 1940.

If Britain should go down all of us in the Americas would be living at the point of a gun ... We must produce arms and ships with every energy and resource we can command. The United States must become the great arsenal of democracy.
US President Franklin D Roosevelt, radio 'fireside chat', 29 December 1940. He had already by-passed the Neutrality Act to sell Britain 500,000 'surplus' rifles and hand over 50 superannuated destroyers; now he wanted US industry to prepare for war production.

~

The Americans cannot build aeroplanes. They are very good at refrigerators and razor blades.
A reassurance for Hitler from Hermann Goering following Roosevelt's 'arsenal of democracy' speech; quoted in Alastair Cooke, America.

1941

The Axis powers invaded Yugoslavia and Greece in April, and Hitler ordered General Rommel's Afrika Corps to reinforce the Italian armies in North Africa. In June, Hitler reneged on the Nazi-Soviet Pact and invaded the USSR; spectacular early gains were followed by the halting of the German advance by winter weather and fierce resistance. Japan's desire for expansion, as an Axis power, was met by the USA with the threat of economic sanctions; as negotiations were proceeding, the Japanese air force bombed the US Hawaiian naval base at Pearl Harbor on 7 December, and America entered the war.

A Kitchen Goes To War

A 'Ration-Time Cookery Book' published by the Ministry of Food. Rationing of butter (4oz (113 g) per person per week), sugar (12oz (340 g)) and bacon (4oz (113 g) uncooked, 3 oz (85g) cooked) began in January 1940; meat followed in March, and by the end of the year the government had become sole buyer of almost all Britain's food; clothing and fuel, too, could only be bought with coupons. Tightened throughout the war, rationing was not to end until 1954.

The tasks of the Party are … to be cautious and not allow our country to be drawn into conflicts by warmongers who are accustomed to have others pull the chestnuts out of the fire for them.

Joseph Stalin, speech to the Sixth Congress of the Communist Party, 6 January 1941.

Give us the tools, and we will finish the job.

Winston Churchill, radio broadcast, 9 February 1941, referring to the 'lease-lend' arrangements with the USA, under which British bases in the West Indies were loaned to the US in exchange for destroyers. The idea was Roosevelt's; he described it as 'lending your neighbour a hose to put out a fire'.

I cannot offer them a delightful life … The first month in a new job will be the worst.

Labour Minister Ernest Bevin orders managers in industry to provide facilities for female employees; 100,000 women were recruited into industry in March 1941, as conscription left vital services and production undermanned. Men aged 41 and 42 were also recruited at a trainee wage of £3 0s 6d (£3.02) a week; women were paid £1 18s (£1.90).

Like German opera, too long and too loud.

Remark attributed to novelist Evelyn Waugh, describing the Battle of Crete, 28 March 1941, in which a large part of the Italian fleet was destroyed by British warships.

The whipped jackal is frisking up by the side of the German tiger.

Winston Churchill, speech, House of Commons, April 1941: following defeat by British-Australian forces at Tobruk and Derna (January) and Benghazi (February), Mussolini's forces were in full retreat from Libya. On 14 February, the advance guard of the German Afrika Korps, the panzer division, arrived in Tripoli under the command of General Erwin Rommel. Benghazi was evacuated in April, and Tobruk was besieged.

Greeks! Be worthy of your history and stand hand to hand, proud and dignified. … We have done our duty. … The heroic exploits of our Allies, the Australians and New Zealanders, are weaving new legends around the slopes of Mount Olympus.

The last statement of the Greek government before the fall of Athens to the Nazis on 27 April 1941; fierce rearguard action on the Mount Olympus line enabled most of the Allied troops to withdraw in safety, amid moving scenes of farewell.

We have finished the job; what shall we do with the tools?

Restored to his throne after driving the Italians out of his country with British help, Emperor Haile Selassie sends a telegram to Churchill from Addis Ababa, 5 May 1941.

It is a reprisal for the methodical bombing of the residential quarters of German towns, including Berlin.

Statement by the Nazi High Command after the

550-plane moonlight raid on London, 11 May 1941. Over 100,000 incendiaries were dropped, and thousands of tonnes of high explosive; some 1400 civilians died, and the chamber of the House of Commons, along with Westminster Hall and the tower of Westminster Abbey, was destroyed; St Paul's Cathedral, though hit, survived. The raid brought the total of London's dead to 20,000, with 25,000 seriously injured.

~

The smell and the stench and the smoke and the fires still burning – I imagine that's what hell would look like ... It was utter despair ... You couldn't even find the road. I felt my youth was gone ... I thought if they can do this to us, do it to our children, we should do it to them.

Midwife Betty Lawrence on the German raid on Plymouth, 20 March 1941; quoted in The People's Century *(BBC, 1995).*

~

You do your worst, and we will do our best.

Winston Churchill addresses Hitler in a speech, July 1941. In addition to the capital, the ports of Liverpool, Belfast, Clydebank, Southampton, Portsmouth and Plymouth also suffered heavy bombing.

Sink the Bismarck!

Admiralty order to all ships in the Western Mediterranean and North Atlantic after the Bismarck, *the pride of the German fleet, sank* HMS Hood *with the loss of over 1300 men; after a three-day, 1750-mile (3000-km) chase from Greenland, the* Bismarck *was sunk some 550 miles (885 km) west of Land's End on 27 May 1941.*

Greenland had been occupied by the still neutral US in April, and US warships deployed to assist in Atlantic convoy duty.

We have only to kick in the door and the whole rotten structure will come crashing down.

Adolf Hitler launching Operation Barbarossa, the invasion of Germany's former ally the USSR by over three million troops, 22 June 1941. Soviet forces, numbering seven million, were caught unprepared and within a few days two Russian armies were encircled in the Ukraine.

~

We will offer whatever help we can, any technical or economic assistance in our power. We are resolved to destroy Hitler and every vestige of the Nazi regime. We will never parley, never. I gave clear and precise warnings to Stalin of what was coming. I can only hope these warnings did not fall unheeded.

Winston Churchill, speech, House of Commons, 24 June 1941.

~

So far as strategy, policy, foresight, competence are arbiters Stalin and his commissars showed themselves at this moment the most completely outwitted bunglers of the Second World War.

Winston Churchill, The Grand Alliance *(see p.71), Chapter 20.*

~

If we see that Germany is winning the war we ought to help Russia, and if Russia is winning we ought to help Germany, and in that way let them kill as many as possible.

Senator Harry S Truman, New York Times, *24 July 1941.*

~

I have only one purpose, the destruction of Hitler, and my life is much simplified thereby. If Hitler invaded Hell I would make at least a favourable reference to the Devil in the House of Commons.

Winston Churchill's mood in July 1941, The Grand Alliance.

~

We must leave them nothing. Our policy is one of 'scorched earth'.

Joseph Stalin, July 1941; retreating in the face of Nazi forces, Soviet troops organized the wholesale destruction of towns and villages and the burning of crops in the fields. Nothing and no one was spared. In August Stalin ordered the blowing-up of the Lenin-Dnjeproges dam, on which all the

....

We'll meet again, don't know where, don't know when,
But I know we'll meet again some sunny day.

Song made famous by Vera Lynn on her BBC radio show Sincerely Yours, *from 1941.*

....

industries of the central Ukraine relied for power; the flat land for miles around was turned into a quagmire, and advancing panzer forces were bogged down. The dam, the pride of Stalin's industrialization policy of the early 1930s (although built with American engineering expertise) was symbolized as the windmill in Orwell's later novel, Animal Farm *(1945).*

. . . —

The Morse signal for the letter 'V', better known as the first four notes of Beethoven's Fifth Symphony, becomes the drumbeat call-sign for overseas services of the BBC as the 'V for Victory' campaign is launched on 20 July 1941; the world was already familiar with Churchill's two-fingered salute.

I commission you to carry out all organisational, material and financial preparations for a total solution of the Jewish question in the German sphere of influence in Europe.
Reichsmarschall Hermann Goering to Reinhard Heydrich, 31 July 1941, ordering the organized destruction of Europe's Jews. On 6 September, Jews were ordered to wear the Star of David.

~

As a human being, a Christian, a priest and a German I demand … that you answer for the crimes that have been perpetrated with your consent, which will bring the vengeance of the Lord on the heads of the German people.
Fr. Bernhard Lichtenberg, Dean of St Hedwig's cathedral, letter to the Reich Chief Physician Leonardo Conti, 8 November 1941. Fr. Lichtenberg, arrested for giving aid and assistance to Jews and other 'sub-human races', died two years later on his way to the Dachau extermination camp.

All men shall be enabled to live in freedom from fear and want.
The central tenet of the Atlantic Charter, signed by Churchill and Roosevelt in a secret meeting off the coast of New England, 14 August 1941.

Do not let us speak of darker days; let us rather speak of sterner days. These are not dark days: they are great days – the greatest days our country has ever lived.
Winston Churchill, speech, Harrow School, 29 October 1941.

It was Goebbels, not the German army, who almost entered the city.
M. Lozovsky, Soviet Vice-Commissar for Foreign Affairs, 12 September 1941, as fierce resistance keeps the encircling German armies out of the city of Leningrad; Britain sent Spitfires and Hurricanes, and let Stalin's commanders in on the secret of radar. There now began a 28-month siege, in temperatures as low as –40°C, during which 630,000 civilians died of cold, disease and starvation, and a further 200,000 were killed by enemy action.

~

All the birds died because of the frost. We tried to catch them but it was very difficult … We ate grass, all kinds of grasses … I brought horse dung home, and I wanted to eat it.
Piano teacher-turned sapper and hospital worker Elena Taranukhina, The People's Century *(BBC, 1995). The daily bread ration in Leningrad fell to 125 g – a slice and a half – before the flour ran out, when bread was made from sawdust; people ate soup made from carpenters' glue, all the cats and dogs disappeared, and dismembered corpses littered the streets. Supplies were occasionally brought in by sledge, under fire and air attack, across the frozen Lake Ladoga.*

~

Moscow will be defended to the last.
Joseph Stalin: order of the day, 20 October 1941, as four panzer armies, each with 5000 tanks, advance on a 300-mile (480-km) front towards the Russian capital, 129 years after Napoleon began his retreat. Elsewhere in the USSR, towns and cities fell daily – but not Leningrad.

~

Squeeze the enemy's throat!
Take Moscow or perish!
Rival slogans in two capitals, November 1941, as the Moscow temperature fell to –27°C.

~

Germany's plans have ended in fiasco.
Moscow radio announces the recapture of Rostov by General Zhukov, who then turned his army on the German forces besieging Moscow, and routed them: 12 December 1941. A new Retreat From Moscow now began as, in 50° of frost, Russian troops started to push the Nazis back along a 1000-mile (1600-km) front.

SAYINGS and SLOGANS of WAR

Coughs and Sneezes Spread Diseases
Keeping healthy was part of war effort, from 1942.

POTATO PETE SAYS...
Don't you know the sight of peelings Greatly hurts Lord Woolton's feelings?
UK poster to combat potato wastage, 1943. Lord Woolton was Minister of Food, 'the father of austerity cuisine'. Potato Pete was a cheery cartoon tuber designed to make austerity fun – or at any rate, more fun than Lord Woolton.

Second Front Now!
Communist-inspired call for a fresh invasion of Europe, from 1942.

We Never Closed
The proud boast of London's Windmill Theatre – venue for 'naughty' shows – after the Blitz.

Wot, no... ?
...beer/char/fags... etc. British graffito, bemoaning shortages.

Overpaid, overfed, oversexed, and Over Here
British resentment of occupation by US allies, attributed to comedian Tommy Trinder.

Kilroy Was Here
US graffito, whose origins are controversial; possibly derived from a US Army quartermaster who chalked it on supplies he had checked. Or, on the other hand, possibly not.

SNAFU
'Situation Normal – All Fucked Up'. US saying, politely – and wrongly – rendered as 'Fouled'.

Got any gum, chum?
British children importune American GIs.

Lend To Defend
British slogan, promoting National Savings.

Somewhere in Europe
The dateline for censored reports after D-Day.

Hitler has only got one ball,
Goering has two, but very small;
Himmler has something sim'lar,
But poor old Goebbels has no balls at all.
Sung in Britain, to the tune of 'Colonel Bogey', throughout the war.

Let's Re-Re-Re Elect Roosevelt
Democrat Party slogan, Presidential election, 1944.

Had enough?
Republican Party slogan, Presidential election, 1944.

Down in the jungle, living in a tent,
Better than a pre-fab – no rent
British children's playground rhyme, c.1945, inspired by Churchill's 'ready-made' dwellings.

Now Let's Win The Peace
Conservative Party election slogan, 1945.

Let Us Face The Future
Labour Party election slogan, 1945.

A son of man has just sent his final message to the Son of God.
President Roosevelt, after appealing for unequivocal assurances of peace to Japanese God-Emperor Hirohito, 6 December 1941.

~

Yesterday, December 7 1941 – a date that will live in infamy – the United States of America was suddenly and deliberately attacked by naval and air forces of the Empire of Japan ... Hostilities exist. There is no blinking at the fact that our people, our territory and our interests are in grave danger ... With confidence in our armed forces, with the unbounding determination of our people, we will gain the inevitable triumph. So help us God.
President Roosevelt, message to Congress after Japanese aircraft destroyed 19 ships and 188 aircraft and killed 2403 US military personnel

in an unprovoked attack on Pearl Harbor, Hawaii, 8 December 1941. At the same time as the Pearl Harbor raid, Japan launched offences against Malaya, Hong Kong, Guam and the Philippines.

~

Praise the Lord and pass the ammunition!
Attributed to Lieutenant Howell M. Forgy during the attack on Pearl Harbor.

~

I fear we have only awakened a sleeping giant, and his reaction will be terrible.
Japanese Admiral Isoroku Yamamoto, December 1941.

'Oh God, another Dunkirk.'
'No, fella. At Dunkirk, they had somewhere to go to.'
Exchange between Canadian soldiers ordered to the defence of Hong Kong against Japanese invasion, 15 November 1941.

When you have to kill a man it costs nothing to be polite.
Winston Churchill explains why the Declaration

of War against Japan was made in traditionally anodyne diplomatic language, 8 December 1941.

So ends a great fight against overwhelming odds.
Christmas Day: after a seven-day battle Hong Kong, along with its 6000 remaining defenders, is surrendered unconditionally to the 40,000-strong Japanese invasion force.

What kind of people do they think we are?
Winston Churchill addresses a cheering Congress, 26 December 1941.

When I warned them [the French] that Britain would fight on alone whatever they did, their Generals told their Prime Minister and their divided Cabinet: 'In three weeks England will have her neck wrung like a chicken.'
Some chicken! Some neck!
Winston Churchill, speech, Canadian Parliament, 30 December 1941.

We must just KBO.
Winston Churchill, remark, December 1941 (KBO = Keep Buggering On).

1942

Within four months of Pearl Harbor, Japan controlled South-East Asia and Burma; US naval successes began to contain the Japanese advance from June onwards. Rommel's Afrika Corps, triumphant in North Africa in the early part of the year, suffered its first significant reverse at El Alamein in October; a fresh German offensive in the USSR was repulsed, and at the end of the year Soviet forces counter-attacked at Stalingrad. The Luftwaffe began its policy of 'Baedeker Raids' against 'historical' towns and cities in Britain; Coventry, where the cathedral was destroyed, was among the tar-

---

I believe that defences of the sort you want to throw up are bad for the morale of troops and civilians.
Lieutenant-General Arthur Percival refuses to countenance landward defences for Singapore, December 1941; it was widely assumed that the jungle-congested Malay peninsula itself would be defence enough against any sort of Japanese 'blitzkrieg'.

~

It is indeed a heavy and far-reaching military defeat ... Here is the moment to display that calm and poise, combined with

grim determination, which not so long ago brought us out of the very jaws of death ... We must remember that we are no longer alone. Three-quarters of the human race are with us.
Winston Churchill, BBC broadcast after the fall of Singapore and the surrender of 130,000 Allied troops to the Japanese, 15 February 1942.

Never before have we had so little time in which to do so much.
President Roosevelt, radio broadcast, 23 February 1942.

The President of the United States ordered me to break through the Japanese lines ... I came through, and I shall return.
US General Douglas MacArthur, pulling out of the Philippines, 11 March 1942.

'The price of petrol has been increased by one penny' – official.
Caption to a Donald Zec cartoon in the Daily Mirror, *26 March 1942; it showed a shipwrecked merchant seaman clinging to a life-raft. Herbert Morrison, Home Secretary, assumed that it implied that seamen were risking their lives for oil-company profits and threatened to close the paper, which also called army commanders 'bone-heads', under the Defence Regulations. The* Mirror *protested that the cartoon merely set in context the grumblings of the British motorist.*

The heroism and devotion of her brave people will long be famous in history.
King George VI awards the George Cross to the Island of Malta, scene of four months' almost continuous air battles, 16 April 1942.

Now the Luftwaffe will go out for every building marked with three stars in Baedeker.
German Foreign Office statement signalling 'Baedeker raids' on British cities of historical and architectural merit, 25 April 1942; on the 29th the lightly defended cities of Exeter, Bath, Norwich and York – where the 15th-century Guildhall was destroyed – were targeted.

From now on the three Great Powers will march step by step together.
Winston Churchill signs a 20-year pact with Stalin, 26 May 1942 – the month in which Germany launched fresh offensives against the USSR, which were largely repulsed.

He has no superior, or even equal, on the field of battle. He carries the story of Waterloo among his identity papers.
US journalist Alexander Sedgwick, covering the Desert War for the New York Times, on the British soldier. In May 1942, Rommel launched a fresh offensive; on 21 June Tobruk fell to the Nazis, and 25,000 Allied troops were taken prisoner; six days later, in Egypt, the Allied Eighth Army abandoned Mersa Matruh. On 6 July, under General Claude Auchinleck, it halted Rommel's advance at El Alamein; one month later, command was passed to General Bernard Montgomery.

America is not training three million troops to play tiddlywinks with Germany. We will pen the German Army in a ring of steel.
US presidential adviser Harry Hopkins, 23 June 1942.

I will scourge the Third Reich from end to end.
Air Marshal Sir Arthur Harris broadcasts, in German, the text of a joint declaration by the RAF and USAF Bomber Commands, 31 July 1942.

We need National Socialist ardour not professional ability.
Adolf Hitler to General Franz Halder sacking him as Army Chief of Staff after he had recommended disengagement from the Russian Campaign, 24 September 1942. A German offensive under General von Paulus against Stalingrad ('The Verdun of the Volga') had driven Russian forces back into the city, which was then defended street by street and house by house; at the end of October a 60,000-strong German offensive gained just 50 yards of territory. Contested areas were reduced to rubble and troops fought hand to hand with bits of twisted steel; enemy soldiers could hear each other breathing in adjoining rooms of the same building. Russian forces then attacked von Paulus's besieging army in November, until by the end of the year they themselves were encircled.

No person shall put sugar on the exterior of a cake after the same has been baked.
UK Ministry of Food regulation. In October 1942, bakers started hiring out cardboard wedding cakes with chalk icing.

The mass of engines labouring in low gear can be heard a great distance away. One imagines that miles of heavy chains are being drawn over sheets of corrugated iron. The guns of the tanks make a metallic ring of flashes that seems to turn the dust cloud into a rosy fire.
Alexander Sedgwick files for the New York Times on the Battle of El Alamein, 23 October–4 November 1942; Rommel's forces were routed.

ONE FOR COVENTRY
Slogan painted on anti-tank shell at El Alamein, 31 October 1942.

~

Rivers of blood are poured out over miserable strips of land that not even the poorest Arab would have bothered about.
Field Marshal Erwin Rommel to his wife Lu, 31 October 1942.

~

Before Alamein we never had a victory. After Alamein we never had a defeat.
Winston Churchill, The Hinge of Fate (see p. 71), Chapter 33.

~

This is not the end. This is not even the beginning of the end. But it is, perhaps, the end of the beginning.
Winston Churchill on victory in the desert, speech, Mansion House, 10 November 1942.

~

Did you hear them in occupied Europe? Did you hear them in Germany?
BBC Overseas Service announcer, after the broadcast of a peal of bells from the ruins of Coventry Cathedral, 15 November 1942, to celebrate victory in the Desert War. The ringing of church bells had previously been forbidden as it was the signal for invasion.

~

In defeat, indomitable; in victory, insufferable; in NATO, thank God, invisible.
The considered – and much later – judgement of Sir Winston Churchill on Earl Montgomery of Alamein. (NATO, the North Atlantic Treaty Organization, was established in 1949, on the principles of the Atlantic Charter.)

———————————

France heard the guns of Toulon, the explosions, the desperate shots fired in a last stand. A tremor of pain, of pity, of rage shook the whole country. On to victory. There is no other road.
General Charles de Gaulle, broadcast to France, 27 November 1942. As German forces arrived in Toulon, the main port of the supposedly independent Vichy France, they were fired on by French

• •

Here's looking at you, kid.
Humphrey Bogart as Rick, in Casablanca (1942).

• •

warships lying at anchor. Sailors blew up the munitions stores, fuel dumps and defence batteries, then scuttled the ships to prevent them falling into Axis hands. Two submarines slipped away to join the Free French forces.

We come amongst you to repulse the cruel invaders who would remove for ever your rights ... to live your own lives in peace and security.
Observing the diplomatic niceties, Lieutenant-General Dwight Eisenhower explains to the people of Vichy-French North Africa why 140,000 US troops have arrived there.

The object of government in peace and in war is not the glory of rulers or of races, but the happiness of the common man.
British Liberal politician and economist William Beveridge, Social Insurance. On 1 December 1942 the 'Beveridge Report' was published, proposing a scheme of compulsory national insurance to give financial protection against sickness, unemployment and old age, and to provide for a National Health Service, free at the point of use; 'social security from the cradle to the grave'. The report was publicized in BBC broadcasts to Occupied Europe, supported by the Labour and Liberal Parties and the TUC, and opposed by insurance companies. Conservative members of the government gave it a qualified welcome but insisted on the retention of private medicine.

Any chortling by officials who have been slothful in pushing this bomb, over the fact that at present it has not succeeded, will be viewed with great disfavour by me.
Said by Winston Churchill to General Ismay in the early stages of the war; Anglo-American co-operation in nuclear fission research – the Manhattan Project – proceeded, and on 2 December 1942 a team led by Enrico Fermi, working in a disused squash court at Chicago University, succeeded in created a sustained, controlled nuclear reaction and producing the atomic explosive, plutonium.

Germany is now carrying into effect Hitler's oft-repeated intention to exterminate the Jewish people in Europe ... Those responsible for these crimes shall not escape retribution.
Statement issued simultaneously in London, Washington and Moscow, 17 December 1942.

1943

German forces were routed at Stalingrad by February, and in May the Soviet army successfully counter-attacked at Kursk. The U-Boat campaign was intensified with heavy losses of Allied shipping, but the Luftwaffe was considered no longer a threat to the British Isles and some anti-invasion provisions were lifted in April; the following month, the RAF 'Dambuster' raid disabled a significant part of the Nazis' war industry. Later in the year, RAF Bomber Command began a series of destructive raids on German cities. The Allied invasion of Italy began in the summer, leading to the resignation of Mussolini; in September, Italy surrendered. Bitter fighting in the Pacific forced Japan into a slow retreat.

• •

Lilli Marlene

German song beamed to the Afrika Corps in 1939, given English words and sung by Marlene Dietrich in 1943.

• •

I imagine all the gunners were tuned into Goering, and had left their posts.

An RAF pilot accounts for the lack of flak during the first ever daylight raid on Berlin, 31 January 1943. Goering was delivering a radio address to mark the tenth anniversary of the Nazi regime. RAF bomber command launched a successful spring offensive with 8000-lb 'Blockbuster' and 4000-lb 'Factory-smasher' bombs against German industrial targets; in March the Air Ministry claimed that 2000 factories had been destroyed and that 20 per cent of Germany's coal production had been lost.

The bitter experience of Stalingrad still weighs heavily on our souls. For the first time we are experiencing the entire tragedy of a reverse. For the first time an entire German army has ceased to exist. What we used to inflict on others has happened to us.

General Dietmar, chief military commentator, Berlin Radio, 5 February 1943. An estimated 250,000 German soldiers died in the Battle of Stalingrad between the beginning of November 1942 and the end of January 1943.

If the German people fails then it does not deserve that we should fight for its future; then we can write it off with equanimity.

Adolf Hitler descends a little further into madness, 6 February 1943.

We entered a gloomy wilderness in our tanks. There wasn't a single man anywhere. Everywhere the forests and marshes are haunted by the ghosts of the avengers ... Night is setting and I feel them stealthily approaching from out of the darkness, they are the ghosts and I am frozen with fear.

Diary of a German officer killed by partisans in Byelorussia, February 1943.

The anti U-boat campaign has been our greatest failure.

UK Cabinet Secretary Lord Maurice Hankey, 24 March 1943. From January 1942 to March 1943, an average of over 600,000 tonnes of Allied shipping was lost each month. The release of convoy escorts and aircraft carriers from North African duty, and developments in radar, asdic (sonar sounding) and depth charge technology, helped to make dramatic reductions in losses from April onwards.

We have reached the conclusion that existing orders can now be relaxed.

Winston Churchill informs the House of Commons that church bells may now be rung to summon people to worship, 20 April 1943. The BBC broadcast the bells of York Minster on Easter Sunday.

Severe damage was done and very serious casualties suffered by the civilian population.

German Propaganda Ministry statement following the 'Dambuster' raid of 17 May 1943, which destroyed the Mohner and Eder dams, flooding the town of Mulheim and inundating coal mines, power stations and steelworks in the Ruhr valley.

We will wage war at your side against Japan while there is breath in our bodies

and while blood flows through our veins.
Winston Churchill addresses a Special Joint Session of Congress, 19 May 1943.

[It is] an offensive of such importance that the whole future of the war may depend on its outcome. More than anything else, your victory will show the whole world that resistance to the German army is hopeless.
Adolf Hitler, Order of the Day, 4 July 1943, launching an offensive in the Kursk region, south of Moscow.

● ●

Don't Let's Be Beastly To The Germans

Noël Coward, song, 1943.

● ●

The enemy's resistance is not shaken to such a degree that it would be justifiable to foresee an early operative German success.
Berlin Radio, 13 July 1943. After the greatest tank battle in history, the Kursk offensive turned into a crushing defeat for the German army and Hitler ordered a cease-fire.

All the well-known streets and squares look as peaceful as ever.
Swedish news report on the US bombing of Rome, 19 July 1943. Crews were under orders to avoid historical buildings, and the Vatican; 1000 tonnes of high explosive was dropped on airfields, factories, railyards and government offices.

~

This is the first page in the story of the liberation of the European continent.
General Dwight Eisenhower, Allied Commander-in-Chief, announces the capture of Palermo and the route of Sicily's 45,000-strong defending army.

~

My dear Duce, my soldiers don't want to fight any more. At this moment you are the most hated man in Italy.
King Victor Emmanuel III invites Mussolini to resign, 25 July 1943; he accepted, and was succeeded by the anti-Fascist Marshal Badoglio.

~

Shut up that Goddam' crying. I won't have brave men here who have been shot seeing a yellow bastard crying. You're going back to the front lines and you may get shot and killed, but you're going to fight. If you don't I'll stand you up against a wall and have a firing squad kill you on purpose. I ought to shoot you myself, you Goddam' whimpering coward.
Lieutenant-General George S. Patton Jr tries out his bedside manner with a shell-shock victim at the 93rd Evacuation Hospital, Sicily, 10 August 1943.

~

All Italians who now act to help eject the German aggressor from Italian soil will have the assistance and support of the Allies.
General Dwight Eisenhower, 8 September 1943, after the Italian surrender to the Allies; the Italian government halted all German troop trains and ships, and the German garrison in Corsica was captured. German forces occupied Rome on the 12th; on the 30th, the Allies entered Naples as the Germans pulled back. Nazi paratroopers sprang Mussolini from gaol on 12 September; on 13 October Italy declared war on Germany. Captured Italian soldiers were taken back to Germany in sealed trains for use as slave labour; in Rome, Nazi officers began crating up art treasures as they prepared to retreat.

Terror, terror, terror. Pure, naked, bloody terror.
German commentator on 'Operation Gomorrah', the Allied destruction of Hamburg in a firestorm in which at least 40,000 people died, 27 July–3 August 1943. Some 10,000 tonnes of explosive fell, more than the total for the 1940–41 London blitz; seven square miles of the city was wiped out, U-boats destroyed on their slipways, shipyards reduced to rubble, and the Elbe tunnel demolished.

Our common tongue is a priceless inheritance and it may well some day become the foundation of a common citizenship.
Winston Churchill proposes a continuing Anglo-US union after the war, speech, Harvard University, 9 September 1943.

The aim is to produce in Germany a state of devastation in which surrender is inevitable … The Battle of Berlin progresses. It will continue as opportunity

serves and circumstances dictate, until the heart of Nazi Germany ceases to beat.
Air Chief Marshal Sir Arthur Harris, Head of RAF Bomber Command, 25 November 1943.

Among ourselves, this once, it shall be said quite frankly but in public we shall never discuss it. I am talking about the evacuation of the Jews, the annihilation of the Jewish people ... In our history,

this is an unwritten and never-to-be-for-gotten page of glory.
Heinrich Himmler addressing the SS, 4 October 1943.

I am entitled to direct anybody anywhere.
Ernest Bevin, UK Minister of Labour, orders one in ten conscripted men aged between 18 and 25 – the 'Bevin Boys' – to work down the coal-mines, 2 December 1943.

1944

The USSR recorded a crushing victory in the Crimea in April, and the retreating German forces abandoned Rome in June. On 6 June – D-Day – the long-awaited Allied 'second front' was opened on the Normandy coastline; after eight weeks the road to Paris was open; the capital was liberated in August, and by September Allied forces were close to the German border. A bomb plot to assassinate Hitler miscarried in July; Field Marshal Rommel, who had been privy to it, later committed suicide. The Warsaw Ghetto rose in armed rebellion at the end of July, encouraged by the nearby Soviet Army, which then failed to assist it. The pilotless plane bomb, the V-1, was deployed against Britain in June; later in the year there followed the first rocket-bomb, the V-2. In October, a huge naval battle in the Pacific resulted in the removal of the Japanese fleet as an effective force. Aachen became, in October, the first German town to fall to the Allies. An Allied plan to seize Netherlands' bridges across the Rhine failed at Arnhem in September; at the end of the year, the German Army launched a counter-offensive in the Ardennes.

Let the Japanese reflect that their war record will not be forgotten.
UK Foreign Secretary Anthony Eden issues an Anglo-American statement on the torture, starva-tion and murder of British, Indian and American prisoners of war, House of Commons, 28 January 1944.

The Fountain of Life will purify the race for all time.
January 1944: Hitler's personal secretary, Martin Bormann, announces the Lebensborn scheme to select suitable unmarried women to breed with 'Nordic' men. Over 200,000 'Aryan' children were taken from their families and sent to Germany to be raised in Nazi orphanages during the war.

If we have to choose between destroy-ing a famous building and sacrificing our own men, then our men's lives count infinitely more and the building must go. Nothing can stand against mil-itary necessity.
General Eisenhower defends the bombing of

Monte Cassino, a German-fortified monastery in Italy. In the House of Lords, Viscount Simon pointed out that most of it dated from the 19th century and was decorated with 'German fres-coes', 16 February 1944.

Lord Winterton (Con):
    I cannot believe that all this wailing about lost babies can possibly have a good effect on the troops.
Mr Thurtle (Parliamentary Secretary to the Minister of Information):
    I do not think a certain amount of crooning is likely to have a serious effect on the British Army.
Parliamentary exchange on the subject of 'female crooners' such as Vera Lynn, 7 March 1944.

The hour of our greatest effort is approach-ing.
Winston Churchill, House of Commons, 26 March 1944, as speculation mounts on the immi-nence of an Allied invasion of mainland Europe. All travel between Britain and Ireland, North and

D–DAY
The Normandy Landings

I don't like it, but there it is. I don't see how we can possibly do anything else. Okay, let's go.
General Dwight D. Eisenhower orders the commencement of 'Operation Overlord' after its 24-hour postponement because of bad weather, 5 June 1944.

Our landings in the Cherbourg-Le Havre area have failed to gain a satisfactory foothold and I have withdrawn the troops. My decision to attack at this time and place was based on the best information available … If any blame or fault attaches to the attempt it is mine alone.
Note written by General Eisenhower on 5 June 1944 in case of failure.

The great battle has begun. After so much conflict, rage and grief the final clash is here. It is of course the Battle of France.
General Charles de Gaulle, BBC broadcast to France, 6 June 1944.

The eyes of the world are upon you. The hopes and prayers of liberty-loving people everywhere march with you.
General Eisenhower, order to troops, 6 June 1944.

Thousands of ships brought tens of thousands of troops to land on the Normandy beaches under cover of the RAF and USAF on 6 June 1944; using prefabricated 'Mulberry harbours', Allied shipping was able to land reinforcements, armoured vehicles and heavy guns before German commanders could bring extra forces to deal with them.

We sure liberated the hell out of this place.
An American soldier surveys the ruins of a Normandy village. On 27 June 1944 the vital port of Cherbourg fell to the Allies, and 20,000 prisoners were taken. By the end of July the road to Paris was open.

South, was banned on 12 March after Eire's Prime Minister de Valera refused a request from President Roosevelt to expel German diplomats from Dublin.

We must have a better word than 'prefabricated'. Why not 'ready-made'?
The British people called them 'pre-fabs': Winston Churchill, memo, 2 April 1944. The first 500,000 steel dwellings, capable of being erected ready for occupation in a few hours, went on display at the end of the month. They were intended to house bombed-out families and returning troops.

The arrogant invaders run like rats, the ground hot beneath their feet. Destroy their ships. Shoot down their planes. Don't allow a single enemy to escape retribution.
Joseph Stalin, Order of the Day, 16 April 1944, as the Soviet army and air force destroy the 100,000-strong Axis army of occupation in the Crimea. With the surrender of Sevastopol on 5 May the Soviet recapture of the Crimea was complete.

When you are sitting by the fireplace with your grandson on your knee and he asks you what you did in the great World War Two, you won't have to cough, shift him to the other knee and say, 'Well, your Granddaddy shovelled shit in Louisiana.' No, Sir. You can look him straight in the eye and say, 'Son, your Granddaddy rode with the great Third Army and a son-of-a-bitch named George Patton.'
General George S. Patton, speech to troops of the Sixth Armored Division, 31 May 1944.

The first Axis capital is in our hands. One up and two to go.
President Roosevelt hails the capture of Rome, 4 June 1944. Retreating German commanders disobeyed Hitler's order to blow up the Tiber bridges.

As they fly overhead we pray that the engine will not stop. Then we feel guilty because we've wished it on someone else. The silence is terrifying.
A London air-raid warden, 14 June 1944, on the new phenomenon of the Vergeltungswaffe-1 – the V-1, known to its victims as the

Doodlebug: a pilotless plane carrying a tonne of high explosive and travelling at 400 mph (645 km/h), the V-1 was powered by petrol and compressed air, and steered – very crudely – by gyroscope. When it ran out of fuel the engine stalled and, around 15 seconds later, it fell to the ground, exploding on impact. Broad swathes of Kent, Surrey and Sussex became known as 'bomb alleys'.

They want to watch it, they do. There'll be trouble if they go on doing that.
Anonymous London taxi-driver after a Doodlebug explosion. On 11 July 1944 Churchill told the Commons that between 100 and 150 V-1 bombs were falling daily on London and its environs, and that 2752 people had been killed. A second mass evacuation of children from the capital was undertaken.

I feel I must do something now to save Germany. We officers must accept our responsibility.
Col. Claus von Stauffenberg speaking to his wife shortly before taking part in a failed attempt to assassinate Hitler, 20 July 1944.

~

A very small clique of ambitious, unscrupulous and, at the same time, criminally stupid officers laid a plot to remove me.
Adolf Hitler, 20 July 1944. The bomb was contained in a suitcase placed under the table at which Hitler was being briefed on the situation in Russia, at his 'Wolf's Lair' headquarters in East Prussia. Three officers were killed, but the Führer escaped with a few scratches. A wide circle of officers, active and retired, was involved in the plot; in the belief that Hitler was dead, orders were issued in Berlin on

---

Warsaw 1940–1944

DANGER – EPIDEMIC ZONE
Sign posted outside the Warsaw Ghetto into which 400,000 Jewish people had been herded, after its sealing with an isolating wall, October 1940.

Killing a Jew by hunger saves a valuable bullet.
Hans Frank, Governor of Warsaw, 31 January 1941.

Brothers, the remaining Jews in Poland live with awareness that in the most terrible days of our history you did not come to our aid. Respond, at least, in the last days of our life.
Message from the Ghetto to US Jews, 21 January 1943. About 60,000 people still remained alive in the ghetto.

The Warsaw Ghetto is no more ... There is a vast amount of stones and scrap metal which could be useful.
SS Major-General Jurgen Stroop, 16 May 1943. As Jews rose up in armed revolt, fighting spread to the sewers, which were then flooded.

Though our hearts are still beating there will never be a joy of life in them.
Ghetto survivor's diary, 16 May 1943

The hour of action is already arrived!
Moscow Radio broadcast to Warsaw, 31 July 1944, signalling the start of the Polish insurrection. In the expectation of Red Army support, Warsaw was captured by the Polish Home Army on 1 August.

The Warsaw action is a reckless, appalling adventure ... This would not have been the case if the Soviet Command had been informed ... The Soviet Command has come to the conclusion that it must disassociate itself from the Warsaw venture.
Kremlin cable to UK Government, 19 August 1944. German attacks drove the Polish Home Army into the sewers on 28 August 1944 while the Red Army remained on the opposite bank of the Vistula, a few miles away; it had orders from Stalin not to intervene. German tanks then set about destroying the city, and the Polish Home Army, having fought from ruin to ruin and sewer to sewer, surrendered on 3 October. Soviet forces occupied what was left of the city the following year.

behalf of 'the new Reich government'. Von Stauffenberg and several others, including a field marshal and 11 generals, were hung from meat hooks with piano wire; the Gestapo's suspect list ran to several thousand names, including that of Field Marshal Erwin Rommel, who had prior knowledge of the plot. He committed suicide on 14 October.

Is Paris burning?
Adolf Hitler, 25 August 1944, as news reached him of the liberation of Paris. He had ordered his commanders to destroy the city before abandoning it; they disobeyed. Free French forces under General Leclerc led the Allied advance into the capital after it had been surrounded by British and Canadian troops and General Patton's US Third Army; Resistance forces then seized the Île de la Cité and the Prefecture before Eisenhower ordered the advance on the evening of the 24th. Charles de Gaulle was flown in by the RAF the following evening, and proclaimed the Fourth Republic on the 26th.

The biggest traffic-jam in history.
The Allied soldiers' description of the scene on the Mons-Brussels road as the liberating army, advancing 25 miles (40 km) a day, ran into the back of retreating German columns; 900 German trucks and 750 horse-drawn vehicles were destroyed. By 9 September 1944, Allied forces were 20 miles (32 km) from the German border.

It was very successful, but it fell on the wrong planet.
The whimsical verdict, 20 years on, of Nazi rocket scientist Wernher von Braun on the V-2, a 46-ft (14-m), 2000 mph (3220 km) rocket bomb with a range of 200 miles (320 km), targeted indiscriminately and flying at an altitude of 60 miles (96 km) before making a powered plunge to earth and arriving before the sound of its flight. The first V-2 fell on a Co-op store in Chiswick, killing 134 peo-

• •

From my mother's sleep I fell into
the State ...
I woke to black flak and the nightmare
fighters.
When I died they washed me out of the
turret with a hose.

From Randall Jarrell's The Death of the Ball
Turret Gunner, *1944.*

• •

• •

But she would weep to see today
How on his skin the swart flies move;
The dust upon the paper eye
And the burst stomach like a cave.

From Vergissmeinicht *by Keith Douglas, who
was killed in action in 1944.*

• •

ple, and the last fell on 27 March 1945, in Orpington; 2754 civilians were killed in all. Von Braun, who obtained Hitler's support for military research in 1936, was indicted as a war criminal for his use of slave labourers, thousands of whom died of malnutrition and chemical poisoning in his underground factory at Peenemünde on the Baltic, but instead was taken to America by US military authorities. In the 1960s he developed the Saturn rocket for the Apollo lunar project.

Sir, we may be going a bridge too far.
Lieutenant General Sir Frederick Browning to Field Marshal Montgomery, September, on the plan to capture strategic bridges across the Rhine in the Netherlands. US airborne divisions were to capture those at Nijmegen and Grave, while the British First Airborne Division captured the bridge at Arnhem; the northern end was taken but the Germans held on to the town. Bad weather prevented the landing of supplies and reinforcements, while supporting Guards divisions, having got through to the American positions, were unable to break through to Arnhem and the British were forced to pull back on 25 September 1944, losing 7600 of their 10,000 men.

I have returned.
General Douglas MacArthur lands at Leyte in the Philippines, 20 October 1944.

~

Our ships have been salvaged and are retiring at high speed towards the Japanese fleet.
Laconic message from US Admiral William F. Halsey, commander of the 3rd Fleet, 25 October 1944; Japanese propaganda had claimed that most of his ships had been sunk or were retiring. In the greatest naval engagement ever seen, the Japanese fleet was effectively put out of action despite its use of kamikaze ('divine wind') tactics: volunteer Japanese pilots, their planes loaded with bombs, flew directly at the decks of the American ships.

Gestapo and soldiers were looting the town, grabbing in mad lust the property of their own people although they had no hope to carry it away.

A Czech reporter in Aachen, the first German town to fall to the Allies, 20 October 1944.

On 18 October Hitler announced the formation of a Home Guard, the Volksturm, *to defend Germany from 'our Jewish international enemies'. Meanwhile, in Britain, the Home Guard – which at its peak numbered over 1.7 million men and nearly 32,000 women – was disbanded on 11 November; on 20 November the lights were switched on in Piccadilly, Fleet Street and the Strand after five years of blackout.*

Whassa matter, Miller, you wanna live forever?

USAF Major Norman Basell to bandleader Glenn Miller, who had asked him where the parachutes were, 15 December 1944. Miller was flying to Paris, to play with his American Air Force Band. The plane vanished; no distress call was received and no wreckage found.

I feel like a fugitive from th' law of averages.
US cartoon caption, Bill Mauldin, Up Front, 1944

He doesn't want anything but security for

his country, and I think that if I give him everything I possibly can and ask nothing from him in return, noblesse oblige, he won't try to annex anything and will work with me for a world democracy and peace.

President Roosevelt assesses Stalin's war aims prior to the 'Big Three' conference at Yalta the following February.

~

This war is not as in the past; whoever occupies a territory also imposes on it his own social system. Everyone imposes his own system as far as his army has the power to do so. It cannot be otherwise.
Joseph Stalin, *quoted in Milovan Djilas, Conversations With Stalin.*

———————

Your hour has struck. Give your all in one last effort.
16 December 1944: With 24 divisions, ten of them armoured, Field Marshal von Runstedt breaks through the Allied lines and advances through the Ardennes, catching the Allies, in Montgomery's words, 'on the hop'. Having created a 'bulge' in the Allied line, von Runstedt's aim was to reach the port of Antwerp and, at the very least, delay the Allies' western offensive by three months. The Germans advanced 60 miles (96 km) before clearing weather enabled Allied planes to bomb their supply lines.

1945

The Ardennes counter-offensive was defeated in January, and the Allies pushed on into Germany; in February, RAF Bomber Command destroyed the militarily insignificant city of Dresden, with colossal loss of life. Later that month, the long and bloody battle of Iwo Jima ended with victory for the US forces, with heavy casualties. The 12th of April saw the sudden death of President Roosevelt; 18 days later, Adolf Hitler committed suicide as Allied forces smashed their way into Berlin. On 4 May Field Marshal Bernard Montgomery accepted the surrender of all German forces in north-west Germany, Holland and Denmark; three days later all Germany's armed forces surrendered unconditionally, and VE Day was celebrated on 8 May. As Japanese troops continued to fight a dogged rearguard action over every inch of every islet in the Japanese archipelago, the US Air Force dropped nuclear bombs on Hiroshima (6 August) and Nagasaki (9 August); Japan surrendered unconditionally on 14 August and the war was at an end. Following a General Election in Britain, called after the end of fighting in Europe, a Labour government was elected with a landslide majority.

Nuts!
US Brigadier General Anthony McAuliffe, commander of the Bastogne garrison, replies to von Runstedt's invitation to surrender Allied fuel dumps there, 9 January 1945. With the Allied

capture of St Vith on 23 January, the Battle of the Bulge was over.

"Ei ssörrender" ... Dies ist die englische und amerikanische Aussprache des

Wortes "I surrender" (Ich ergebe mich). Macht davon Gebrauch, wenn sich Gelegenheit ergibt.
'Make use of it if you have the opportunity': millions of these leaflets were dropped behind German lines from D-day onwards.

We have learned that we cannot live alone, at peace; that our own well-being is dependent on the well-being of other nations far away. We have learned that we must live as men, not as ostriches, nor as dogs in the manger ... We have learned to be citizens of the world.
President Roosevelt makes his fourth Inaugural Address to Congress, 20 January 1945.

The Third Reich has aroused the envy of our impotent democratic onlookers.
Still inveighing against the Treaty of Versailles, Adolf Hitler broadcasts to Germany on the 13th anniversary of his coming to power, 30 January 1945. As he spoke, Nazi documents were being removed to Bavaria and troops in Berlin were firing on crowds to prevent looting of food.

The destruction of Dresden remains a serious query against the conduct of Allied bombing.
Winston Churchill, memo, April 1945, on the raid on Dresden, 13–14 February. 800 RAF Lancasters deluged the city with incendiaries and explosives, setting up a huge, intense firestorm; in the morning, 400 US B-17s resumed the bombardment. The ancient city, much of it wooden, was substantially destroyed, along with its 17th– and 18th–century artistic treasures. Its peacetime population of 600,000 had swollen to around one million because it was considered, as a mostly non-industrial city with no military establishment, to be safe from attack, although it was a meeting point for rail communications to the Eastern Front. Estimates of deaths vary from 50,000 to 130,000. Air Chief Marshal Sir

• •

The creatures outside looked from pig to man, and from man to pig, and from pig to man again; but already it was impossible to say which was which.
George Orwell: Animal Farm, *1945.*

• •

Arthur Harris's policy of 'terror bombing' to sap German morale was criticized at the time, especially by USAF chiefs.

Six thousand Allied bombers began pounding German transport targets on 22 February; on 11 March, 1000 bombers destroyed the Krupps factory.

~

I do not personally regard the whole of the remaining cities of Germany as worth the bones of one British Grenadier.
Air Chief Marshal Sir Arthur Harris, letter to Sir Norman Bottomley, Deputy Chief of Air Staff, April 1945.

The United States flag was raised on the summit of Mount Suribachi at 10.35 a.m. today.
A terse statement from Admiral Chester Nimitz, 23 February 1945, the fifth day of fighting for control of the island of Iwo Jima. The 21,000-strong Japanese garrison had tunnelled into the volcanic island, and defended it pillbox by pillbox; 5372 US troops had died at the time of Nimitz's announcement. Japanese troops were told by their commanders that Allied soldiers would torture and even eat them if they were captured.

We should shake hands with the Russians as far to the East as possible.
Winston Churchill to General Eisenhower following the Yalta Conference of 4–11 February 1945, at which it was understood that the USSR would exercise close post-war control over territory conquered by the Red Army; Stalin promised to declare war on Japan as soon as Germany could be defeated.

'This is my eighth child. What are you going to do about it?'
'I am forwarding my marriage certificate, and my two children. One of them is a mistake, as you can see.'
'I am told that my husband sits in the YMCA every night with the piano playing in his uniform. I think you will find him there.'
A selection of letters received by a US admiral, published in the Los Angeles Times *of 25 February 1945.*

He figured the men would have a better chance swimming, since they would then

••••••••••••••••••••••••••••••••••

Walk on, walk on, with hope in your
heart
And you'll never walk alone.

Oscar Hammerstein II, song from Carousel,
1945.

••••••••••••••••••••••••••••••••••

present only the tops of their heads as targets to the enemy gunners.
Staff Sergeant Thomas J. Defibaugh on General Patton's method of crossing the icy River Sure to attack Bettendorf, 7 March 1945.

The noise you can hear in the background is frying chicken.
Wynford Vaughan-Thomas records a BBC broadcast with US forces who crossed the Rhine, which Allied armies reached on 8 March 1945, after a 58-hour dash; Cologne had fallen two days earlier. It was announced that over one million German prisoners of war had been taken on the Western Front since D-Day.

The Werewolf has been born of National Socialism. It makes no allowances and knows no considerations as imposed on regular troops ... Hatred shall be our prayer and revenge our battle cry.
Martin Bormann, organizing 'Werewolf' guerrilla groups in Germany, 26 March 1945.

More than an end to war, we want an end to the beginnings of all wars.
President Franklin D. Roosevelt, speech in anticipation of the founding of the United Nations; broadcast on 13 April 1945, the day after his death from cerebral haemmorrhage. Vice-President Harry S Truman was sworn in as his successor.

My Führer, I congratulate you! Roosevelt is dead! It is written in the stars that the second half of April will be the turning point for us.
Josef Goebbels, memo to Adolf Hitler, 13 April 1945.

In Franklin Roosevelt there died the greatest American friend we have ever known and the greatest champion of freedom who has ever brought help and comfort from the New World to

the Old.
Winston Churchill, Triumph and Tragedy *(1948–54).*

They entered the war to prevent us from going into the East, not to have the East come to the Atlantic.
Hermann Goering profoundly misunderstands Britain's war aims, April 1945; in the dying weeks of its existence, the Nazi regime tried to sue for peace with Britain and an 'anti-Bolshevik alliance' to fight the USSR.

————————————

The enemy is being met with formidable artillery and infantry, replenished with numerous fresh formations.
Adolf Hitler, Order of the Day, 14 April 1945. Berlin was 'defended' by boys and old men, as SS troops shot soldiers who tried to surrender or desert as Allied forces raced to encircle the Reich capital. Hitler took to a deep bunker underneath the Chancellery as three million people found what shelter they could amidst the rubble created by continuous air and land bombardment; Soviet troops entered the city on 22 April.

~

I die with a happy heart ... There will spring up the seed of a radiant rebirth of the National Socialist movement and hence of a truly united nation.
Hitler's last testament, 29 April 1945. He committed suicide, together with Eva Braun, his wife of 24 hours, the following day. Joseph Goebbels killed his wife and seven children, and then himself. On 28 April Mussolini and his mistress Clara Petracci were shot by Italian partisans and strung up by their heels in Milan; German forces in Italy surrendered the next day. On 30 April, Grand Admiral Karl Dönitz, Hitler's choice as successor, announced that the war would continue.

————————————

We must make certain by your work here that another war will be impossible.
President Harry S Truman, cable to the inaugural meeting of the United Nations in San Francisco, 25 April 1945.

Who are you? I've never heard of you. Major! How dare you bring a major into my headquarters!
Lüneburg Heath, 3 May 1945: Field Marshal Montgomery dismisses Gestapo Major Friedl from

••••••••••••••••••••••••••••••••

Very stupid to kill the only servant in the house. Now we don't even know where to find the marmalade.

Judith Anderson, And Then There Were None, 1945.

••••••••••••••••••••••••••••••••

his tent. The following day he took the unconditional surrender of German forces in north-west Germany, Holland and Denmark.

If we must die, let us fall as true heroes, not as cowards crying for mercy.

Hitler's ally Dr Ante Pavelic, leader of Croatia's Ustachi militia, Zagreb, 4 May 1945. So saying, he fled to the Austrian border; he subsequently escaped to Argentina, where he died in 1958.

JUST IN TIME

British newspaper headline over a report that Spain had broken off diplomatic relations with Germany on 7 May 1945.

We walked on the railroad tracks because the roads were full of Americans. We had our Hitler Youth winter uniforms on, since we had no civilian clothes. We spent the night on straw in a signal box. The next morning we heard the news that the war was over.

7 May 1945: aged 16, the future Chancellor of Germany, Helmut Kohl, spends his last night as a boy soldier of the Third Reich; quoted in Steinhoff, Pechel and Showalter (eds), Voices From the Third Reich, An Oral History, Regnery Gateway (US, 1989).

~

While we were still wandering, we found one of our guards, severely wounded on the Eastern Front before being made a guard, and he said, 'I have completely wasted the last ten years of my life.'

Author Kurt Vonnegut was taken prisoner in the Battle of the Bulge; his experiences as a prisoner held underground in Dresden during the bombing form the basis of his novel Slaughterhouse-Five. Letter to Martin Gilbert, quoted in The Day the War Ended (1995).

~

With this signature, the German people and the German armed forces are, for better or worse, delivered into the victors' hands.

General Alfred Jodl, German Army Chief of Staff, after signing the instrument of unconditional surrender to Allied Supreme Commander General Dwight Eisenhower in Rheims at 2.41 on the morning of 7 May 1945. V-E (Victory in Europe) Day was celebrated on 8 May in Britain and the US, and a day later, following a separate surrender to Soviet forces in Berlin, in the USSR.

~

The Russian soldiers reached our cellar the next morning, May 8. Women of all ages were raped openly, in sight of everyone, including their own small children. A drunken soldier pushed me to the floor and raped me, but he was only the first. The next day the women didn't ask one another, 'Were you raped?' They just asked, 'How many times?'

The first Soviet forces to reach Berlin pushed on in pursuit of the retreating German army; the second wave of Russian troops fully justified the epithet of 'brutal and licentious soldiery'. Thousands of German schoolgirls, indoctrinated by their teachers and parents with the slogan 'Honour lost, everything lost', committed suicide. An anonymous woman quoted in Martin Gilbert, The Day the War Ended (1995).

IT'S OVER
OVER HERE

Headline in the European editions of the American forces' newspaper Stars and Stripes, 8 May 1945.

~

The German war is therefore at an end ... but let us not forget for a moment the toil and efforts that lie ahead. Japan, with all her treachery and greed, remains unsubdued.... Advance, Britannia! Long live the cause of freedom! God save the King!

Winston Churchill broadcasts to Britain and Europe at 3 p.m. on 8 May 1945, V-E Day.

~

This is your victory. This is not a victory of any party or of any class. In all our long history we have never seen a greater day than this.

Echoing the words of Mrs Miniver, Winston

Churchill addresses the crowds from the balcony of the Health Ministry on V-E Day.

~

This is a solemn but glorious hour. My only wish is that Franklin D. Roosevelt had lived to witness this day.
President Truman broadcasts to the USA on V-E Day.

~

When Winston Churchill said, 'Our dear Channel Islands are to be freed today,' we had big lumps in our throats and tears in our eyes. Someone, my mother I think, blew their nose and said, 'Thank God for that, let's have a cup of tea.'
Channel Islander Dorothy Wallbridge, then aged 17, recalls V–E Day in Martin Gilbert, The Day the War Ended (1995).

~

It is the end of one war ... At the end we should have sung 'God Save the King' but we were silent as the full orchestra played ... There is no holiday for us, no relief from a long day in an oppressive climate. And tomorrow more lives will be lost.
The diary of Major Alfred Doulton, serving with IV Corps in Pegu, Burma, 8 May 1945; quoted in Martin Gilbert, The Day the War Ended (1995).

~

When a report on Churchill's speech and the surrender of Germany came in at midday, prisoners on the smaller production floor where the boilers were made burst into consultations. ... It was Schindler who provided a little encouragement and dispelled our apprehensions ... he noted with satisfaction that he had succeeded in keeping his promise to help and protect us to the best of his ability ... and repeated several times that, just as he had promised, he would stay with us until five minutes after midnight, until after the SS guards left the camp and endangered us no longer ... Schindler kept his word.
At Brünnlitz in the Sudetenland, made famous by the film Schindler's List (US 1994), Oscar Schindler provided the 1200 Jewish inmates with arms and ammunition to defend themselves against the threat of a 'Death March' in flight from Allied forces; hundreds of thousands of concentration camp inmates died in this way in the last weeks of the war. Moshe Bejski,

quoted in Martin Gilbert, The Day the War Ended (1995).

———————————

I crossed Poland from east to west, I entered many towns and cities including Cracow, and I found no Jews anywhere. There are no Jews in Poland ... Don't head east; they don't like us there. But don't head west either, because they don't like us anywhere.
A Jewish lieutenant in the Red Army addresses the newly-liberated inmates of Brünnlitz, 11 May 1945; quoted in Martin Gilbert, The Day the War Ended (1995).

~

I don't even want to think of what the sight of all these terrible things is doing to me. How can I ever have the tenderness to worry about your scratched finger, or the other little things which will now seem so insignificant to me?
US Sergeant Benjamin Ferencz writes to his fiancée in New York from Mauthausen concentration camp, 10 May 1945; quoted in Martin Gilbert, The Day the War Ended (1995).

~

10,000 UNBURIED DEAD WERE FOUND HERE, ANOTHER 13,000 HAVE SINCE DIED, ALL OF THEM VICTIMS OF THE GERMAN NEW ORDER IN EUROPE AND AN EXAMPLE OF NAZI KULTUR.
Sign outside Belsen concentration camp, liberated by British forces on 15 April 1945.

~

Hitler has lost every battle on every front except the battle against defenceless and unarmed men, women and children. He won the war against the Jews of Europe.
Dr Zalman Grinberg addresses survivors of Dachau concentration camp, 27 May 1945; quoted in Martin Gilbert, The Day the War Ended (1995).

~

• •

Did anyone ever tell you that you have a dishonest face – for a priest, that is?

Ingrid Bergman, The Bells of St Mary's, 1945.

• •

After the last war people were inclined to kiss off atrocity stories as propaganda. The thing that impressed me most was that the actual sight was worse than any atrocity story. What we saw proved our own reporters during the war told the absolute truth without exaggeration. The things we saw could not be exaggerated.
Los Angeles Times *publisher Norman Chandler, after visiting Dachau, 6 May 1945.*

In a planned and organized programme of extermination, prefigured in Mein Kampf *and ordered by the Führer, the Nazis killed approximately six million Jewish people in Europe during the Third Reich. 'Revisionist historians' in Europe and the US continue to contest this fact; in Germany itself it is a crime to deny it.*

~

I am completely confident of my acquittal. The people of France will give me a vote of thanks.
Pierre Laval, former Vichy Chief of Government, 5 May 1945. He was tried for treason and shot on 15 October. Other collaborators, including future President François Mitterrand, were more fortunate. Pétain, who had ordered de Gaulle's death in 1940, was spared execution.

A good thing, too. It was just an opera anyway.
Albert Speer, Hitler's architect and Minister of Armaments, is arrested in his bath on 23 May 1945.

~

I was motivated not by a desire for personal gain, but solely from political conviction.
William Joyce, whose braying upper-class tones in Nazi propaganda broadcasts to Britain earned him the nickname of 'Lord Haw-Haw', arrested by British troops on the Danish border, 26 June 1945. He was tried for treason, and executed.

It provides for a peace with teeth; for the unity of peace-loving peoples against future aggressors; for a united front amongst the greatest powers, backed by the forces of the smallest powers as well.
Elder statesman Jan Smuts, President of South Africa, on the signing of the Security Charter of the United Nations, 26 June 1945. The General Assembly, in which each member nation – 50, at first – would have one vote, was to be the ruling body, with a two-thirds majority needed on all important issues. Rapid decisions were to be made by the Security Council, with five permanent members – Great Britain, the USA, the USSR, China and France – and six others, elected for two-year periods.

There can be no doubt that Socialism is inseparably interwoven with totalitarianism and the abject worship of the State. No Socialist government ... could afford to allow free, sharp, or violently-worded expressions of public discontent. They would have to fall back on some form of Gestapo.
Winston Churchill on the Labour Party in an election broadcast, 4 June 1945. He had wanted to continue the Coalition government until after the defeat of Japan, but Labour ministers forced a dissolution of Parliament.

~

He wanted the electors to understand how great was the difference between Winston Churchill, the great leader in war of a united nation, and Mr Churchill, the party leader of the Conservatives.
Labour leader Clement Attlee, election broadcast, 5 June 1945.

~

Actually I vote Labour, but my butler's a Tory.
Admiral Earl Mountbatten of Burma, to a Conservative Party canvasser.

~

We are facing a new era. Labour can deliver the goods.
Clement Attlee, speaking as early election results on the night of 25–26 July 1945 predicted a Labour victory.

~

The decision has been recorded. I have therefore laid down the charge which was placed upon me in darker times. It only remains for me to express my profound gratitude for the unflinching support they have given their servant through these perilous years.
Winston Churchill, after tendering his resignation to King George VI in the early hours of 26 July 1945. Thanks in large part to the forces' postal

votes, Labour won the election with a landslide: 393 Labour MPs were returned, 213 Tories, 13 Liberals and 22 others.

~

At the moment it seems quite effectively disguised.
Winston Churchill to his wife, who suggested his election defeat might be a blessing in disguise.

[...] The battle of Okinawa had to be fought. No-one doubted the need to bring Japan to its knees. But some Americans came to hate the things we had to do, even when convinced that doing them was absolutely necessary; they had never understood the bestial, monstrous and vile means required to reach the objective – an unconditional Japanese surrender.
William Manchester: 'Okinawa: The Bloodiest Battle of All' in The New York Times Magazine, *14 June 1987. After 83 days of ferocious fighting, in which US forces advanced using flamethrowers against Japanese soldiers holed up in fissures in the rocks, the Japanese commander committed hara-kiri in front of his troops and the island was surrendered on 21 June 1945; the US lost 12,000 men, including their commander, Lieutenant-General Simon Buckner, and Japan 110,000. With US forces now established only 325 miles (520 km) south of the 'homeland' island of Kyushu, Japan was invited to surrender or face 'prompt and utter destruction'.*

~

I am become Death, the destroyer of worlds.
J. Robert Oppenheimer, Director of the Manhattan Project, quoting the Bhagavad-Gita *after the first atom bomb test, 16 July 1945.*

~

This is the greatest thing in history.
President Truman, 6 August 1945, after the dropping of an atomic bomb on the Japanese city of Hiroshima, population 250,000, at 8.15 a.m. local time that morning. Ninety per cent of the city was destroyed; some 60,000 people were killed instantly. One hundred thousand people were injured, most of whom died from radiation sickness.

~

Hiroshima suffered considerable damage as a result of an attack by a few B-29s. It is believed that a new type of bomb was used. The details are being investigated.
Japanese radio broadcast, early morning, 7 August

The Price of War

Approximately 55 million people – roughly equivalent to the entire population of Great Britain today – were killed in the Second World War. The figures for the combatants (civilian deaths in brackets) include:

Great Britain and Commonwealth:	445,000 (65,000)
France:	250,000 (350,000)
USA:	300,000 (nil)
USSR:	13,600,000 (7,700,000)
Poland:	120,000 (5,260,000)
Yugoslavia:	300,000 (1,300,000)
China:	3,500,000 (10,000,000)
Germany:	3,250,000 (3,800,000)
Austria:	210,000 (100,000)
Japan:	1,700,000 (350,000 – not including subsequent deaths from radiation-induced cancers)

1945. Reported in John Hersey's 'Hiroshima', a 30,000-word essay occupying an entire edition of The New Yorker, *31 August 1946, and reprinted in Britain in an edition of 250,000 copies by Penguin Books that November.*

~

A rain of ruin from the air, the like of which has never been seen on this earth.
In a short-wave broadcast to the Japanese people, President Truman warns of further attacks if Japan does not surrender, 7 August 1945.

~

The atomic bomb literally scorched to death all living things, human and animal. People outdoors were burned to death and those indoors were killed by the indescribable pressure and heat. The dead were simply uncountable. It is not possible to distinguish the men from the women among the killed. The power of destruction of the atom bomb is beyond words.
Japanese radio account of the bombing of Nagasaki, 9 August 1945.

~

If I had only known, I would have become a watchmaker.
Albert Einstein: apparently uttered soon after the bombing of Hiroshima and Nagasaki; reported in the New Statesman, *16 April 1965. Other sources substitute 'locksmith'.*

~

I for one hold little brief for the future of civilisation.
RAF Group-Captain Leonard Cheshire, VC, on the bombings.

~

The last of our enemies is laid low.
Newly elected as Prime Minister, Clement Attlee broadcasts to Britain at midnight, 14 August 1945.

~

It is my earnest hope, and indeed the hope of all mankind, that from this solemn occasion a better world shall emerge out of all the blood and carnage of the past.
US General Douglas MacArthur, on the deck of the USS Missouri, *14 August 1945 – the day the US suffered its final military casualties when the USS* Indianapolis *was sunk with almost all hands, off the Philippines. MacArthur's forces then occupied Japan. As British, Commonwealth and American POWs were liberated, new atrocities were uncovered: tens of thousands of Allied troops had died as a result of starvation, untreated disease, forced labour and cannibalism while in captivity, and 'medical' experiments had been conducted on civilians in detention camps.*

~

The war situation has developed not necessarily to Japan's advantage.
The God-Emperor Hirohito announces Japan's surrender in a radio broadcast, 15 August 1945.

~

The Bomb brought peace but man alone can keep that peace.
Winston Churchill, Leader of the Opposition, House of Commons, 16 August 1945.

Let MacArthur have my corpse. I will not be judged by a conqueror's court.
General Hideki Tojo, former Japanese dictator, arrested by US troops on 8 September 1945, shot himself in the heart but survived despite a Japanese doctor's refusal to treat him. He was tried for war crimes and executed in 1948.

We have had our last chance. If we do not devise some greater and more equitable system, Armageddon will be at our door.
General Douglas MacArthur, US radio broadcast, 2 September 1945.

Properly speaking, there is no such thing as revenge. Revenge is an act which you want to commit when you are powerless and because you are powerless: as soon as the sense of impotence is removed, the desire evaporates also.
George Orwell, 'Revenge is Sour', Tribune, 6 November 1945.

In the aftermath of the Second World War, two million German nationals were expelled from East Prussia, newly annexed by Poland. Stalin rounded up all German nationals living within the new boundaries of the USSR, and transported them to the Asian states of the Soviet Empire as punishment.

All the returning Soviet prisoners of war were sent to labour camps as suspected spies. Among them was a soldier named Alexander Solzhenitsyn, sentenced to ten years' hard labour for referring to Stalin in a letter to a friend as 'Old Whiskers'.

In accordance with the Potsdam Agreement, the British military authorities disarmed and returned tens of thousands of Cossack troops who had fought under

General Vlasov against the USSR in the belief that they would secure independence, together with their families. All, except those who had first committed suicide and children killed by their parents, were shot.

In Paris, women known to have slept with Nazi occupiers were shaved, tarred, feathered, and paraded naked through the streets. Most of France's collaborationist politicians and officials were rehabilitated.

More than 23 million people, including 12 million Germans, became 'Displaced Persons' after the war, and a new body, the United Nations Relief and Refugee Agency (UNRRA) was set up to deal with them. Mass starvation broke out in Germany and, with the need to send emergency supplies to some 30 million former enemies, food rations in Britain were cut to below wartime levels. The off-white 'Victory Loaf' was replaced by darker bread with a lower wheat content which, for the first time ever, was itself rationed. President Truman of the USA cancelled the wartime 'Lend-Lease' arrangements, and Britain became a contributor to the Marshall Plan to provide monetary aid to the defeated Axis nations of central Europe, so preventing them from falling under the Soviet aegis. Food rationing in Great Britain was not to end until the spring of 1954, by which time Winston Churchill, now knighted, was once again Prime Minister.

The USA entered the post-war era with a strong economy, a political commitment to New Deal policies, and a 'GI Bill' to retrain returning soldiers at the public expense. Britain embarked on it with widespread bomb damage, high ideals, an exhausted economy, and a Labour government pledged to implement in full the recommendations of the Beveridge Report and usher in the age of the 'Welfare State', while continental Europe fell under the shadow of the 'Cold War' between rival ideologies, as a result of which the western half of the newly divided Germany was given every encouragement to become a strong and sustainable capitalist democracy.

When I look back on all these worries I remember the story of the old man who said on his deathbed that he had had a lot of trouble in his life, most of which had never happened.

Winston Churchill, Their Finest Hour *(1948–54).*

From War's End to Decade's End
1945-1949

Man is condemned to be free.

~ *Jean-Paul Sartre*, Existentialism is Humanism, *1947*

After the end of the wartime alliance between the Soviet Union and the Western allies, newly organized into the North Atlantic Treaty Organisation (NATO), relations cooled rapidly. British and American forces had not advanced as far to the East as Churchill had desired and, as he foresaw, the 'Iron Curtain' that descended between Communism and democracy soon cut off the newly liberated countries of Eastern Europe. When US Secretary of State George Marshall announced financial aid for Europe's reconstruction, Czechoslovakia and Poland at first agreed to meetings of the 'Marshall Plan' committee; after 'consultations' with Stalin they withdrew. Both countries subsequently became Soviet 'puppet states', as the USSR attempted, by blockading Berlin, to force the scrapping of plans for the creation of an independent, democratic state of West Germany.

In China, the long campaign of Mao Tse-tung was rewarded with success with the fall of Shanghai and Peking to his forces, and the creation of the People's Republic of China at the end of the decade. In Malaya, which subsequently gained independence, British forces defeated the Communist guerrilla army.

Britain's Labour government, beset by severe material deprivation and financial difficulties following the immediate withdrawal of US assistance as the war ended, set about acting on wartime and election plans and promises. Against strong opposition from the Medical and Dental Associations, the National Health Service was introduced, along with reforms in education and welfare. The steel industry, mines and railways were included in a programme of nationalization.

The Indian subcontinent gained independence, at the cost of pogrom and bloodshed, and the state of Israel came into being after a concerted campaign of Zionist terrorism aimed at British forces trying vainly to fulfil the terms of Britain's mandate in the interests of the Palestinian population.

The decade ended with the commercial exploitation of three technological breakthroughs: the transistor and the 'vinylite' gramophone record, both in the USA, and the jet airliner. Amid great secrecy, the British De Havilland company developed the Comet, which made its maiden flight at 500 mph (800 km/h) in July 1949.

1945

Does that mean that because Americans won't listen to sense, you intend to talk nonsense to them?

The economist John Maynard Keynes in conversation with a UK Treasury official before a meeting in Bretton Woods to establish the International Monetary Fund and the World Bank, July 1945. Against fierce opposition from Imperialists, the UK Parliament passed the enabling legislation on 13 December of that year, and accepted a £1100 million loan from the USA.

The privilege of opening the first trial in history for crimes against the peace of the world imposes a grave responsibility. The wrongs we seek to condemn and punish have been so calculated, so malignant and so devastating that civilisation cannot tolerate their being ignored.

Justice Jackson, Chief US Prosecutor, opens the Nuremberg War Crimes trial on 20 November 1945.

1946

It is for the peoples of the world to make their choice between life and death. Our aim is the negation of war and the creation of social justice and security.

Prime Minister Clement Attlee addresses delegates from 51 nations at the inaugural session of the United Nations General Assembly, held in Central Hall, Westminster, 30 January 1946.

~

Our agenda is now exhausted. The Secretary General is exhausted. All of you are exhausted. I find it comforting that, beginning with our very first day, we find ourselves in such complete unanimity.

The Belgian delegate to the UN, Paul Henri Spaak, concludes the inaugural session, February 1946.

Brides are requested to keep out of the kitchen.

If only.... Notice at a camp in Tidworth, Hampshire for the first of 50,000 British 'GI Brides' en route for New York, 22 January 1946.

From Stettin in the Baltic to Trieste in the Adriatic, an Iron Curtain has descended across the Continent ... The Dark Ages may return on the gleaming wings of science. Beware, I say. Time may be short.

Winston Churchill addresses an audience at Fulton, Missouri, 5 March 1946. The phrase 'Iron Curtain' is traceable to the 1920s, and Churchill himself had used it in the Commons. On 11 March, Pravda denounced the USSR's former ally as 'an anti-Soviet warmonger'; by the end of the month, the BBC had started Russian-language broadcasts, which were jammed.

We are the masters at the moment, and not only at the moment but for a very long time to come.

Sir Hartley Shawcross, Nuremberg prosecutor and Labour's Attorney-General, House of Commons, 2 April 1946. Frequently misquoted as 'We are the masters now', and often misattributed to Aneurin Bevan.

Should the Government prove obdurate ... the doctors of this country might have to decide not to work in the new service.

Jealous of its members' fees, the British Medical Association sets up a £1 million fighting fund to oppose the introduction of a National Health Service, 7 March 1946.

~

I would rather be kept alive in the efficient if cold altruism of a large hospital than expire in a gush of warm sympathy in a small one.

Aneurin Bevan, Secretary of State for Health, presents the National Health Service Bill to the Commons, 30 April 1946.

~

I stuffed their mouths with gold.
Privately, Mr Bevan explains how he overcame BMA opposition to the NHS; doctors working within it were permitted to spend a proportion of their time in private practice.

The British mandate shall continue until Arab–Jewish hostility disappears.
UK-US declaration on Palestine, 1 May 1946. Both Arabs and Jews objected to it.

It is as easy today to obtain a marriage licence as to buy a dog licence.
The Baby Boom begins: Mr Skeffington-Lodge MP, 11 May 1946, on Marriage Guidance Council figures suggesting that 40 per cent of women under 20 were pregnant on their wedding day. As contingents of the 50,000 GI Brides left Britain, some 80,000 British servicemen and their wives waited to obtain divorce, and 35 legal teams were appointed by the government to speed the process.

This is a movement of Jewish Resistance. We are about to blow up the Government offices. We have warned them.
A two-minute warning from the 'Stern Gang' as the King David Hotel in Jerusalem is bombed on 22 July 1946 killing or injuring 150 British Mandate personnel. Britain favoured a partition of Palestine into self-governing Muslim and Jewish states; the Arabs wanted the Jews to remain a minority in a unified state, while the vast majority of Jews everywhere responded to the Zionist call for the Jewish national home of Israel, which they believed had been promised them as a nation-state by the Balfour declaration. In an atmosphere of increasing terrorism, British civilians began to be evacuated from Palestine in January 1947.

Bloodshed and civil war must be avoided if possible. But now there is no more room left. … If you want war, we accept it.
In India, the Moslem League demands a separate

•••••••••••••••••••••••••••••••••••••

Tell me why it is that every man who seems to be attractive these days is either married or barred on a technicality.

Celeste Holm in Gentleman's Agreement, *1946.*

•••••••••••••••••••••••••••••••••••••

Islamic state and accuses the British of colluding with Gandhi's Congress Party to turn an independent India into a Hindu Raj, 29 July 1946.

The atom bomb is a paper tiger which the United States reactionaries use to scare people.
Mao Tse-tung, interviewed in August 1946 as civil war breaks out in China.

Time may be short. At present there is a breathing space, but if we are to form a United States of Europe – or whatever name it may take – then we must begin now. I say to you: Let it arise.
Winston Churchill, speech broadcast worldwide from Zurich, 19 September 1946.

I wish peace to the world.
Last words of Hitler's Foreign Minister, Joachim von Ribbentrop, executed at 1.11 a.m. on 16 October 1946 after being sentenced at Nuremberg. Also hanged were Field Marshal Keitel, who had stuck to a defence that he was 'only obeying orders', Ernst Kaltenbrunner (Heydrich's successor as Nazi Governor of Prague), Alfred Rosenberg, leading exponent of the Master Race Theory, Hans Frank, Governor of Poland (who pleaded guilty and converted to Roman Catholicism in prison), Wilhelm Frick, 'Protector' of Bohemia, Julius Streicher, slave labour boss Fritz Saukel, General Alfred Jodl, and Arthur Seyss-Inquart, Nazi Governor of Austria, who called for 'peace and understanding between peoples' as he was led to the scaffold. Hermann Goering committed suicide with a cyanide pill before sentence could be carried out; Martin Bormann, believed dead, was tried in absentia. Albert Speer, Hitler's former architect and Minister of Supply, was sentenced to 20 years' imprisonment after expressing his contrition.

If you have no sword, arm yourselves with axes and sticks.
Fleeing Hanoi under bombardment, Vietnamese President Ho Chi Minh calls his people to arms after a breakdown in negotiations with France, 28 December 1946.

British designers have nothing to learn from this brand of design.
A delegate from the Ford Motor Co. of Great Britain, one of several representing the British car industry, tours the Volkswagen Wolfsburg factory

in 1946. Britain had been offered first refusal of the plant, machinery and design patents, but was not interested. The following year, ICI considered Agfa's colour film technology 'commercially uninteresting'; Agfa's technicians went to work for Kodak in the USA instead.

1947

The proposed five-day week for miners is difficult. Coal exports are down to vanishing point.

Emmanuel Shinwell, Minister for Fuel, issues a warning as ownership of Britain's coal mines – and the communities of the men who work in them – passes from private hands to the State, in the form of the National Coal Board, 1 January 1947. As a severe winter took its grip on Britain, coal stocks dwindled. The birth of the NCB on New Year's Day was marked by mass absenteeism.

NO BREAD SINCE JAN. 27. STARVING *Telegram received from a hamlet near Widecombe-in-the-Moor, Devon, 12 February 1947. Severe blizzards, huge snowdrifts, prolonged sub-zero daytime temperatures and an acute fuel shortage brought Britain's economy to a virtual standstill, as the nation got used to living by candlelight and over four million workers were laid off; even Channel shipping was halted. In Yorkshire, 500 prison inmates were put on a work detail to clear a way to snowbound communities. The meat ration was cut by tuppence, to one shilling's-worth per person per week.*

In all the history of Parliament, such a matter has never been denied discussion.

Winston Churchill, from the Opposition benches, tries unsuccessfully to persuade the Prime Minister to reveal to the Commons the 'differences, divergencies or disagreements' that led to the premature retirement on 20 February 1947 of Field Marshal Lord Wavell as Viceroy of India, and his replacement with Lord Mountbatten, a man with no experience of the complexities of Indian polity. The government announced that Britain would quit India by July 1948.

Let us not be deceived – we are today in the midst of a cold war.

US presidential adviser Bernard Baruch addresses the South Carolina legislature, 16 April 1947; an early recorded use of the phrase that was to dominate international relations for more than four decades.

It just rained steel out there.

Anonymous nurse, 19 April 1947, 714 people are killed and 90 per cent of Texas City destroyed as fire on a French ship in the harbour spreads to a chemical plant, several oil refineries, and then to the High Flyer, a ship packed with nitrate explosive.

Even Solomon would find this task beyond him. And I'm afraid the V. is no Solomon.

Anonymous Indian Army officer, May 1947, as the British government, advised by Mountbatten, announces the partition of India, and its armed forces, into two independent states provisionally named 'Hindustan' and 'Pakistan'. Muslims viewed with deep suspicion the cordial relationship that existed between the Viceroy and Gandhi, and what was widely seen as cronyism between the Hindu Congress leader, Nehru, and both Lord and Lady Mountbatten, as the details of partition began to be worked out, frequently – and in the face of Civil Service advice to the contrary – to Pakistan's disadvantage. In British government circles, beset by acute economic crisis, the pressure to be rid of the expensive Jewel of Empire was immense.

We will have the state of Israel.

The Zionist Irgun terrorist group, counting among its leading activists the future Israeli Prime Minister, Menachem Begin, continues its campaign by blasting into a prison in Acre and releasing 251 inmates, driving them away in stolen British army trucks, 4 May 1947.

We know that you, the organized workers of the country, are our friends … As for the rest, they do not matter a tinker's cuss.

Emmanuel Shinwell, Minister for Fuel, woos the workers at the annual congress of the Electricians' Union, 7 May 1947.

Export Or Die
Work Or Want

Profoundly non-Socialist slogans of the British government in June 1947, as the latest dollar loan

• •

I do not like to be interrupted in the middle of an insult.

Charles Laughton in The Paradine Case, *1947.*

• •

••••••••••••••••••••••••••••••••••

I have always depended on the
kindness of strangers.

Vivien Leigh in A Streetcar Named Desire,
1947.

••••••••••••••••••••••••••••••••••

runs out. Petrol imports were cut, newspapers
reduced to the wartime quota of four pages, the
tinned meat ration was cut to 2d worth a week,
and the weekly milk ration to 2 pints per person.

Our policy is directed not against any
country or doctrine but against hunger,
poverty, desperation and chaos. Its purpose should be the revival of a working
economy in the world so as to permit the
emergence of political and social conditions in which free institutions can exist.
US Secretary of State George Marshall, in a speech
at Harvard University, 5 June 1947, launches the
'Marshall Plan' to 'kick start' the economies of con-
tinental Europe; after it was immediately rejected
by the USSR, the scheme was aimed particularly at
those most likely to be on Stalin's 'shopping list' of
satellite countries. Britain, the first country to
endorse the plan when Foreign Secretary Ernest
Bevin announced to the Commons that 'Europe can
wait no longer', became, despite near-bankruptcy, a
contributor. Germany, which the USSR sought to
cripple for a second time in 30 years through repa-
rations, was the main beneficiary. Czechoslovakia
and Finland, still outside the Soviet bloc, declined
the offer.

No annihilation without representation.
The historian Arnold Toynbee urges Britain to
take a more active role in the United Nations.

————————

At this solemn moment, when the people
of India, through suffering and sacrifice,
have secured freedom, I, as a member of the
Constituent Assembly of India, dedicate
myself in all humility to the service of India
and her people to the end that this ancient
land attain her rightful place in the world.
Oath sworn by Indian Assembly members; on the
stroke of midnight on 15 August the State of India
– a secular parliamentary democracy, eschewing
the British suggestion of 'Hindustan' – came into
existence.
~

In thus achieving your independence by
agreement you have set an example to the
freedom-loving peoples throughout the
world.
Message of congratulation to the new state of
Pakistan from King George VI, 15 August 1947.
Celebrations in both States were marred by vio-
lence and, as great treks of populations began
between countries, many observers doubted
Mountbatten's assurances that there would be no
bloodbath. By the year's end at least 400,000
people, mostly Muslim, out of 8 million refugees,
had been slaughtered, and India and Pakistan
were fighting a proxy war in Kashmir.
~

So long as there are tears and suffering, so
long our work will not be over.
Pandit Jawaharlal Nehru, first Prime Minister of
India, first speech to the Indian Constituent
Assembly.

————————

I have no easy words for the nation. I cannot say when we shall emerge into easier
times.
British Prime Minister Clement Attlee, 27
August 1947. Foreign holidays were banned,
and businessmen abroad restricted to spending
no more than £8 a day; under the Supplies and
Services Act – christened the 'SS Act' by the
Opposition – the government reserved the right,
without parliamentary sanction, to direct
labour and restrict materials for non-essential
industries; miners were awarded bigger meat
rations and farmers and fishermen were
allowed extra bread and cheese. Washington
criticized the action for its leniency; the follow-
ing month, Britan began to spend its gold
reserves to pay for imports.

————————

I hope that we are never prompted by fear
or resentment of Communism into compromising any of our democratic principles in order to fight them.
Hollywood actor Ronald Reagan gives evidence
to the House Committee on Un-American
Activities, 23 October 1947; nonetheless it
began a witch-hunt of 'Reds' in the film indus-
try, beginning the following month with
Hollywood's 'voluntary blacklisting' of ten
screenwriters and producers.
~

The Communist plan for Hollywood was
remarkably simple. It was merely to take

over the motion picture business. Not only for its profits, as the hoodlums had tried, but also for a grand worldwide propaganda base.
Looking back.... Ronald Reagan, now a Republican politician, in his autobiography Where's The Rest Of Me? *(1965).*

~

Before every free conscience in America is subpoenaed, please speak up.
Judy Garland stands out against the witchfinders, November 1947.

In the name of Allah I proclaim a Holy War against the Jews.
Dr Hussein Khalidi, Palestinian Arab leader, 30 November 1947, after the United Nations announced a plan to partition the region into a Jewish state, an Arab state, and a separate, undefined, regime for Jerusalem, sacred to both communities. The UN did not, however, make any provision for enforcing the plan.

I would rather be an opportunist and float than go to the bottom with my principles round my neck.
Attributed remark of Stanley Baldwin, three times British Prime Minister, who died on 14 December, aged 80.

1948

Friends and comrades, I do not quite know what to tell you and how to say it. Our beloved leader, Bapu as we called him, the father of the nation, is no more. The light has gone out...
Prime Minister Nehru, his voice breaking, broadcasts on All-India Radio, 30 January 1948. After

• •

God have mercy on us. Christ have mercy on us. White man, have mercy on us.

Alan Paton: Cry, The Beloved Country, *1948 - the year veteran Prime Minister Jan Smuts lost his seat in the South African elections and the National Party – fighting on an apartheid ticket of racial segregation and white supremacy, formed the government.*

• •

fasting for six days in the cause of Hindu-Muslim tolerance, Mahatma Gandhi was shot dead in his garden by a fanatical Hindu separatist, Nathuram Godse. After Gandhi's funeral there were serious outbreaks of arson and rioting in which many died.

We are at a critical moment in the organisation of the postwar world. The Communist process goes ruthlessly on.
British Foreign Secretary Ernest Bevin, 22 January 1948. A month later, on Stalin's orders, Communists seized power in Czechoslovakia having earlier pledged to share it with the elected pre-war government, now returned from wartime exile in London. Armed members of the 'Trades Union Militia' prevented government supporters from reaching its headquarters at Hradcany Castle; President Eduard Benes resigned and died shortly afterwards. His close ally, Foreign Minister, Jan Masaryk, was reported to have retained his post; on 10 March his body was found beneath the window of his office. 'Suicide caused by nervous strain' was the official explanation.

The Government considers the British title to the Falkland Island Dependencies to be well-founded, and has been willing that it should stand the test of international arbitration.
Foreign Office statement, 16 February, as a Royal Navy cruiser is dispatched to shadow an Argentinian naval operation ordered close to the islands, over which Argentina claimed sovereignty, by President Juan Péron. On this occasion, nothing further happened.

We will submerge England in eggs and bury her in bacon.
Irish Agriculture Minister James Dillon promotes his own brand of 'export or die' policy, 18 February 1948, after strikes and shortages bring down the Prime Minister, Eamon de Valera. He was replaced by John A. Costello at the head of a coalition administration.

We, members of the National Council, representing the Jewish people in Palestine and the Zionist movement of the world ... by virtue of the natural and historic right of the Jewish people, and by resolution of the General Assembly of the United Nations, hereby proclaim the

establishment of a Jewish state in Palestine to be called 'Israel'.
As the British Mandate ends and troops withdraw, Jewish Agency leader David Ben-Gurion proclaims the new state of Israel on 14 May 1948 but does not define its borders. President Truman immediately recognized the new state; all its Arab neighbours immediately declared war on it. During periods of UN-negotiated ceasefire interspersed with periods of intense conflict, the various Zionist terrorist organizations either voluntarily disbanded or – as in the case of the Stern Group – were suppressed, and subsumed into the Hagana organization to form the Israeli Army.

~

They should settle this problem in a true Christian spirit.
A rather unhelpful suggestion in October 1948 from Warren Austin, US delegate to the UN, as Israeli military superiority and ad hoc *negotiation forces a withdrawal of Arab forces and a defining of the borders of the new Jewish State, albeit with disputed territories in Gaza Strip and the Negev, and a divided city in Jerusalem. As Jews from all over the world took advantage of Israel's unrestricted immigration policy, Palestinian Arabs began a mass migration to refugee camps in neighbouring states, taking their keys and title deeds with them.*

This strike is not against capitalists and employers. It is a strike against your mates.
Prime Minister Attlee broadcasts to Britain as the government employs the Emergency Powers Act 1920 to bring troops in to break an unofficial dock strike that held 232 ships in port, 28 June 1948.

We are in Berlin to stay.
US Secretary of State George Marshall, 30 June 1948. In April, the USSR began a blockade of Allied sectors of the former German capital, now isolated in the Communist Eastern Zone. By June, supplies in the city were down to one month's consumption and flights of food and medicine – supplied by the USA and, despite its own acute shortages, Britain – were landing at the rate of one every four minutes. For many former RAF pilots, the Berlin Airlift provided welcome post-war employment. On 18 September a record 7000 tonnes of supplies were landed, with 895 flights in 24 hours. The blockade was lifted in May 1949; it cost some $200 million to break it.

Anti-Sovietism, Trotskyism, leanings towards capitalist states, inordinate ambition, and grandeeism.
A mixed bag of charges levied against the Yugoslavian leader, Marshal Tito, by Cominfor (the international organization of Communist Parties) as Yugoslavia is expelled from it, 4 July 1948. 'Healthy elements' in the country were urged to overthrow him.

In a great plan like this, there must be some rough edges, but these will be overcome with patience and goodwill.
Health Minister Aneurin Bevan launches the National Health Service with the opening of 992 local offices of the Ministry of National Insurance, as 2751 hospitals come under the control of Regional Health Boards, 5 July 1948. Despite rearguard action from the old guard of the BMA, 19,000 doctors had already registered with the NHS; the British Dental Association, however, has prevented full implementation of the NHS to this day.

DEWEY DEFEATS TRUMAN
But he didn't; Truman won by 303 College votes to 189. Headline in the early edition of the Chicago Daily Tribune, *3 November 1948; Truman even won the paper's own state of Michigan. The* Washington Post, *whose own headline had read 'Mounting Dewey Vote Indicates Victory', invited all the erring pundits, and the President, to a banquet at which 'Humble Pie' was on the menu.*

I know of no other man … who so convincingly demonstrated the power of the spirit over material things.
A tribute to Mahatma Gandhi from Britain's Chancellor of the Exchequer, the economist Sir Stafford Cripps, a deeply spiritual man who exer-

• •

In Italy for thirty years under the Borgias they had warfare, terror, murder, bloodshed – they produced Michelangelo, Leonardo da Vinci, and the Renaissance. In Switzerland they had brotherly love, five hundred years of democracy and peace, and what did that produce? The cuckoo clock.

Orson Welles memorably departs from Graham Greene's script for The Third Man, *1949.*

• •

cised austere control over material things in his own country – and who, in December 1948, persuaded the Trades Union Congress to impose a voluntary wage freeze for the common good.

All human beings are born free and equal in dignity and rights.
Article 1 of The Universal Declaration Of Human Rights, 1948.

1949

I am going home to sweep the graves of my ancestors.
President Chiang Kai-shek announces his retirement, as Communist troops march into Peking on 22 January 1949. Mao Tse-tung rejected his call for peace talks, and in May Shanghai fell to the Communists.

I have never seen a human being who more perfectly represented the modern conception of a robot.
Winston Churchill, in The Second World War (1948-54), on Vyacheslav Molotov, who became an eponym for a sort of petrol bomb, and whose 'Nyet' at the United Nations had become an international byword for unthinking intransigence. He was replaced by Andrei Vishinsky, chief prosecutor in the pre-war Show Trials.

You may now consign your clothing coupons to the appropriate salvage channel.
Harold Wilson, a youthful President of the Board of Trade, announces the end of clothes rationing, 15 March 1949. The 'cloth quota' scheme for utility clothing remained, however, as did price controls. Sweet rationing was also eased.

A national property in which every man has a right and interest who has an eye to perceive and a heart to enjoy.
The words of William Wordsworth are invoked as a Bill is introduced naming the Lake District as one of 12 National Parks in England and Wales.

I commend the Bill to the House as a practical solution, if not a very logical one.
Clement Attlee moves the acceptance of the Ireland Bill, 11 May 1949, whereby Britain recognized Eire, as the post-Dominion status republic now became, and citizens of each country, resident in the other, enjoyed all its rights. It passed by 317 votes to 14.

It is closing time in the gardens of the West and from now on an artist will only be judged by the resonance of his solitude or the quality of his despair.
Cyril Connolly, in the last issue of Horizon *magazine, 1949.*

With the adoption of this constitution I look forward to the eventual reunification of Germany.
Konrad Adenauer, Mayor of Cologne and soon to be elected first Chancellor of West Germany, formed from the British, French and US zones of the former Reich, 23 May 1949. Stalin set up the Communist Republic of East Germany in October.

• •

It was in fact the combination of public service motive, sense of moral obligation, assured finance and the brute force of monopoly which enabled the BBC to make of broadcasting what no other country has made of it.

Lord Reith, first Chairman of the BBC, in Into The Wind, *1949.*

• •

The country didn't go to hell then, and it won't now.
President Truman, on 30 June 1949, urges Americans to get over 'post-war hysteria' and stop hunting 'Reds', citing the case of the Alien and Sedition Acts of 1798: designed to protect the 'safety and dignity of the Republic' by expelling distasteful foreigners and imprisoning anyone guilty of bringing it into 'disrepute'. They were criticized as oppressive and quickly repealed. Witch-hunting continued in Congress 150 years later, particularly against Alger Hiss, a State Department official who testified to the Un-American Activities Committee that he had never been a Communist and had never passed on State secrets to Whittaker Chambers – an editor of Time, *and a self-confessed former Soviet spy – who claimed that he had.*

No attempt at ethical or social seduction can eradicate from my heart a deep

burning hatred for the Tory Party ... So far as I am concerned they are lower than vermin.
Aneurin Bevan, speech, Manchester, 4 July 1949.

Have rejoined the Fleet south of Woosung. No damage or casualties. God Save The King.
Lieutenant-Commander J. S. Kerans signals the Admiralty from HMS Amethyst on 30 July 1949 after making a 140-mile (235-km) dash down the River Yangtse under cover of darkness, four months after being shelled and trapped by the Communist armies.

This is just something dreamed up by a lot of long-haired boys from Bloomsbury.
Lord Lyle, Chairman of the sugar refiners Tate & Lyle, opposes Labour's manifesto plans for the nationalization of the sugar industry, 16 August 1949. The company adopted 'Mr Cube', a sugar cube armed with shield and sword, as its trademark, and refused Board of Trade requests to remove anti-nationalization slogans from its packaging.

If ever he went to school without any boots it was because he was too big for them.
Ivor Bulmer-Thomas MP, referring to Harold Wilson's claims to humble origins, at the Conservative Party Conference in September 1949.

We thus start upon another stage in the magnificent struggle of our people to overcome the crushing difficulties imposed upon them by their sacrifices in the world war.
18 September 1949: Sir Stafford Cripps announces a 30 per cent devaluation of the pound in order to end speculation, restore confidence in the currency, and boost British exports; warning of a resulting rise in domestic prices and no increase in subsidies, he reaffirmed the need for a wage freeze. The devaluation was prepared for in great secrecy, with those briefed beforehand being summoned to unconnected government departments and then escorted through secret tunnels to the Treasury. Cripps explained as 'a necessary deception in a wicked world' his nine-times-repeated assertion that there could be no question of devaluation.

Banks and stock exchanges were closed the following day.

Not while I'm alive, he ain't.
Foreign Secretary Ernest Bevin, on being told that his government colleague Herbert Morrison (or perhaps Aneurin Bevan, or Emmanuel Shinwell) was his own worst enemy; c. 1949.

This Government is willing to observe the principles of equality, mutual respect and territorial sovereignty.
Mao Tse-tung proclaims the People's Republic of China at the Gate of Heavenly Peace in Peking, 1 October 1949.

Communism is a very emotional subject in our country right now.
US Secretary of State Dean Acheson explains why the USA will not be following Britain's lead in recognizing Communist China, 26 October 1949. China's seat at the United Nations, however, was occupied by the ousted Nationalist government, now resident in the island of Taiwan (formerly known as Formosa).

Think nothing of it. It's a family idiosyncrasy. My sister Mary was a horse until she 'came out'.
King George VI on his young daughters' equine obsession, according to Marion Crawford – 'Crawfie' – the former Royal governess whose memoirs were published in December 1949. She was subsequently ostracized by the Palace.

Oh no, thank you, I only smoke on special occasions.
Alleged to have been spoken by a Labour minister when asked if he would like a cigar, while dining with King George VI.

• •

Two gin-scented tears trickled down the sides of his nose. But it was all right, everything was all right, the struggle was finished. He had won the victory over himself. He loved Big Brother.
The closing words of Nineteen Eighty-Four by George Orwell, 1949.

• •

The Century's
Middle Age
1950~1959

My definition of a free society is a society where
it is safe to be unpopular

~ *Adlai Stevenson, October 1952*

The 1950s was a decade of growing prosperity, especially in the USA where the phrase 'You never had it so good' was coined in the 1952 presidential election campaign; Britain, which began the decade with a cut in food rationing, first heard it five years later. Europe, and particularly West Germany, recovered strongly from the devastation of war with the aid of the Marshall Plan and through the agency of what was to become the 'Common Market', the European Economic Community; Britain declined the invitation to join towards the end of the decade, when the Liberals, who divided the House of Commons on the issue, found themselves in a single-figure minority.

The 'Red Scare' of the late 1940s intensified in the USA during the first half of the 1950s thanks largely to the relentless and largely fraudulent campaigning of Senator Joseph R. McCarthy and his henchman, the future Vice-President Richard M. Nixon. During this period US forces were in action, under the auspices of the UN, against Communism in Korea. A popular uprising against Communist rule in East Berlin was quickly put down in 1953. Some thawing of NATO–Soviet relations had been hoped for after the new Soviet leader Nikita Khrushchev denounced Stalinism, but in 1956 a full-scale national revolt in Hungary was suppressed by military invasion. The Cold War intensified with the development of nuclear fusion warheads – the 'H-Bomb' – deployed on intercontinental missiles; 1958 saw the formation in Britain of the Campaign for Nuclear Disarmament. At the end of the decade the USSR took an early lead in the 'space race' with the successful launching of *Sputnik-1*, the first man-made object to be sent into orbit. In January 1959 Communism came to America's back door with the victory of Fidel Castro's guerrillas in Cuba.

Britain and France sent troops to the Middle East in 1956 after President Nasser of Egypt announced the nationalization of the Suez Canal; although the intervention was partially successful in military terms it proved damaging to Britain's international relations and ended Prime Minister Anthony Eden's career.

President Eisenhower's attempts to enforce 'desegregation' of schools in the American South met with partial success and fierce resistance from white racists; in Britain, intimidation of black people by gangs of white youths led to race riots in Nottingham and Notting Hill in 1958. Institutionalized racism was given a formal Afrikaans name, 'apartheid', by the governing National Party in South Africa.

The 1950s saw the birth of rock'n'roll and a boom in sales of television sets as radio audiences began to slump. In architecture, commericial art and interior design, the decade was marked by the almost complete absence of good taste.

1950

At 50, everyone has the face he deserves.
One of the last entries in the notebook of George Orwell, who died on 21 January 1950.

While I cannot take the time to name all the men in the State Department who have been named as members of the Communist Party and members of a spy ring, I have here in my hand a list of 205 that were known to the Secretary of State as being members of the Communist Party and who nevertheless are still working and shaping policy in the State Department.
Senator Joseph R. McCarthy, speech, Wheeler, W. Virginia, 9 February 1950. In another speech in Wheeler on the same day, he quoted the number as 57.

~

Last night I discussed Communists in the State Department. I stated that I had the names of 57 card-carrying members of the Communist Party ... Now, I want to tell the Secretary this: If

• •

When a white man in Africa by accident looks into the eyes of a native and sees the human being (which it is his chief preoccupation to avoid), his sense of guilt, which he denies, fumes up in resentment and he brings down the whip.

Doris Lessing, The Grass is Singing, 1950.

• •

he wants to call me tonight at the Utah Hotel, I will be glad to give him the names....
Joseph R. McCarthy, speech, 10 February 1950.

~

I frankly feel in view of the number of cases – there are 81 cases – that it would be a mistake for me to disclose these names on the floor.
Joseph R. McCarthy, speech, US Senate, 20 February 1950.

~

Those of us who shout the loudest about Americanism... are all too frequently those who... ignore the basic principles of Americanism: The right to criticize; The right to hold unpopular beliefs; The right to protest; The right of independent thought...

I do not like the way the Senate has been made a rendezvous for vilification, for selfish political gain at the sacrifice of individual reputations and national unity.
Senator Margaret Chase Smith, speech, US Senate, 1 June 1950. But the witch-hunt went on.

Parliament will be in an unstable condition now.
More in glee than in sorrow: Winston Churchill views the aftermath of the General Election of 23 February 1950, in which Labour's overall majority was cut to five.

He is a man suffering from petrified adolescence.
Aneurin Bevan's view of Winston Churchill, c. 1950.

The end of rationing will be a great boon to holiday resorts.
The Mayor of Buxton lets off fireworks to usher in

the Age of the West Country Traffic Jam, as petrol rationing is abolished in time for the 1950 Whitsun Bank Holiday. At 11 p.m. on 30 May, the Automobile Association reported all roads into London choked from ten miles out. On 1 June the price of petrol went up to 3 shillings (15p) a gallon, its highest level since 1920.

There is no question whatever about the outcome of this struggle. We shall win.
General Walton Harris Walker of the US Far Eastern Command 8th Army, 31 July 1950. On 25 June the armies of Communist North Korea invaded the South; the United Nations Security Council (in the absence of the USSR, who had walked out in protest at the presence of Nationalist China) condemned the action and called for international assistance. General Douglas MacArthur became Commander in Chief of the UN 'police action'.

~

If there ever was a time when we should stand shoulder-to-shoulder, it is now.
British Prime Minister Clement Attlee sends 4000 British troops to aid the US forces in Korea, July. By the end of the month, North Korea had effectively occupied all but the south-west corner of its neighbour; Seoul, the Southern capital, was occupied.

~

These cookies are beaten!
Major-General Hobart Gay, commander of the US First Cavalry Division, 23 October 1950. A daring seaborne invasion at Inchon on the west coast by US forces under MacArthur on 16 September then drove the North Koreans back in spectacular retreat to the Chinese border; Pyongyang, the Northern capital, was occupied by UN troops and the North Korean army seemed to be falling apart.

~

We are not at war.
It was, of course, a Police Action: President Truman, October 1950.

~

They came over just like a crowd at a football match.
Anonymous RAF gunner, November/December 1950 – but even pre-war Wembley never witnessed a crowd of 300,000. Chinese troops stationed in Manchuria crossed the border and drove UN forces back; Pyongyang was abandoned as the Chinese advanced south of the national North-

South border at the 38th Parallel, and Seoul fell again.

~

If they ever meant it, they don't now.
An unattributable informed source in the British delegation as Attlee flies to Washington to plead with President Truman not to drop the atom bomb on North Korea. Truman assured him that he 'hoped never to do so'.

~

We will have victory in fifteen months.
Not Korea, but Vietnam, where France was fighting Communist Vietminh forces under Ho Chi Minh: General Jean de Lattre de Tassigny, C-in-C French forces in Indo-China, December 1950. An immediate victory was scored as the French beat off an attack on Hanoi on 18 January 1951, killing 6000 Vietminh.

You can hear every word he sings – which is sometimes a pity, considering the material. It is like being force-fed with treacle.
A London critic on the British debut concert of Frank Sinatra, who had recently signed a record-breaking radio contract for $1 million, July 1950.

Perhaps it is better to be irresponsible and right than responsible and wrong.
Winston Churchill, Party Political Broadcast, 26 August 1950.

1951

People do not like momentous events such as war and disaster to be read by the female voice.
Regional accents were also infra dig. *A BBC spokesman announces a reduction in the number of newsreaders from 19 to 8, in the interests of 'consistency of pronunciation', 23 January. The John Lewis Partnership was more enlightened; on 16 February it appointed Miss M. J. Ahern managing director.*

••••••••••••••••••••••••••••••••••••••

The slave begins by demanding justice and ends by wanting to wear a crown. He must dominate in his turn.

Albert Camus, The Rebel, 1951.

••••••••••••••••••••••••••••••••••••••

••••••••••••••••••••••••••••••••

I hate the idea of causes, and if I had to choose between betraying my country and betraying my friend, I hope I should have the guts to betray my country.

E. M. Forster, 'What I Believe' in Two Cheers for Democracy, 1951.

••••••••••••••••••••••••••••••••

Certainly we are going to stay in Korea. We are going to stand here and fight.

General Collins, US Army Chief of Staff, 26 January 1951, as the Chinese advance slowed down and ran into supply problems. In February, advancing UN forces pushed back over the 38th Parallel.

A desiccated calculating machine.

Aneurin Bevan's opinion of Labour's Chancellor, Hugh Gaitskell. On 22 April Bevan resigned as Health Minister after Gaitskell pushed through a Treasury plan to impose charges for NHS false teeth and spectacles; Harold Wilson, President of the Board of Trade, resigned the next day, and a period of civil war ensued in the Labour Party. The charges were imposed against a background of increased defence spending and a worsening economic situation; the meat ration was cut, by tuppence, to 1s 4d (7p) a week, enough for about 4 oz (120 g). Whisky went up by 1s 8d (8p) to £1 15s (£1.75) a bottle.

—————————————

I have therefore considered it essential to relieve him so that there would be no doubt or confusion as to the real purpose of our policy ... So far it has been successful. So far we have prevented World War Three.

President Truman broadcasts to America, explaining why he has sacked General MacArthur, 11 April 1951. The White House published sheaves of documents to demonstrate that the general had repeatedly made 'political statements'.

~

I didn't fire him because he was a dumb son of a bitch, although he was, but that's not against the law for generals. If it was, half to three-quarters of them would be in gaol.

President Harry S Truman, quoted in Merle Miller, Plain Speaking (1951).

~

The wrong war, at the wrong place, at the wrong time, and with the wrong enemy.

General Omar Bradley gives evidence at a Senate inquiry into the war, 23 May 1951.

—————————————

My policy is to be able to take a ticket at Victoria station and go anywhere I damn well please.

Foreign Secretary Ernest Bevin, who died on 14 April 1951.

This action is necessary to avoid the collapse of white civilisation in the whole of Africa.

Dr Theophilus Donges, South Africa's Minister for the Interior, announces the abolition of the right to vote for 'Coloureds' – people of mixed racial origin – on 14 May 1951.

No visible means of support, and only good for scrap – it symbolises Britain, really.

Anonymous verdict on the Skylon, a gigantic aluminium exclamation mark over the 27-acre bombsite on the South Bank of the Thames that became the Festival of Britain in May 1951, a jamboree designed, in the words of Herbert Morrison, 'to let the people pat themselves on the back'. The only structure not afterwards broken up for scrap was the Royal Festival Hall, designed by Robert Matthew of the London County Council.

We are taking a long Mediterranean holiday.

Telegram, 8 June 1951, from Guy Burgess and Donald MacLean, two British spies who defected to the USSR; they turned out to be KGB 'moles'. Theirs was the latest in many 'Red Spy' cases both

••••••••••••••••••••••••••••••••

I bring you warning – to everyone listening to the sound of my voice. Tell the world, tell this to everyone wherever they are: Watch the skies, watch everywhere, keep looking – watch the skies!

Look out for aliens, especially from the Red Planet... The Thing, 1951. 'Watch the Skies' was the working title of the 1977 film, Close Encounters of the Third Kind.

••••••••••••••••••••••••••••••••

in Britain and the USA, where McCarthy's witch-hunt continued unabated.

How can we account for our present situation unless we believe that men high in the government are concerting to deliver us to disaster? This must be the product of a great conspiracy, a conspiracy on a scale so immense as to dwarf any previous venture in the history of man. A conspiracy of infamy so black that, when it is finally exposed, its principals shall be forever deserving of the maledictions of all honest men.
Senator Joseph R. McCarthy, speech, US Senate, 14 June 1951.

WHOSE FINGER? Today YOUR finger is on the trigger ... VOTE FOR THE PARTY YOU CAN REALLY TRUST ... The *Daily Mirror* believes that Party is Labour.
Front page of the Daily Mirror *on election day, 25 October 1951. The phrase, which recalled Attlee's when he went to Washington to discuss deployment of the atom bomb, so annoyed Churchill that he sued for libel; the* Mirror *settled out of court for £1250. Churchill's Conservatives won the election with an overall majority of 17.*

The French will only be united under a threat of danger. Nobody can simply bring together a country that has 265 kinds of cheese.
General Charles de Gaulle, speech, 1951.

1952

My decision to remove myself completely from the political scene is definite and positive.
General Dwight D. Eisenhower, 1948: but in January 1952, in a long and carefully worded statement, he allowed it to be understood that, if called, he would serve as the Republican candidate for that year's Presidential election.

There will soon be only five kings left – the Kings of England, Diamonds, Hearts, Spades and Clubs.
King Farouk, the last King of Egypt; remark to Lord Boyd-Orr. Mass protest against the King, and

the British presence in Egypt, led to rioting in which a number of British institutions, including Barclay's Bank and the Turf Club, were looted and burned in January 1952. Farouk was deposed on 26 July.

~

We're not a family; we're a firm.
King George VI, who died on 15 February, five months after having a cancerous lung removed, coined the expression which his daughter, as Queen Elizabeth II, was to make her guiding principle. George was the third of Queen Mary's sons to predecease her.

The way to win an atomic war is to make certain it never starts.
General Omar Bradley, quoted in 'Sayings of the Week' in the Observer, *20 April 1952. The USA was at that time testing prototypes of the Hydrogen Bomb, a fusion device several hundred times more powerful than the fission bomb that destroyed Hiroshima and Nagasaki. The existence of Britain's own fission bomb, developed in secret by the Labour regime, was only revealed to Churchill after he became Prime Minister; he accused Labour of practising 'the Machiavellian Art'.*

If the Communists win in Indochina, the whole of Southern Asia will fall like a row of dominoes.
The first airing for the 'Domino Theory', Jean de Tourneau, French Minister Resident in Indo-China, 26 April 1952, as French forces launched a new offensive against the Vietminh.

I cannot and will not cut my conscience to fit this year's fashions, even though I long ago came to the conclusion that I was not a political person and could have no comfortable place in any political group.
The dramatist Lillian Hellman, letter to the US House of Representatives Committee on Un-American Activities, May 1952.

~

McCarthyism is Americanism with its sleeves rolled.
Senator Joseph R. MacCarthy, campaigning for re-election to the Senate, 1952.

~

Sole purpose of visit.
British broadcaster Gilbert Harding, written answer to US Immigration Authority question, 'Is

it your intention to overthrow the government of the US by force?'

~

To continue my lifelong search for naked women in wet mackintoshes.
Dylan Thomas, on being asked why he had come to the US.

Our spiritual leader has gone!
Eva Perón – 'Evita' – is mourned by the Argentinian radio station she controlled, after dying at the age of 33 on 26 July 1952. The former nightclub singer, wife of Argentina's President Juan Perón, championed the cause of the underclass – the 'shirtless ones' – and won Argentinian women the right to vote and seek divorce, but was also the moving force behind a campaign of torture and corruption, and the practice of 'disappearing' dissidents.

There is a small articulate minority in this country which advocates changing our national symbol, which is the eagle, to that of the ostrich, and withdrawing from the United Nations.
Eleanor Roosevelt, speech, Democratic National Convention, 22 July 1952.

~

Let's talk sense to the American people. Let's tell them the truth, that there are no gains without pains.
Adlai Stevenson, the Democrats' choice as Presidential candidate, speech, Chicago, 26 July 1952.

~

Man has wrested from Nature the power to make the world a desert or to make the deserts bloom. There is no evil in the atom, only in men's souls.
Adlai Stevenson, speech, 18 September 1952.

~

Adlai is the appeaser ... who got his PhD from Dean Acheson's College of Cowardly Communist Containment.
Joe McCarthy's sidekick, Richard M. Nixon,

....

A man's gotta dream; it comes with the territory.

Frederic March, Death of a Salesman, 1952.

....

now Dwight Eisenhower's Vice-Presidential running-mate, speech, September 1952. Nixon entered politics in response to an advertisement for a Republican candidate, 'preferably a veteran, fair education', and had advanced through his vigorous prosecution of 'Un-American activities'.

~

He is not only completely vindicated as a man of honour but, as far as I am concerned, he stands higher than ever before.
Dwight Eisenhower, after Richard Nixon had broadcast on TV to rebut allegations that he had illegally misused an $18,000 campaign fund, 14 September 1952. He told viewers that his wife wore 'a good Republican cloth coat', and appealed to their emotions by refusing to hand back a cocker spaniel puppy called 'Checkers', a gift to his six-year-old daughter.

~

I'm not a quitter and incidentally Pat's not a quitter. After all, her name was Patricia Ryan and she was born on St Patrick's Day.
The 'Checkers Speech', 14 September 1952. In fact, Patricia Nixon was born the day before St Patrick's Day.

~

My definition of a free society is a society where it is safe to be unpopular.
Adlai Stevenson, speech, October 1952.

~

I will undoubtedly have to seek what is happily known as 'gainful employment', which I am glad to say does not describe holding public office.
Dean Acheson leaves the office of Secretary of State after Eisenhower wins the Presidential election, 5 November 1952.

~

The Buck Stops Here.
The retiring President, Harry S Truman, tells an audience at the national War College about the sign he kept on his desk during his term of office, 19 December 1952.

When the reed-buck horn is blown, if I leave a European farm before killing the European owner, may this oath kill me.
One of the oaths sworn by the Mau-Mau who, by October 1952, had brought the British colonial administration in Kenya to crisis; British troops

SLOGANS and CATCHPHRASES of THE FIFTIES

I was only obeying orders.
Often spoken by defendants at Nuremberg but ruled out by the War Crimes Tribunal as a valid defence; it became a catchphrase in the 1950s, usually in a cod-German accent.

All human life is here.
This really was the advertising slogan of the News of the World *from 1958–59.*

Ban the Bomb
Originally US and traceable to 1953; became the most popular slogan of marchers for the Campaign for Nuclear Disarmament (founded 1958) whose symbol (allegedly a colophon of the letters C, N and D) quickly became a worldwide icon of protest.

Better red than dead.
Another CND slogan, from 1958. Supporters of nuclear weapons favoured the opposite.

Go to work on an egg.
An enduring slogan, devised for the British Egg Marketing Board by the novelist Fay Weldon in her 'poor and struggling' days, back in 1958.

It's fingerlickin' good!
Col. Sanders Kentucky Fried Chicken, since 1958.

Communism, Corruption, and Korea
Presumably intended to get the McCarthyite vote: anti-Democrat Republican campaign slogan, Presidential election, 1952.

... I Like Ike
Republican campaign slogan for Eisenhower, Presidential election, 1952.

... You Never Had It So Good
Democrat campaign slogan for Adlai Stevenson, Presidential election, 1952; Macmillan pinched it for the Tories in the 1959 General Election in Britain.

... Everything's booming but the guns.
Republican campaign slogan for Eisenhower, Presidential election, 1956.

I Still Like Ike.
Republican campaign slogan for Eisenhower, Presidential election, 1956.

... We Need Adlai Badly.
I'm Madly For Adlai.
Democrat campaign slogans for Stevenson, Presidential election, 1956. The British Liberal MP and future Party leader, Jo Grimond, recalled wearing a badge with the latter slogan and 'feeling a little foolish, among all those very pretty girls who really were' in New York.

... Life's better under the Conservatives ... Don't let Labour ruin it.
General election campaign slogan for the Conservatives, 1959.

flew out to Nairobi on 21 October, and a bitter war began in earnest. In the 'White Highlands' a militia force, the 'European Home Guard', was formed.

Let him have it Chris.

Words spoken by Derek Bentley (19) to Christopher Craig (16) before Craig shot dead Police Constable Sidney Miles on the rooftop of a Croydon warehouse after a botched attempt at robbery. Both were charged with wilful murder but Craig was too young to hang. On 11 December 1952 the jury had to decide if the words Bentley spoke meant (a) 'Give him the gun' or (b) 'Shoot him'. They decided on the latter and Bentley, although he did not pull the trigger, was hanged on 28 January 1953. After a long campaign to clear his name, Bentley was finally pardoned by the Home Secretary. Craig was sentenced to be detained during Her Majesty's Pleasure.

… I have now reached the stage where I don't care whether I live or die. What is going to happen will happen.

July 1944, from The Diary of Anne Frank, *published in 1952.*

1953

For many years I thought what was good for our country was good for General Motors, and vice versa.

Probably the first use of the well-worn phrase, US engineer Charles Irwin Wilson in testimony to the Senate Armed Services Committee, 15 January 1953.

Whatever America hopes to bring to pass in the world must first come to pass in the heart of America.

From the inaugural address of President Dwight D. Eisenhower, 20 January 1953. One of the first acts of the new President was to meet General MacArthur, sacked by Truman, to discuss plans for ending the war in Korea.

That is a good question for you to ask, not a wise question for me to answer.

UK Foreign Secretary Anthony Eden, on being asked by a reporter what effect Stalin's death would have on international affairs, 4 March 1953. Stalin died next day, of a brain haemorrhage; his death came as a reprieve for nine leading Soviet

Are you sitting comfortably? Then I'll begin.

Introduction to the story on Listen With Mother, *BBC programme for tinies, presented by (among others) Daphne Oxenfoorde.*

physicians, six of them Jewish, who had been arrested by the KGB and accused of promulgating a 'Doctors' Plot' to poison leading members of the Soviet government, Stalin included. They were released on 4 April, along with thousands of prisoners in Gulag labour camps including a former army officer called Alexander Solzhenitsyn. After Stalin's death, titular power passed to Georgi Malenkov but the real authority was vested in Politburo member Nikita Khrushchev as head of the Party secretariat. Lavrenti Beria, Stalin's long-serving KGB chief, was arrested in July and charged with being a Western spy; he confessed, and was shot in December.

I am not a Communist and I never have been. I have been the object of vicious propaganda.

Charlie Chaplin, attempting to return to the USA, where he had lived for 40 years, after travelling in Europe to publicize his new film, Limelight, *is refused a re-entry permit and vows never to return, 17 April 1953. With his wife Oona and four children he settled at Vevey in Switzerland.*

We have discovered the secret of life!

Cambridge scientist Francis Crick, with his colleague James D. Watson, discover the 'double helix' structure of deoxyribonucleic acid – DNA – the lock and key to all living things; their findings were published in Nature, *25 April 1953.*

The countries of Western Europe are no longer in a position to protect themselves individually.

West German Chancellor Dr Konrad Adenauer, speech, May 1953.

It will be said of this generation that it found England a land of beauty and left it a land of beauty spots.

British philosopher and broadcaster Professor Cyril Joad bemoans the rise of the motor car and the 'holiday destination'; quoted in the Observer, *31 May 1953.*

Be proud of Britain on this day,
Coronation Day
ALL THIS – AND EVEREST TOO!
Briton First On The Summit
Headline in the Daily Express, *2 June 1953 as Mount Everest is finally conquered, by Edmund Hillary (a New Zealander) and Tenzing Norgay (a Nepalese); the final ascent had been made the previous day. The expedition's leader, Colonel John Hunt, was English.*

~

We done the bugger!
Tenzing Norgay, June; quoted by Sir Edmund Hillary in High Adventure.

Ivan, go home!
One hundred thousand people gather in the Wilhelmstrasse and jeer Soviet tanks as a workers' uprising, fuelled by severe food shortages and sparked by an order to increase productuion by 10 per cent, shakes the governments of both East Germany and the USSR, 15 June 1953; many government buildings were occupied and some set alight. Since the beginning of May, thousands of refugees, often under fire, had been fleeing to the West. The USSR sent in tanks, and the revolt was crushed.

A long and difficult road lies ahead. There are no short cuts. We must continue our efforts to seek and defend peace.
The UN Allied Commander, General Mark Clark, 27 July 1953, as an armistice signed in Panmunjom at 10.01 a.m. brings the Korean War to an end; some two million people had been killed. Korea was partitioned along the 38th Parallel, which became a four-mile-wide Demilitarized Zone under the authority of the United Nations.

A year ago none of us could see victory. There wasn't a prayer. Now we can see it clearly – like light at the end of the tunnel.
Lieutenant-General Henri-Eugene Navarre, C-in-C of French Union Forces in Indo-China, 28 September 1953.

~

We have taken the place and we shall stay there. I foresee final victory in the Spring of 1956.
General René Cogny, commander of French Union

Forces in Indo-China, 20 November 1953, *speaks of the place where the light at the end of France's Vietnamese tunnel – Dienbienphu – turned out to be the onrushing train; see May 1954 (p.116).*

An alcoholic is someone you don't like who drinks as much as you do.
The poet Dylan Thomas, who died of drink, aged 39, in a New York hotel on 9 November 1953.

I have consistently urged my friends to abstain from reading it.
Winston Churchill on his only novel, Savrola. *On 10 December 1953 he was awarded the Nobel Prize for Literature while still part-way through writing his six-volume* History of the Second World War *(1948–54). The prize was collected by his wife; the 79-year-old Prime Minister, having made a partial recovery from a stroke suffered in June, was said to be attending a conference in Bermuda. News of his illness was voluntarily suppressed by the British press.*

1954

Just a summer storm which, thank Allah, is now over.
Egypt's President Neguib, 28 February 1954, after regaining the Presidency from his rival, Gamal Abdel Nasser. But seven weeks later Nasser seized full control over the country, arresting Neguib's supporters while he was on a visit to Sudan.

The bomb's brilliant gleam reminds me of the brilliant shine GLEAM gives to floors. It's a science marvel!
In the Pittsburgh Press, *an advertisement cashes in on the US test of a fusion Hydrogen bomb 600 times more powerful than the fission bomb dropped on Hiroshima in March 1954, on Bikini Atoll in the Pacific. The crew of a Japanese fishing boat, the* Lucky Dragon, *which had been operating 70 miles (113 km) from the Atoll and outside*

••

Heeeeeeeeeere's Johnny.

Ed McMahon, introducing The Tonight Show
with Johnny Carson, *1954, US.*

••

••••••••••••••••••••••••••••••••

ESTRAGON: Let's go
VLADIMIR: We can't.
ESTRAGON: Why not?
VLADIMIR: We're waiting for Godot.

Samuel Beckett, Waiting for Godot, *1954.*

••••••••••••••••••••••••••••••••

the exclusion zone, suffered severe radiation burns; their heavily contaminated boat was destroyed.

Now our witch-hunters are trying to drive students and teachers into conformity with a rigid concept of Americanism defined by ignorant and irresponsible politicians. If we do not check this movement, we shall become a totalitarian state like the Fascist and Communist models and our colleges and universities will produce frightened rabbits instead of scholars with free minds.
Virginia Gildersleeve, 'The Inescapable Desert' in Many a Good Crusade *(1954). On 29 April President Eisenhower announced that on 23 December the previous year he had withdrawn the security clearance for Dr J. Robert Oppenheimer, leader of the wartime Manhattan Project, and nicknamed 'The Father of the Atom Bomb', after allegations that he 'consorted with Communists and deliberately delayed H-bomb development'. Oppenheimer, who admitted that some of his friends were Communists but denied sabotaging the research, was found to be 'loyal and discreet' by a government enquiry that reported in June – but his security clearance was not restored.*

~

If none of us ever read a book that was 'dangerous', had a friend who was 'different', or joined an organisation that advocated 'change', we would all be just the kind of people Joe McCarthy wants. Whose fault is that? Not really his. He didn't create this situation of fear. He merely exploited it, and rather successfully ... No one can terrorize a whole nation, unless we are all his accomplices.
The beginning of the end for Senator McCarthy: Ed Murrow winds up his CBS TV programme, See It Now, *7 March 1954. McCarthy had by then started accusing the US Army and the CIA of*

being 'riddled with and even run by card-carrying Communists'. President Eisenhower then publicly gave his support to those accused.

~

Until this moment, Senator, I think I never really gauged your cruelty or your recklessness. If it were in my power to forgive you for your reckless cruelty I would do so. I like to think that I am a gentle man, but your forgiveness will have to come from someone other than me. Let us not assassinate this lad further, Senator. You have done enough. Have you no sense of decency, sir, at long last? Have you left no sense of decency?
Representative Joseph Nye Welch interrupts McCarthy during a session of the House Committee on Un-American Activities, March 1954.

~

The junior senator from Wisconsin, by his reckless charges, has so preyed upon the fears and hatreds and prejudices of the American people that he has started a prairie fire which neither he nor anyone else may be able to control.
Senator J. William Fulbright speaks to the Motion of Censure of Senator Joseph R. McCarthy, 30 November 1954. The motion was carried on 2 December, by 67 votes to 22.

With a united will created, it will diminish, I hope, the need for united action. But there should be a willingness to have united action if events should be such as to require that.
Statement by US Secretary of State John Foster Dulles, 8 April 1954; it was interpreted as a warning to China not to assist the Vietminh General Giap, then beginning his encirclement of French forces at Dienbienphu.

~

Dienbienphu has fulfilled the mission that was assigned to it by the High Command.
A spokesman for Lieutenant-General Henri-Eugene Navarre after the French garrison had fallen to the Vietminh on 7 May 1954; all 16,000 French troops were either killed or captured. The following day, the French government called an end to hostilities; a pact was signed on 21 July.

~

The Vietnamese have ample manpower and even today outnumber the enemy by 100,000. This matter can be resolved without bringing in one single American soldier to fight.
General John W. O'Daniel, Head of the US Military Mission of Advisers to the government of South Vietnam, 7 July 1954.

In the field of public education the doctrine of 'separate but equal' has no place. Separate educational facilities are inherently unequal.
Chief Supreme Court Justice Earl Warren hands down judgment in the case of Brown v. The Board of Education, Topeka, 17 May 1954, in a decision affecting 8.5 million white children and 2.5 million black children in racially segregated schools in the Southern States – most of whose leaders immediately rejected it.

To jaw jaw is better than to war war.
Sir Winston Churchill, recently knighted, speech, Washington, 26 June 1954.

If we find that prices are not falling, we will hold protest meetings.
Statement issued by the National Federation of Housewives, 3 July 1954, after meat rationing was abolished. This brought to an end 14 years of rationing in Britain; ration book burning parties were held in many places, including Trafalgar Square.

It is certainly a remarkable example of modern art.
Sir Winston Churchill damns Graham Sutherland's portrait of him with faint praise when presented with it at a televised ceremony at Westminster Hall, 30 November 1954. It was later burned by his wife.

What you said hurt me very much. I cried all the way to the bank.
Wladziu Valentino Liberace puts his critics in their place, 1954.

1955

This means that men who have killed inoffensive civilians by panga slashing, men who have disembowelled babies before their mothers' eyes, men who have eaten the brains of their human victims, will not even be prosecuted.
Humphrey Slade, member of the Legislative Council of Kenya, after the government announces an amnesty for Mau Mau terrorists who give themselves up, 19 January 1955. Slade's claims for Mau Mau atrocities were numerously instanced; a long military campaign had failed to eradicate the threat to white farmers and their families. In the three years to October 1955, 13,000 people died and some 70,000 had been imprisoned.

They were among the cleanest, most respectable and intelligent passengers I have ever carried.
Captain George Gladioli of the cruise liner SS Fairsea lands 380 Jamaican immigrants at Plymouth on 23 January 1955; the ship's band played them ashore. The British government, beset by labour shortages in the post-war years, had advertised for immigrants in the West Indies, and tens of thousands had answered the call. By 1955, politicians had begun to talk about immigration controls.

These proposals fall far short of the nation's urgent need.
The British Roads Federation greets a government announcement that £212 million is to be spent over four years on road improvements and motorways, 2 February 1954. A 15-year plan to modernize the railways, replacing steam with electricity and diesel, was also announced.

No two men will ever change guard more smoothly.
Shortly after delivering a memorable Commons speech on the British H-bomb, Sir Winston Churchill, now 80 and visibly frail, steps down as Prime Minister and hands over to his Foreign Secretary, Sir Anthony Eden, who called a General Election for 26 May. The Conservatives won, with an increased overall majority of 58 – the first time since 1865 that a Party in office had been re-elected with a bigger majority. Churchill, campaigning with relish as a backbencher, was returned as MP for Woodford.
~

Not a gentleman; dresses too well.
Bertrand Russell on Sir Anthony Eden; remark made to Alastair Cooke and recalled in his Six Men *(1956).*

You have got the impression that contemporary physics is based on concepts somewhat analagous to the smile of the absent cat.

The one Schrödinger put in his box, perhaps. A comment by Albert Einstein on Viscount Samuel in his Essay on Physics. *Einstein died on 18 April, aged 76.*

I love you, David.

Words spoken by Ruth Ellis, former model and nightclub hostess, and mother of two, as she shot her lover, David Blakely, after pleading with him not to leave her for another woman. She was sentenced to death by Mr Justice Havers on 21 June and, despite protests and petitions, hanged in Holloway Prison on 13 July, the last woman to be executed in Britain.

We are far more concerned with research and the general behaviour and design of craft at these speeds than we are with merely breaking the world's record.

But he broke it anyway: Donald Campbell, whose hydroplane Bluebird *averaged 202.32 mph on Ullswater, 23 July 1955.*

• •

Good evening, all!

'PC George Dixon' salutes farewell: Dixon of Dock Green, BBC. The character was a spin-off from the film The Blue Lamp.

• •

Some television programmes are so much chewing-gum for the eyes.

The US critic John Mason Brown quotes a friend of his young son on 28 July 1955; chewing-gum and television came together in Britain with the first broadcast of Independent Television on 22 September; Associated Rediffusion and Associated Broadcasting, both in the London area, co-screened a variety show – although the first commercial was not for gum but for Gibbs' SR Toothpaste. BBC TV aimed to steal ITV's thunder with The Donald Duck Story, *while on the wireless Grace Archer, one of the principal characters in* The Archers, *was burned to death trying to rescue her horse from a stable fire. BBC switchboards were jammed with calls of condolence and distress.*

Mindful of of the Church's teaching that marriage is indissoluble and conscious of my duty to the Commonwealth, I have resolved to put these considerations above all others.

The Queen's sister, Princess Margaret, announces on 31 October that she will not marry the man she loves. Group Captain Peter Townsend, a Royal equerry and much decorated wartime RAF hero, was a divorcee, albeit as the 'innocent party'; the Palace was mindful of the damage done by the abdication of Edward VIII, while the Princess was mindful of the fact that she would lose her place in the Succession and her Civil List payments. In the end, it was duty to 'The Firm' that prevailed.

I have never been a Communist, although I know people who were Communists at Cambridge and for a year afterwards. The last time I spoke to a Communist, knowing him to be one, was in 1934.

11 November 1955: Harold 'Kim' Philby, until recently First Secretary at the British Embassy in Washington, liaising with the CIA, and from 1944-46 head of anti-Communist counter-espionage, rejects the accustation, made under House of Commons privilege by Labour MP Colonel Marcus Lipton, that he was a Soviet agent and the 'Third Man' who gave orders to the Soviet double-agents Burgess and MacLean. Lipton pronounced himself satisfied with the rebuttal, and withdrew his remarks; Philby went on, with the connivance of British Intelligence, to be a foreign correspondent for the Observer *and the* Economist, *based in Beirut. Faced with exposure in 1963, he admitted to having been the Third Man and fled to Moscow. It emerged that he had been recruited at Cambridge in the 1930s and had been the head of a Soviet spy ring; as such he, and the others, had seriously compromised much of the work of MI6 and the CIA.*

Few thought he was even a starter –
There were many who thought
   themselves smarter –
But he ended PM, CH and OM,
An Earl and a Knight of the Garter.

Lines written about himself (in April 1956) by Clement Attlee, who at 72 resigned as Leader of the Labour Party and as an MP on 7 December 1955. His elected replacement was the 49-year-old Hugh Gaitskell, beating Aneurin Bevan (who had anathematized him as 'a desiccated calculating machine') by 157 votes to 70. Herbert Morrison, architect of the Labour landslide of 1945, polled only 30, and at once resigned in tears as Deputy Leader, as Labour Party feuding continued unabated.

Yes.
December 1955: The hasty reply of the Conservative politician R. A. Butler to a reporter's question, 'Is Mr Eden the best Prime Minister we have?'; Butler had been boarding a plane at the time. This was quoted in the report as 'Butler says Eden is the best Prime Minister we have', which was far from complimentary; Butler protested, but to little avail. He was himself to become known as 'the best Prime Minister we never had'.

1956

Five Greek lives for every Turk.
Slogan of the Turkish crowds in Nicosia and Limassol in the British colony of Cyprus, 12 January 1956, after Greek-Cypriot EOKA terrorists seeking 'enosis' – full union with Greece – continued their campaign of bombing, killing and arson by shooting dead a Turkish Cypriot policeman in Paphos; hitherto, British troops and officials had been the targets. Another contingent of British troops was sent out, as the Governor met in secret with the Greek Cypriot leader, Archbishop Makarios. On 9 March the British deported him to the Seychelles.

To the gallows, Mollet.
Slogan chanted by supporters of the National Liberation Front (FLN) as the French premier arrives in Algiers for talks with Arab and Colonial leaders on 6 February 1956; an escalating guerilla war had been in progress for 18 months.

Here we see no wisdom, but only a demonstration of brutal force ... odious falsifications and criminal violations of legality ... all-consuming vanity and the glorification of his own person ... What could we do? There was a reign of terror. You just had to look at him wrongly and the next day you lost your head.
At a closed session of the USSR 20th Party Congress on 14 February 1956, Nikita Khrushchev denounces his predecessor Joseph Stalin. He told a stunned Congress that, of 139

members of the Central Committee elected in 1934, 97 had been shot on trumped-up charges of 'counter-revolution'. He accused Stalin of military incompetence, in not heeding warnings of Hitler's 1941 invasion, and cowardice: the Wise Father of the People, he declared, only dared to visit the front on one occasion, and never visited a liberated city; he also divulged details of the 'Gulag Archipelago' of slave-labour and punishment camps. The speech sparked rioting in Stalin's home state of Georgia even though only a heavily censored version of it was officially reported on 18 March.

The nation must pause in its pursuit of a higher living standard.
The UK Chancellor of the Exchequer Harold Macmillan raises bank rate – the basic rate for credit – to 5 per cent, its highest level since the crisis of 1931, 17 February 1956.

We aint gonna ride in the back no more.
Slogan chanted by black people in the streets of Montgomery, Alabama, in February 1956 after Rosa Parks, a black woman, had cocked a snook at segregation and sat in the 'Whites Only' front section because, she said, she was tired after a day's work on her feet and didn't want to stand; she was arrested and gaoled. A widespread bus boycott led to the arrest of 119 people on 29 February; meanwhile Autherine Lucy, the first black student to be admitted (under great protest) by the University of Alabama, was stoned and spat on when she attempted to attend classes; the University suspended her 'for her own protection'.

~

It is incumbent on the South to show some progress towards racial integration.
President Eisenhower lends lukewarm public support to the campaign to de-segregate the Southern states, 22 March 1956. On 1 March, the University of Alabama, defying a Federal Court order, permanently expelled Ms Lucy for 'making outrageous, false and baseless accusations' against it; she had accused the University authorities of racism. The Reverend Martin Luther King, organizer of the bus boycott, urged that racist practices be countered with 'passive resistance and the weapon of love'.

The Hungarian Uprising

Today, my friends, we have begun negotiations which are to lead to the total evacuation of Soviet troops from Hungary. We have begun negotiations for the annulment of our remaining obligations under the Warsaw Pact. Please show patience. Such negotiations cannot be completed today or tomorrow. But surely the results I have achieved already since I took power entitle me to your confidence.

Speech from the balcony of the Parliament building in Budapest to cheering crowds below: Hungarian President Imre Nagy, 29 October 1956, after a momentous week. Encouraged by rumours of Khrushchev's 'secret speech', Hungarian workers and students had begun a spontaneous uprising, tearing down Soviet symbols and overthrowing the 25-ft statue of Stalin in Budapest, and demanding the immediate withdrawal of all Soviet troops. The authorities replied by bringing in more Soviet troops – although Nagy vehemently denied this as 'a dastardly lie' – and with the machine-gunning by the AVH, Hungary's equivalent of the KGB, of unarmed protestors; 80 people, mostly women and children, were slaughtered in Magyarovar, whose people replied by massacring their oppressors. Rebellion took fire across the country, and by the 26th it was estimated that 3000 Hungarians were dead, although much of the country and most of the capital was in rebel hands, often after heavy fighting between armoured Soviet forces and civilians armed with rifles, scythes and clubs. Nagy promised free elections and an effective, negotiated independence, but the Soviet forces did not withdraw.

A thing which no one in all the world, not even the big powers, dared to do, was done by small and forlorn Hungary.

Cardinal Josef Mindszenty, imprisoned since the end of the War and released by rebel fighters on 28 October; a week later he was to seek indefinite sanctuary in the US embassy in Budapest.

This is Imre Nagy speaking. Early this morning Soviet troops started to attack the Hungarian capital with the apparent purpose of overthrowing the democratic government of the Hungarian People's Republic.

The President broadcasts in Hungarian and English, 4 November 1956, as Soviet tanks begin to surround the Parliament building; as they advanced into the city, the tank crews were seen to destroy whole buildings in order to silence a single sniper.

What is the United Nations doing? Give us a little encouragement. We will hold out to our last drop of blood ... Planes are flying overhead, but can't be counted, there are so many. The roar of the tanks is so loud ... Now I have to run over to the next room to fire some shots ... Our boys are on the barricades ... There is most bitter fighting in the inner city ... Don't worry about us. When the fighting is over we will rebuild our unhappy, much oppressed country.... Goodbye friends. Save our souls.

A Hungarian reporter in the besieged building of the newspaper Szabad Nep on the morning of 4 November taps out a commentary on the teleprinter to the Associated Press; five minutes later the line was cut.

Help Hungary. Help. Help. Help.
Broadcast from Radio Budapest, 8.10 a.m., 4 November; it then fell silent.

Our ship is sinking. The light vanishes.
The last broadcast to be monitored in Vienna, mid-afternoon, 4 November.

Fascist and reactionary elements have been crushed.
First broadcast on Radio Budapest on the morning of 5 November 1956.

Hungary was, is, and will remain in the Socialist camp as a free and independent country.
Soviet Praesidium member Mikhail Suslov, statement, 6 November.

The Soviet troops are assisting the Hungarian people to retain their independence from Imperialism.
Their masters' voice: the British Communist Party Daily Worker *– some of whose staff resigned in protest at their paper's coverage of events – 7 November 1956.*

Some 200,000 Soviet troops, mostly Mongolian, and 4600 tanks were used, with the assistance of Soviet air force fighter-bombers, to crush the Hungarian rebellion; at least 30,000 people were killed in Budapest alone, while Hungarians in their hundreds of thousands fled across the Austrian border; thousands of young Hungarians, captured in the fighting, were taken back to Russia. The USSR installed János Kádár as a puppet president as the last pockets of resistance were overcome by 12 November, and Imre Nagy went into hiding in the Yugoslav embassy in Budapest. He was eventually handed over, and executed for treason in June 1958.

We have received assurances from Mr Khrushchev that the Soviet armies in Poland will return to their regular bases within two days. Please leave the square in an orderly manner ... Be disciplined. Prove what the proletariat of Warsaw are like. Enough of public meetings and demonstrating.
Polish President Gomulka addresses a crowd, 25 October 1956; the protests died down, and on 18 November, mindful of the Hungarian experience, Gomulka asked Soviet forces to remain in Poland 'in order to assist with the protection of the people'.

We will bury you.
Nikita Khrushchev to a Western diplomat at a Kremlin reception, 26 November 1956; he insisted afterwards that he had meant that Communism would outlive Capitalism.

Your grandson will certainly be a Communist.
Soviet leader Nikita Khrushchev to Sir William Hayter, November 1956.

These extraordinary measures have become necessary owing to the continued activities of counter-revolutionary elements.
10 December 1956: President Kádár of Hungary – who, on 1 November, had declared that 'the Communist Party has degenerated into perpetuating despotism and national slavery' – dissolves the Workers' Council, institutes summary courts, and declares Martial Law.

JIMMY: Oh, heavens, how I long for just a litle ordinary enthusiasm. Just enthusiasm, that's all. I want to hear a warm, thrilling voice cry out, Hallelujah! Hallelujah, I'm alive! ... There aren't any good brave causes left. ... When they put me up against the wall, along with all the other poor old liberals ... it'll be in aid of the brave new nothing-very-much-thank-you.

John Osborne, Look Back In Anger, *1956.*

You do not like Communism. We do not like capitalism. There is only one way out – peaceful co-existence.
Nikita Khrushchev visits Britain in April 1956 and gives a farewell speech on the 22nd. Earlier, after a heated argument with an emotional George Brown, then one of Labour's 'shadow cabinet', at a dinner, he declared that if he was British he would vote Tory.

In an apparent 'thaw' in the Soviet satellite countries, Bulgaria's Stalinist leadership was purged, and Wladislaw Gomulka, the post-war Polish Communist leader imprisoned in 1949, was rehabilitated; Khrushchev had revealed in his 'secret speech' that Stalin had ordered the entire pre-war Polish Communist leadership to be shot, as well as the massacre of 12,000 Polish officers in the forest of Katyn during World War Two, an atrocity still officially blamed on Hitler's Germany. After workers' riots and the assassination of many secret policemen, Gomulka was installed as Polish Prime Minister on 21 October.

EGGHEAD WEDS HOURGLASS
Headline in Variety *as the playwright Arthur Miller marries the film star sex-symbol Marilyn Monroe, 29 June 1956.*

Let them choke to death on their own fury.
After mortgaging Egypt's cotton crop for years ahead in order to buy $200 million worth of arms from the Communist bloc, President Nasser announces the nationalization of the Anglo-French Suez Canal Company on 26 July 1956; shareholders were to receive 'appropriate compen-sation', he said. Britain and the USA had earlier refused to finance Nasser's prestige project, the Aswan High Dam.

~

We cannot allow a man with Colonel Nasser's record to have his thumb on our windpipe.
UK Prime Minister Sir Anthony Eden, 28 July 1956, announcing that all Egyptian assets in London had been frozen. Control of the Suez Canal was considered vital to Britain's oil imports. An Anglo-French military force began to assemble in the region at the end of August; on 29 September Nasser rejected two plans for international, UN-supervised control of the canal, put to him by the US Secretary of State, John Foster Dulles.

Nothing in this great, free continent is going to make me put that boy on my programme.
3 September 1956: American TV chat-show host Ed Sullivan refuses to have Elvis Presley on the show. A week later, for a fee of $17,000, Presley appeared and was viewed by 82 per cent of the potential 54 million audience.

Nasser is a papier-mâché Hitler, a puppet manipulated by the same criminals who have just dealt out death in Hungary. Britain and France, after long forebear-ance, finally found the courage to act. They are entitled to American support. The struggle against Communism is indivisible ... Coexistence is a fraud, a tactic of deception, a mirage in the desert of Western confusions ... We must fight Communism in the satellites, in the Middle East, in our own country.
Putting a spin on it: sponsored advertisement in Cry Hungary *– a special issue of* Picture Post *to raise money for the Lord Mayor's Refugee Fund – and in other publications on both sides of the Atlantic, 'presented as a public service by Playtex' and signed by A. N. Spanel, Chairman of the International Latex Corporation, November 1956.*

~

It is too big for a reprisal and too small for a war.
Israeli government spokesman, as 30,000 Israeli troops seize the Sinai peninsula from Egypt and advance towards the Suez canal, 29 October

1956. In Britain, Prime Minister Eden, after holding talks with the ambassadors of Israel, France and the USA, urged both sides to withdraw from the Canal Zone and hand it over to international control; Egypt at once rejected this.

~

We are not at war with Egypt. We are in a state of armed conflict.
Sir Anthony Eden, 4 November 1956, as first the RAF and then the Royal Marines, in conjuction with French forces, bombard, invade and occupy the Canal Zone; the governments of Britain, Israel and France vehemently rejected accusations – which were widely believed in the USA – that they had engineered the crisis caused by the Israeli invasion the previous month in order to take Suez from Nasser's Egypt. On 8 November, with the canal in Anglo-French control, the UN imposed a cease fire as Royal Navy frogmen began to clear Egyptian blockships from the waterway.
    In Britain, opposition politicians – and some on the Conservative backbenches – viewed the whole operation as having been disgracefully stage-managed, and mismanaged. A run on sterling began, and it was made clear to the Chancellor, Harold Macmillan, that the US Treasury would not intervene to prevent a total collapse unless Britain withdrew.

~

We deserve some credit for stopping a small war. We will leave as an act of good faith.
UK Foreign Secretary Selwyn Lloyd announces Britain's withdrawal to a hostile United Nations, 23 November 1956. Anglo-French forces began to withdraw from the front line of Suez operations on 7 December; on the 10th, the IMF authorized a $1.3 billion loan to Britain. Parts of the canal became navigable by the end of the year; Israel refused to withdraw from the Gaza Strip. Eden, whose health had not been good for some months, left Britain on 19 November to recuperate in Jamaica, leaving the Leader of the House, R. A. Butler, in charge; he returned on 14 December.

· ·

You aint nothin' but a hound dog,
Cryin' all the time.

Written by Jerry Leiber and Mike Stoller, sung by Elvis Presley, 1956.

· ·

The worst govenment is the most moral. One composed of cynics is often very tolerant and human. But when fanatics are on top there is no limit to oppression.
H. L. Mencken, Notebooks (1956).

Let a hundred flowers bloom and a hundred schools argue.
Mao Tse-tung defuses unrest in China, 1956; for a while, it was permitted to disgree a little.

1957

The Communist Party lost their hold over so many people by raising the Iron Curtain even for a month. It was as if we were discovering a new planet, stepping into the future. We were stunned. We couldn't believe that people lived like that.
Soviet and other Communist countries' citizens were not allowed to travel to the West – but, just occasionally, the West was allowed to travel to them – as on this occasion, when the USA staged a 'cultural exhibition' in Moscow in 1957. Alexei Kozlov – quoted in The People's Century (BBC 1995) – was there.

If my services are of value, they will be put at Mr Macmillan's disposal.
R. A. Butler, after the arcane process of 'taking the soundings' had produced Harold Macmillan as leader of the Conservative Party and Prime Minister on 10 January 1957, in succession to Sir Anthony Eden, who retired with chronic ill-health.

Tennis, anyone?
To his dying day – which was 14 January 1957, aged 57, Humphrey Bogart denied that this was the first line he ever spoke professionally.

Its appeal is its simplicity. Everyone wants to get into the act. With rock'n'roll they can join in.
Bill Haley, who gave his first British concert in front of 3000 rapturous fans at London's Dominion Theatre, and celebrated record sales of 22 million, 7 February 1957.

We seek to strengthen the long-term bonds that bind together the British Empire and my country.
President Dwight D. Eisenhower, who met Harold

Macmillan for a four-day summit in Bermuda to repair the damage caused to Anglo-American relations by Suez, 14 March 1957.

If I am a traitor, kill me.
King Hussein of Jordan attempts to foil a republican army coup by saving the life of its leader, and confronting rebel troops at the Fourth Infantry Headquarters, 14 April 1957. It worked.

I think it is a shoddy, unusual thing to do to use the floor of the Senate to attack your opponent without any proof whatsoever.
Why, yes indeedy-doody! Senator Joseph R. McCarthy protests in 1956; he died largely unlamented on 2 May 1957.

There is no reason to attack the monkey when the organ-grinder is present.
Aneurin Bevan, interjection in a Commons debate, 16 May 1957: the monkey was Chancellor Selwyn Lloyd, the organ-grinder Macmillan, the Prime Minister.

I have no statement to make. Neither has my wife.
Arthur Miller and Marilyn Monroe still have nothing to say as the playwright is granted bail after refusing to name names to the House Committee on Un-American Activities, 31 May 1957. He risked a year's imprisonment for contempt.

The people are charming, not yet spoiled by easy money. The Germans are fond of it and they have built a magnificent hotel on the hill above it.
The quiet, unspoiled 'beauty spot' of Benidorm, eulogized by a travel writer, 7 June 1957; strangely enough, it became quite popular after that.

Surely the right course is to test the Russians, not the bombs.
Labour leader Hugh Gaitskell in a Commons

. . . .

The official world, the corridors of power, the dilemmas of conscience and egotism – she disliked them all.

C. P. Snow coins a phrase in Homecomings, 1957; he afterwards used it as a book title.

. . . .

debate on Britain's independent nuclear deterrent, quoted in the Observer, 23 June 1957.

The anti-Party group has been routed.
Khrushchev foils a coup on 3 July 1957; ex-Premier Malenkov was sent to run a hydro-electric plant in Kazakhstan, while ex-Foreign Minister Molotov became ambassador to Mongolia.

Being a champion is all well and good, but you can't eat a crown.
The view on retirement in 1968 – but on 6 July 1957 Althea Gibson became Wimbledon's first black champion when she won the Ladies' Singles 6-3, 6-2; she and the beaten finalist, Darlene Hard, then went on to win the Ladies' Doubles.

Let us be frank about it. Most of our people have never had it so good.
Harold Macmillan, speech, Bedford football ground, 20 July 1957. 'You Never Had it So Good' was Adlai Stevenson's campaign slogan in 1952.

He was like a brother to me.
Stan won't get Ollie into any more fine messes: Laurel mourns Hardy, who died on 7 August 1957, aged 65.

We were blessed with a good administration. Let this legacy left by the British not suffer in efficiency or integrity in the years to come.
Malaya's first Chief Minister, Tengku Adbul Rahman, celebrates independence at midnight, 29/30 August 1957.

Two, four, six, eight –
We won't integrate.
Racist white students protest in Little Rock, Arkansas, 25 September 1957. Three black boys and six black girls – the Little Rock Nine – attempted to attend the Central High School, as the ruling in Brown v. Board of Education entitled them to do. Governor Orval Faubus ordered the State Militia to bar their way, and when they arrived they were greeted by a screaming mob of 500 white townspeople. President Eisenhower, in a move that stunned Southern racists and gave heart to the cause of integration everywhere, ordered 1000 US paratroopers to put the Arkansas State Militia under Federal control. With bayonets fixed, they formed a guard for the nine children to go to school, while a crowd of 1500 bayed abuse.

We're really all of us bottomly broke. I haven't had time to work in weeks.

Jack Kerouac, On The Road, *1957*.

Others provide cocktails; I serve only plain water.

The Finnish composer Jean Sibelius, who died on 20 September 1957, aged 91.

If you carry this resolution and follow out all its implications and do not run away from it, you will send a Foreign Minister, whoever he may be, naked into the conference chamber.

Amid heckling and accusations of treachery from the Left of the Labour Party, its hero Aneurin Bevan appeals successfully for the throwing-out of a unilateral nuclear disarmament motion at the Labour Party annual conference, 3 October 1957.

The USA has lost a battle more important and greater than Pearl Harbor.

Atomic physicist Dr Edward Teller bewails the success of Sputnik–1, *Earth's first man-made satellite, which went into orbit on 4 October 1957.*

Most of the radioactivity has dispersed. The public are at no direct risk of contamination.

Sales of milk from cows grazing 14 square miles of land at Windscale, Cumberland, are banned after one of the reactors at Britain's first nuclear power station goes on fire, 17 October 1957. It was revealed some 35 years later that contamination was much more severe than was admitted at the time.

Women are most fascinating between the ages of thirty-five and forty, after they have won a few races and know how to pace themselves. Since few women ever pass forty, maximum fascination can continue indefinitely.

Couturist Christian Dior, who died on 24 October 1957, aged 52.

How long can this Tommy Steele last? Five months?

Mr Justice Harman tries a contractual lawsuit involving Britain's first rock'n'roll star, 1957. Mr Steele is still performing.

If you don't dig, you lose your superiority over the square and so you are less likely to be cool.

Norman Mailer, who called them 'white negroes', pretty well invents Cultural Studies single-handed as he analyses the 'Beat Generation' in 1957.

I thought that the best thing to do was to settle up these little local difficulties and then turn to the wider vision of the Commonwealth.

Prime Minister Harold Macmillan makes light of the resignation of his entire Treasury team – Chancellor Peter Thorneycroft, and Ministers Enoch Powell and Nigel Birch – after he refused, in the run-up to an election year, to peg government spending at its 1957 level, 7 January 1958.

Hardly the kind of performance any parent could wish their child to witness.

The Musical Express *does not like Cliff Richard, Britain's answer to Elvis, 1958.*

I think it will be a great experience for me.

But not for his fans, who must wait for him until 1960: Elvis Presley answers his draft and checks in for two years with the armed services – and a haircut – on 24 March 1958.

I have provisionally taken into my hands the destinies of French Algeria. I ask you to put your trust in the army and show your trust and determination.

General Salan, C-in-C of the army in Algeria, seizes power as head of the French Nationalist 'Committee of Public Safety' on 13 May 1958, after years of bitter fighting with Algerian nationalists. The crisis in France brought Charles de Gaulle to power as Premier, under his own terms.

~

I have understood you. I know what has happened here. I see what you have wanted to do. I see that the road you have opened in Algeria is that of renovation and brotherhood.

In what seems to be a case of government by confusion, de Gaulle addresses French nationalists in Algiers, 4 June 1958. He made it clear that he stood for integration and equal rights for

••••••••••••••••••••••••••••••

'A novel of today with a freshness and raw fury that makes *Room at the Top* look like a vicarage tea party.'

The Daily Telegraph *reviews Alan Sillitoe's* Saturday Night and Sunday Morning, *1958.*

••••••••••••••••••••••••••••••

all in Algeria, but was hazy on the constitutional form this might take. On 28 September de Gaulle had the support of 80 per cent of voters for a Fifth Republic, giving him wide-ranging extra-parliamentary powers as Prime Minister. Algerian Arabs who voted were promised full constitutional rights as French citizens, though de Gaulle stopped short of calling for full union of the two countries. On 21 December he became President.

———————

It was the most unopposed landing in the history of amphibious warfare.

Anonymous onlooker as 1700 US Marines wade ashore, by invitation, in Beirut, and are handed ice-creams by bikini-clad Lebanese bathing beauties, 31 July 1958; 2000 British paratroopers landed in Amman, Jordan, at the invitation of King Hussein, whose Iraqi colleague in the Arab Union, King Feisal, had been assassinated by young army officers inspired by Nasser's call for a greater United Arab Republic; reports said that Nasser-backed units of the Syrian army were massing to attack Jordan, while Lebanon's President Chamoun was fighting 'Nasserist' terrorists in his own country. The USSR protested vehemently against the West's intervention, but was ignored. The crisis passed.

I am tied to Russia by birth, by life and by work. Leaving my motherland would equal death for me.

Further evidence of a false thaw: 68-year-old Boris Pasternak, expelled as a 'traitor' from the Soviet Writers' Union for his novel Doctor Zhivago *(1958), which was banned in the USSR, is forced to reject the Nobel Prize for Literature, and writes a grovelling letter to Khrushchev in order to avoid expulsion from his homeland, 31 October 1958.*

One test of a mature personality is the capacity to face reality and tackle difficult situations with courage and determination.

Thirty-five years before Prozac, Sir John Charles, Chief Medical Officer at the Department of Health, warns against excessive use of sedatives and tranquilizers, many of which, he says, have not been adequately tested, 12 November 1958.

Introducing Super-Mac

A Vicky cartoon in the Evening Standard, *6 November, invents the Caped Conservative. Macmillan did not hide his pleasure at the soubriquet.*

More die in the United States of too much food than of too little.

John Kenneth Galbraith, The Affluent Society *(1958).*

I give Castro a year. No longer.

January 1959: from his exile in the Dominican republic, former dictator Fulgencio Batista foresees a return to power that never came. In fact, the guerrilla army of Fidel Castro installed Dr Manuel Urrutia as President on 2 January.

Want authority to rent barn in place called Hollywood for $75 a month.

Telegram from movie director Cecil B. de Mille to his boss Sam Goldwyn in 1913. De Mille died on 21 January 1959, aged 77, in the town that was built around the barn.

The biggest no-talent I ever worked with.

The 1956 verdict of Decca's Paul Cohen on the rock star Buddy Holly, who died in a plane crash on 3 February 1959, aged 22.

I am here on a voyage of discovery.

Prime Minister Harold Macmillan deploys his 'first use' patrician charms to the full on a visit to the Soviet Union in February 1959. In August, President Eisenhower came to London for a four-day 'Ike–Mac' summit; it was noted that their long motorcade procession took the two leaders through cheering crowds in a lot of marginal constituencies.

She gave me a smile I could feel in my hip pocket.

Raymond Chandler, who went down his last mean street on 26 March 1959, aged 70. He attended

Dulwich School with P.G. Wodehouse and began
his career as a member of the 'Bloomsbury Group',
writing poetry, before the idea of Philip Marlowe
occurred to him.

I balanced each floor like a teatray on a waiter's finger.

*Architect Frank Lloyd Wright, whose Imperial
Hotel was the only building to survive the
1927 Tokyo earthquake intact. He died on 9
April 1959, aged 89, as his Guggenheim
Museum on New York's Fifth Avenue was nearing completion.*

The British public did not appreciate, having seen her in the role of the dying swan, seeing her in the role of decoy duck.

*Shadow Foreign Secretary Aneurin Bevan, 21 April
1959, on the ballerina Dame Margot Fonteyn,
whose husband Roberto Arias was in hiding, suspected of plotting to overthrow the government of
Panama and install a Communist regime in a coup
designed to coincide with a British Royal visit in
HMS Britannia; Fonteyn spent a night in a
Panamanian police cell but was released after she
had convinced the authorities of her innocence. The
couple were reunited in Brazil in June.*

It takes twenty years or more of peace to make a man; it takes only twenty seconds of war to destroy him.

*King Baudouin I of Belgium, address to US
Congress, 12 May 1959.*

You can be up to your boobies in white satin, with gardenias in your hair and no sugar cane for miles, but you can still be working on a plantation.

*Billie Holiday on the black woman's lot in her
autobiography* Lady Sings The Blues *(1956); she
died on 17 July 1959, aged 44.*

We've got all that in our kitchens. I've got everything in my home that you've got here.

*Nikita Khrushchev tours an American exhibition
in Moscow on 25 July 1959 and spends an hour
among the gadgets, debating the virtues of
Capitalism and Communism with US Vice
President Richard Nixon. They agreed to differ on
everything.*

I am with you all the way.

*Arkansas Governor Orval Faubus addresses a
crowd of 1000 white racists gathered on 12
September 1959 to prevent another two black
children enrolling at the Central High School,
Little Rock. Police kept them at bay using truncheons and fire hoses.*

I can promise you only one thing. It will rain in October.

*Harold Macmillan goes on the stump after calling
a General Election for 8 October 1959.*

We now know that space is not a vacuum but contains gas, cosmic dust and some larger particles of matter.

A TASS news agency report after the Soviet spacecraft Lunik II *crashed into the Moon on 14
September 1959; it had sent a stream of data
back to Earth during its journey.*

It has gone off rather well.

*Prime Minister Harold Macmillan is quietly triumphant after winning the General Election, 9
October 1959. The Conservatives now had a
majority of 100 over all other parties.*

The rest of my life will be devoted to women and litigation.

*Towards the end of his life, Errol Flynn promised
to cut down on under-age girls and booze; he died,
aged 50, on 14 October 1959.*

We must work together in a spirit of great sincerity, with great respect for the natural rights of each other.

*Archbishop Makarios, elected President of the
Republic of Cyprus, 14 December 1959.*

I am still an atheist, thank God.

Film director Luis Buñuel, quoted in Le Monde,
16 December 1959.

* * *

An Aston Martin, three-guinea shirts and a girl with a Riviera sun-tan.

*Laurence Harvey finds what he wants in John
Braine's* Room at the Top, *1959.*

* * *

The Century's
Second Youth
1960-1969

There is always inequality in life. Some men are killed in
a war and some men are wounded and some men never
leave the country. Life is unfair.

~ *J.F. Kennedy, 1962*

The 1960s was a decade marked by the apparent ascendancy – some would say
'invention' – of youth. The USA elected its youngest-ever President, John F. Kennedy,
and Britain the relatively youthful Harold Wilson, with his promises of vigour and
modernity, as Prime Minister, and 'youth culture' – radical, irreverent, progressive
and 'alternative' – seeemd to set the social and, to some extent, political trends as the
post-war 'baby boom' generation moved into adolescence. The far-reaching social and
political changes of the 1960s were, however, the work of an older generation:
Martin Luther King led a huge and successful Civil Rights Movement in America, and
the retreat from colonial rule in Africa was led by Harold Macmillan for Britain, and
in a much less orderly fashion, by General Charles de Gaulle for France.

The USA become embroiled in the proto-colonial nightmare of the Vietnam War,
which by the end of the decade had succeeded in moving almost every other consideration off America's political agenda. One exception was the space programme:
President Kennedy announced at the beginning of the decade, after the USSR had put
a man into orbit, that Americans would walk on the Moon before 1970: in 1969, his
promise was kept by two members of the crew of *Apollo 11*.

In the Western world, and especially in Britain, the decade was generally a period
of great optimism, as economies prospered, society became more open and more free,
and it seemed possible for the rising adult generation to do, and have, and be whatever
it chose. Television came of age and began to produce popular dramas and comedies of
lasting quality, rock'n'roll evolved and produced The Beatles, The Rolling Stones and a
host of groups and performers whose output, especially in the years 1966–68,
remains unrivalled both for quality and quantity; theatre in Britain revelled in the lift-
ing of censorship and produced work to build on the foundations of Osborne and the

Absurdists of the 1950s. 'Progress' – the evolution of things towards the freer, easier and better – seemed, not only to the generation that matured in those years, to be a natural and universal law. Ugly events, such as the assassinations of Kennedy and King, and even the brutal suppression of the liberalizing regime in Czechoslovakia, once again by Soviet military invasion, appeared as the dying manifestations of an old order that could and would be defeated. But one event of the mid-decade, the 'Six Day War' between Israel and her Arab neighbours, was to have consquences that brought the party to an abrupt end in the early years of the Seventies.

1960

One does not arrest Voltaire.
Attributed to French President Charles de Gaulle: reply when asked why he had not ordered the arrest of philosopher and polemicist Jean-Paul Sartre for urging French soldiers to desert rather than fight Algerian nationalist forces – but in January 1960 he faced the prospect of civil war, as French settlers in Algeria rebelled against his plans for Algerian 'self-determination'.

The wind of change is blowing through this continent and, whether we like it or not, this growth of national consciousness is a political fact. … We may sometimes be tempted to say to each other, 'Mind your own business'. But in these days I would expand the old saying so that it runs, 'Mind your own business but mind how it affects mine, too.'
British Prime Minister Harold Macmillan addresses the all-white South African Parliament to snarls of disapproval, Cape Town, 3 February 1960, and urges a move towards policies of racial equality throughout the Commonwealth.

There has to be justice not only for the black man in Africa but also for the white man.
South African Prime Minister Hendrik Verwoerd replies, to loud applause.

The Germany of today is not the Germany of yesterday. We remember the past not in order to brood upon it but in order that it shall never recur.
Israeli Prime Minister David Ben-Gurion, after his New York meeting with West German Chancellor Konrad Adenauer, 14 March 1960.

If they do these things, they must learn their lesson the hard way.
Colonel D. H. Pienaar, Police Commissioner for

the Transvaal, 21 March 1960. Fifty-six black South Africans were killed and 162 were injured in the 'native township' of Sharpeville when police opened fire on a crowd of 15,000 demonstrating against the Pass Laws, which required Africans to carry identity cards at all times; they were not permitted to travel outside their 'designated areas'. The 'Sharpeville Massacre' was followed by strikes and widespread rioting as black leaders were arrested and gaoled for sedition.

I'm off on a pub crawl.
Harold Macmillan, attending the four-power Summit in Paris on 16 May 1960, clambers over the wall of the British Embassy garden – and goes to see Charles de Gaulle. The talks achieved nothing, largely because Khrushchev demanded, as a prerequisite, a public apology from the US for sending a U-2 reconnaissance plane to spy on the USSR; Soviet fighters had shot it down and its civilian pilot, Gary Powers, was eventually sentenced in Moscow to 10 years' imprisonment. The USA insisted at the time that the plane was on a meteorological misssion to photograph clouds, and had strayed off course.

I have to inform you that the State of Israel has taken into custody one of the greatest of the Nazi war criminals.
Israel's Prime Minister David Ben-Gurion informs the Knesset on 23 May 1960 of the arrest of the former SS Colonel Adolf Eichmann, 'the technician of death' who planned and organized the mass transportation of Jews to the death camps from all over occupied Europe. It later emerged that he had been kidnapped by the Israeli secret service, Mossad, in Argentina, where he had been living since the end of the war, and smuggled out on an official Israeli plane. Nineteen months later, on 15 December 1961, he was sentenced to death. (See 31 May 1962, p. 134.)

For 80 years we sent you the best of our sons.
King Baudouin of Belgium dwells at length on all the

benefits of occupation as he addresses Patrice Lumumba, Prime Minister of the newly-independent Congo after a long and brutal war, at a formal ceremony on 30 June 1960. Lumumba replied with a long and passionate diatribe cataloguing all the wrongs inflicted on his country and his people since the 'Grab for Africa'; Belgium's record is widely recognized as the worst of all the colonial powers. Congo descended almost at once into anarchy and civil war as a thrice-bankrupt businessman, Moise Tshombe, declared independence for the copper-rich province of Katanga. United Nations forces were dragged into the conflict at the end of July, and on 14 September the army seized power under Colonel Joseph-Desire Mobutu. (See 13 February 1961, p. 131.)

Nigeria gained independence from Britain on 1 October 1960.

I read the newspaper avidly. It is my one form of continuous fiction.

Aneurin Bevan, quoted in the Observer, *3 April 1960. He died, aged 62, on 6 July 1960.*

We stand today on the edge of a New Frontier … But the New Frontier of which I speak is not a set of promises – it is a set of challenges. It sums up not what I intend to offer the American people, but what I intend to ask of them.

The 43-year-old John F. Kennedy accepts the Democratic nomination for the Presidency, Los Angeles, 15 July 1960. His main challenger, Hubert Humphrey, had withdrawn from the contest after Kennedy took 70 per cent of the votes in the Maryland primary election of 17 May. The Republicans nominated the former Vice-President and McCarthy aide Richard M. Nixon.

There are some of us … who will fight, fight, fight, and fight again to save the party we love.

Labour leader Hugh Gaitskell, missing the support of his left-wing colleague Aneurin Bevan, fails to prevent a nuclear disarmament motion being passed at the Labour Party Conference, 3 October 1960.

* * *

Has anyone here been raped and speaks English?

Anonymous BBC TV reporter to Belgians waiting to be evacuated from the Congo, 1960.

* * *

What a genius the Labour Party has for cutting itself in half and letting the two parts writhe in public.

William Neil Cannon – 'Cassandra' of the Daily Mirror *– writes during the week of the Labour Conference in October. Labour's left wing made no secret of its desire to get rid of Gaitskell.*

Politicians are the same all over. They promise to build a bridge even when there is no river.

In genial mood, Nikita Khrushchev engages in badinage at Glen Close, New York, in October.

This liar, this imbecile, this jerk, this American stooge.

In uncongenial mood on 12 October, Nikita Khrushchev removes his shoe and bangs it on his desk at the UN as Philippine delegate Lorenzo Sumulong accuses the USSR of imperialism in Eastern Europe; later, he waved his shoe at the US Assistant Secretary of State. The session came to a chaotic end when the Assembly President smashed his gavel as he was banging it in fury at the Romanian Foreign Minister.

The expression 'positive neutrality' is a contradiction in terms. There can be no more positive neutrality than there can be a vegetarian tiger.

The Indian writer and jurist V. K. Krishna Menon, The New York Times, *18 October 1960.*

Would you approve of your young sons, your young daughters – because girls can read as well as boys – reading this book? Is it a book that you would leave lying around your own house? is it a book that you would wish your wives or even your servants to read?

Mr Mervyn Griffith-Jones, senior Treasury Counsel, addresses the (mixed) jury as he opens the case for the Prosecution in the case of Regina v. Penguin Books Ltd, *publishers of D. H. Lawrence's novel* Lady Chatterley's Lover, *banned in the UK for 30 years. The trial became an extended seminar in literary criticism, and ended on 2 November with victory for Penguin, who sold the entire print run of 200,000 copies the next day.*

Do you realize the responsibility I carry? I'm the only person standing between Nixon and the White House.

John F. Kennedy to Arthur Schlesinger, 10 October 1960.

You don't set a fox to watching the chickens just because he has a lot of experience in the hen house.

Harry S Truman on Richard Nixon's bid for the Presidency, speech, 30 October 1960. By a narrow margin, John F. Kennedy was elected President on 9 November with just 120,000 more of the popular vote than Nixon.

There is only one policy for Algeria: self-determination and reconciliation.

President de Gaulle completes a campaigning tour through the French colony on 13 December 1960; he was cheered by Muslims, but French Algerians rioted and 123 people were killed. In the Referendum that followed, voters in both countries backed his Home Rule policy by 15 million to 5 million.

1961

Let the word go forth from this time and place, to friend and foe alike, that the torch has been passed to a new generation of Americans ... unwilling to witness or permit the slow undoing of those human rights to which this nation has always been committed, and to which we are committed today at home and around the world.

Let every nation know, whether it wishes us well or ill, that we shall pay any price, bear any burden, meet any hardship, support any friend, oppose any foe to ensure the survival and the success of liberty. ...

Let us never negotiate out of fear, but let us never fear to negotiate. ...

In your hands, my fellow citizens, more than mine, will rest the final success or failure of our course ... And so, my fellow Americans, ask not what your country can do for you; ask what you can do for your country.

A memorable inauguration address, President John F. Kennedy, 20 January 1961.

A revolution is not a bed of roses. A revolution is a struggle to the death between the future and the past.

Fidel Castro, speech marking the second anniversary of the Cuban revolution, January 1961.

I would be lying if I said the death of Mr Lumumba makes me sad. He was an ordinary criminal responsible for thousands of deaths.

Godefroid Munongo, Katangan Minister for the Interior, statement, 13 February 1961. Lumumba, whose followers pursued a policy of wholesale extermination of Europeans in Congo, had been sent to Katanga after his arrest because it was feared that he would persuade his guards to release him; the European pilot who flew him there reported that he had been badly beaten on the flight. Congolese authorities reported that he and two companions were killed by unnamed villagers – who reportedly received a £3000 reward – after fleeing from captivity; the doctor who signed their death certificate gave 'Died in the bush' as the cause of death.

It is clear after the lead given by a group of Afro-Asian nations that we will be no longer welcome.

On 15 March 1961, South African Prime Minister Dr Hendrick Verwoerd informs Commonwealth leaders in London that his country will leave the British Commonwealth when it becomes a republic at the end of the month. South Africa's Apartheid policies had been publicly criticized by all other Commonwealth states, particularly after the Sharpeville shootings.

———————

The sky looks very very dark and the earth bluish.

A message from orbit from the Russian Major Yuri Gagarin, the first man in space, 12 April 1961. His Vostok craft made a hard-surface landing after a flight lasting 108 minutes.

~

I believe that this nation should commit itself to achieving the goal, before this decade is out, of landing a man on the moon and returning him safely to earth.

President John F. Kennedy, Supplementary State of the Union Address, 25 May 1961. On 5 May, Alan B. Shepard Jr, became the first American in space, with a 15-minute sub-orbital flight.

———————

The Irish don't know what they want and are prepared to fight to the death in order to get it.

Sidney Littlewood, President of the Law Society, speech, 13 April 1961, as the UK entered the fourth year of an IRA bombing campaign.

I have taken careful note of your statement that events in Cuba might affect

peace in all parts of the world. I trust that this does not mean that the Soviet government … is planning to inflame other areas of the world. I would like to think that your government has too great a sense of responsibility to embark on any enterprise so dangerous to general peace.
Prelude to a crisis: President Kennedy's cable to Nikita Khrushchev, 19 April 1961, after a counter-revolutionary force of Cuban exiles had invaded Cuba at the Bay of Pigs. The extent to which Kennedy was actively involved with the attempted coup – which was sponsored and largely planned by the CIA – is disputed; it was easily defeated by Cuban government troops.

The worse I do, the more popular I get.
President Kennedy, April 1961, quoted in The People's Almanac, D. Wallechinsky.

Frenchmen and women, help me. In the name of France I order the use of all means, I repeat all means, to bar the route to these men until they are defeated.
President de Gaulle broadcasts to the nation, 24 April 1961, as riot police and Republican Guards stand by to repel the threat of a paratroop invasion of France by rebel French Algerian forces, led by General Challe. Airport runways were blocked, the air force was ordered to shoot down hostile French planes, and Sherman tanks ringed the Elysée Palace; de Gaulle also ordered a naval blockade of Algeria. The rebellion crumbled before an invasion could be launched, and de Gaulle, who had already had several near-miraculous escapes from assassination attempts, opened talks with Algerian nationalist leaders the following month.

When you are skinning your customers you should leave some skin on to grow, so that you can skin them again.
Nikita Khrushchev, speech to British businessmen, May 1961.

King Charles I was at least given a hearing at his trial.
Anonymous MP, 8 May 1961, after the House of Commons voted to disbar the absent Viscount Stansgate; peers are not permitted to sit in the Commons. Viscount Stansgate, who had sat as Anthony Wedgwood Benn for the constituency of Bristol South-East before his father's death, contested the by-election caused by his elevation and doubled his majority. In July the High Court

declared his defeated Tory rival to be the elected MP. By a subsequent Act of Parliament he was permitted to renounce his title, and he re-entered the Commons – as Tony Benn – after a by-election in 1963.

Your treachery has rendered much of this country's efforts completely useless.
With Kim Philby yet to be unmasked as a Soviet spy, Lord Chief Justice Parker sentences George Blake, a 38-year-old naval diplomat, to 42 years' imprisonment on 8 May 1961. Blake confessed to passing to the USSR 'every document I could get hold of' over a period of nine years while working in Germany and Lebanon. It was alleged that he had been 'brainwashed' after his capture by Korean Communists in 1951, after which he was held for 3 years. On 22 October 1966, Czech intelligence agents organized his escape from Wormwood Scrubs prison; within 80 minutes he was on a plane to Frankfurt, thence to East Berlin. He surfaced eventually in Moscow.

Protect me! protect me!
16 June 1961: as the touring Kirov ballet company prepares to board a London flight at Le Bourget airport, Paris, one of its dancers rushes across to a group of French Police. His name was Rudolf Nureyev, and he was granted asylum after an interview with Soviet officials had failed to persuade him to reconsider.

SLOGANS and CATCHPRASES of THE SIXTIES

Black Power!
US Black Militant slogan, from c.1960.

Up against the wall, motherfucker.
Black Militant slogan, US, from 1960.

Beanz means Heinz
Advertisements, UK, from early 60s.

Burn, baby, burn!
Black extremist slogan, mainly US, from 1965.

Hell no, we won't go!
US draft-resisters' chant, from 1965.

If you are lucky enough to have lived in Paris as a young man, then wherever you go for the rest of your life, it stays with you, for Paris is a moveable feast,
Ernest Hemingway, A Moveable Feast, published posthumously in 1964; on 2 July 1961 the 61-year-old writer committed suicide, as his father had done, with his own shotgun.

I ask you not to revolt, and not to despair. You cannot be held in slavery forever.
Willi Brandt, Mayor of West Berlin, broadcasts to East Berlin, 31 August 1961 after East Germany had sealed off the border with the West and begun the rapid building of the Berlin Wall as a physical barrier between the two worlds; tens of thousands of East Germans, particularly agricultural workers, had fled to the West in the preceding months, while many of the 50,000 East Berliners who worked in the Western sector were failing to return home.

During the wall's construction many thousands more, including East German security guards, also fled.

It was my first trip in a Black Maria as the last time I had been gaoled I had been taken to Brixton in a taxi, but I was too tired to enjoy the novelty.
Bertrand Russell, Autobiography, Volume III (1969). In August 1961 the 88-year-old philoso-pher was sentenced to a week's imprisonment (which he spent in the prison hospital) for inciting a breach of the peace by addressing an anti-nuclear rally in Hyde Park. In September, 850 people were arrested as a 15,000-strong CND rally, assisted by 3000 policemen, had blocked Trafalgar Square. Among the detainees were John Osborne, George Melly and Vanessa Redgrave.

Never let success hide its emptiness from you, achievement its nothingness, toil its desolation. ... Do not look back. And do not dream about the future, either. It will neither give you back the past, nor satisfy your other daydreams. Your duty, your reward – your destiny – are *here* and *now*.
Dag Hammarskjöld, Secretary-General of the United Nations: Markings, published posthumously in 1965. On 18 September 1961 Hammarskjold was one of 13 passengers to die as his plane crashed near Ndola airport in Northern Rhodesia. He had been on his way to negotiate a cease-fire with the Katangan leader Moise Tshombe, whose forces were at war with UN troops; Hammarskjöld himself had been opposed to direct UN military involvement. The sole survivor, an American security guard, said that Hammarskjöld had changed his mind at the last moment and ordered the pilot to alter course; soon after, there was a large explosion and the plane fell out of the sky. The cause of the crash has never

The East is red.
Chinese Communist anthem and slogan, from c.1965.

Hey, hey, LBJ, how many kids did you kill today?
US Vietnam protestors' chant, from 1965.

Make love, not war.
Attributed to a G. Legman of the Kinsey Institute for Sexological Research; adopted by Vietnam protestors and youth generally from the mid-Sixties.

We shall overcome.
From a very old song; revived in the US, it became the anthem of Civil Rights movements worldwide from the mid-Sixties.

Bombs away with Curt Lemay
US Peace Movement chant, from 1967.

I'm backing Britain
Short-lived in 1968.

If you're not part of the solution, you're part of the problem.
Black activist slogan, US, attributed to Eldridge Cleaver, from 1968.

Out of the closets and into the streets.
Adopted by the US Gay Liberation Front; first aired in San Francisco, 1969.

Power to the People!
Coined by US Black Panther Movement in 1969.

been established. Hammarskjöld was posthumously awarded the 1961 Nobel Peace Prize, and was succeeded at the UN by the Burmese diplomat, U Thant. In December the Irish diplomat who had ordered the military action in Katanga, Dr Conor Cruise O'Brien, was sacked by the UN.

A joke in very bad taste.

President de Gaulle, 8 September 1961, on a failed attempt by the OAS Secret Army to blow up his car with plastic explosive near his home at Colombey-les-Deux-Eglises; the disgraced former General of French Algerian forces, Raoul Salan, was implicated in the attack. The following month, Muslim women in France took part in mass passive demonstrations while their husbands went on strike in protest at the curfew imposed to deal with terrorism. Over 1000 women and children were detained for identity checks. In January 1962 the OAS launched a bombing campaign in Algiers and Paris, where 25,000 armed troops patrolled the streets.

I wonder how it is with you, Harold? If I don't have a woman for three days, I get a terrible headache.

President Kennedy reveals a hidden aspect of Camelot to Harold Macmillan during discussion at Chequers, the Prime Minister's country residence, in December 1961: quoted in Macmillan 1957–1986, A. Horne. The rapport between the two leaders revived the wartime phrase, 'The Special Relationship'.

I'd like to manage those four boys. It wouldn't take me more than two half-days a week.

Record shop owner Brian Epstein, after attending a performance by the Beatles at the Cavern Club, Liverpool, 9 November 1961.

1962

We don't like their sound. Groups of guitars are on the way out.

An early setback for Mr Epstein, as Decca Records reject his boys' demo tape, January 1962.

Conservatism is young, virulent, and alive: the wave of the future.

Senator Barry Goldwater addresses a 'Young Americans for Freedom' rally in New York, 7 March 1962.

There were three thousand six hundred and fifty-three days like that in his stretch. From the first clang of the rail to the last clang of the rail.
The three extra
days were for leap years.

One Day in the Life of Ivan Denisovich, *Alexander Solzhenitsyn's account of a Soviet labour camp: published during the 'Kremlin thaw' by the magazine* Novy Mír *in November 1962, it sold out in three hours.*

It's fantastic. I can hardly believe it.

With no opportunity for the traditional speech of thanks, the newly-elected MP Eric Lubbock gasps a few words of astonishment at overturning a Tory majority of 14,760 to win the Orpington by-election for the Liberals with a majority of 7855, 15 March 1962.

We did not want our wives to crawl, but to walk unbowed to freedom.

The 81-year-old spokesman for a group of 11 elderly East Berliners explains why the tunnel they dug under the Berlin Wall to escape to the West had such a high roof, 5 May 1962.

We shall meet again. I have believed in God. I obeyed the laws of war and was loyal to my flag.

The last words of Adolf Eichmann, spoken to the official witnesses at his execution, 31 May 1962.

Greater love hath no man than this, that he lay down his friends for his life.

Liberal MP Jeremy Thorpe comments in the House of Commons on a new Night Of The Long Knives, 13 July 1962: Prime Minister Harold Macmillan cleared up another little local difficulty by sacking seven of his cabinet colleagues.

Everybody is always tugging at you. They would all like sort of a chunk of you.

Marilyn Monroe, quoted in Life *for the week in which she was found dead in bed, an empty bottle of sleeping tablets nearby; she was 36, 5 August 1962.*

They really are bad shots.

President de Gaulle, having declared Algerian independence after a referendum vote of 99 per cent in favour, survives the fourth assassination attempt in a year on 22 August 1962; OAS hitmen opened fire on his car from three positions at a crossroads near Versailles, but nobody was injured. With ex-General Salan sentenced to life imprisonment, the crackdown against the OAS continued.

I want to be the white man's brother, not his brother-in-law.
US Civil Rights leader, Rev. Martin Luther King, interview, New York Journal-American, 10 September 1962. On 30 September three people were killed in a riot at Mississippi University as a white racist mob broke in to protest against the registration of a black student, James Meredith. Governor Ross Barnett had used State Troopers to prevent Meredith entering campus, but President Kennedy ordered Federal Marshals to escort him in. At a huge racist rally at Jackson Stadium, the college band turned out in Confederate uniforms to lead the crowd in the singing of 'Dixie'.

The training, transportation and logistical support we are providing in Vietnam has succeeded in turning the tide against the Vietcong.
An upbeat assessment from US General Barkside Hamlett, Army Vice Chief of Staff, 10 October 1962. US military advisers had been sent to South Vietnam at the end of the Fifties to assist with the campaign against the Communist North.

———————

I guess this is the week I earn my salary.
President Kennedy, October 1962, as news breaks of the Cuban Missile Crisis: US spy planes had photographed Russian medium-range nuclear missiles installed at a launching base in Cuba, and a Soviet ship was on its way with more. Kennedy personally informed Nikita Khrushchev that the USA would regard the basing of the missiles so close to its own territory as an act of war, and react accordingly by invading Cuba. On 28 October, Khrushchev publicly ordered the dismantling of the missiles and their return to the USSR. Kennedy praised the Soviet leader's statesmanship; for Khrushchev it proved politically fatal.
~
They talk about who won and who lost. Human reason won. Mankind won.
Nikita Khrushchev, speech, November 1962. His Kremlin colleagues were not impressed with this interpretation of the outcome of the Cuban crisis. On 21 December, at a meeting with Harold

Macmillan, Kennedy announced that British and French submarines would be equipped with US 'Polaris' nuclear missiles as part of a NATO 'deterrent force'. The British Prime Minister accepted at once, but France did not reply.

———————

He was entrapped by his lust and thereafter cash kept him crooked. He had neither the moral fibre nor the patriotism to alter his conduct.
UK Attorney General Sir John Hobson, 22 October, comments on the 18 year gaol sentence for William Vassall, an Admiralty clerk who photographed secret documents for the USSR. He had been lured, during a period of service in Moscow six years previously, into a homosexual 'honey trap' and thereafter blackmailed; on his return to London the KGB paid him enough to double his salary of £700 a year. A few days after Vassall's trial ended, government member Thomas Galbraith resigned when a newspaper published his letters to the spy. On 2 November the KGB in Budapest arrested the British businessman and MI6 agent Greville Wynne; a few days later they arrested his Soviet contact, KGB Colonel Oleg Penkovsky.

Just think about how much you're going to be missing, you won't have Dick Nixon to kick around anymore because, gentlemen, this is my last press conference.
An embittered Richard Milhous Nixon speaks to the press after being rejected by the voters of California in the election for Governor, 2 November 1962.

She would rather light candles than curse the darkness, and her glow has warmed the world.
Adlai Stevenson pays tribute at the UN to the former chairman of the UN Commission on Human Rights and widow of the four-times US President, Eleanor Roosevelt, two days after her death on 7 November 1962.

Members rise from CMG (known sometimes in Whitehall as 'Call Me God') to the KCMG ('Kindly Call Me God') to ... the GCMG ('God Calls Me God').
Anthony Sampson, in Anatomy of Britain, 1962, on the progess of the Great and the Good in the Honours System.

The struggle is my life.
The lawyer and African Nationalist leader Nelson Mandela, sentenced to five years' imprisonment on 7 November 1962 by the Pretoria Court for 'inciting subversion' by organizing a strike, and for leaving South Africa illegally to address a conference in Addis Ababa. Mandela, then nicknamed 'The Black Pimpernel', had been evading arrest for several months.

Great Britain has lost an Empire and has not yet found a role.
The US Secretary of State Dean Rusk coins a contentious phrase in a speech at the West Point Military Academy on 5 December 1962.

Power corrupts, but lack of power corrupts absolutely.
Adlai Stevenson adapts Lord Acton, January 1963.

———————

Britain neither thinks nor acts like a continental nation, and so is not yet qualified for membership of the European Economic Community.
Monsieur Non: on 14 January 1963 President Charles de Gaulle rejects Britain's application for EEC membership, but Britain's chief negotiator, Edward Heath, plugs on regardless. France also rejected the USA's proposals on the arming of France's submarines with Polaris warheads. De Gaulle said France preferred to organize her own defences.

~

It does mean, if this is the idea, the end of Britain as an independent European state … It means the end of a thousand years of history.
Labour leader Hugh Gaitskell addresses his October 1962 Party Conference on the subject of Britain's proposed EEC membership. After returning from a trip to the USSR he fell ill with a mysterious virus; as his condition worsened, an artificial kidney was used in a vain atempt to keep him alive. He died, at the age of 56, on 18 January 1963.

———————

In Western Europe, there are now only small countries – those that know it, and those that don't know it yet.
Belgian statesman Théo Lefèvre, speech on Britain's application for EEC membership, January.

They say I have a good memory. I intend to become famous for my short one.
Harold Wilson, elected as Labour leader on 14 February 1963, replies to questions about his previously uneasy relationship with the Deputy Leader, George Brown, whom he defeated by 144 votes to 103.

Let us drop blaming Beeching. … All that has happened has been at the injunction of the Tory government. Public attention was deliberately diverted to Beeching in order to save the government. We must not fall for this trap.
The Railway Review *on the Beeching Report, published on 27 March 1963. Dr Beeching had been brought in from ICI 'to increase efficiency' on British Railways: his report recommended cutting the network by one quarter, losing 67,700 jobs, and closing 2128 stations, most of them in rural areas. Most of his recommendations were subsequently implemented, as a politically sponsored and ultimately fatal blow to the postwar concept of the railways as a public service.*

I wish I could bring Stonehenge to Nyasaland to show there was a time when Britain had a savage culture.
Dr Hastings Banda, President of Malawi – formerly Nyasaland, which the British Government detached from the Central African Federation: on 29 March 1963, it was announced that Northern Rhodesia (now Zambia) would also leave. This left a substantial element of Southern Rhodesia's whites-only administration, which had been fighting a guerilla war against Zimbabwean Nationalists, pressing for full independence along South African apartheid lines.

He mobilized the English language and sent it into battle.
President Kennedy confers honorary US Citizenship on Sir Winston Churchill, 9 April 1963; in fact, the words were those of broadcaster Ed Murrow, nine years earlier.

It's like a foreign country; there's no communication.
The US President's brother, Attorney-General Robert Kennedy, 25 April 1963, having failed to persuade the Governor of Alabama, George

Wallace, to obey the anti-segregation laws. Civil Rights leaders Drs Martin Luther King and Ralph Abernathy had been arrested, along with 58 others, for parading without a permit on a peaceful march through the streets of the state capital, Birmingham, two weeks previously. In May, 1000 people were similarly arrested in one day; riots followed.

My accident last year has decreased my mobility. I'm very sad.
Sir Winston Churchill, MP for Woodford in Essex, at the age of 88 and approaching 60 years' membership of the House of Commons, announces on 1 May 1963 that he will not contest the next General Election. He had broken his thigh in a fall the previous June.

There was no impropriety whatsoever in my acquaintanceship with Miss Keeler ... I shall not hesitate to issue writs for libel and slander if scandalous allegations are made or repeated outside the House.
John Profumo MP, Secretary of State for War, statement to the House of Commons, 22 March 1963. Rumours were rife about a 'relationship' between Profumo and Christine Keeler, a 21-year-old model and call-girl whose name had also been sexually linked with that of a Soviet naval attaché, Eugene Ivanov, and who had gone missing when called as a witness against her ex-lover, who was accused of trying to shoot her. As news began to break about the defection of the British secret agent and 'Third Man' Kim Philby, Opposition MPs were keen to exploit anything that might link the government to breaches of national security; many government MPs were profoundly uneasy. The Prime Minister announced that he accepted the truth of Profumo's statement, and regarded the matter as closed.

This is a great tragedy for you, your family and your friends.
Prime Minister Harold Macmillan, on holiday in Scotland, writes to John Profumo on 5 June 1963; Profumo admitted that he had lied to the House of Commons about his relationship with Christine Keeler, though he continued to deny that there had been any security risk. His denial ten weeks earlier had been challenged in a letter to Macmillan and Labour leader Harold Wilson from Dr Stephen Ward, a society artist and osteopath. Ward asserted that the two had first met at a party (at which Ivanov, along with several call-girls and various 'public figures', was also present) at his cottage on

And so, there is the choice for the electorate: on the one hand, Lord Home – on the other hand, Mr Harold Wilson. Dull Alec versus smart-alec.
David Frost closes a show in the second series of That Was The Week That Was, 19 October 1963. The BBC received 310 letters of complaint, and 599 phone calls; the show was 'pulled' the next month.

Lord Astor's Cliveden estate, where Miss Keeler had frolicked naked in the swimming pool, and that he had subsequently arranged for the two to meet at his Hampstead flat. In what has since come to be seen as an Establishment vendetta, Ward himself was then arrested and put on trial for living off immoral earnings. Profumo resigned his office and his seat in the Commons, and began what was to prove a 30-year process of social rehabilitation through charitable work.

~

A great party is not to be brought down because of a scandal by a woman of easy virtue and a proven liar.
In a BBC interview on 13 June, cabinet member Lord Hailsham (Quintin Hogg) attempts to reduce the Profumo Affair to trifling proportions.

~

The members of our secret service have apparently spent so much time looking under the beds for Communists, they haven't had time to look in them.
The comment of Labour politician Michael Foot; according to Miss Keeler, she had told the police six months earlier that Dr Ward had asked her to find out 'when West Germany would get nuclear weapons'; she had ignored the request and they, apparently, had ignored her report. On 30 June, 30 Tory MPs refused to back the government on an Opposition censure motion on the affair, and a judicial enquiry under Lord Denning was set up to consider the security implications; after interviewing over 160 witnesses in private (including a man who had attended 'dinner parties' as a waiter dressed only in a mask, whom Denning said was not a minister) he concluded that there had been no security threat.

~

Well, he would, wouldn't he?
Mandy Rice-Davies, 18-year-old model and call-girl, when told on 29 June that Lord Astor had

repudiated her evidence at the trial of Dr Ward. Largely relying on the evidence of two other prostitutes – who both claimed afterwards that they had committed perjury under pressure – Ward was found guilty, but not before he had taken a fatal overdose of sleeping pills; he died a few days later. Police began investigating their allegations, but soon dropped the enquiry. In December, Keeler herself began a nine-month prison sentence for perjury at the trial of another ex-boyfriend, Aloysius 'Lucky' Gordon. Her Counsel blamed the dead Dr Ward for being 'a perverted Professor Higgins'.

~

The so-called new morality is too often the old immorality condoned.
Lord Shawcross sums up in November.

~

Both the Government and the police have played a curiously passive role in this shabby record of gangsterism [and of] growing fat by battening on human misery.
Opposition leader Harold Wilson, House of Commons, 22 July, in a debate on 'Rachmanism', the practice of buying up tenanted slum property and terrorizing its inhabitants into leaving, thereby making it available for profitable 'gentrification' and resale. The practice took its name from the late Peter Rachman, a criminal slum landlord who turned out to be yet another ex-lover of Christine Keeler. The government set up an inquiry into privately rented housing, which led to reforms.

All free men, wherever they may live, are citizens of Berlin. And therefore, as a free man, I take pride in the words, *Ich bin ein Berliner.*
US President John F. Kennedy receives rapturous applause for a speech at the City Hall, West Berlin, on 26 June 1963. He ought strictly to have said 'Ich bin Berliner', since 'ein Berliner' is a sort of doughnut.

I say to you today, my friends, that in spite of the difficulties and frustrations of the

....

Please get out of the way if you can't lend your hand -
For the times they are a-changin'.

Bob Dylan, song, 1963.

....

moment I still have a dream. It is a dream deeply rooted in the American Dream.

I have a dream that one day this nation will rise rise up and live out the true meaning of its creed: 'We hold these truths to be self-evident; that all men are created equal.' [...]
I have a dream that my four little children will one day live in a nation where they will not be judged by the colour of their skin but by the content of their character. I have a dream today. [...]

When we let freedom ring, when we let it ring from every village and every hamlet, from every state and every city, we will be able to speed up that day when all of God's children, black men and white men, Jews and Gentiles, Protestants and Catholics, will be able to join hands and sing in the words of the old Negro spiritual, 'Free at last! Free at last! Thank God Almighty, we are free at last!'
The Rev. Martin Luther King addresses a quarter of a million people, black and white, at the Lincoln Memorial, Washington, DC, 28 August 1963 – the centenary of the signing of the Emancipation Proclamation. The following month, Alabama Governor George Wallace ordered State Troopers to seal off Tuskegee High School to prevent integration, and President Kennedy took control of Alabama's National Guard to enforce it.

~

The blood of four little children and thirteen others critically injured is on your hands. The irresponsible and misguided actions have created the atmosphere that induced continued violence and now murder.
Rev. Martin Luther King, telegram to George Wallace, 15 September 1963, after white supremacists in Birmingham, Alabama, bombed the 16th Street Baptist Church; Wallace responded by sending riot squads to quell black protest. When stones were thrown at them they opened fire, killing one youth and injuring three others.

A nuclear test ban treaty does not mean the end of the arms race. You do not like our social system and we do not like yours. No treaties can overcome the concrete contradictions between the two social systems.
Nikita Khrushchev, 8 August 1963, after signing the Moscow Treaty to outlaw nuclear weapons

testing in the atmosphere, outer space, and underwater, but not the nuclear arms race itself. Britain's Foreign Secretary, Lord Home, said he hoped it would mean that people could be free of the fear that 'the health of their unborn children is in danger from man-made poisons in the air'. The USA and USSR, with large unpopulated land masses, did not wish to ban testing underground; France refused to sign the treaty altogether.

In bygone days, commanders were taught that when in doubt, they should march their troops towards the sound of gunfire. I intend to march my troops towards the sound of gunfire.
Jo Grimond gives his fellow-Liberals a whiff of grapeshot at the Party's Annual Assembly in Llandudno, 14 September 1963.

We are redefining our socialism in terms of the scientific revolution. The Britain that is going to be forged in the white heat of this scientific revolution will be no place for restrictive practices or outdated methods on either side of industry.
Harold Wilson, addressing a rather puzzled Labour Party conference on 1 October 1963, aims to usher in the age of the classless technocrat.

After half a century of democratic advance, the whole process has ground to a halt with a Fourteenth Earl.
18 October 1963: Harold Wilson welcomes the new Conservative Party leader and Prime Minister, Sir Alec Douglas-Home, formerly Lord Home, who renounced his title in order to sit in the Commons, using the process pioneered by the socialist Tony Benn. With his administration tottering under the weight of the Profumo Affair and other scandals, Harold Macmillan was persuaded to resign, on the grounds that he might not have long to live, after a prostate operation: a prognosis that was to prove hugely premature. Deputy Leader R. A. 'Rab' Butler had been expected to succeed, but was rejected after 'the soundings' had been taken: chiefly instrumental in this process was the Chairman of the 1922 Committee, John Morrison MP, who, claiming proudly that he had never read a book in his life, was known to dislike Butler's 'cleverness'. Douglas-Home rewarded him later with one of the last hereditary peerages, the Barony of Margadale in Islay, where Morrison was an absentee landlord. Senior Tory MPs Iain MacLeod

and Enoch Powell – both also considered rather too 'clever' – refused to serve under the new PM.

~

I suppose Mr Wilson, when you come to think about it, is the fourteenth Mr Wilson.
Sir Alec Douglas-Home, TV interview, 21 October.

~

He is used to dealing with estate workers. I cannot see how anyone can say he is out of touch.
Caroline Douglas-Home, the PM's daughter, quoted in the Daily Herald, 21 October 1963.

~

Everybody should have an equal chance – but they shouldn't have a flying start.
Harold Wilson defines Labour's egalitarianism; quoted in the Observer's 'Sayings of the Year', 1963.

Christ in this country would quite likely have been arrested under the Suppression of Communism Act.
Joost de Blank, Dutch-born British churchman, comments on South Africa; quoted in the Observer, 27 October 1963.

Well, Mr President, you can't say that the people of Dallas haven't given you a nice welcome!
Mrs John Connally, wife of the Governor of Texas, welcomes John F. Kennedy, 22 November 1963; the visit had been undertaken with some trepidation on the part of Presidential staff in view of Texan hostility to many of Kennedy's policies, particularly his pursuit of racial integration. Security men were particularly anxious about the planned drive in an open car, but Kennedy had insisted it go ahead as planned.

This monstrous act has taken from us a great statesman and a valiant man.
Sir Winston Churchill.

~

A piece of each of us died at that moment.
Senator Michael J. Mansfield.

The real 1960s began on November 22nd, 1963. ... It came to seem that Kennedy's murder opened some malign trap door in American culture, and the wild bats flapped out.
Lance Morrow, Time, 14 November 1983. The moment most people over 45 can always remember,

POLITICAL SLOGANS of THE SIXTIES

I'M VOTING
FOR
NIXON
NO GIVE AWAYS!
Remember Yalta?
NO APOLOGIES!
Remember the Summit?
NO PIE IN THE SKY!
Remember, it's YOUR money
Jack Will Play Poker With
Perhaps he wrote it himself: Republican Presidential campaign, 1960.

Experience Counts
Slightly snappier: Republican Presidential campaign, 1960.

New Frontier
Democrat Presidential campaign, 1960.

Let's get America moving again.
Democrat Presidential campaign, 1960.

Let's Go With Labour
Labour Party slogan, general election, 1964.

Thirteen wasted years...
... of 'Tory misrule': never an official Labour slogan, but widely used by Harold Wilson in the 1964 election.

All the Way with LBJ
Democrat Presidential campaign slogan, 1964.

In Your Heart You Know He's Right
Republican Presidential campaign slogan (of Barry Goldwater), 1964.

You know Labour Government works.
Labour Party, general election, 1966.

Action not words.
Conservative Party slogan, general election, 1966.

Nixon's the One
Republican Presidential campaign slogan, 1968.

and the beginning of several conspiracy theories: US President John Fitzgerald Kennedy is shot in the head as he is driven through Dallas, Texas, in an open car, and dies as his wife cradles his head. Governor Connally, also aged 46, was seriously wounded. Hours later, Vice-President Lyndon Baines Johnson was sworn in as President, as Jackie Kennedy, suddenly a widow, stood at his side, her pink dress still stained with her husband's blood. Police arrested Lee Harvey Oswald, said to be the chairman of a pro-Castro 'Fair Play For Cuba Committee', alleging that he had fired the shots from a book depository. Two days later, as he was being transferred to the County Gaol, he was shot dead in front of TV cameras by Jack Rubinstein, known as Jack Ruby, a night-club owner who, as an old buddy of the Dallas Police, had been allowed to mingle with reporters as Oswald was being led from police head-quarters via an underground car park. Rubinstein had advanced stomach cancer; he was found guilty and sentenced to death in March 1964 and died in prison hospital pending appeal.

The publication of the Warren Commission's report in September 1964, which found that both Oswald and Rubinstein acted alone and were not part of any conspiracy, did little to quell speculation; the Mafia, the CIA, the FBI, the KGB and the Ku Klux Klan – individually, and in various permutations – form the basis of most alternative theories.

Originally, the Africans had the land and the English had the Bible. Then the missionaries came to Africa and got the Africans to close their eyes and fold their hands and pray. And when they opened their eyes, the English had the land and the Africans had the Bible.
Jomo Kenyatta, former Mau Mau internee and President of Kenya, which achieved independence on 12 December 1963, the 34th African territory to do so since Harold Macmillan's 'wind of change' speech of January 1960. (The above quotation has also been attributed, in various forms, to Chief Dan George and Archbishop Desmond Tutu.)

I myself have become a Gaullist only little by little.
President Charles de Gaulle, quoted in the Observer's 'Sayings of the Year', 1963.

1964

Young people are tired of wearing essentially the same as their mothers.
British designer Mary Quant, who opened the country's first 'boutique', lambasts Paris fashion on 13 January 1964 – the year Britain started to swing.

This Administration here and now declares unconditional war on poverty in America.
President Lyndon B. Johnson in his State of the Union message, 8 January 1964, launches the 'Great Society'.

We don't think they'll do anything in this market.
Capitol Records' chief Alan Livingston is pessimistic on the eve of The Beatles' first US tour, which began on 8 February. Thousands of screaming fans broke security barriers at Kennedy Airport, their song 'I Want to Hold Your Hand' went to Number 1, and they appeared to a record TV audience on the Ed Sullivan Show.

We aim to achieve a negotiated independence, but we can visualise circumstances which would drive us to do something else.
Ian Smith, 44, elected Prime Minister of Rhodesia in a whites-only ballot on 13 April 1964; Britain insisted that the African population 'be brought fully into the electoral process' in a Rhodesian Constitution before independence could be granted.

I do not deny that I planned sabotage. We had either to accept inferiority or fight against it by violence.
Nelson Mandela, whose diaries were found at ANC headquarters by South African police, is brought from prison to be tried for treason on 20 April 1964, and pleads guilty. He was sentenced to life imprisonment on Robben Island on 6 June.

It is inconceivable that the Viet Cong could ever defeat the armed forces of South Vietnam.
General William C. Westmoreland marks his appointment as Commander of some 20,000 US forces in Vietnam with a news conference in Saigon, 25 April 1964.

One fifth of the people are against everything all the time.
US Attorney-General Robert F. Kennedy, brother of the assassinated President, speech, University of Pennsylvania, 6 May 1964.

I shall soon become an apprentice again, though whether in heaven or hell I do not know.
The 'hands-on' newspaper proprietor Lord Beaverbrook, who died at the age of 85 on 9 June 1964.

I call on all citizens to eliminate the last vestiges of injustice in America. Let us close the springs of racial poison.
President Lyndon B. Johnson signs the Civil Rights Act on 2 July 1964, after fighting a tough rearguard action to prevent it being weakened by Congress. It outlawed racial discrimination in employment, public accommodation, publicly-owned facilities, union membership, and federally funded programmes.

I didn't just screw Ho Chi Minh. I cut his pecker off.
President Johnson rejoices at the US bombing of North Vietnam, 12 July 1964.

I would remind you that extremism in defence of liberty is no vice. And let me remind you also that moderation in the pursuit of justice is no virtue!
The right-wing McCarthyite and racist, Senator Barry M. Goldwater, nominated as Republican Party Presidential candidate in a bid to reverse integration and halt welfare programmes, speech at the Republican Convention, San Francisco, 16 July 1964. An attempt by the liberal Nelson Rockefeller, Governor of New York State, to condemn the activities of the fanatical John Birch Society was howled down by delegates.

The world must never forget that aggression unchallenged is aggression unleashed. We of the United States have not forgotten.
President Lyndon B. Johnson, TV broadcast, 7 August 1964, after US planes bombed North Vietnamese installations in retaliation for an abortive attempt to torpedo the USS Maddox in the Gulf of Tonkin. Congress voted approval for him to take 'all necessary action' against the Communist regime.

I am the most fortunate self-taught harpist and non-speaking actor who ever lived.
Harpo Marx, who died during the course of a heart operation on 28 September 1964, aged 70.

If you start throwing hedgehogs under me, I will throw two porcupines under you.
It was remarks like these that made Western diplomats wonder if Nikita Khrushchev made up Old Russian Proverbs as he went along. He was ousted in a carefully planned Kremlin coup on 15 October, denounced as a 'wilful meddler', sent into retirement and purdah, and succeeded by Leonid Brezhnev (Party leader) and Alexei Kosygin (Prime Minister).

I am restless with remedies for the problems the Tories have criminally neglected in thirteen years of misrule.
Prime Minister Harold Wilson, whose Labour Party secured an overall majority of four in the General Election, 16 October 1964, promises 'purposive planning' and 'dynamic action'.

We are not about to send American boys nine or ten thousand miles away from home to do what Asian boys ought to be doing for themselves.
President Lyndon B. Johnson seeks, in Akron, Ohio, on 21 October 1964, to allay fears that the powers Congress has granted him will lead to an escalation in the number of US troops in Vietnam. Between 1964 and 1968, however, their numbers grew from c. 20,000 to c. 500,000.

It is a tribute to the discipline, wise restraint and majestic courage of the millions of Negroes and white persons of goodwill ... seeking to establish a reign of justice and the rule of love.
Dr Martin Luther King, awarded the 1964 Nobel Peace Prize, 24 October 1964.

I am going to build the kind of nation that President Roosevelt hoped for, President Truman worked for, and President Kennedy died for.
President Lyndon B. Johnson, on beating Senator Barry M. Goldwater with 60 per cent of the popular vote, 3 November 1964.

My Government will protect all liberties but one – the liberty to do away with other liberties.
President Gustavo Diaz Ordaz of Mexico, inaugurated in 1964, on the basic conundrum of democracy.

This case has no precedent and will, I hope and believe, have no successor.
Roy Jenkins, British Home Secretary, recommends a Royal Pardon for Timothy Evans, wrongly hanged in 1950 for the murder of his baby daughter; it was granted in 1966. On 16 December 1964, the House of Commons voted by 355 to 170 to abolish the death penalty for murder; the Lords did not seek to reverse the vote as it had been carried by such a large margin of 'unwhipped' MPs.

1965

How pleasant to meet Mr Eliot – with his conversation so nicely restricted to What precisely and If and Perhaps and But.
The poet and critic Thomas Stearns Eliot, who died on 4 January 1965, aged 76.

Try Belfast.
A postal worker's amendment to a letter from Seán Lemass, Prime Minister of the Irish Republic, to Terence O'Neill, Prime Minister of Northern Ireland, accepting the latter's invitation to talks on 15 January 1965 and addressed to 'Stormont Castle, Dublin'. It was the first ever meeting on Irish soil between the leaders of North and South.

The nation had the lion's heart. I had the luck to give the roar.
Sir Winston Churchill, in a speech on his 80th birthday, 30 November 1954. He died on 24 January 1965 and lay in state in Westminster Abbey for three days, where at one stage the chiefs of the armed services kept the watch. After a service at St Paul's, attended by 3000 people and watched on television by 350 million people in Europe alone, his coffin was taken up the Thames from Tower Pier to Waterloo Station; then, adhering to precise arrangements Churchill himself had made, it was transported to the village churchyard near his ancestral home of Blenheim Palace, where he was buried on 30 January.

A girl's real gone on Crimplene!
Arguably the nastiest dress fabric ever invented: it began to be heavily advertised in 1965, and has been heavily stocked in charity shops ever since.

If Negroes could vote ... our children would not be crippled by segregated schools and the whole community might live together in harmony.

Eleven years after Brown v. Board of Education of Topeka, *Dr Martin Luther King is arrested yet again on 1 February 1965 for parading without a licence in Selma, Alabama; the following month, he and his wife led 25,000 people on a civil rights march in Montgomery, while in Selma itself, 50 large bombs were discovered in black institutions and shops, and at the homes of leading black citizens. In April, Home Secretary Roy Jenkins announced that it would become a criminal offence to incite racial hatred; the first of Britain's Race Relations Acts followed in November.*

~

It is a great shock at the age of five or six to find that in a world of Gary Coopers you are the Indian.

The black US writer James Baldwin addresses the Cambridge Union, 17 February 1965.

———————

Many will call me an adventurer – and that I am, only one of a different sort: one of those who risks his skin to prove his platitudes.

The Argentinian-born revolutionary Che Guevara leaves his home in Cuba to join guerrillas in Bolivia, 1965: from his last letter to his parents.

We will keep political power in white hands in order to maintain civilized standards in our country.

Financed by cattle ranchers and tobacco growers, Ian Smith's white supremacist Rhodesian Front Party gains all 50 'European seats' in the General Election, 7 May 1965.

It is dedicated in perpetuity to the American people ... in memory of a man whom in death my people still mourn and whom in life they loved and admired.

Queen Elizabeth II dedicates an acre of meadow and woodland in Runnymede, close to the spot where the Magna Carta was signed, to the memory of John Fitzgerald Kennedy, 14 May 1965.

The Soviet people sincerely congratulate the two cosmonauts and the American scientists.

Moscow TV spokesman, 3 June, as Major Edward White carries out the first American

'spacewalk'; *the USSR had achieved the feat in March. But an attempt at an orbital rendezvous between the Titan launcher and the* Gemini 4 *spacecraft, essential to Moon landing plans, was cancelled.*

I do not wish to be the holder of an award that places me on the same level as these vulgar nincompoops.

Canadian MP Hector Dupuis returns his OBE as the Beatles are each awarded the MBE in the Queen's Birthday Honours, 15 June 1965.

We have learned at a terrible and brutal

••••••••••••••••••••••••••••••••••

I can't get no satisfaction.

Jagger/Richard – The Rolling Stones, song 1965.

••••••••••••••••••••••••••••••••••

cost that retreat does not bring safety and weakness does not bring peace.

A month after US troops were used in combat in Vietnam for the first time, President Johnson orders 50,000 more to be posted there on 28 July 1965.

———————

The vote is the most powerful instrument ever devised by man for breaking down injustice and destroying the terrible walls which imprison men because they are different from other men.

President Johnson's address on signing the Voting Rights Bill, 6 August 1965.

~

This strikes from the hand of the Negro the very weapons with which he is achieving his own emancipation.

President Johnson on rioting in Watts, Los Angeles, 15 August 1965: 28 people died and 676 were wounded, over 1000 fires were started and 2157 looters were arrested. The trouble began after Los Angeles police beat up a black man whom they suspected of driving while drunk.

———————

I too had thoughts once of being an intellectual, but I found it too difficult.

Attributed reply to an African who refused to undertake a menial duty on the grounds that he was an intellectual: Albert Schweitzer, the Doctor of Philosophy, Theology and Music, who founded a leper hospital, and died aged 90 on 4 September 1965.

Vinland – a new land discovered by Bjarni and Leif Eriksson, extremely fertile, even having vines.
Inscription on a map dated by radiocarbon tests to 1440, 50 years before Columbus, and published on 11 October 1965; Eriksson is known from other sources to have lived in the 11th century. Subsequent archaeological excavations on the eastern seaboard above and below the US-Canadian border have confirmed that the Vikings did indeed get there first.

~

Nidma
Harold Wilson's acronym for Britain's basic pre-condition for the future of Rhodesia: No independence without majority rule. He flew to Salisbury (now Harare) on 28 October for a crisis meeting with Ian Smith, who did not yield to Wilson's demands.

~

Whereas in the course of human affairs history has shown that it may become necessary for a people … to assume amongst other nations the separate and equal status to which they are entitled....
In this case, for 'a people' read '220,000 whites' rather than '4 million Africans': Ian Smith apes the US Declaration of Independence and hijacks the hour and day of Remembrance to broadcast his 'unilateral declaration of independence' for Rhodesia: 11 a.m., 11 November 1965. Smith ordered Britain's colonial Governor, Sir Humphrey Gibbs, to resign, and he responded by sacking Smith; each ignored the other.

~

Don't sell the white man down the river.
According to Smith, this is what Queen Elizabeth II said to Harold Wilson before he left for talks in Salisbury; Downing Street denounced the claim as a lie. On 16 November the Queen gave Royal Assent to the Southern Rhodesia Bill, and economic sanctions against the rebel state were declared throughout the Commonwealth. South Africa, which officially recognized Smith's regime as the lawful government, at once set up ways in which they could be broken, often by British companies, and particularly in the case of oil

and petroleum. Britain ruled out the use of armed force; a scheme to destroy Rhodesia's main rail supply route from the air earned the Liberal MP for North Devon the soubriquet 'Bomber Thorpe'.

The cumulative effects of the economic and financial sanctions may well bring the rebellion to an end within a matter of weeks rather than months.
UK Prime Minister Harold Wilson, to Sierra Leone Prime Minister Sir Albert Margai, at a Commonwealth conference in Lagos on 16 January 1966. The rebellion continued for another 14 years.
In the March 1966 General Election, Labour's majority was increased to 96.

I doubt if there are any rational people to whom the word 'fuck' would be particularly diabolical, revolting or totally forbidden. I think that anything that can be printed or said can also be seen.
The first clearly audible use of the f-word on British television: the BBC programme BBC3, 13 November 1965. Critic and producer Kenneth Tynan was asked by Richard Dimbleby if he would allow a play depicting sexual intercourse on stage to be put on at the National Theatre. Dimbleby died of cancer, aged 52, on 22 December.

There are moments when I have such an eagerness for death that I could fly to it as to the arms of a lover. It seems to me to offer the final absolute freedom.
William Somerset Maugham, in a 90th birthday interview in January 1964; he died, a few weeks short of his 92nd, on 16 December 1965.

1966

We wanted to get rid of rotten and corrupt ministers and political parties.
Major Chukwuma Nzugwa, an Ibo officer who led an army coup against the predominantly Hausa (and Muslim) government of Nigeria on 16 January 1966; at least 50 officers and senior politicians – including Prime Minister Sir Abubakar Tafawa Balewa – were killed. Following a counter-coup, Hausa troops declared open season on Ibo people; more than a thousand were hunted down and shot in the city of Kano on 3 October.

I shall strive to create what my father used to call a climate of peace.
Indira Gandhi, daughter of Nehru, who became Prime Minister of India on 19 January 1966 following the death of Lal Shastri, who had just signed a peace agreement with Pakistan; the two countries had been at war over Kashmir.

You rebuild a bridge which for centuries has lain fallen between the Church of Rome and the Church of Canterbury; a bridge of respect, of esteem and of charity.
Pope Paul VI welcomes Archbishop Ramsey to the Sistine Chapel on 23 March 1966, the first meeting between the leaders of Roman and Anglican Catholicism in 400 years.

A typical triumph of modern science to find the only part of Randolph that was not malignant and remove it.
Evelyn Waugh, March 1964 diary entry. Randolph Churchill had entered hospital to have a suspected cancerous lung removed, but the growth turned out to be benign. Waugh, the reactionary satirist and novelist, died aged 62 at Combe Florey, Somerset, on 10 April 1966.

There are a million Negroes in Mississippi. I think they'll take care of me.
James Meredith, who became the first black student at the University of Mississippi in 1962, prepares to join a civil rights march into the State on 7 June 1966. He was shot in the back and legs shortly after a car carrying white supremacists waving Confederate flags had 'buzzed' the marchers. Saying, 'The day for the Negro man being a coward is over,' he recovered to rejoin marchers at Jackson on the 25th.

The time has come to call a halt.
Harold Wilson makes a Prime Ministerial TV broadcast on 20 July 1966, and announced a six-month freeze on pay and dividends, followed by another six months of 'severe restraint'; prices were to be frozen for a year but purchase tax was increased, and there were to be new curbs on hire purchase buying and sterling allowances for holidaymakers.

We have decided it is my duty to stay.
George Brown, Minister for Economic Affairs, is noticeably 'tired and emotional' as he reads a statement on the steps of Number 10 at midnight on 20 July. He had offered his resignation at least five times in the previous 48 hours; Frank Cousins, the former trade union leader, had

Space – the final frontier.

Star Trek, *with William Shatner as Captain James T. Kirk, split its first infinitive in 1966.*

already resigned as Minister of Technology in protest at what he called 'two-faced leadership'.

Some people are on the pitch – they think it's all over. It is now!
Kenneth Wolstenholme, BBC TV commentator. At the end of extra time in the World Cup Final at Wembley Stadium, London, on 30 July 1966, the referee blows his whistle twice: once for an infringement, and then to signal England's victory, by 4 goals to 2, over West Germany. The rest is nostalgia.

A revolution is not a dinner party, or writing an essay, or doing embroidery. A revolution is an insurrection, an act of violence by which one class overthrows another.
Spelling it out in August in wall posters all over the People's Republic of China: the words of Chairman Mao Tse-tung in 1927 herald the 'Cultural Revolution', a great terror in which gangs of Red Guards, many of them teenagers, began an organized pogrom against the country's 'bourgeois reactionary elements': teachers, lawyers, writers, artists, doctors, engineers, and other intellectual and professional people were forced to leave their work, homes and regions to be 're-educated' in slave labour programmes; some were simply beaten to death. Mao's do-it-yourself Stalin Purge cost millions of lives.

The North Vietnamese cannot take the punishment any more in the South. I think we can bring the war to a conclusion within the next year, possibly within the next six months.
US General S.L.A. Marshall, 12 September 1966. The following month, President Johnson paid a morale-boosting visit to US forces in Vietnam.

I did it because the government is doing too much for the coloureds and nothing for the poor whites.
An ironic end for Prime Minister Hendrik Verwoerd, the father of apartheid: stabbed to

death in the National Assembly by the Bible-quoting Demetrio Tsafeñdas, a Greek-Portuguese racist fanatic and parliamentary messenger. Verwoerd was succeded by Balthazar Johannes Vorster on 19 September – the same day that singer Joan Baez led a procession of black children to an all-white school in Mississippi.

I can tell you how to make money in newspapers – own them!

On 30 September 1966, Lord Thomson of Fleet – famous for describing his ownership of Scottish Television as 'a licence to print money' – acted on his own 1961 dictum by buying The Times from the Astor family to add to his portfolio of titles: the Thunderer now became the sister paper of the Sunday Times, which he already owned. In May 1967 the paper started to carry news on its front page; two years later, circulation had doubled to 451,000.

••••••••••••••••••••••••••••••••••

All the lonely people, where do they all come from?

Lennon/McCartney – The Beatles,
'Eleanor Rigby', 1966.

••••••••••••••••••••••••••••••••••

We demand that Art be free of all control exercised by reason, aesthetics or morals.

The poet André Breton, who wrote the 1924 Surrealist Manifesto, died on 28 September 1966, aged 70.

I don't think any of us can find words to describe this tragedy.

Prime Minister Harold Wilson visits the Welsh coalmining village of Aberfan on 27 October 1966. A simple description of what happened is shattering enough: after days of heavy rain activated a spring deep in a spoil heap above the village school, millions of tonnes of slag and slurry engulfed the building and nearby houses, killing 116 children and 28 adults. On 3 August 1967 the report of the Official Enquiry pinned the blame on the National Coal Board for ignoring warnings of the tip's instability.

In a season of torrential rain all over Europe, northern Italy experienced its worst storms for a millennium and tens of millions of pounds' worth of books and art treasures were destroyed or damaged

when the River Arno burst its banks in Florence, tearing the Door of Paradise from the Cathedral.

The people of Rhodesia find these terms utterly repugnant.

On 6 December 1966, rebel leader Ian Smith rejects British proposals for independence put to him on board HMS Tiger by Prime Minister Wilson, who demanded an end to UDI, the placing of Rhodesian armed forces under British command, and the inclusion of at least two Africans in the government.

1967

She's going – she's going – I'm almost on my back....

The last words of Donald Campbell, who died on 4 January 1967 while trying to break his own world water-speed record in Bluebird on Coniston Water. The boat, which probably hit a semi-submerged piece of wood, reared into the air, somersaulted and broke up as it re-entered the lake; Campbell's body was never recovered.

Life is much easier, being an Earl. It has changed me a lot. I'm much nastier now.

Columnist and publisher the Earl of Arran, Sunday Times, 15 January 1967.

You've got to forget about this civilian. Whenever you drop bombs, you're going to hit civilians.

Senator Barry Goldwater talks tough to 'liberals' disturbed at scenes of 'collateral damage' in Vietnam in the TV news programmes, 23 January 1967. On 26 February, 25,000 airborne US troops attacked 'War Zone C', a Viet-Cong-held area running right up to the Cambodian border.

But of course, it was all fun … I do not want to cross swords with the peasants.

A piece of UK television history: on David Frost's TV show on 5 February 1967, Emil Savundra makes light of his business adventure and declines to face some of its victims – though he was obliged to all the same. He ran the cut-price Fire, Auto & Marine Insurance Co., which collapsed with debts of £1.4 million (shortly after a Board of Trade Inquiry had found there to be 'no immediate danger of insolvency') leaving tens of thousands of people uninsured and uncompensated. Arrested on 10 February, Savundra was subsequently convicted of fraud, fined £50,000, and gaoled for eight years.

This is the greatest ever peacetime threat to Britain.
Harold Wilson holds a crisis 'mini-cabinet' meeting at RAF Culdrose, Cornwall, before ordering the RAF to bomb the broken-backed oil tanker, Torrey Canyon, with 1200 gallons of napalm on 30 March 1967, after much of the 100,000 tonnes of crude oil it was carrying had washed up, along with thousands of bedraggled seabirds, on West Country tourist beaches.

We shall suppress any resistance to our efforts to save Greece from internal enemies.
Colonel Georges Papadopoulos leads a right-wing military coup on 21 April 1967; King Constantine's attempted counter-coup in December failed, and Greece began a seven-year reign of Colonels, in which strikes were outlawed and resistance suppressed through censorship, arrest, torture, indefinite imprisonment and 'disappearance'.

I ain't got no quarrel with them Viet Congs. No Viet Cong ever called me nigger.
The appeal against his draft (based on grounds of religious conscience) of boxer and Muslim convert Muhammad Ali (formerly Cassius Clay) falls on deaf ears on 30 April 1967; he was stripped of his title and sentenced to imprisonment. Both rulings were revoked in 1970.

There will be boundless joy in France when Britain joins the Common Market, but there are formidable obstacles to this application.
President de Gaulle again says, 'Non', this time to Harold Wilson on 16 May 1967. He demanded an end to the Sterling Area, and to the British-American 'special relationship'.

I can honestly say that I was never affected by the question of the success of an undertaking. If I felt it was the right thing to do, I was for it regardless of the possible outcome.
Golda Meir, who had recently retired as Israeli Foreign Minister, quoted in Golda Meir: Woman With a Cause, Marie Syrkin.
Towards the end of May 1967 President Nasser of the United Arab Republic (of Egypt and Iraq) ordered UN peacekeeping forces to leave the Egypt–Israel border and closed to Gulf of Aqaba to Israeli shipping; on 30 May he signed a military treaty with Jordan. Sensing an imminent invasion, Israel launched a pre-emptive air strike against

Egypt on 5 June; the Six Day War had begun with the destruction of 374 Egyptian warplanes on the ground. In a few days' fighting Israel was triumphant, taking the Gaza Strip and the Sinai peninsula from Egypt and advancing to the Suez Canal, and seizing Bethlehem, Hebron, Jerusalem and much of the West Bank from Jordan; despite Syria's acceptance of a UN-brokered cease-fire, Israel then advanced into Syria and captured the Golan Heights. Fighting ended on 10 June, with over 100,000 casualties, and with Israel in possession of territory many times greater than its own, much of it occupied by Palestinian Arabs.

I'm the world's original gradualist. I just think ninety-odd years is gradual enough.
In 1958, this was US judge Thurgood Marshall's reaction to President Eisenhower's call for black people to be patient. On 13 June 1967 Marshall became the first black member of the US Supreme Court.

WHO BREAKS A BUTTERFLY ON A WHEEL?
Editorial in The Times, *1 July 1967, is critical of the prison sentences given to Rolling Stones Keith Richard (one year) and Mick Jagger (three months) for possession of marijuana. The sentences were quashed by the Court of Appeal on 31 July.*

A riot is at bottom the language of the unheard.
Dr Martin Luther King, in Chaos or Community *(1967). Race riots broke out all over the USA in the summer of 1967; one of the worst was in Detroit on 27 July. After two black women were shot dead by police, a raid on a party at an illegal drinking club to celebrate the homecoming from Vietnam of a black soldier was the spark that ignited a riot that the 101st and 84th Parachute Divisions were sent to deal with. President Johnson ordered a commission of enquiry.*

Vive le Québec libre!
Referring also on 25 July 1967 to 'the century

If you are goin' to San Francisco,
Be sure to wear some flowers in your hair.

Scott McKenzie: invitation to the Summer of Love, and an Annus Mirabilis of music, 1967.

of oppression which followed the British conquest', President de Gaulle so offended his Canadian government hosts that they cut short his visit.

Prick Up Your Ears.
Title of an unmade film by the playwright Joe Orton; it was suggested by his companion Keith Halliwell, who murdered him on 9 August 1967. He was 34.

The House of Lords is like a glass of champagne that has stood for five days.
The attributed opinion of Clement (later Earl) Attlee, who died on 8 October, aged 84.

From now on the pound abroad is worth 14 per cent or so less in terms of other currencies. This does not mean, of course, that the pound here in Britain, in your pocket or purse or in your bank, has been devalued.
Harold Wilson, Prime Ministerial broadcast, 19 November 1967. Devaluation became inevitable as Britain's gold and currency reserves were used up in an attempt to keep sterling at $2.80. The 'credit squeeze' was tightened, the bank rate went up to 8 per cent, and taxes were increased by £200 million; arrangements were made for huge international loans and credits. Chancellor of the Exchequer James Callaghan, who had opposed this reversal of the previous three years' fiscal policy, swapped places with Roy Jenkins at the Home Office.

I don't know how much money I've got. I did ask the accountant how much it came to. I wrote it down on a bit of paper. But I've lost the bit of paper.
John Lennon, interviewed by Hunter Davies for The Beatles, *1967. In the year that saw the release of the album* Sergeant Pepper's Lonely Hearts Club Band *it must have been a biggish bit of paper.*

● ●

C'mon parents, throughout the land,
Pack your boys off to Vietnam....
Be the first ones on your block
T'have your boy come home in a box!

McDonald – Country Joe & The Fish, 'I-Feel-Like-I'm-Fixin'-To-Die Rag', 1967.

● ●

Come and see the light at the end of the tunnel.
The wording on the invitations to a New Year's Eve party at the US Embassy in Saigon, Sotu Vietnam, 31 December 1967. New Year is 'Tet' in Vietnamese; and in January 1968 the Viet Cong launched a 'Tet Offensive' against South Vietnamese cities, including the capital where the US Embassy was captured. US parachute troops fought from room to room to capture it back, and the Viet Cong remained in possession of the suburb of Cholon. Thirty US aircraft were destroyed at the Da Nang airbase, and the US military headquarters at Bien Hoa was cut off from the capital.

1968

To save the town, it became necessary to destroy it.
Attributed by Associated Press to 'a US army officer in Ben Tre' on 8 February 1968. On 24 February, US-South Vietnamese forces recaptured the second city, Hue, after virtually destroying the occupied Imperial Palace in the process.

~

Buddha will understand.
Comment of South Vietnamese General Loan after shooting a 'suspected Viet Cong' in the head in a street in Saigon. The killing was broadcast on TV news programmes in the USA, and helped to fuel the growing anti-war movement, which was equally strong in Britain: on 17 March 1968, around 100,000 people assembled in Trafalgar Square and marched to the US Embassy in Grosvenor Square, where there were violent confrontations with mounted police; when 250,000 marched there in October there was very little trouble. On 12 March the liberal anti-war Democrat Eugene McCarthy gained 40 per cent of the votes in the New Hampshire primary, the first ballot of the 1968 US Presidential campaign; four days later, Senator Robert F. Kennedy, also a 'dove', announced his own candidacy for the Democrat nomination. On the same day, Johnson ordered another '35,000–50,000' men to Vietnam.

~

It is true that a house divided against itself is a house that cannot stand. There is a division in the American house now and believing this as I do, I have concluded that I should not permit the

Presidency to become involved in the partisan divisions that are developing in this political year. Accordingly, I shall not seek, and I will not accept, the nomination of my party for another term as your President.
His Presidency weighed down by Vietnam and with visions of the Great Society receding over the political horizon, 'LBJ' bows out in a US television broadcast, 31 March 1968.

It is possible that the five girl typists of Surbiton will, when the history of these confused times is written, become as famous as the six martyrs of Tolpuddle.
On the other hand, maybe not. The Daily Mirror enthusiastically applauds the five 'girls' who in January 1968 offered to work an extra half-hour a day for no pay as their contribution to the 'I'm Backing Britain' campaign. Prime Minister Wilson quietly abandoned the bandwagon as it sank into the sands of public indifference; the revelation by a rival newspaper that the Mirror's *'I'm Backing Britain' T-shirts were made in Portugal did not help.*

We have a responsibility to our own people at home as well as to a million holders of British passports abroad.
British Home Secretary James Callaghan announces the first of a succession of increasingly restrictive Immigration Bills; this, on 22 February 1968, restricted the number of work vouchers allocated to Kenyan immigrants to 1500 a year. Kenyan Asians, persecuted at home by their African government, were at that time arriving in the UK at the rate of 1000 a week.

Most British statesmen have either drunk too much or womanised too much. I never fell into the second category.
The former is, of course, well-known as an inhibitor of the latter; George Brown (later Lord George-Brown) looks back in 1974. On 15 March 1968 he resigned as Foreign Secretary, blaming the Prime Minister's 'dictatorial style of government'. In an all-night Commons sitting on 14–15 March he had appeared notably 'tired and emotional', and he was alseep at home in the morning when required to attend a Cabinet meeting.

Longevity has its place, but I'm not concerned about that right now. I want to do God's will and He's allowed me to go the mountain, and I've looked over, and I've seen the Promised Land. I may not get there with you, but I want you to know tonight that we as a people will get to the Promised Land. So, I'm happy tonight. Mine eyes have seen the glory of the coming of the Lord!
Dr Martin Luther King, speech, Memphis, Tennessee, where he had gone to support a strike of garbage workers, 3 April 1968. He was gunned down the following day by a white man in a white Mustang; there were riots all over the USA as news of the killing broke. On 6 June 1968 police in London arrested James Earl Ray, wanted by the FBI for King's murder. The fact that Ray, who appeared to have no visible means of support, was able to buy the car and travel in five countries in the previous year raised suspicions that he was a hired gunman.

Be sure to sing 'Precious Lord' tonight, and sing it well.
According to the Rev. Jesse Jackson, one of the contenders for Dr King's mantle, these were the civil rights leader's dying words to him.

As I look ahead I am filled with foreboding. Like the Roman, I seem to see 'the River Tiber foaming with much blood.'
Enoch Powell MP, UK Opposition spokesman on Defence, in a speech on immigration policy in Birmingham, 21 April 1968, chooses his quotation (from Virgil's Aeniad, Book VI) with great care – but it was not the classical allusion that registered with his audience, nor with his racist supporters in Britain. Tory leader Edward Heath at once sacked him from the 'Shadow Cabinet'; Powell then embarked on a crusade to save 'the British character'; a Gallup poll on 6 May suggested his anti-(coloured) immigration views had the support of 74 per cent of the people whose character he sought to protect.

La réforme, oui; la chienlit, non. [Reform, yes; bed-shitting, no.]
Oft-repeated mantra of President Charles de Gaulle as the mythical alliance of students and workers actually came to pass in France in May 1968, the 'Month of the Barricades' in Paris. After growing student unrest, much of anti-American, the authorities at the Sorbonne locked out all its students; about 30,000 of them took to streets in the first week of May and their demands became more generalized – and more philosophical, as their principal leader, Daniel Cohn-Bendit,

● ●

If you take the game of life seriously, if
you take your nervous system seriously,
if you take your sense organs seriously,
if you take the energy process seriously,
you must turn on, tune in,
and drop out.

Dr Timothy Leary, The Politics of Ecstasy,
1968.

● ●

*was joined by Jean-Paul Sartre. On 14 May,
French trade unions ordered a one-day general
strike in sympathy with the students and in
protest against unemployment, poor state
salaries, censorship and stifling centralization.
The Communist Party – which took very little part
in any of the action – reminded anyone who cared
to listen that it stood for the overthrow of the system, and de Gaulle put the armed forces on alert to
enforce Martial Law. The franc plummeted and
France's gold reserves dwindled.*

The voice we have just heard is that of
dictatorship; the French people will
silence that voice.
*Francois Mitterrand, French Socialist leader,
accuses the President of inciting civil war as, on
30 May 1968, de Gaulle tells France that it is
threatened with Communist dictatorship – and
that to prevent this he has renamed all regional
Prefects 'Commissioners of the Republic' and
given them full powers to suppress subversion,
and has also dissolved the National Assembly so
that he can rule by decree, pending a General
Election on 30 June. The result proved Mitterrand
wrong: de Gaulle's UD-V Party secured a majority
over all other parties combined, while the
Socialists and Communists saw their representation cut by half. But unrest persisted.*

My thanks to all of you. And now it's on
to Chicago and let's win there.
*Just before midnight on 4 June 1968 at the
Ambassador Hotel, Los Angeles, Robert F.
Kennedy thanks supporters who helped him win
the California primary with 50 per cent of the
vote.*

~

Oh God! Not again!
*A Kennedy aide screams as 24-year-old
Palestinian immigrant Sirhan Sirhan fires five*

*shots into the candidate at close range just after
midnight on 5 June, in a kitchen passage of the
hotel; his bodyguards had avoided the public
areas as a security risk. He was pronounced dead
20 hours later, at the age of 42.*

In the service of the people we followed
such a policy that socialism would not
lose its human face.
*Aleksandr Dubcek, the 46-year-old President of
Czechoslovakia, interviewed in* Rudé Právo, *19
July 1968. Since he came to power in March,
Czechoslovaks had enjoyed greater economic,
political and cultural freedom; they had even
begun to read real news in the papers. President
Brezhnev of the USSR, claiming that American
spies were in Czechoslovakia preparing for a West
German invasion, moved 1000 tanks and
75,000 troops up to the border, and began
'manoeuvres' there. On 29 July he suggested they
be invited in 'to help protect the Czechoslovak
people'.*

~

I was asked at the airport whether our
sovereignty was jeopardized and I am
saying frankly that it is not.
*Aleksandr Dubcek, 30 July 1968, after inconclu-
sive negotiations with Brezhnev. On 9 July
President Tito of Yugoslavia arrived for talks in
Prague, and on 16 July Dubcek signed a 20-year
pact with Romania.*

~

... when internal and external forces that
are hostile to socialism try to turn the
development of some socialist country
towards the restoration of a capitalist
regime; when socialism in that country
and the socialist community as a whole is
threatened...
*Part of the 'Brezhnev Doctrine' used to justify
Soviet 'intervention' in the affairs of another
Communist country.*

~

How could they do this to me? My entire
life has been devoted to co-operation
with the Soviet Union. This is my own
profound personal tragedy.
*Aleksandr Dubcek, as news came through that sev-
eral hundred thousand Soviet troops and tanks had
invaded his country on 22 August 1968; it was
reported on clandestine radio stations, which added
that three members of Dubcek's cabinet – who had
earlier urged a return to the old ways of government
– seemed quite satisfied to hear the news. The people*

of Prague crowded the streets and attempted to tell the troops that they were not invited, and should leave. Within a few hours the National Assembly and Communist Party HQ were occupied and the Czech news agency shut down. Telephone and telex lines were cut: it was a repeat of Hungary in 1956. Dubcek was arrested and taken to Moscow, where he was led from the airport in chains.

Sporadic resistance continued in the form of strikes, mass protests and non-cooperation for some months. Press censorship was reimposed by a regime more authoritarian than the one Dubcek had replaced; the ex-President himself was given a new job, as a clerk in a remote office of the Forestry Commission.

Let us begin by committing ourselves to the truth, to see it like it is and to tell it like it is, to find the truth, to speak the truth and live with the truth. That's what we'll do.
Richard Milhous Nixon accepts the Republican Party nomination for the Presidency in Miami on 8 August 1968 and unveils his campaign theme.

A Nixon-Agnew administration will abolish the credibility gap and re-establish the truth, the whole truth, as its policy.
Spiro T. Agnew, Nixon's running-mate, pursues the theme in his acceptance speech, 8 August 1968.

Get this thing straight once for all. The policeman isn't there to create disorder. The policeman is there to preserve disorder.
As the Democrat National Convention, where the anti-war vote was split between Eugene McCarthy and George McGovern, voted 3:2 against putting peace in Vietnam 'on the platform' and, on 29 August 1968, adopted Hubert Horatio Humphrey as candidate for the Presidency, anti-war protestors took to the streets of Chicago, where the police set about beating them up. Delegates accused their host, Mayor Richard Daley, of organizing 'Gestapo tactics' and a 'police riot': this was Daley's public reply to reporters.

This is not a cricket team, but a team of troublemakers for South Africa's separate development policies.
On 17 September 1968, South African Prime Minister Vorster cancels the MCC's four month Test tour of his country after English cricket selectors pick all-rounder Basil d'Oliveira, a 'coloured' player born in Cape Province.

What we now expect – what we have a right to expect – are prompt, productive, serious and decisive negotiations in an atmosphere conducive to peace.
President Johnson announces a cessation of US bombing operations in North Vietnam on 1 November 1968 in an attempt to revive the notoriously unproductive Paris peace talks, which had stalled on – among other things – the issue of what size and shape the negotiating table should be.

I won without having to pay the price or make any deals.
Richard M. Nixon signals a 'clean administration' on 6 November 1968 as he defeats H. H. Humphrey by just over half a million popular votes and by 301 College votes to 191; the racist George Wallace, running as an 'American Independent', won 46.

We have reached an important point where the end begins to come into view.
General William C. Westmoreland, Commander of US forces in Vietnam, on prospects for victory, 21 November 1968.

We thought we could put the economy right in five years. We were wrong. It will probably take ten.
Possibly intended as a joke...? Tony Benn, Minister for Technology, 1968.

1969

The *News of the World* is as British as roast beef, and we intend it should remain so.
Stafford Summerfield, the paper's editor, wrote this as a hint to Czech-born Robert Maxwell that his owenership of the title would be unwelcome; on 1 January 1969 it was sold to Australian Rupert Murdoch instead.

It has been a very nasty and disappointing affair. Everyone is very upset.
Anonyomous Northern Ireland Civil Rights leader, after a Civil Rights march in Claudy was attacked by a Protestant mob, resulting in a pitched battle and a call-out for the riot squad on 3 January 1969. The Civil Rights movement campaigned for an end to discrimination against Roman Catholics, particularly in employment and housing, and in the franchise: only householders were

permitted to vote in local government elections, while Protestant- and Unionist-dominated local authorities ensured that the majority of householders in Council housing were Protestants and Unionists. The police – particularly the 'B-Specials' called in on this occasion – were seen as rabidly anti-Roman Catholic.

In a separate incident on the same day, a crowd of Nationalists attacked the Guildhall in Londonderry, where they had trapped the abrasive Unionist politician and Free Presbyterian minister, the Rev. Ian Paisley, who was later gaoled for three months on a conviction for unlawful assembly. In the General Election of 24 February Paisley ran Northern Ireland's Unionist Prime Minister, Sir Terence O'Neill, a close second in the Bann constituency, gaining 38 per cent of the vote; for 23 years O'Neill had been returned unopposed. On 29 April O'Neill advocated the introduction of one-person-one-vote for local government elections, and then resigned; he was succeeded by Major James Chichester-Clarke.

The coach has turned into a pumpkin and the mice have all run away.

Lady Bird Johnson, as her husband yields the Presidency to Richard M. Nixon on 20 January 1969.

Of all the men running, Richard Nixon is the most dangerous to have as President. I would never work for that man. That man is a disaster.

Professor Henry Kissinger on Nixon the candidate, 1968; in January 1969 he became the new President's adviser on National Security.

The conventional army loses if it does not win. The guerrilla wins if he does not lose.

Henry Kissinger on the Vietnam Peace negotiations, January 1969.

• •

You only have power over people so long as you don't take everything away from them. But when you've robbed a man of everything, he's no longer in your power – he's free again.

Alexander Solzhenitsyn, The First Circle, 1969. He was expelled from the Soviet Writers' Union the following year.

• •

My act has fulfilled its purpose, but let nobody else do it.

The dying words of Czech student Jan Palach, aged 21, as reported by a weeping announcer on Czech TV on 21 January 1969. Palach had set fire to himself in Wenceslas Square on 19 January as a protest against the Soviet invasion and occupation of his country; a week later, students occupied central Prague, painting out signs for the newly-named Red Army Square and replacing them with 'Jan Palach Square'. Hundreds were arrested.

I respect their strength of feeling, even though I know rather more of the facts of this question.

Prime Minister Harold Wilson, 12 February 1969, on West German students protesting against the British government's military and financial support for the Nigerian government forces in their civil war – and, in many instances, campaign of genocide – against the self-proclaimed Ibo state of Biafra, one of the country's principal oil-producing regions. British oil companies had at first co-operated with the Biafran regime, but the Nigerian government then prevented tankers leaving Nigerian waters. Wilson claimed that British support for Nigeria was a Commonwealth obligation, and necessary in order to deter Soviet interference; France sent arms to the Biafran separatists.

As Nigerian authorities banned Red Cross flights to Ibo areas, claiming they were being used to ship arms, some four million people in the war zone began to starve.

I will see you later.

A message for someone in the public gallery from a member of the Kray Brothers' gang as they are taken down to the cells at the Old Bailey on 5 March 1969. The psychopathic Kray twins, Ronnie and Reggie – society figures and charitable benefactors for much of the Sixties – were each sentenced to life imprisonment for the murder of George Cornell and the attempted murder of Jack 'The Hat' McVitie; the judge recommended they serve a minimum of 30 years.

It proves that clinical efficiency never beats honest-to-God enthusiasm for a good cause.

Bernadette Devlin, returned to Parliament as Nationalist MP for Mid-Ulster with a 4211 majority in a by-election on 18 April 1969; the former Unionist majority had been frantically defended by party workers from all over the province. On 20 April, British troops were sent to Northern Ireland to guard key installations after a night of bombings in which nine Belfast post offices, the main bus station and the city's reservoir were seriously damaged.

We have the enemy licked now. He is beaten. We have the initiative in all areas. The enemy cannot achieve a military victory; he cannot even mount another offensive.
Admiral John S. McCain, C-in-C US Pacific Forces, February 1969; the year the Viet Cong launched 159 simultaneous attacks in South Vietnam. On 24 April the US forces' death toll in Vietnam officially reached 33,641, equalling that in Korea in the Fifties. President Nixon announced a scaling-down of bombing raids, for 'economic reasons'.

Politics is too important to be left to the politicians.
General Charles de Gaulle, who resigned as President on 28 April after falling short by 3 per cent in a referendum seeking public approval for his plans to reform the Constitution by abolishing the Senate, reorganize the regions, and concentrate power centrally. Quoted in Clement Attlee: A Prime Minister Remembers *(1961).*

This aphorism has also been used by Tony Benn (of broadcasters), Georges Clemençeau (of Generals) and Iain MacLeod (of historians).

NOTE: In some of our copies the article *The Power of the Papacy* described the Pope as His Satanic Majesty. This should have read The Roman Antichrist.
The sectarian heritage of Northern Ireland: correction in a 1969 edition of the Belfast Protestant Telegraph.

By yesterday morning British troops were patrolling the streets of Belfast. I fear that once Protestants and Catholics get used to our presence they will hate us more than they hate each other.
Richard Crossman, leader of the House of Commons, Diaries, 17 August 1969. As British troops entered the Roman Catholic district of Bogside, Londonderry, they were cheered by crowds in the streets, and given cups of tea; they had been sent to erect a 'peace line' of barbed wire to protect the residents against attacks from Protestant gangs. The Protestant police reserve, the B-Specials, was disbanded shortly afterwards.

$\mathcal{T}$*o Boldly Go...*

Houston – Tranquility Base – The Eagle has landed.
Neil Armstrong, commander of Apollo 11, reports Moonlanding, 21 July 1969.

That's one small step for a man, one giant leap for mankind.
This is what Neil Armstrong said as he set foot on the Moon on 21 July 1969; owing to a 'transmission blip' it is not what the hundreds of millions of people watching and listening on Earth heard him say. The indefinite article disappeared somewhere in between.

HERE MEN FROM THE PLANET EARTH
FIRST SET FOOT UPON THE MOON
JULY 1969 AD
WE CAME IN PEACE FOR ALL MANKIND
Plaque left behind, together with the Stars and Stripes, in the Sea of Tranquility, 22 July 1969.

This is the greatest week in the history of the world since the Creation.
A curiously deflationary piece of hyperbole: President Richard M. Nixon welcomes the Apollo astronauts on board USS Hornet, 24 July 1969.

On 28 September, as a 'temporary measure', troops erected a 'peace wall', complete with checkpoints, between the Shankhill Road and the Falls Road in Belfast. On 12 October, troops were permitted to retaliate if attacked; they fired tear-gas at a crowd of Protestant rioters.

PIG
The word smeared in blood across the front door of the Beverly Hills home of film actress Sharon Tate on 9 August 1969. Miss Tate, who was eight months pregnant, was shot dead with four others and their bodies mutilated; the next day, there were two similar murders in a house nearby. On 24 December, four

members of a 'hippy commune' – teenagers Patricia Krenwinkel, Susan Atkins, Leslie van Houten, and Charles 'Tex' Watson – were charged with first-degree murder, along with their leader, 35-year-old Charles Manson. (See January 1971, p. 157)

Three days of love, peace, dope, sex and rock'n'roll.
A promise more or less fulfilled at the Isle of Wight Festival; 150,000 people listened as Bob Dylan played a two-hour set in the gloaming of 31 August 1969.

We sold off a small yacht and I may have to give up polo. We may have to leave Buckingham Palace next year if we go into the red.
HRH Prince Philip, Duke of Edinburgh and consort of Queen Elizabeth II, interviewed on US television on 9 November 1969, complains of the Civil List allowance of £475,000 a year.

As far as criticism is concerned, we don't resent that unless it is absolutely biased, as it in most cases.
South African Prime Minister John Vorster defines the limits of free speech; quoted in the Observer, 9 November 1969. In Britain, anti-apartheid protestors mounted a campaign to disrupt the all-white Springboks rugby tour.

… And we huddled them up. We made them squat down and Lieutenant Calley came over and said, 'You know what to do with them, don't you?' And I said yes. So I took it for granted that he just wanted us to watch them. And he left, and came back about ten or fifteen minutes later and said, 'How come you ain't killed them yet? … I want them dead.' So I started shooting. I poured about four clips into the group....
The testimony of GI Paul Meadlo at the Court Martial of Lt. William Calley, Indiana, 24

November 1969, for the murder of 109 of the 347 old men, women, children and babies who were killed in the Vietnamese village of My Lai in 1968; most of the girls were raped first.
The US Army knew of the atrocity but covered it up until an army photographer, Ron Haeberle, published an article in a Cleveland newspaper with photographs of the bodies.

~

It was no big deal, Sir.
Lieutenant Calley – who insisted he was only obeying orders to 'neutralize subversive elements' – shrugs off the incident during cross-examination, November 1969.

~

There was a crucifixion 2000 years ago of a man named Jesus Christ. I don't think we need another crucifixion of a man named Rusty Calley.
The Word of God according to the Rev. Michael Lord, pastor at Fort Benning. As Calley was convicted of murdering 'at least 22' civilians and sentenced to hard labour for life, the Governor of Indiana ordered flags to be flown at half-mast. President Nixon commuted the sentence to three years' house arrest at Fort Benning, where his girlfriend was allowed to visit him.
The coverage of the My Lai massacre added to Americans' growing revulsion at their country's conduct of the Vietnam War; many wondered openly how many similar atrocities there might be. Others took a different view: the record 'The Battle Hymn of Lt. William Calley' sold well, especially in Indiana.

Abolition of capital punishment once and for all will help create a more civilized society. It will rebound to the advantage and honour of the nation.
Dr Michael Ramsey, Archbishop of Canterbury, speech, House of Lords, 18 December 1969, as the Lords agreed that the 1965 suspension of the death penalty should become permanent.

A Decade of Disaffection
1970~1979

Only the man who finds everything wrong and expects it to get
worse is thought to have a clear brain.

~ *J.K. Galbraith*, The Age of Uncertainty, *1977*

The 'Sixties Dream' turned sour when Arab oil-producing countries, outraged at the
West's support for Israel during the 'Yom Kippur War', acted against it by massively
increasing the price of oil: the effect of this was to put enormous strain on Western
economies, especially that of Britain, which was almost entirely dependent for its supplies on the Middle East, and recession and unemployment inevitably followed. As social
relations became increasingly strained and violent, the 'Summer of Love' seemed a long
way in the past. Arab terrorism became a feature of life for many people, especially international travellers; in the UK, a state of virtual urban guerrilla warfare arose in Northern
Ireland after the thwarted aims of the Civil Rights movement gave way to an unprecedented campaign of terrorism and counter-terrorism.

Disillusionment became a keynote in the USA after the Watergate Scandal removed
President Nixon under threat of impeachment and brought into question the Presidency
itself, and the whole apparatus of American politics; people began to abstain from voting
or taking any serious interest in the democratic process, setting a trend that continues in
the closing years of the century. In Britain the decade ended, as it had begun, with industrial strife and widespread discontent, and many who voted out of office the Labour government in 1979 were voting not only against a party but against the whole post-war
polity, which was reckoned to have failed beyond the possibility of mitigation.

The UK joined the European Economic Community in 1972 and voted in a referendum to remain a member in 1975; at the end of the decade, the incoming political leadership was known to be, at best, coolly enthusiastic for its plans for expansion and
enhancement, and the wilder promises of pro-Marketeers showed no signs of being kept.
Eastern Europe and the USSR seemed to be regressing into a sort of neo-Stalinism under
President Leonid Brezhnev as Soviet dissident movements were crushed and their most
eloquent spokesman, the novelist Alexander Solzhenitsyn, was hounded, arrested, and
finally deported; less well-known in the West but at least as important was the nuclear
physicist Andrei Sakharov, who was sent into internal exile. South Africa's apartheid
regime continued its policy of suppressing all movements, whether peaceful or not,

towards a sharing of power between black and white South Africans; elsewhere the growing anti-apartheid movement in Britain and the Commonwealth began to co-ordinate activities designed to isolate it. Islamic fundamentalists in Iran led a huge popular uprising against the Shah, who fought a desperate and vain campaign for survival in the closing days of the decade.

1970

One man's wage rise is another man's price increase.
UK Prime Minister Harold Wilson urges restraint, 11 January 1970. At the turn of the year it was announced that the minimum fare on the London Underground was to be increased by 50 per cent – to one shilling (5p). Large pay rises followed.

Nothing I have here is mine or is generated by me.
The pain of exile: General Ojukwu, granted asylum in Ivory Coast after the surrender of Biafra to Nigerian Federation troops on 21 January 1970. Journalists and Western observers reported widespread starvation, murder, and rape as the conquerors moved in; Britain's 'special envoy'. Lord Hunt, called these reports 'exaggerated and irresponsible'. He had seen many people looking 'in no way undernourished'.

Three passions have governed my life: the longing for love, the search for knowledge and unbearable pity for the sufferings of mankind.
Bertrand Russell, who died on 2 February 1970 at the age of 97.

Houston, we have a problem.
James Lovell – or it may have been John Swigert – sends a message from Apollo XIII *after an explosion in the service module, carrying the main engine and the bulk of the crew's oxygen supply. The Moon landing was abandoned; unable to turn back and with vital supplies running low, the crew moved to the landing module as the whole craft orbited the Moon and returned, crippled, to Earth. On 17 April they moved back in to the main craft for re-entry and a safe splashdown in the Pacific.*

I would rather be a one-term President than a two-term President at the cost of seeing America become a second-rate power and accept the first defeat in its history.

US President Richard M. Nixon announces a US troop invasion of neutral Cambodia in order to attack North Vietnamese and Viet Cong bases there, on 30 April 1970. In March, the Cambodian leader, Prince Sihanouk, was ousted in an anti-Communist right-wing coup while in the USSR trying to persuade Soviet leaders to assist in a North Vietnamese withdrawal.

~

They're just scum.
President Nixon on students at Kent State University, Ohio, who had staged an 'occupation' of the campus in protest at the US invasion of Cambodia. On 4 May 1970, the National Guard opened fire, killing four of them and injuring 11; on the same day, troopers shot dead two students at Jackson State University in Mississippi.

~

When dissent turns to violence it invites tragedy.
President Nixon comments on the Kent State killings. On 5 May 1970, as Congress prepared to debate Senator George McGovern's proposal to cut off war funding, he promised that US troops would be withdrawn 'in three to seven weeks'.

~

We are all the President's men.
Henry Kissinger expresses solidarity over Cambodia; recorded in The Sunday Times Magazine, *4 May 1975.*

~

If we just keep up the pressure, these little guys will crack.
US General Earl Wheeler, June 1970.

Nor would it be in the interests of the Community that its enlargement should take place except with the full-hearted

Love, love, love – all the wretched cant of it ...
Germaine Greer, The Female Eunuch, *1970.*

consent of the Parliament and people of the new member countries.
But he didn't mean by referendum: Edward Heath addresses the Franco-British Chamber of Commerce, 5 May 1970. On 19 June his Conservative Party brought six years of Labour government to an end at the general election, securing an overall majority of 30. The new government was dealt a severe blow with the death of the new Chancellor, Iain MacLeod, on 20 July. He was succeeded by Party Chairman Anthony Barber.

Around nine million working days were lost to strike action in 1970, the highest total since 1926.

This would, at a stroke, reduce the rise in prices, increase productivity and reduce unemployment.
Conservative Central Office election campaign press release number GE228, 16 June 1970; a phrase that was to haunt Prime Minister Edward Heath, even though he never actually said it.

A very friendly boom, like a pair of gleeful handclaps.
UK government scientific adviser Sir James Lighthill tries to allay fears about the 'sonic boom' of Concorde, the world's first supersonic passenger aircraft. But it was subsonic engine noise that drew protests as Concorde made its debut at Heathrow on 12 September 1970.

I am what I feel. I play as I feel and I act as I feel. I can't express myself in any conversation. I can't explain myself like this or that. It doesn't come out like that. But when I'm up on stage, it's all the world. It's my whole life … When I die I want people just to play my music.
Blues guitarist Jimi Hendrix, who died on 18 September 1970 at the age of 27. Quoted in Tony Palmer, All You Need Is Love *(1976).*

Get Johnny Cash on the phone. I'm the biggest singer in America, I'm the biggest singer in the world!
A frantically insecure Janis Joplin screams at a telephone operator. She died of a heroin overdose on 4 October 1970, at the age of 27.

The universal, obligatory force-feeding with lies is now the most agonizing aspect of existence in our country – worse than all our material miseries, worse than any lack of civil liberties.
Alexander Solzhenitsyn, Letter to Soviet

Leaders. *In October 1970 he resisted pressure from the authorities to reject his award of the Nobel Prize for Literature.*

It is time for the great silent majority of Americans to stand up and be counted.
President Nixon campaigns in the US mid-term elections, October 1970. He had used the phrase 'silent majority' in a TV broadcast the previous November but it became current in this form.

I always thought I was Jeanne d'Arc and Buonaparte – how little one knows oneself.
Charles de Gaulle, on being compared with Robespierre in 1958. He died, two weeks short of his 80th birthday, on 9 November 1970. Six thousand people, including past and present world leaders, crowded into Notre Dame Cathedral for a Requiem Mass, but de Gaulle had instructed that only ordinary 'men and women of France and of elsewhere' should attend the funeral at Colombey-les-Deux-Églises. Tens of thousands did, in a ceremony described by a French radio commentator as 'grandiose in its rustic simplicity'.

1971

You won't outlive this, old man.
Charles Manson, convicted along with his three acolytes and co-defenders of killing Sharon Tate and six others, addresses the judge after the verdict is announced on 25 January 1971. They then began an indefinite sojourn on Death Row.

General Amin, a beefy, soft-spoken man of the Madi tribe, sets an example of self-restraint. First reports seem to suggest … a military government which, with any luck, may turn out to be of like nature and ambitions to those which have successfully brought law and order and relatively clean administration to Ghana and Nigeria.
Echoing the government view, the UK Daily Telegraph *welcomes the coup that brings to power Major-General Idi Amin while Uganda's leader, Milton Obote, attends the Commonwealth Prime Ministers' Conference (where he had attacked Britain's links with apartheid South Africa and the sanctions-busting activities of UK companies in Rhodesia) on 25 January 1971. Amin pledged to abolish corruption and tribalism, to restore civilian*

● ●

Politics is the art of the possible.

*R. A. Butler, The Art of the Possible, 1971;
the phrase was used by Bismarck,
among others.*

● ●

*government as soon as possible, and to release pris-
oners held on 'false or unspecified charges'.*

*In February it was announced that Britain
would sell seven military helicopters to South
Africa.*

———————

There they were, all the lovely sisters,
giggling and shivering and bawdy and
prim, and I turned and turned again,
gloating at the numbers before and
behind my motley, frost-defying sex.
Because sex is all we really had in common.

Jill Tweedie, writing in the Telegraph Weekend
Magazine *about the 'Women's Liberation' march
from Hyde Park to Number 10, Downing Street,
on 6 March 1971; 4000 took part.*

~

No one ever mentions these millions of
women. I declare that I am one of them. I
declare that I have had an abortion.

*Simone de Beauvoir and 343 other French women
sign a letter to* La Nouvel Observateur, *5 April
1971.*

~

Eliminating the patriarchal and racist
base of the existing social system requires
a revolution, not a reform.

The first issue of Ms *magazine, USA, 1971.*

———————

Why do you do nothing to help us? The
outside world says this is an internal
affair. … This is not an internal affair. It
is a pogrom.

*Muhammed Eunus Ali, a member of the self-styled
Bangladeshi Assembly, berates foreign correspondents on 17 April 1971. The eastern part of
Pakistan had ceded from the larger, more powerful, western part the previous month, and Sheikh
Mujibur Rahman declared the independent state
of Bangladesh. West Pakistan troops launched a
large offensive, shelling and bombing indiscriminately; at least 7000 people died in Dacca in 48
hours of bombardment. Over two million refugees*

*fled to India where, herded into refugee camps in
monsoon rains, they began to succumb to cholera;
by June the epidemic was out of control and India
attempted to seal the border.*

*As the plight of the refugees worsened, rock
stars George Harrison, Eric Clapton and Ringo
Starr were among those who, along with Ravi
Shankar, raised $250,000 in a charity concert
for aid agencies on 1 August.*

I would not like to leave contraception on
the long finger too long.

*Using an Ulster expression for procrastination,
Republic of Ireland Prime Minister Jack Lynch is
quoted in the* Irish Times, *23 May 1971; the sale
of contraceptives was prohibited in Ireland.*

● ●

My father made him an offer he
couldn't refuse.

Al Pacino, The Godfather (1972).

● ●

Things will never be quite the same
again.

*Anonymous French government official, 24 June
1971, as Geoffrey Ripon, Britain's chief negotiator, announces 'a very satisfactory deal' on membership of the European Economic Community.
On 28 October, the House of Commons voted by
356-244 in favour of a government motion on
membership; 69 Labour MPs supported the government, 39 Tories voted against.*

They played the tune, he sang the words,
then blasted the roof off with his golden
obbligato. He spoke to the heart of
Greenlander and Japanese alike. He had
world stature.

*British poet and jazz fan Philip Larkin on Louis
'Satchmo' Armstrong, who died on 6 July 1971,
aged 71.*

Those who have murdered in cold blood,
created situations which have led to
death or injury to people quite unin-
volved in disorder, maimed numerous
people including young children and put
at risk their jobs and the whole future of
entire communities.

*Northern Ireland Prime Minister Brian Faulkner
lists those who will be affected by his policy of*

internment without trial, simultaneously announced and enforced on 11 August 1971; the newly-created 'breakaway' Provisional IRA responded by murdering 12 people within hours. After four days of rioting, 5000 Catholic and 2000 Protestant homes were burned out on 12 August. At a Belfast press conference, IRA chief Joe Cahill dismissed the damage done by internment to his organization as 'no more than a pinprick'.

On 7 September 1971 Annette McGavigan, aged 14, became the 100th fatal victim of the 'Troubles' when she was caught in crossfire between troops and IRA rooftop snipers in Londonderry. She had gone into the street to find a rubber bullet to add to her collection of souvenirs.

We are men. We are not beasts. We only want to live.

A banner at Attica gaol, New York State, which in September 1971 was the scene of rioting in protest against caging, beating and other brutalities; 32 inmates and 10 warders were killed.

You cannot shake hands with a clenched fist.

India's Prime Minister, Mrs Indira Gandhi, 19 October 1971, as negotiations over East Pakistan ground to a halt. Frequent clashes between Indian and Pakistani troops along the East Pakistan border became more serious over the next few weeks; three Pakistani military planes were shot down over Indian territory, and on 23 November Pakistan reported Indian troops 30 miles (50 km) inside their territory. Pakistan launched a full-scale war against India on 3 December and Mrs Gandhi declared a State of Emergency; on 6 December India recognized the state of Bangladesh. The government of East Pakistan resigned as Indian troops closed in on Dacca on 14 December, and three days later President Khan of Pakistan accepted India's cease-fire terms. Bangladesh was born amid scenes of bloody revenge; the Indian army allowed surrendering Pakistani soldiers to keep their arms in order to avoid being lynched.

I don't think one can speak of defeating the IRA, of eliminating them completely, but it is the design of the security forces to reduce their level of violence to something like an acceptable level.

Saying the unspeakable: Reginald Maudling, UK Home Secretary, on a visit to Northern Ireland, 15 December 1971. Unionist politicians seized on the phrase 'an acceptable level of violence' in their demands for 'tougher action'.

1972

We have the happiest Africans in the world.

Ian Smith, head of the rebel racist regime in Rhodesia: but on 18 January 1972 it seemed that some European Rhodesians were less than happy. Police arrested the former Prime Minister, Garfield Todd, and his daughter Judith, as 'a threat to public order'. They had opposed a proposed settlement with Britain, the precise details of which had not been made public, for granting legal independence to the former colony.

There is absolutely no doubt that the Parachute Regiment opened up only after they were fired on.

But who fired? The balance of eyewitness evidence suggests it was a 'loyalist' gunman, not a republican terrorist: 13 are killed and 17 wounded as the Paras open fire on a Civil Rights rally that had begun to degenerate into stone-throwing on 30 January 1972, a day that came to be known in the extensive annals of Irish history as 'Bloody Sunday'. Three days later, a mob burned down the British Embassy in Dublin. On 22 February the IRA bombed the Aldershot HQ of the 16th Parachute Brigade; five female members of the kitchen staff, a gardener, a Roman Catholic padre and an army Major were killed.

~

Now is your chance. A chance for fairness, a chance for prosperity, a chance for peace: a chance at last to bring the bombings and killings to an end.

UK Prime Minister Edward Heath, TV broadcast, 25 March 1972, announcing the abolition of the Northern Ireland Parliament at Stormont and the imposition of direct rule from London; the Irish government responded by restoring diplomatic relations, suspended after Bloody Sunday.

~

• •

It's not the voting that's democracy, it's the counting.

Tom Stoppard, Jumpers, *1972.*

• •

I do not intend to prejudge the past.
William Whitelaw, appointed Secretary of State for Northern Ireland after the dissolution of Stormont. His appointment was greeted with a gun battle between loyalist and nationalist paramilitary forces on 21 May 1972, in which eight people died; on 22 June he agreed a cease-fire with the Provisional IRA, who demanded 'a public reciprocal response'. The government promised that it would reciprocate, but did not specify how. The cease-fire lasted two weeks, at the end of which British troops stormed the barricades that had been erected around 'no-go areas' while it had lasted.

Let us join in a long march together on our different roads towards world peace.
President Nixon, visiting China in February and taking a stroll along the Great Wall, speaks as a guest of Prime Minister Chou-En-lai at a banquet in the Great Hall of the People in Peking. In May 1972 he paid an amicable visit to Moscow.

I'd much rather have that fellow inside my tent pissing out, than outside my tent pissing in.
Lyndon Baines Johnson on J. Edgar Hoover, founder of the FBI and its director for nearly 50 years, who died on 2 May 1972, aged 77, his propensity for dressing up in women's clothing still unguessed at.

Today I am one trillionth part of history.
Or, as Andy Warhol put it, famous for 15 minutes: Arthur Bremer, who shot and crippled Governor George Wallace during the presidential campaign on 16 May 1972.

We intend to remain alive. Our neighbours want to see us dead. This is not a question that leaves much room for compromise.
Israeli Prime Minister Golda Meir, interviewed in Reader's Digest in 1971; on 30 May 1972, three Japanese terrorists belonging to the 'Red Army Faction' and trained by Wadi Hadad's Popular Front for the Liberation of Palestine, opened fire with auto-

---

Watergate – Part One

In 1972, when Watergate was still mostly smoke and little flame, Kissinger is reported to have quipped, 'The illegal we do immediately. The unconstitutional takes a little longer.'
Bill Gulley (with Mary Ellen Reese), Breaking Cover, (1980).

This raises the ugliest questions about the integrity of political processes.
Lawrence O'Brien, chairman of the Democratic National Committee, on the arrest of five men who had broken into Democrat headquarters in the Watergate Building in Washington, DC, on 17 June 1972. One of the men, former CIA agent James McCord, was the 'security co-ordinator' of the Campaign to Re-elect the President (CREEP).

A predictable election year Mickey Mouse, of course, but surely the

Democrats are pushing our sense of humour too far.
The Richmond News, 22 June 1972, on the Watergate break-in.

Within our own staff, under my direction, Counsel to the President Mr Dean has conducted a complete investigation of all leads which might involve any present members of the White House or anybody in Government. I can say categorically that no one in the White House staff, no one in this administration, presently employed, was involved in this bizarre incident.
President Richard M. Nixon, public statement on the Watergate break-in, 29 August 1972. (See 21 March 1973, p. 162.)

On 11 August President Nixon ordered the withdrawal of the last US ground troops from Vietnam as part of his 'Vietnamization-of-the-war' policy; US air attacks on North Vietnam were stepped up.

matic weapons at Tel Aviv airport, killing 25 people. On 5 September, members of the Palestinian 'Black September' group (named after the explusion of Palestinian guerrillas from Jordan in September 1970) opened fire on the Israeli 'village' at the Olympic Games in Munich, taking ten athletes hostage. German security forces opened fire as terrorists and hostages were boarding a plane; in all, 16 people, 11 of them Israelis, were killed.

There comes a time in every man's life when he must make way for an older man.
Reginald Maudling, already dogged by rumours over his involvement with a collapsed offshore bank, was implicated in the scandal of the municipal architect John Poulson, who used bribery and corruption to secure local government building contracts. Poulson, and Newcastle Council leader T. Dan Smith, were both jailed for their actions; Maudling resigned as Home Secretary on 18 July 1972.

I am one thousand per cent for Tom Eagleton and I have no intention of dropping him from the ticket.
George McGovern, Democrat candidate for the Presidency, 25 July 1972, on his Vice-Presidential nominee who had admitted that he had twice undergone electric shock therapy to treat depression. After it was revealed that Eagleton had been a hospital in-patent on three occasions for 'nervous exhaustion', McGovern dropped him and chose Sargent Shriver, John F. Kennedy's brother-in-law.

We always thought that Amin was a decent chap. After all, he served in the British Army for more than 15 years.
A spokesman from the British Home Office reacts to Amin's announcement that he is to expel 50,000 UK passport-holding Ugandan Asians, 6 August 1972. He blamed them for 'conspiring to wreck Uganda's economy'.

One word of truth shall outweigh the whole world.
The speech Alexander Solzhenitsyn could not deliver personally at the Nobel Prize Awards; it was published on 24 August 1972, Soviet authorities denied him a visa to travel to Stockholm.

We are not prepared to allow inflation to take control of events.
After budgets in which taxes were cut and credit unsqueezed, prices began to rise alarmingly in 1972 – and so did wage demands, and the number of days lost through strike action. As his govern-

ment tried to steer an Industrial Relations Bill through Parliament, Prime Minister Edward Heath – speaking here to the Press Club on 26 September – was faced with public sector wage rise demands of £5.50 per week (power workers), £4 (dustmen) and £4.50 to £7 (miners). He called for a £2 limit on wage rises and a 5 per cent limit on price rises.

Have you taken leave of your senses?
Dissident backbench Tory MP Enoch Powell questions his Prime Minister on 6 November 1972 as Heath announces a compulsory 90-day freeze (extendable by 60 days) on wages, prices, rents and dividends, following a breakdown in negotiations for a voluntary code with the TUC and the CBI. While emergency legislation was passing through Parliament there was a rush to 'beat the freeze'; Fleet Street printers extracted a 16 per cent rise from the Newspaper Publishers' Association.

Even if the bombs don't coerce the enemy into successful peace talks, they're destroying his will to fight.
Anonymous US army officer, 7 November 1972. President Nixon, re-elected by a crushing margin over George McGovern (albeit on a poll of only 55.7 per cent) promised 'peace with honour in Vietnam' and hoped to bomb the North into concluding a peace. Hanoi was blitzed for 12 days, although many US planes were lost. On 30 December Nixon ordered the suspension of all bombing operations.

Your pigmentation would make you more allergic to frostbite in our frozen food.
Race discrimination in employment – as reported here by the Daily Telegraph – became illegal in Britain with the passing of the Race Relations Act on 26 November 1972.

I am sorry to see such intelligent and educated people in your situation. Undoubedly a warped understanding of sociology has brought you to the state in which you are.
On 6 December 1972 Mr Justice James sentences four members of the 'Angry Brigade' to 10 years' imprisonment for bombing offences between 1969 and 1971. The trial lasted 111 days, and the jury took 52 hours to bring in majority verdicts; four others were acquitted.

If you can't stand the shit, get out of the shithouse.
Sanitized to 'heat' and 'kitchen', but this is what

he actually said: Harry S Truman, who died on 26 December 1972, at the age of 88.

If Jesus, at the Last Supper, offered His body and blood to all the apostles, He was giving us to understand that we must do the same.
Sr Alfredo Delegado, press conference, Montevideo, 29 December 1972. On 13 October a Uruguayan plane carrying 45 people crashed in the Andes; 16 people, most of them members of a rugby team called The Christians, survived after food supplies ran out on day two by eating the bodies of the victims, at the rate of one every five days. They were rescued after ten weeks.

Right has triumphed over wrong.
The interpretation of the chief North Vietnamese negotiator, Le Duc Tho, as a cease-fire agreement is signed with the USA in Paris on 23 January 1973. There was to be an exchange of POWs and the withdrawal of all US troops and military advisers within 60 days; South Vietnam would be allowed to settle its own political future. A 1160-strong force from Canada, Poland, Hungary and Indonesia would supervise the agreement on the ground. The last known US prisoner was released on 27 March.

1973

Did y'ever think, Ken, that making a speech on economics is a lot like pissing down your leg? It seems hot to you, but it never does to anyone else.
Lyndon Baines Johnson in conversation with J. K. Galbraith; quoted in the latter's A Life in Our Times (1981). LBJ died on 22 January, at the age of 64.

There is no reason to feel guilty.
Israeli Defence Minister Moshe Dayan, 22 February 1973. An Israeli Air Force fighter shot down a Libyan Airlines Boeing 727 over occupied territory in the Sinai Desert, claiming it had ignored radio instructions to land; all 74 passengers and crew were killed. Cairo ground control, which had been in radio contact with the French pilot, denied that any warning had been given. On 25 February Israel agreed to pay compensation.

The only way to enjoy life is to work. Work is much more fun than fun.
Noël Coward, quoted in the Observer, 21 June 1963. On 26 March 1973 he died, still working at the age of 73.

Watergate – Part Two

We have a cancer within, close to the Presidency, that is growing. It is growing daily. … I can give a show we can sell them, just like we were selling Wheaties.
John Dean, special counsel to the President – the man Nixon said had 'conducted a complete investigation' – in conference with the President, 21 March 1973. On 8 February the Federal prosecutor had ordered a fresh inquiry into the Watergate burglary and 'related issues'. (From the Watergate Tapes.)

I don't give a shit what happens. I want you all to stonewall, let them plead the Fifth Amendment, cover-up or anything else, if it'll save it, save the plan. That's the whole point.
President Nixon in conference with John Dean, 22 March 1973. Dean afterwards claimed Nixon had offered $1 million to fund a 'cover-up' of the fact that he himself had organized the Watergate break-in – and of other illegal activities, including tapping the telephones of several hundred political opponents and 'subversives'. (From the Watergate Tapes.)

There can be no whitewash at the White House.
The public face of President Nixon, TV broadcast, 17 April 1973, promising a thorough investigation of alleged links between 'dirty tricks' and presidential staff.

When I was their age I could draw like Raphael. It had taken me a lifetime to learn how to draw like them.
Pablo Picasso, on children's paintings. He died on 8 April 1973, at the age of 91.

It is the unpleasant and unacceptable face of capitalism, but one should not suggest that the whole of British industry consists of practices of this kind.
Prime Minister Edward Heath, House of Commons,

They are two of the finest public servants it has been my privilege to know.
President Nixon, on TV, announcing the resignations of Bob Haldeman, his Chief of Staff and John Erlichman, chief domestic affairs adviser, along with the Attorney-General, Richard Kleindienst, and John Dean, chief Counsel.

Boys, give me hell every time you think I'm wrong.
President Nixon speaking to members of the press corps after the broadcast. Nixon accepted responsibility for Watergate on the 'buck stops here' principle, and admitted that there had been a cover-up, but he denied any knowledge of either scandal.

The new Attorney-General, Elliot Richardson, was authorized to appoint a Special Prosecutor.

The burglars who broke into the Democratic National Committee were in effect breaking into the home of every American. They were trying to steal not the jewels, money or other property of American citizens, but something much more valuable – their most precious heritage, the right to vote in a free election.
Senator Sam Ervin of North Carolina, chairman of the Senate Select Committee hearing into the Watergate Affair, 17 May 1973. On 7 May, Carl Bernstein and Bob Woodward of the Washington Post *were awarded the Pulitzer Prize for their investigations, without which the affair would have been quickly forgotten. On 25 June, John Dean told Senator Ervin's committee that Nixon had played an active role in the cover-up for the previous eight months, but that 'he did not realize or appreciate at any time the implications of his cover-up'.*

I was hoping you fellows wouldn't ask me about that.
On 17 July 1973, Alexander Butterfield, a middle-level White House aide, responds at the Senate Committee hearings to an enquiry about a rumour concerning tapes of conversations at the White House. He went on to tell astounded Senators and viewing millions that Nixon had personally installed bugging devices in the Oval Office, other offices, and his own telephone line and that he had kept all the tapes. There then began an epic struggle to force the President to hand the tapes over intact. The Watergate Special prosecutor, Archibald Cox, ordered him to surrender them; Nixon then ordered his Attorney-General, Elliot Richardson, to dismiss Cox. Richardson refused, so Nixon sacked him; then Richardson's deputy, William Ruckelshaus, also refused, so Nixon sacked him, too. Finally, the Solicitor-General, Robert Bork, sacked Cox – but on 23 October 1973, Nixon agreed to hand the tapes over. It became swiftly apparent that he had kept some back.

–[expletive deleted]–
A phrase frequently encountered in Watergate Tape transcripts, denoting frequent presidential obscenities.

I made a terrible mistake. I pressed the wrong button but Mr Nixon said it didn't matter.
On 26 November 1973, President Nixon's secretary, Rose Mary Woods, tells the Senate Committee that she accidentally erased 18 minutes from the Watergate Tapes. Coincidentally, they appeared to be vital to the Committee's investigations.

15 May 1973, on revelations that the international mining conglomerate Lonrho (one of whose directors, Edward du Cann, was a Conservative MP) made extensive use of a Cayman Islands tax haven in order to avoid UK taxes.

This is a very fine country to be acutely ill or injured in, but take my advice and do not be old and frail or mentally ill here – at least not for a few years. This is definitely not a good country

to be deaf or blind in either.
Keith Joseph, UK Secretary of State for Social Services, in candid mood; quoted in the Observer, *1 July 1973.*

Mr Chancellor, you are being welcomed in Israel with the esteem due to one who, in the darkest period for the human race and especially for the Jewish people, joined forces with those who fought the Nazis.
Israeli Prime Minister Golda Meir greets West

German Chancellor, and former Resistance fighter, Willi Brandt, 7 July 1973.

Despite the inevitable ups and downs, we know we are going to make it.
Bahamian Prime Minister Lynden Pindling celebrates independence, 10 July 1973.

The charges against me are, if you'll pardon the expression, damned lies. I am innocent of these charges. If indicted I shall not resign.
US Vice-President Spiro T. Agnew, under investigation in his home state of Maryland on bribery charges, 8 August 1973. (See below.)

I don't know of any foreign leader that was ever assassinated by the CIA. ... There were always discussions of everything ... things that may not be acceptable to the American people.
Richard Helms, director of the CIA, 1975, quoted in Lois and Alan Gordon, American Chronicle. On 11 September 1973 the elected Marxist government of Chile was overthrown in a military coup and the President, Salvador Allende, killed. The CIA organized it.

My writing is not allegorical. I deplore allegory, whenever I smell it out.
J.R.R. Tolkien, the man who created a universal myth in The Lord of the Rings(1954) died on 3 September 1973, at the age of 81.

To the man-in-the-street, who, I'm sorry
    to say,
Is a keen observer of life,
The word Intellectual suggests straight
    away
A man who's untrue to his wife.
W. H. Auden, 'Notes on Intellectuals', 1947. He died on 28 September 1973, at the age of 66.

That Gerald Ford. He can't fart and chew gum at the same time.
Lyndon Baines Johnson on the Republican Repre-

• •

That's the way it's been in town, Ever since they tore the juke box down.

Hunter/Garcia – The Grateful Dead, Stella Blue, 1973.

• •

sentative who became Vice-President on 12 October 1973 after Spiro T. Agnew, indicted for corruption, resigned; quoted in J. K. Galbraith, A Life of Our Times (1981).

———————————

It is a miracle at any military level.
Egyptian President Anwar Sadat, as Egyptian troops hold a patch of land on the East Bank of the Suez Canal; on 6 October Egypt crossed the canal to invade the Sinai during the Jewish holiday of Yom Kippur and on 14 October, 100,000 Egyptian troops pushed eastwards. Israel pushed them back and gained territory on the West Bank of Suez, but Egypt held its gain.
~

There wasn't one country in Europe which wouldn't have let Israel go under.
A Pentagon spokesman gives voice to US disapproval of Europe's attitude to the Yom Kippur war, 31 October 1973. Five days earlier, alleging intelligence that the USSR was about to send its forces to the Middle East, President Nixon put US forces on worldwide alert. A few hours later he said the situation had been 'defused' by a personal message from Soviet President Brezhnev. The US organized a military airlift to Israel but other NATO members, including Britain, refused to co-operate by allowing bases in their countries to be used for it. Arab oil-producing countries in the OPEC cartel responded to US support for Israel by raising the price by 70 per cent overnight; a complete embargo on the USA was immediately put in place. Britain, dependent on Arab oil for 80 per cent of its consumption, with a weak currency and rampant inflation, prepared for petrol rationing; 16 million ration books were printed, but never used. Rationing was by price, up to 42p a gallon by New Year, and a 50 mph (80 km/h) speed limit was imposed on all roads. Ugandan President (and Field Marshal) Idi Amin started a 'Save Britain' fund.

———————————

Ah well, they say the situation isn't as bad as they say it is.
Overheard in Belfast in 1973. After a year of bombings and shootings on both sides of the Irish Sea, Northern Ireland Secretary William Whitelaw secured the agreement of Loyalist and Nationalist politicians to take part in a 'power-sharing executive' in the former Parliament building of Stormont Castle. It seemed like a breakthrough to peace. On 9 December 1973, political leaders from Ireland, Britain and the North agreed at the Civil Service Training College,

Small Is Beautiful.

E. F. Schumacher's book, 1973.

• •

Sunningdale, to set up a Council of Ireland comprising a seven-a-side Ministry and a 30-a-side Consultative Assembly. A very similar body had been provided for in the original settlement of the 1920s but it was vetoed on that occasion by the Ulster Unionists. On 22 January 1974, fighting between rival Unionists – in which the Rev. Ian Paisley, leader of the Democratic Unionists, was removed by police – reduced the new Assembly to a shambles. Unionist leader and former Northern Ireland PM Brian Faulkner resigned.

People have got to know whether or not their President is a crook. Well, I am not a crook. I've earned everything I have got.
President Nixon defends himself to reporters against charges of tax evasion, 17 November 1973.

If we have to have oil and pay more for it, the country will have less to spend on other things from abroad.
UK Prime Minister Edward Heath faces an emergency in the Commons on 17 December 1973: strikes are paralysing the coal mines, power stations and railways, the trade deficit is growing alarmingly under the impact of the OPEC oil price rise, and there is a run on the pound on the foreign exchanges. The government announced a three-day working week, beginning on 1 January 1974, to save fuel; TV stations were ordered to close transmission at 10.30 p.m. and street lighting was reduced; hire purchase and credit controls were tightened, and surtax increased. VAT and excise duty were left untouched, for fear of triggering 'Phase III' of the Incomes Policy, which allowed for automatic wage increases above the current 7 per cent per annum level if the cost of living index rose.

Labour will tax the rich until the pips squeak.
As Britain prepared in December for an inevitable General Election, Labour's Shadow Chancellor, Denis Healey (to whom the above quote is attributed) targeted 'excess wealth' and business profits.

I owe my life to the good old NHS.
Joseph Sieff, 68, British Jewish leader and Chairman of Marks and Spencer, narrowly escapes death at the hands of Palestinian gunmen at his home on 30 December 1973, and insists the bullets were deflected by his false teeth. He underwent surgery to remove a bullet from his jaw.

I would not wish to be Prime Minister, dear. I have not had enough experience for that job. The only full Ministerial position I've held is Minister for Education and Science. Before you could even think of being Prime Minister you'd need to have done a good deal more jobs than that.
Margaret Thatcher MP in conversation with a juvenile interrogator on BBC children's television, 1973.

In our country the lie has become not just a moral category but a pillar of the State.
Alexander Solzhenitsyn, whose chronicle of the Soviet labour camp system, The Gulag Archipelago, was published in Paris on 1 January 1974. KGB agents had tortured a woman friend of the author and obtained a manuscript of the book, which Solzhenitsyn had suppressed for five years in order to protect former inmates whose names appeared in it; she afterwards committed suicide. On 13 February the KGB broke into the author's flat and took him away; the next day he was sent into exile. He arrived in Frankfurt, stayed at the house of German author Heinrich Böll, then settled in Switzerland. His wife and three children followed him shortly after his expulsion.

If you want to see the acceptable face of capitalism, go out to an oil rig in the North Sea.
Edward Heath, campaigning in the general election, 14 February 1974. Huge reserves of oil and gas had been discovered in the North Sea during the Sixties, and a massive programme of investment, exploration and extraction set in progress, although it was to be some years before the refined product began to make a difference to Britain's economy.

Labour and the Tories have no God-given monopoly of power. You have a third choice.
Liberal Party leader Jeremy Thorpe: election cam-

paign message. The general election of 28 February 1974 produced a 'hung Parliament'; Labour had 301 seats, the Conservatives 297, Liberals 14 and Scottish and Welsh Nationalists 9. Thorpe, complaining bitterly about the 'first-past-the-post' election system that gave his party so few seats to show for their six million votes (more than half as many as each of the other two main parties) went to 10, Downing Street for talks with the Prime Minister, who hoped to be able to construct some sort of coalition with Thorpe himself in the Cabinet. Electoral reform was not on offer and, citing the fact that an incumbent government had in effect been rejected at the polls, Thorpe rejected the proposal and Edward Heath tendered his resignation to the Queen.

~

Looking around the House, one realizes that we are all minorities now.

Jeremy Thorpe, as the House of Commons reconvenes, 6 March 1974. A minority Labour government under Harold Wilson moved immediately to settle the miners' strike – at the cost of a pay increase of up to 35 per cent – and return the country to a five-day working week.

Rutland, Cumberland, Huntingdonshire, Westmorland, the Ridings, Cardiganshire, Clackmannanshire.

What the Beeching Report did to the railways, the Local Government Act 1972 did to the counties of Britain: some of the many names to disappear as its effects came into force on 1 April 1974. Only ten English counties and one Welsh one remained unchanged in a process that involved the invention of such entities as Avon, Clwyd, Tyne and Wear – and Highland, with an area larger than that of Belgium.

Every time someone shakes my hand I feel they are trying to take my pulse.

After a long and unexplained illness, French President Georges Pompidou (quoted above by Henry Kissinger) died on 2 April 1974, at the age of 62. In the ensuing election, the centrist Valéry Giscard-d'Estaing took 51 per cent of the vote to beat his Socialist rival, Francois Mitterrand.

I am now called Tania.

The rather suburban revolutionary name apparently adopted by publishing heiress Patty Hearst, who, kidnapped by the 'Symbionese Liberation Front', was photographed by a security camera in

the act of joining in an armed robbery on a San Francisco bank on 15 April 1974. The organization itself professed somewhat chaotic aims, one of which was to give poor people free food.

I have never issued an inflammatory statement in my life.

Free Presbyterian Minister and Ulster politician Rev. Ian Paisley, who gave vociferous support to the seven-day Protestant Workers' Strike that brought the province to a standstill – and brought down the Northern Ireland Assembly on 28 May 1974, as it was intended to. As a Trade Unionists' 'back-to-work' march attracted only 250 people there were widespread reports of intimidation by 'loyalist' paramilitaries; armed and hooded men had blocked the road to Aldergrove airport. Direct rule from London was reimposed by default; in the following weeks there were IRA bombings in Birmingham and Manchester, and at Westminster Abbey and the Tower of London.

One feels that Uganda cannot afford General Amin's warmhearted generosity.

A London Times editorial, 1972; on 4 June 1974 the International Committee of Jurists reported that some 250,000 people had been killed in Uganda since Amin came to power.

I do not mind the Liberals, still less do I mind the Country Party, calling me a bastard. In some circumstances I am only doing my job if they do. But I hope you will not publicly call me a bastard, as some bastards in the Caucus have.

Australian Prime Minister Gough Whitlam, beset with opposition on all sides, addresses his Labor Party, 9 June 1974.

In view of the exceptional circumstances with which our motherland is faced, the armed forces have decided to entrust the government of the country to a civilian government.

Greek President General Phæton Gizikis renounces power on 30 July 1974 after a seven-year rule by 'Colonels' Junta', characterized in equal measure by repression and incompetence. Around 100,000 people crammed into Constitution Square in Athens to proclaim Democracy as the former PM, Constantine Karamanlis, returned from exile in France. In November he beat his Socialist rival, Andreas Papandreou, in free elections; the following month, Greece voted to abolish the monarchy and become a republic.

Watergate ~ Part Three

I urge the Congress to join me in mounting a major new effort to replace the discredited president....
A whole generation learns the meaning of the term 'Freudian slip': President Nixon, giving the State of the Union Address in January 1974, had intended to say 'precedent'.

The crimes to which Richard M. Nixon was a willing accessory threatened the system of law and justice, and for this alone they are impeachable offences; but more fundamentally, this President has undermined the very basis of our government. If we do not impeach him for this, then we will be accessories to his crime and jointly responsible for raising the Presidency above the law.
Representative Charles B. Rangel moves the First Article of Impeachment against President Nixon; when it was approved by 27 votes to 11 on 27 July 1974, the way was cleared for a Bill of Impeachment to be introduced. On 24 July the US Supreme Court ruled, by 8 to 1, against Nixon's use of 'executive privilege' in withholding the last remaining 'Watergate Tapes' required in the prosecution of six others; what they contained proved fatal to Nixon's Presidency.

I have no intention of resigning. The President is not going to leave the White House until January 20th 1977.
Following the Supreme Court ruling and the Impeachment vote, Nixon is still in fighting mood.

You fellows, in your business, you have a way of handling problems like this. Somebody leaves a pistol in the drawer. I don't have a pistol.
Richard M. Nixon to General Alexander Haig, 7 August 1974.

I have never been a quitter. To leave office before my term is completed is abhorrent to every instinct in my body. But as President I must put the interests of America first ... Therefore, I shall resign the Presidency, effective at noon tomorrow.
Richard M. Nixon, radio and television address, 8 August 1974.

This country needs good farmers, good businessmen, good plumbers ... .
Another Nixon slip, this time addressing staff on the White House lawn, 9 August 1974: 'The Plumbers' was the conspirators' code term for the Watergate burglars.

Our long national nightmare is over. Our Constitution works.
President Gerald R. Ford, sworn in on 9 August 1974. He chose Nelson Rockefeller, Governor of New York and the moderate Republican candidate in the 1964 and 1968 primaries, to be his Vice-President. On 16 September, President Ford granted Nixon a pardon.

President Nixon's motto was: If two wrongs don't make a right, try three.
US editor Norman Cousins, writing in the Daily Telegraph, 17 July 1979.

As a black American, I have been especially struck by the poetic justice of the discovery of the Watergate burglars by a black man. Black people were not considered by the Founding Fathers of this nation when they undertook to issue the Declaration of Independence in the name of freedom. Although a black man was among the first to fall in the American Revolution and blacks fought alongside the revolutionary heroes for freedom, we were not included when citizenship was defined in the Constitution. We have spent the one hundred and ninety-eight year history of this nation trying to become covered by the guarantees of freedom and equality contained in the Constitution. We therefore value, perhaps to a greater extent than most Americans, the guarantees of freedom and equality expressed in the Constitution and the structure of government that provides, through democratic participation, for the will of the people to prevail.
Representative Charles B. Rangel, Congressional Record, July 1974.

The plan was simple. In the run-up to the election which, given the level of instability in Parliament, must be due within a matter of months, MI5 would arrange for selective details of the intelligence about leading Labour Party figures, but especially Wilson, to be leaked to sympathetic pressmen. … 'We'll have him out,' said one of them, 'this time we'll really have him out.'

Peter Wright, Spycatcher *(1987). On 25 October 1974 personal papers including tax documents were stolen from the home of the Prime Minister in Lord North Street – he had moved there from Number 10 in March – although there were no signs of a break-in; Wilson suspected a British Intelligence involvement at the time. (See 16 March 1976, p.171.)*

Oh dear, what a pity. Nannies are so hard to come by these days.

A genteel old lady in Belgravia responds to police enquiries into the murder of Sandra Rivett, nanny to the children of Lord and Lady Lucan, who was battered to death on 7 November 1974; Lady Lucan was also attacked, and police worked on the theory that Lucan, who has never been seen since, murdered one woman in mistake for the other. Numerous 'sightings' of Lord Lucan are still reported from around the world although a court has now ruled that he must be presumed dead.

Do not let the olive branch fall from my hands.

Yasser Arafat, leader of the Palestinian Liberation Organisation, addresses the United Nations, 13 November 1974.

The loss of civilian life is regrettable, but Oglaigh na hEirann has no alternative but to continue the armed struggle so long as Britain remains an occupying force in Ireland.

Statement attributed to the IRA, 22 November 1974. On 4 November Judith Ward was jailed for 30 years for the bombing of a bus carrying soldiers and their families along the M62 in February, in which 11 people died. On 7 November an IRA bomb destroyed a pub frequented by soldiers in Woolwich; one person was killed and 28 injured. On 15 November, IRA member James McDade was killed by the premature explosion of his own bomb; permission was refused for a 'military funeral' in the Midlands. On 21 November bombs exploded in two pubs in Birmingham, the Mulberry Bush and the Tavern in the Town: 17 people

were killed outright. Police arrested five Irishmen travelling back to Ireland from Birmingham on 22 November and – as it was finally admitted nearly two decades later – beat them up until they got a confession. On 29 November the Prevention of Terrorism Act was passed through Parliament.

To ask the Home Secretary whether he will review arrangements for preventing drowning accidents.

Written parliamentary question in the name of John Stonehouse MP, May 1974. Stonehouse, a former Postmaster-General, was presumed drowned shortly afterwards when his clothes were found abandoned on a beach; on Christmas Eve 1974 he was arrested in Australia, where he had been living under an assumed name with his secretary. Investig-ations proceeded into a Bangladesh bank of which he had been chairman.

You mustn't take out a man's appendix when he's moving a grand piano.

According to Philip Ziegler in Mountbatten *(1985) this is a favourite expression of Lord Healey who, as Denis Healey, was Chancellor of the Exchequer in Harold Wilson's 1974–76 government. Healey found himself moving something resembling a mighty Würlitzer at the end of 1974: inflation, fuelled by wage rises of 13.5 per cent (local government workers), 28 per cent (senior civil servants), and 32 per cent (teachers) and by his own Budget, which lifted price controls on nationalized industries and slapped a hefty rate of VAT on petrol, was running at 20 per cent. The price of steel had risen by 45 per cent in 12 months, and bakery workers were out on strike for a 66 per cent wage rise; the average annual wage increase was 26 per cent.*

In 1974, scientists in the USA developed a technique for performing 'cut-and-paste' operations on DNA, and the British Antarctic Survey, using what it cheerfully described as 'Heath Robinson equipment' discovered a small hole in the ozone layer.

1975

I will not be influenced by any views which are backed by the bomb and the bullet.

Northern Ireland Secretary Merlyn Rees, 16 January 1975, as the IRA calls off a 25-day cease-fire and calls for 'direct negotiations' with the UK government.

I owe nothing to Women's Lib.

Margaret Thatcher, 1 December 1974, quoted in the Observer. *On 11 February 1975 she polled the votes of 146 Tory MPs, against 79 for William Whitelaw, to become leader of the Conservative Party; Edward Heath, having been defeated on the first ballot, had resigned.*

If there's a hell, I've seen it.

Anonymous doctor, after spending hours working in the wreckage of a 'tube' train at Moorgate on the London Underground, 28 February 1975. The train had accelerated into a 'blind' tunnel at 30 mph (50 km/h)and crashed through sand piles and buffers, compressing the first three carriages. Thirty-five people, including the driver, were killed.

I will abide by the wishes of the British people.

Prime Minister Harold Wilson, his Cabinet split on the issue of continued British membership of the EEC, which was to be the subject of Britain's first national referendum, 18 March 1975.

There is pandemonium everywhere.

The last telex message out of the South Vietnamese city of Da Nang – once the main US military base – before it fell to advancing Communist forces on 29 March 1975; they had taken the city of Hue three days earlier. The road to Saigon now lay open.

~

We enter as conquerors and are not here to talk about peace with the traitors of the Phnom Penh clique.

A statement from the Khmer Rouge and their leader, Pol Pot, as they entered the capital on 17 April 1975 as direct heirs of Richard Nixon's war strategy. Pol Pot proclaimed 'Year Zero', abolished money, shackled peasants to buffalo-ploughs – and the killing began.

~

If you Americans think you are going to just walk away and leave us, you'll never make it to the airport.

Colonel Luan, Chief of the South Vietnamese Police, as North Vietnamese troops advanced on Saigon. As US Embassy guards threw Vietnamese employees off the last helicopter on 29 April 1975, and after 25 years of fighting, the Vietnam War was over. On 1 May, Saigon was renamed Ho Chi Minh City.

Mum's out, Dad's out, let's talk rude – Pee po belly bum drawers!

A late lyric by Michael Flanders, who died on 15 April 1975 at the age of 53; after serving with the Royal Navy in the Second World War he was a noted athlete at Oxford University before being crippled by polio; his sparkling stage performances from a silver wheelchair, accompanied by Donald Swann, are treasured by all who saw them.

These figures are disappointing, alarming, and an absolute tragedy.

A milestone is passed as unemployment in Britain passes the one million mark on 24 April 1975, Engineering Union leader Hugh Scanlon. The average wage increase for the previous 12 months was 32 per cent. Inflation hit 25 per cent in June – the same amount by which sterling was devalued from its 1971 value on the foreign exchanges.

In a revolutionary process the vote is not the only or even the most significant expression of the strength and influence of a party.

After a year in which dictatorship gave way to military rule, which in turn gave way to elections, Portugal elected a Socialist government under Mario Soares; the Communists – whose leader, Alvaro Cunhal, is quoted above – came third: 26 April 1975.

This going into Europe will not turn out to be the thrilling mutual exchange supposed. It is more like nine middle-aged couples with failing marriages, meeting in a darkened bedroom in a Brussels hotel for a Group Grope.

The unsettling image evoked by historian E. P. Thompson as Britain prepared for the EEC Referendum campaign: quoted in The Sunday Times, *27 April 1975.*

Television brought the brutality of war into the comfort of the living room. Vietnam was lost in the living rooms of America, not the battlefields of Vietnam.

Marshal McLuhan, Canadian sociologist and media guru, Montreal Gazette, 16 May 1975.

There exists no politician in India daring enough to attempt to explain to the masses that cows can be eaten.

Indira Ghandi, who was expelled from the Indian parliament, the Lok Sabha, and disbarred from public office for six years after being found guilty of

SAYINGS, SLOGANS and CATCHPHRASES of THE SEVENTIES

Burn your bra!
Feminism in the Mesolithic era, US from c.1970.

Clunk, click, *every* trip.
UK Department of Transport advert, from 1971.

Heineken refreshes the parts other beers cannot reach.
UK, Heineken beer advert, from 1975.

I ♥ New York
1977, then everywhere (and everything) else.

I'm Mandy, fly me.
A target for feminists: US and UK advert for Trans World Airlines.

I quit school when I were sixteen.
US public service ad.

Save water – bath with a friend. Don't pull for a pee.
Semi-official exhortations from the UK drought year of 1976.

That'll do nicely, sir.
UK, American Express advert, from the US 'Accepted Everywhere'.

Your flexible friend.
UK, advert for Access credit card.

electoral fraud on 12 June 1975; quoted in Oriana Fallaci, New York Review of Books.

I hold the future of Britain in my hand.
Tony Benn, Energy Secretary, holds up a bottle of crude oil as North Sea production begins to flow on 18 June 1975.

Something had to be done to bring this madman's merry-go-round of inflation to a stop.
Denis Healey, 11 July 1975, as the government

announces a limit of £6 a week on wage increases and an upper limit on pay of £8500 a year; inflation had hit 26 per cent a year.

In view of the success of my economic revolution on Uganda, I offer myself to be appointed Head of the Commonwealth.
Field Marshal President Idi Amin offers his services, July 1975.

No one should try to dictate to other peoples the manner in which they ought to conduct their internal affairs.
Looking very ill and with slurred speech, Leonid Brezhnev puts his signature on a pact recognizing post-war borders in Europe and committing all signatories – the USA, the USSR, Canada, and 35 European states – to uphold human rights, Helsinki, 1 August 1975. Dissidents in the Soviet Union and its satellites set up 'Helsinki Monitoring Groups'.

There are too many guns in the hands of people who don't know how to use them.
A bit of a faux pas: Hubert Horatio Humphrey comments on the unsuccessful attempt by Sarah Jane Moore to assassinate President Ford, 5 September 1975. On 22 September there was another attempt, by a member of Charles Manson's 'family', Lynette 'Squeaky' Fromme.

It is my intention to encourage far-reaching improvements.
King Juan Carlos, General Franco's designated successor, takes over as Head of State in Spain after the 82-year-old dictator's death on 20 November 1975 and declares a general amnesty of political prisoners.

Let our children grow tall, and some taller than others if they have it in them to do so.
Tory leader Margaret Thatcher, on the first of many US speaking tours, 1975.

They are tired but unharmed, and drinking gallons of tea.
Hospital bulletin on John and Sheila Matthews, who were held hostage for six days by IRA gunmen in their flat in Balcombe Street, London W1, and freed on 12 December 1975.

An Act to render unlawful certain kinds of sex discrimination and discrimination on the ground of marriage and establish a Commission with the function of working

towards the elimination of such discrimination and promoting equality of opportunity between men and women generally.
The long title of the Sex Discrimination Act, passed into law in Britain, along with the Equal Pay Act on 29 December 1975.

1976

The presence of the SAS in Northern Ireland will not be helpful.
Nonetheless, on 7 January 1976, they were sent in to the 'bandit country' of South Armagh, where 15 people had been shot dead that week: Gerry Fitt, leader of the Social Democratic and Labour Party.

These little grey cells – it is 'up to them', as you say over here.
Shortly after switching off their life support in the last Poirot adventure, Curtain, *the creator of Hercule Poirot, Dame Agatha Christie, died on 13 January 1976, at the age of 85, Britain's richest author.*

The Iron Lady of British politics is seeking to revive the Cold War.
Captain Y. Gavrilov, writing in the Soviet Defence Ministry newspaper Red Star *on 23 January 1976 after Margaret Thatcher had accused the USSR of being 'bent on world dominance' and 'putting guns before butter'. In a speech on 31 January she accepted the title.*

Tell the lobby correspondents you've got a little story that might interest them.
UK Prime Minister Harold Wilson pulls one last rabbit out of his hat by resigning on 16 March 1976, saying that he had been planning it for a long time, and had now established Labour as 'the natural Party of Government'. In ballots of Labour MPs Wilson was succeeded by James Callaghan, who beat Chancellor Denis Healey and left-wing candidate Michael Foot.

I don't believe in black majority rule ever in Rhodesia... not in a thousand years.
Ian Smith, leader of the rebel regime, March 1976; on 20 March he called up Rhodesia's white army reservists after nationalist guerrillas, now aided by the Marxist regime in neighbouring Mozambique, finally acted on Jeremy Thorpe's recommendation and blew up the railway line to South Africa. On 24 September, under pressure from the USA and South Africa, Smith annouced a two-year progression to black majority rule, and the immediate replacement of the government by a half-white, half-black Council of State.

Bunnies *can* (and *will*) go to France.
Liberal Party leader Jeremy Thorpe; letter to male model Norman Scott, 13 February 1961, published after Scott alleged in a Magistrate's Court that he and Thorpe had had a homosexual relationship. He later accused Thorpe of killing his dog and attempting to murder him in order to cover up the liaison. Thorpe resigned as leader on 10 May 1976, vowing to defend himself against a 'press witch-hunt and campaign of denigration'. He was later charged with attempted murder. When Peter Hain, leader of the Young Liberals and prominent anti-Apartheid campaigner, was (as it turned out) falsely accused of robbing a branch of Barclay's Bank, Harold Wilson said he suspected the South African security organization BOSS of carrying out 'dirty tricks' campaigns against selected Liberal and Labour politicians, including himself, and with help from 'elements' in British Intelligence.

It is the language of pass laws, permits and police.
Black social worker in the township of Soweto, South Africa, after authorities ordered that Afrikaans was to enjoy equality with English as the language medium in black schools; three days of protests and rioting from 15–18 June 1976, during which police were ordered to fire on crowds without warning, left 100 dead and 1000 wounded.

Uganda has among the best prisons in the world and people from many countries are eager to visit them.
President Idi Amin of Uganda grants an interview to a Guardian *journalist, January 1976; among these enlightened penal policies was the practice of obliging the prisoners themselves to carry out executions, using sledgehammers. On 27 June, five Palestinians and two Germans hijacked an Air France plane, most of whose passengers were Israeli, and ordered it to fly to the Ugandan airport of Entebbe; on arrival one passenger, Mrs Dora Bloch, was taken off and murdered by Ugandan police. Ugandan troops then helped the kidnappers to guard the plane. On 4 July an Israeli airborne commando raid rescued all but three of the hostages and flew them out in a Hercules; one commando, all the hijackers and 20 Ugandan soldiers were killed, and 11 MiG fighters – 25 per cent of the Ugandan Air Force – destroyed.*

• •

Love is two minutes fifty-two seconds of squishing noises. It shows your mind isn't clicking right.

'Johnny Rotten', whose punk group The Sex Pistols adorned the late Seventies with such numbers as Anarchy in the UK *and* Never Mind the Bollocks.

• •

A simple and proper function of government is just to make it easy for us to do good and difficult for us to do wrong.

Jimmy Carter, peanut farmer and Governor of Georgia, accepts the Democrat Party nomination for the Presidency, New York City, 15 July 1976.

Britain has lived too long on borrowed time, borrowed money and even borrowed ideas.

UK Prime Minister James Callaghan, quoted in The Observer, *3 October 1976. On 29 September Britain applied to borrow $3.9 billion from the International Monetary Fund in order to prop up sterling, which had sunk to $1.69. With the IMF now, in effect, running Britain's economic policy, the bank rate went up to 15 per cent on 7 October, and the mortgage rate to 12.25 per cent the next day. The loan was granted on 3 January 1977.*

On 17 December, OPEC raised the price of crude oil by 15 per cent.

Don't be a gang of four.

Alleged to have been said to his wife, Chiang Ching, of her attempts to plot with senior Communist Party officials, by Mao Tse-tung, who died on 29 September 1976 at the age of 82.

The 'Gang of Four' were then arrested, described officially as 'dog dung', paraded in effigy through Peking, and jailed on 23 October.

————————

There is no Soviet domination of Eastern Europe and there never will be under a Ford administration.

A celebrated gaffe, as President Ford and Jimmy Carter engage in a campaign debate on US television, 7 October 1976.

~

A strong nation, like a strong person, can afford to be gentle, firm, thoughtful and restrained. It can afford to extend a helping hand to others. It's a weak nation, like a weak person, that must behave with bluster and boasting and rashness and other signs of insecurity.

Jimmy Carter puts a psychological spin on realpolitik in a speech in New York City, 14 October 1976; on 2 November he was elected President, with 40.8 per cent of the popular vote to Ford's 39.1 per cent, and by 297 electoral college votes – half of them from Southern and border states – to 240. His Vice-President was Walter Mondale.

The new President's local Baptist church in Plains, Georgia, started to admit black worshippers on 14 November.

————————

A lie can be halfway round the world before the truth has got its boots on.

A misquotation of the 19th-century Baptist preacher, the Rev. C.H. Spurgeon, who put it rather more decorously: Prime Minister James Callaghan, House of Commons, 1 November 1976, on the effect of 'media distortion'.

The world is here today.

Mairead Corrigan, who, with Betty Williams, led the Northern Ireland 'Women for Peace' campaign and won the 1976 Nobel Peace Prize, addresses a 30,000-strong rally in London, 27 November 1976. The movement later changed its name to 'Peace People', and eventually fizzled out.

Power is the ultimate aphrodisiac.

Henry Kissinger, then briefing President-elect Carter on foreign policy, and no stranger to the company of very much younger women: quoted in the Guardian, *28 November 1976.*

1977

During the past few weeks I have felt sometimes that the Suez Canal was flowing through my drawing-room.

Lady Clarissa Eden, November 1956, whose husband Anthony Eden, later Lord Avon, died on 14 January 1977, at the age of 79.

Let's do it.

The last words of Gary Gilmour, executed by firing squad at the Utah State Penitentiary for the murder of two students at Brigham Young

University, 17 January 1977; he was the first person to be executed in the USA for ten years. He had requested death rather than imprisonment for life.

Britain is no longer in the politics of the pendulum, but of the rack.
Margaret Thatcher, speech to the Institute of Public Relations. On 26 February 1977, the government-owned vehicle makers British Leyland closed down all its factories after a succession of strikes had crippled output; their effect on quality did much to boost sales of imported Japanese cars.

Turkeys don't vote for Christmas.
Liberal MP David Penhaligon explains on 24 March 1977 why his party did not vote against the government on a motion of confidence and thus bring about a general election; instead the Liberals entered a pact with Labour under which they were supposed to have influence in the formulation of policy.

A piece of the ceiling fell on my wife, and as I was trying to unfasten her seat belt there was another explosion. People just started raining down from the lounge above on top of me. It was just like a movie.
Californian Jim Naik, a passenger on a Pan Am Boeing 747 jumbo jet that collided with a KLM 747 on the runway at Tenerife on 27 March 1977; both had been diverted from Las Palmas because of a bomb explosion. It was the worst accident in aviation history: 547 people died. It emerged afterwards that the KLM airliner had not been cleared for take-off.

As the Prime Minister put it to me … he saw his role as being that of Moses.
A case of 'the son-in-law also rises' as Peter Jay, husband of the Prime Minister's daughter, is propelled from his job as an economic journalist with Independent Television to be Britain's Ambassador in Washington, DC, on 13 May 1977; at a meeting of the 'Group of Seven' five days earlier, Callaghan and President Carter had agreed to make the reduction of inflation and the creation of employment their top priority.
The 'Social Contract' between government and Unions was finally declared dead in July, as the TUC refused to adhere to a voluntary 10 per cent wage-rise limit; miners' union delegates demanded £135 for a four-day week, and railwaymen submitted a 63 per cent claim.

Much of the world's work, it has been said, is done by men who do not feel quite well. Marx is a case in point.
J. K. Galbraith, The Age of Uncertainty, 1977.

Whenever you accept our views, we shall be in full agreement with you.
Israeli General Moshe Dayan to US negotiator Cyrus Vance, 14 August 1977. Israel's Prime Minister, Menachem Begin, a former terrorist, had permitted Jewish settlement on the West Bank of the River Jordan, captured in 1967.

Listen, son, you ain't goin' nowhere. You oughta go back to drivin' a truck.
Jim Denny, manager of Grand Ole Opry, fired Elvis Presley after one performance, 25 September 1954. On 16 August 1977, having grossed $1 billion in earnings, the King died of a surfeit of drugs and junk food, at the age of 42.

Please accept my resignation. I don't care to belong to any club that will have me as a member.
Letter to the Secretary of the Friars Club, Beverly Hills, from Groucho Marx, who died on 20 August 1977, at the age of 86.

The most potent weapon in the hands of the aggressor is the mind of the oppressed.
The South African black leader Steve Biko, who died in custody on 12 September 1977 after being stripped naked and put in leg irons and handcuffs before a five-day interrogation. According to police, he threw a chair at them and then, during a 'struggle', collided with walls and tables; he was afterwards 'found injured in his cell' and driven, naked, 750 miles (1250 km) from Port Elizabeth to Pretoria, where he died. On 2 December a magistrate ruled that police were not to blame for his death, which was from 'self-inflicted brain injuries'. Riots followed.

All they have managed to do is to improve our licence and open the floodgates for lower-price air travel all over the world.
Entrepreneur Freddy Laker on the 'big six' air-

lines who tried to block his application to run a 'walk-on' service between Heathrow and New York. On 26 September 1977 the first Laker Skytrain took off: the single fare was £59 plus an optional supplement of £1.75 for a three-course meal with wine. The normal single fare at the time was £186.

Either back us or sack us.
UK Prime Minister James Callaghan throws down the gauntlet to his own left-wingers at the Labour Party Conference, Brighton, 5 October 1977.

All I need to make a comedy is a park, a policeman and a pretty girl.
From the Autobiography (1964) of Charlie Chaplin, who died as Sir Charles Chaplin on Christmas Day 1977, at the age of 88. On 2 March 1978 his coffin was exhumed and stolen; seven weeks later it was found reburied ten miles away.

1978

Of course they have, or I wouldn't be sitting here talking to someone like you.
Dame Barbara Cartland, interviewed on BBC radio, was asked if she thought that British class barriers had broken down: quoted in Jilly Cooper, Class (1978).

I stuck on a stage moustache and dyed my grey hair black. Then I climbed over the back fence.
Donald Woods, editor of the South African Daily Despatch, had incurred the displeasure of the state by his reporting of the death of Steve Biko, and had been warned by police not to leave his home; an ill-wisher sent his young daughter a Steve Biko T-shirt impregnated with acid. He escaped by hitch-hiking to Lesotho, 300 miles (500 km) distant, by posing as, among other things, an Afrikaner who could speak no English, and an Australian on the bum; then he swam 75 yards across the Tele River, which was in spate. His wife and five children joined him on 1 January 1978 by a more conventional route, and the family settled in England.

Andy shoots from the lip a bit, but he's fundamentally on-side.
UK Foreign Secretary David Owen on Andrew Young, US Ambassador to the United Nations, who criticized Britain for appearing to acqui-

esce in Ian Smith's plan for eventual black majority rule in Rhodesia, which did not include the two main nationalist guerrilla leaders, Joshua Nkomo and Robert Mugabe: 15 February 1978. A month later, Mugabe led his forces out of Mozambique and began to wage war on the regime.

We expect to stay here for quite a while.
Israel joins in Lebanon's complex of bloody conflicts by invading and occupying the south of the country, ostensibly in response to the hijacking of three buses by Palestinian guerrillas based in the region, and the murder of 30 passengers: Israeli Army spokesman, 14 March 1978.

Your experience will be a lesson to all of us men to be careful not to marry ladies in very high positions.
A message of condolence from President Idi Amin to Lord Snowdon, on his divorce from Princess Margaret, which was petitioned on 14 May 1978.

We have a public relations disaster on our hands. We really must behave. The nation cannot stand this shock.
William Price MP, in charge of the experimental radio broadcasting of proceedings in the House of Commons, alerts his colleagues to the listening public's response to their 'bellowing, abuse, baying, hee-hawing and the rest', 6 June 1978.

Poor poor Peru!
What're we going tae do to you?
Too true!
The poet Alan Bold pens a triumphalist verse in The Scotsman in advance of Scotland's World Cup match against Peru. Peru won and the Scots, having drawn 1–1 against Iran, came home again. Argentina won the final 3–1 against Holland on 25 June 1978.

As we Jews say, 'Next year in Jerusalem'.
Anatoly Scharansky, a founder member of the Helsinki Group, is sentenced to 11 years' detention in prison and labour camp for 'treason and anti-Soviet agitation'; his parting words to the judge on 14 July 1978.

Human rights is the soul of our foreign policy, because human rights is the very soul of our sense of nationhood.
President Jimmy Carter at the 30th anniversary of the UN Declaration of Human Rights, 6 December

1978; in September the US urged the Nicaraguan dictator, Anastasio Somoza, to step down, and on 18 September President Carter brokered the 'Camp David Agreement' between Israeli Prime Minister Menachem Begin and the Egyptian President Anwar Sadat, who had already survived an assassination attempt by Muslim extremists for his recognition of the state of Israel – which, under the agreement, surrendered its occupied territories in Sinai to Egypt. Both men received that year's Nobel Peace Prize.

We shall go forward in faith and humble obedience to God. We will not bend on our knees before Marxism or revolution.
The 'laager mentality': new South African Prime Minister Pieter Willem Botha, 28 September 1978.

We will all remember him for his lovely smile.
Cardinal Basil Hume mourns the death of Pope John Paul on 30 September 1978 after only 33 days in the Vatican; rumours abounded as to the cause of the 65-year-old pontiff's unheralded death, which was ascribed to 'a heart arrest'; it was known that he was keen to distribute a sizable portion of the Vatican's immense wealth, and had intended to investigate the Papacy's banking arrangements. On 16 October the College of Cardinals elected Karol Wojtyla, a fiercely anti-Communist Pole, and the first non-Italian Pope since Adrian VI in 1542; he was also, at 58, the youngest this century. He took the pontifical name of John Paul II.

There was I, waiting at the church.... Can't get away to marry you today, my wife won't let me.
Prime Minister James Callaghan has them rocking in the aisles with an old music-hall number at the Labour Party Conference in October 1978, as he confirms that there will not be an autumn General Election.

~

I have to warn my colleagues in the Labour Movement that this winter will be make or break time for the government.
James Callaghan, 1 November 1978, after the TUC had rejected the government's 5 per cent pay limit proposals; he had reminded trade union leaders that the outcome of pay negotiations would almost certainly settle the outcome of the general election, now due in 1979.

This is an act of revolutionary suicide.
After killing Congressman Leo Ryan and his five colleagues, who had gone to investigate his activities, the Rev. Jim Jones of the 'Jonestown' commune of the People's Temple in Guyana gave his cult followers Kool-Aid laced with cyanide and ordered them to drink it; then he shot himself. Investigators found this note, and the bodies of 913 men, women and children on 29 November 1978.

There Will Be An Interruption
The Times, leader, 30 November 1978. Following a series of industrial disputes and the breakdown of

---

SAYINGS, SLOGANS and CATCHPHRASES of THE SEVENTIES

Nixon: Now More Than Ever
Republican Presidential campaign, 1972.

Come Home, America.
Democrat Presidential campaign, 1972.

Grits and Fritz.
Democrat Presidential campaign, 1976. (The Southern diet, and Walter Mondale's nickname)

Yesterday's Men
Labour, 1970: caption to a photomontage of Tory politicians.

Who governs?
Conservative, February 1974 – inviting a dusty answer.

It's YOUR choice. Take Power – Vote Liberal
Liberal, February 1974.

One Nation
Labour, October 1974; recycling the phrase of (Tory) Stanley Baldwin.

One more heave
Liberal, October 1974.

Labour isn't working
Conservative, 1979: caption to a portrayal of a very long dole queue.

●●●●●●●●●●●●●●●●●●●●●●●●●●●●●●●●

With Nixon in the White House, good health seemed to be in bad taste.

Jane Fonda, California Suite, 1978.

●●●●●●●●●●●●●●●●●●●●●●●●●●●●●●●●

negotiations over pay and manning levels, Times Newspapers Ltd suspended publication. The next edition was dated 12 November 1979.

Because of the greatness of the Shah, Iran is an island of stability in the Middle East. This is a great tribute to you, Your Majesty, and to your leadership, and to the respect, admiration and love which your people give to you.

President Jimmy Carter, 31 December 1978 – a month that saw the imposition of martial law in Iran after a wave of rioting and arson by Islamic militants, and demonstrations in which several million Iranians took to the streets to condemn the Shah for his oppressive regime and encouragement of 'Western practices' in Iranian social life; large numbers of protestors carried portraits of the septuagenarian fundamentalist Shi'ite leader, Ayatollah Ruhollah Khomeini, then in exile in a suburb of Paris. As Soviet troops massed for highly conspicuous military exercises on Iran's border, the Shah installed the Opposition leader Shahpur Bakhtiar as Prime Minister and appealed to Western self-interest to keep him in power.

1979

I should very much like to take a vacation.

Mohammed Reza Pahlavi, Shah of Iran, as he left for Egypt on 16 January 1979. He did not return.

~

I will strike with my fists at the mouths of this government. From now on it is I who will name this government.

Ayatollah Ruhollah Khomeini, Tehran, 1 February 1979. He was as good as his word.

I don't think that other people in the world would share the view that there is mounting chaos.

Prime Minister James Callaghan, arriving at Heathrow from a four-power economic summit in

Guadalupe, *in response to a reporter's question about 'mounting chaos in the country at the moment', 10 January 1979. The* Sun *ran the story under the headline,* CRISIS? WHAT CRISIS? *The 'Winter of Discontent', marked by series of mostly unofficial strikes over which the trade unions exercised little or no control, saw Britain in a chaotic and miserable state, with garbage in the streets and urban open spaces, such as Clapham Common, being used as emergency rubbish dumps; hospitals turned away patients when ancilliary staff walked out and, for a while, the dead in parts of Liverpool were left unburied as gravediggers withdrew their labour. A strike of lorry drivers disrupted food and fuel distribution and on 12 February over 1000 schools were closed because they had run out of heating oil. Two days later the government struck a deal of sorts with union leaders: long-term 'goals' for the reduction of inflation were set, but there was no agreement on a maximum for wage increases.*

Well, that's understandable when you consider that Scotland is a foreign country from their point of view.

Jo Grimond, Liberal MP for Orkney and Shetland, after his constituents voted 'No' in the Scottish devolution referendum of 2 March 1979. The proposal to establish a devolved Scottish Assembly, responsible for administering Scotland's affairs, in the Old High School in Edinburgh was supported by 51.5 per cent of those voting – but 36 per cent of the electorate did not vote. The government, under pressure from Labour anti-devolutionists, had declared that devolution would fall if it failed to be supported by 40 per cent of the whole electorate. In Wales, where 41 per cent stayed away from the polls, similar proposals were rejected by 4 to 1. Scottish and Welsh Nationalists withdrew their support for the government in the Commons and, with the ending of the Lib–Lab pact the previous year, an early election became inevitable.

We have won, at least, the first step of peace, a first step on a long and difficult road.

On the White House lawn, President Carter seals the 'Camp David Accord' between Anwar Sadat and Menachem Begin, 26 March 1979.

Now that the House of Commons has declared itself we shall take our case to the country.

Prime Minister James Callaghan, House of

Commons, as his government loses a confidence motion by one vote at 10.19 p.m. on 28 March 1979. The following day, the Liberal David Alton was elected MP for Alton, Merseyside, in a by-election already pending: he overturned a Labour majority with a swing of 32 per cent.

(1) A normal aberration. *(28 March 1979).*
(2) The coolant leakage is nothing – just a small amount. ... Everything worked. *(28 March).*
(3) This accident is not out of the ordinary for this kind of reactor.
(4) I would not call it an accident. I would call it a malfunction.
(5) The only accident is that this thing leaked out. You could have avoided this whole thing by not saying anything.

The words of: (1) and (3) Jack Herbein, Vice-President of Consolidated Edison; (2) Don Curry, Head of Public Relations for Consolidated Edison; (4) Atom-bomb guru Edward Teller, interviewed in Playboy; (5) Craig Faust, reactor control room operative. On 28 March 1979 the nuclear reactor at the Three Mile Island generator in Pennsylvania suffered catastrophic overheating when coolant valves failed to function; a mistake by an operator compounded the problem, and a process of meltdown began. A large bubble of hydrogen gas then formed inside the crippled reactor; an explosion was avoided when a jet of the radioactive gas was released into the atmosphere and drifted 16 miles (27km) downwind. A quantity of contaminated water – 250,000 gallons – leaked on to the reactor floor, and radiation levels inside the plant rose to 1000 times the normal level. The Three Mile Island reactor was permanently shut down; eight similar reactors in other parts of the USA were kept open.

Oh Lord, help me, for I am innocent.
The last words of former Pakistan Prime Minister Zulfikar Ali Bhutto, hanged on 4 April 1979 after being convicted of the murder of a political opponent – a conviction that was almost certainly false, and obtained on the orders of the new regime, led by the fundamentalist General Zia ul-Haq.

We will never know. This is one small spot in one small place. It is a nation of skulls.
Anonymous Cambodian government spokesman as 2000 skeletons, roped together and weighted, are

found in a lake near the town of Stung Treng, 2 April 1979. Pol Pot's Chinese-backed regime had been overthrown by Vietnam, although the Khmer Rouge still controlled large parts of the country. In July, after numerous 'skull mines' had been been unearthed, Cambodian leader Heng Samrin formally indicted Pol Pot for the murder of three million people.

The latest estimated population is seven million.

As conqueror of the British Empire I am prepared to die in defence of the Motherland, Uganda.
So saying, General Idi Amin fled to Libya as Tanzanian forces and opposition militias liberated the country. On 13 April 1979 Yusuf Lule, a former Vice-Chancellor of Kampala University, returned from exile to become President.

~

We must not indulge in the evil acts of the regime we have removed. Respect for life and individual rights must be paramount. The rule of law must be established.
President Lule of Uganda, 13 April 1979. Amin's regime is conservatively estimated to have murdered 300,000 Ugandans.

I would just like to remember some words of St Francis of Assisi which I think are really just particularly apt at the moment: 'Where there is discord, may we bring harmony; where there is error, may we bring truth; where there is doubt, may we bring faith; and where there is despair, may we bring hope.'
Margaret Thatcher becomes Prime Minister in the early hours of 4 May 1979, with an overall majority of 43. A letter to the Church Times from a former Bishop of Ripon suggested that the prayer was of 19th-century origin, and probably French.

Any woman who understands the problems of running a home will be nearer to

•••••••••••••••••••••••••••••••••••••••

I love the smell of napalm in the morning – it smells of victory.

Robert Duvall, Apocalypse Now, *1979.*

•••••••••••••••••••••••••••••••••••••••

understanding the problems of running a country.
Prime Minister Margaret Thatcher, quoted in the Observer, *8 May 1979.*

Communism and capitalism are realities, but underneath stand the people. This is human reality.
Pope John Paul II visits Poland on 2 June 1979, and kisses the ground at the airport; he was welcomed in Warsaw by Cardinal Wyszynski and President Jablonski, and by two million people who lined the route from the airport.

Aw, this truly was the Son of God.
Possibly apocryphal: John Wayne, playing a centurion, was asked to deliver his lines at the foot of the Cross 'with awe'. Wayne, whose real name was Marion Morrison, died on 11 June 1979, at the age of 72.

You strike me as the sort of person who has a cocktail bar in his sitting-room.
At the Old Bailey trial of former Liberal leader Jeremy Thorpe, Mr Justice Cantley addresses one of the co-accused, gaming machine salesman George Deakin. On 22 June 1979, and after the jury had been out for 52 hours, all four were found not guilty of conspiring to murder Norman Scott; Thorpe, who did not give evidence, was also acquitted of incitement to murder. It had emerged during the trial that a chief prosecution witness, former Liberal MP Peter Bessell, was under contract to the Sunday Telegraph *for serialization of his book on the affair; had Thorpe been convicted he would have earned more money.*

We are helping to defend the most sacred right of every man, the right to live.
Soviet leader Leonid Brezhnev, whose own life was being heavily defended by a battery of Kremlin doctors, signs the SALT-2 Treaty with President

Carter in Vienna on 18 June 1979. The treaty equalized the number of strategic nuclear missiles each side could hold, and restricted them to 2250 – but there was no limit on the number of warheads each could carry.

Not every problem someone has with his girlfriend is necessarily due to the capitalist mode of production.
Professor Herbert Marcuse, radical guru of the Sixties, quoted in the Listener; *he died on 29 July 1979, at the age of 81.*

I can think of nothing more counterproductive and less likely to succeed than an attempt of this kind to move government policy on South Africa.
UK Foreign Secretary Lord Carrington, 31 July 1979, as the military regime in Nigeria seizes the oil assets of British Petroleum, ostensibly in order to force Britain's hand on the issue of sanctions against apartheid.

What would they want with an old man like me?
Earl Mountbatten of Burma refused to employ bodyguards while in Mullaghmore, Co. Sligo, where he had holidayed for 30 years. On 27 August 1979 a remotely controlled 50 lb (23 kg) bomb blew his fishing boat apart as it was leaving harbour and, along with a 15-year-old boatman, his grandson Nicholas (14) and his daughter, Lady Bradbourne, he was killed instantly; he was 79. On the same day, a half-tonne IRA bomb hidden in a haycart at Warrenpoint, Co. Down, killed 15 soldiers as they were passing it in convoy.

On my knees I beg you to turn away from violence. Further violence will only drag down to ruin the land you claim to love and the values you claim to cherish.
Pope John Paul II, visiting Ireland, addresses a huge crowd in Drogheda, 30 September 1979; 250,000 crossed the border from the North to hear him.

Tell me why – I don't like Mondays, I wanna shoot the whole day down.

Bob Geldof – The Boomtown Rats, I Don't Like Mondays, *1979. Brenda Spencer, a 14 year old San Diego schoolgirl, killed and wounded several people in the playground; asked why she'd opened fire, she said, 'I don't like Mondays.'*

If 2,225,000 Americans were starving to death, this ad would be a lot bigger. Feed Cambodia.
Billboard, USA, October 1979. The Cambodian government and the Khmer Rouge agreed to allow UNICEF and the Red Cross to organize famine relief.

In the name of the Prophet I call upon American Muslims to take this acolyte of Satan from his bed and dismember him.
Ayatollah Khalkhali, the 'Judge Jeffreys' of revolutionary Iran, reacts to the news that the exiled Shah has entered a New York hospital for the removal of his gall bladder and treatment for thyroid cancer, 23 October 1979.

~

No More Iranian Students Will Be Permitted On These Premises Until The Hostages Are Released.
Sign outside a licensed brothel near Reno, Nevada, November 1979. On 4 November a mob of 'students' invaded the US Embassy in Tehran and seized nearly 100 staff, who were paraded blindfold before TV cameras before being led away to be held hostage for the return of the Shah. A vast crowd surrounded the Embassy, burning American flags and chanting slogans. Eleven days later, Khomeini ordered the release of all black and female hostages; for the others, the wait was to prove longer.

On 13 November a Shi'ite mob, taking inspiration from Khomeini, stormed and seized the Grand Mosque in Mecca; they were ejected by Saudi troops 11 days later, and 64 were later executed. On 21 November a huge mob laid seige to the US Embassy in Islamabad, Pakistan, killing a Marine guard, and the British Council library in Rawalpindi was badly damaged in another mass attack.

I was not prepared to settle for a third of the loaf.
Prime Minister Thatcher, Dublin, 30 November 1979. She had demanded a £1000 million rebate on Britain's £1100 million EEC budget contribution, and had been offered a rebate of £350 million. She rejected it. In the New Year she threatened to withhold VAT payments to the EEC and, in June, settled for around two-thirds of the loaf: Britain's contribution was cut to £250 million. Also in November, the government announced a £3500 million public spending cut and a large increase in NHS prescription charges, and building societies put the mortgage rate up 3.5 per cent to 15 per cent. The National Union of Mineworkers threatened strike action over a 65 per cent wage claim.

The Soviet Union has been requested to render urgent political, moral, military and economic assistance to the people of Afghanistan.
On Christmas Eve 1979 airborne forces seized control of Kabul airport to clear the way for a rapid air and land invasion of the country, while a KGB hit squad stormed the Darulaman Palace and assassinated President Hafizullah Amin and his family; Moscow named Babrak Karmal as the the new leader of the country. It was presumed that the Kremlin feared Amin was not sufficient guarantee against another Islamic revolution on its borders. A long, bitter, and – for both countries – ruinous war began, which was to be called 'Russia's Vietnam'.

Aspects of Liberty
1980-1989

Greed is all right. Greed is healthy. You can be greedy and still
feel good about yourself.

~ *Ivan Boesky, US financier, 1986*

As the decade opened, the USSR seemed to have become involved in 'another
Vietnam' in its neighbour, Afghanistan, where it found itself fighting a ferocious
guerrilla war on several fronts against a bewildering number of armed Islamic
groups. In Iran, fundamentalist Shi'ite Islam triumphed as the Shah fled into
exile and the Ayatollah Rohalla Khomeini, fresh from his own exile in Paris, took
over.

In Britain and America, which elected the former film actor and Californian
governor Ronald Reagan as President in 1980, the keyword of the decade was
'market' as 'market forces' and the 'discipline of the market' were assumed to
reign supreme in all areas of politics and society. The first manifestation of this
was recession and high unemployment in the 'rust belts' – the areas of both countries in which the older heavy industries, as well as some of the newer ones, were
located; to some extent, this was part of an inevitable 'technological revolution'
brought about by the commercial exploitation of developments in computing and
digital communication. Direct taxes were cut (and government deficits raised,
despite large cuts in 'headline' areas of government spending) as part of both
administrations' interpretation of 'monetarist' economic philosophy. In Britain,
a significant part of the post-war 'political settlement', including the Welfare
State, was to be dismantled as nationalized industries, including all the public
utilities, were returned to shareholder ownership through 'privatization', and
the social security and National Health systems were reorganized along 'market
economy' lines. Even government departments – and in turn, institutions such as
the BBC – found themselves subject to the 'internal market' philosophy, while
huge areas of local government, from the setting of local charges to the provision
of school dinners, were removed from local democratic control. Throughout this
period, both in the UK and the USA, political opposition was weak, fragmented
and poorly organized and neither Mrs Thatcher, throughout the whole decade,
nor President Reagan from 1980 to 1988, was seriously threatened by scandal,
although the 'Iran-Contra Affair' in the USA might well have toppled a less pop-

ular and self-assured politician. For Mrs Thatcher, the Falklands War of 1982 was an undoubted boost, as well as being an undeniable fillip for national pride; and the miners' strike of 1984–85 gave her government a perfect and well-planned opportunity to take on and defeat an aspect of British Socialism that enjoyed little popularity in the country; the sea-change in the Labour Party that has produced the 'New Labour' of Tony Blair in the 1990s may be dated to the crushing defeat of the National Union of Mineworkers and its former Communist leader, Arthur Scargill.

Following the succession of Mikhail Gorbachev as Soviet leader in 1985, the decade ended with some of the most extraordinary and moving events, of this or any other century, as the countries of eastern Europe freed themselves from totalitarian rule and declared themslves independent and sovereign democracies. A similar attempt, also inspired by the Soviet leader, to shrug off the dictatorship of an oligarchy in China failed horribly and appallingly in Peking's Tiananmen Square.

1980

Let's get down to the nitty-gritty. You are being arrested on the same charges.
Former Rhodesian Prime Minister Garfield Todd is arrested on 9 February 1980 as he attempts to intercede on behalf of a local schoolmaster under arrest for 'assisting terrorists'. A new interim colonial administration was in charge in the country now called Zimbabwe, under Bishop Abel Muzorewa and Governor Lord Soames – who intervened to have Mr Todd released. Guerrilla leaders Robert Mugabe and Joshua Nkomo were to contest elections, which began on 27 February.

It could never be a correct justification that, because the whites oppressed us yesterday when they had power, that the blacks must oppress them today because they have power.
Robert Gabriel Mugabe, Prime Minister of Zimbabwe. On 4 March 1980, Mugabe's ZANU was declared the winner, with 57 of the reserved 'black' Parliamentary seats; the ZAPU party was represented by Nkomo, who became Home Affairs minister in a 'reconciliation cabinet' which included two members of Ian Smith's Rhodesian Front, winners of all 20 'white' seats. The Rev. Dr Canaan Banana was President.

The soil of our country is destined to be the scene of the fiercest fight and the sharpest struggles to rid our continent of the last vestiges of white minority rule.

South Africa was now the last bastion of white supremacy in Africa; Nelson Mandela, message from prison to mark the transference of power in Zimbabwe, March 1980.

It is difficult to go on strike if there is no job in the first place.
Lord George Brown, quoted in the Observer *of 24 February 1980; on 14 February the government announced that state benefit to strikers would be halved. In April, unemployment stood at 1.5 million; it reached 2 million in August, 2.5 million in April 1981, and 3 million thereafter. Many changes were made in the Eighties to the methodology of calculating unemployment. The March 1980 budget raised VAT to a single rate of 17.5 per cent; inflation rose to 22 per cent in May.*

~

There is no easy popularity... I believe people accept that there is no alternative.
The phrase that acquired for Mrs Thatcher the nickname 'Tina': There is no alternative. Speech to the Conservative Women's Conference, 21 May 1980.

The proverbial man in the street says the street's no place for anyone anymore.

New York Times *editorial, 1980.*

The rich hate signing cheques. Hence the success of credit cards.

Graham Greene, Dr Fischer of Geneva, or, The Bomb Party, 1980.

Hell is other people.
Jean-Paul Sartre, Huis Clos, 1944. On 15 April 1980 Sartre was released from earthly torment, at the age of 74.

It was my decision to attempt the rescue operation, it was my decision to cancel it when a problem developed in the placement of our rescue team. The responsibility is purely my own.
President Carter, 25 April 1980, after an attempt to rescue the US Embassy hostages in Iran ended in hideous failure after being aborted in the desert, hundreds of miles from Tehran, when sand clogged the engines of the rescue helicopters, one of which was hit by a tanker aircraft. The burned bodies of eight US troops were left behind to be gloated over on Iranian TV.

The incumbent President had lost the Massachussetts primary election to Edward Kennedy on 4 March.

What I said was, actors should be treated like cattle.
Alfred Hitchcock, denying in 1943 that he'd said actors were cattle. He died on 29 April 1980 at the age of 80.

No one knows more about this mountain than Harry. And it don't dare blow up on him! This goddamned mountain won't blow. Scientists don't know shit from apple butter!
'Mountain Man' Harry Truman, 83, refuses to be evacuated from Mount St Helens, Washington,

What a man does defiles him, not what is done by others.

William Golding, Rites of Passage, 1980.

which 'blew' on 19 May 1980, killing eight people – including Harry Truman – and sending a 60,000 ft column of ash into the atmosphere.*

Voodoo economics.
Republican Presidential contender George Bush on the 'supply side' and 'trickle-down' theories advocated by his rival, Ronald Reagan (or, perhaps, advocated on his behalf), May 1980.

My ambition is to be remembered as the greatest player of all time. I guess you could say I have come close.
Björn Borg wins the Wimbledon Men's Singles for the fifth time, 5 July 1980.

Like the sorry tapping of Neville Chamberlain's umbrella on the cobblestones of Munich.
Ronald Reagan, adopted as Republican candidate for the Presidency on 17 July 1980, on the foreign policy of President Carter, as the US hostages in Iran remained in captivity. Reagan chose ex-CIA boss (and 'voodoo economics' critic) George Bush as his running mate.

A professional girlfriend and an amateur actress.
Britt Ekland according to Peter Sellers, who died on 24 July at the age of 54, two weeks after the release of the film of Being There (US), in which he played the human 'tabula rasa', Chauncey Gardiner. He got his first job at the BBC by fooling a producer into believing he was Kenneth Horne.

I can win much better with him.
President Carter appealed for the support of Edward Kennedy, who divided the Democrats with a superb speech advocating unity at the National Covention on 14 August 1980. Carter won the nomination, but chose Walter Mondale as his running mate.

We are now co-masters of this land.
Lech Walesa, leader of a two-month campaign of strikes and demonstrations in the Gdansk shipyard, celebrates an agreement with the Polish government on 30 August 1980: the release of political prisoners, an easing of censorship, the right to strike, and recognition of Walesa's 'Solidarity' free trade union movement. Communist Party leader Edward Gierek 'retired' the following month.

She is the Enid Blyton of economics. Nothing must be allowed to spoil her simple plots.
Richard Holme on Margaret Thatcher, at the Liberal Party Assembly, 10 September 1980.

~

To those waiting with bated breath for that favourite media catch-phrase, the U-turn, I have only one thing to say: you turn if you want to. The lady's not for turning.
Margaret Thatcher addresses the Conservative Party conference, 11 October 1980.

~

I love argument, I love debate. I don't expect anyone just to sit there and agree with me, that's not their job.
Margaret Thatcher on letting a thousand flowers bloom in Cabinet discussions: quoted in The Times.

~

If a woman like Eva Perón with no ideals can get that far, think how far I can go with all the ideals I have.
A comparison to conjure with: Margaret Thatcher, interviewed in The Sunday Times.

~

She is clearly the best man among them.
Former Labour minister and now a member of the European Parliament, Barbara Castle, on Margaret Thatcher: The Castle Diaries *(1980).*

There you go again!
Ronald Reagan gets slightly the better of Jimmy Carter in a TV debate on 28 October 1980: Carter had accused Reagan of intending to cut the Medicare budget. In the 4 November election, Reagan won 43.9 million votes; Carter, who carried only six of the 50 States, received 35.4 million. The US hostages were released on 21 January 1980, after 444 days in captivity.

Men of power have not time to read; yet men who do not read are unfit for power.
Debts of Honour (1980) by Michael Foot, who became leader of the Labour Party on 10 November, defeating Denis Healey. Foot's aphorism echoes that of Jon Wynne Tyson: 'The wrong sort of people are always in power because they

would not be in power if they were not the wrong sort of people."

Life is what happens to you while you're making other plans.
John Lennon, song, 'Beautiful Boy', 1980. On 8 December 1980 Lennon was shot dead outside his home in the Dakota building, New York, by 25-year-old Mark Chapman, who had stalked Lennon for three days and obtained his autograph; he sat on the sidewalk and read The Catcher in the Rye *while waiting to be arrested. The former Beatle was 40.*

No-one would have remembered the Good Samaritan if he'd only had good intentions. He had money as well.
Margaret Thatcher, TV interview, 1980.

1981

The experimental plane may well finish up a few fields from the end of the runway. If so, the voluntary occupants will have only inflicted bruises or worse on themselves. But the reverse may occur and the experimental plane may soar into the sky. The politics of the left and centre of this country are frozen in an out-of-date mould [...] Can this mould be broken?
Roy Jenkins, former Labour Chancellor, Home Secretary and Deputy Prime Minister, now an EEC Commissioner, speaks at a House of Commons Press Gallery lunch, 8 June 1980; on 25 January 1981 the experimental plane began to taxi gently down the runway as Jenkins and three senior serving Labour politicians – Shirley Williams, David Owen and William Rodgers – issued the 'Limehouse Declaration' and founded a 'Council for Social Democracy'. They were then expelled from the Labour Party.

I have never understood why one's affections must be confined, as once with women, to a single country.

John Kenneth Galbraith, A Life in Our Times, *1981.*

•••••••••••••••••••••••••••••••••••

Politicians can forgive almost anything in the way of abuse; they can forgive subversion, revolution, being contradicted, exposed as liars, even ridiculed, but they can never forgive being ignored.

Auberon Waugh, the Observer, *1981.*

•••••••••••••••••••••••••••••••••••

If ever there's any emergence of a fourth party in this country, the task of the Liberal Party is to strangle it at birth.
Liberal MP Cyril Smith, quoted in the Guardian, *reacts to the launch of the SDP.*

I have ordered the armed forces to take all necessary measures to deal with this situation and to ensure the continuance of democratic order.
King Juan Carlos saves Spain's democracy, TV broacast, 23 February 1981, after a group of Civil Guards burst into the Spanish Parliament, the Cortes, fired shots into the ceiling, and took all 350 MPs hostage. The right-wing General presumed to be behind the attempted coup then ordered his men back to barracks.

Yes … whatever that may mean.
HRH the Prince of Wales, interviewed on 24 February 1981 about his engagement to Lady Diana Spencer, is asked whether he is 'in love' with her.

———————————

There's a lot of romantic bullshit about the Secret Service. And they're still living off their finest hour – the Kennedy assassination, when they protected Lyndon Johnson and Jacqueline Kennedy, who weren't the targets anyway, while the President got killed. The most dangerous thing about it is that if you didn't know, you might even feel safe with those guys around. The truth is that the Secret Service is the worst, most inefficient, badly run, highly political outfit in the United States government.
Bill Gulley, former Director of the White House Military Office, Breaking Cover *(1980). On 30 March 1981 President Ronald Reagan was shot in the chest at close range by John Hinckley III, a rich Yale drop-out; the bullet missed the 70-year-*

old President's heart by three inches and lodged in his left lung. Three others – including a Secret Service man – were wounded.

~

Please tell me you're Republicans.
The wounded President quips as he is wheeled into an operating theatre at George Washington Hospital, 30 March 1981.

~

What makes you think I'd be happy about that?
Recovering from surgery, Reagan is told that the government is running smoothly, 31 March 1981.

~

As of now, I am in charge of the White House.
An over-excited Alexander Haig, Secretary of State, reacts to the news of the President's shooting on 30 March 1981. He wasn't.

———————————

Marxism is like a classical building that followed the Renaissance: beautiful in its way, but incapable of growth.
The Earl of Stockton (Harold Macmillan), speech to the Primrose League, 29 April 1981. The Eighties, culturally something of a 'retro decade', saw a pseudo-Classical revival in architecture.

During my seven years in office, I was in love with seventeen million French women … I know this declaration will inspire irony and that English language readers will find it very French.
Valéry Giscard d'Estaing, Le Pouvoir et la Vie (1988). On 10 May 1981, following his defeat in Presidential elections, he gave way to François Mitterrand.

To demonstrate to the world the imperialistic crimes of the Soviet Union and the United States.
Note written in advance of the act by Mehmed Ali Agca, a Turk described by the Turkish authorities as an Armenian, who shot Pope John Paul II four times on 13 May 1981; two of the bullets lodged in the 60-year-old Pope's intestines but he made a recovery after five hours of surgery. Two women were also wounded.

Mehmed was afterwards reconciled with the Pope, who visited him in gaol in Rome. An Italian judge claimed that he had been a 'hit man' for Bulgaria, who had employed him to 'discredit Solidarity'.

My advice was delicately poised between the cliché and the indiscretion.

Robert Runcie, Archbishop of Canterbury, on his 'pre-nuptial counselling' of Their Royal Highnesses the Prince and Princess of Wales, who were married in St Paul's Cathedral, 29 July 1981. The Royal romance was described by Dr Runcie as 'the stuff of which fairy tales are made'.

There is no place in this nation for deviants from Islam.

Grand Ayatollah Ruhollah Khomeini, 30 August 1981, after a bomb killed President Mohammed Ali Rejai and Prime Minister Dr Mohammed Javad Bahomar. It was blamed on exiled members of Iran's Opposition, who 'force people to carry out sabotage'.

I know all about these problems. I grew up in the thirties with an unemployed father. He didn't riot. He got on his bike and he looked for work. And he found it!

Norman Tebbit, Secretary of State for Trade and Industry, addresses the Conservative Party Conference, September 1981. High unemployment – particularly among young males in inner cities – had been cited as one of the causes of a wave of rioting in Britain during that summer.

This so-called message to the working people of Eastern Europe, adopted at Gdansk, has become an outrageous provocation. We expect the Polish Communist Party leadership and the Polish government immediately to take determined radical steps to cut short the malicious anti-Soviet propaganda and actions hostile to the Soviet Union.

Statement released by Poland's official news agency on 18 September, one week after it was received from the Politburo in Moscow. The Solidarity Movement braced itself for a crackdown, and on 13 December President Jaruzelski duly declared martial law. Within two days, 14,000 trade unionists had been arrested, including Lech Walesa; Poland's former leader, Edward Gierek, was also arrested, along with other prominent Communists, for abusing his post for personal profit. On 20 December, Poland's ambassador to the USA was granted political asylum.

~

My father still reads the dictionary every day. He says your life depends on your power to master words.

Arthur Scargill, President of the National Union of Mineworkers, the Sunday Times, 1981.

If we resign today we will bury our hopes for freedom for many years to come. Several thousand people cannot overcome ten million.

Solidarity's message to Polish workers at the end of December 1981.

In the New Year, prices in Poland increased at a stroke by between 100 and 500 per cent and there was fresh rioting.

I have always said about Tony that he immatures with age.

Sir Harold Wilson on Tony Benn, in The Chariot of Israel, 1981.

A triumph of the embalmer's art.

Gore Vidal on Ronald Reagan, quoted in the Observer, 1981.

1982

I'm flying high and couldn't be more confident about the future.

Sir Freddie Laker, 4 February 1982. Three days later his cut-price Laker Airways collapsed after banks withdrew support; it had been troubled by high interest rates during the recession, and the strength of the dollar against the pound. Sir Freddie blamed his competitors among the big airlines for 'ganging up' against his Skytrain operation and, in some cases, using 'dirty tricks'; a decade later, evidence emerged to support his claim. The following year, both People Express and Virgin Atlantic offered single fares of £99 on the London–New York route.

My conscience is very, very clear.

John De Lorean, US entrepreneur, and another business collapse: this time of De Lorean Cars on 19 February 1982, after losing upwards of £17.8 million invested in its Belfast factory by the British taxpayer. The gull-winged sports car, made from a material previously used in the manufacture of lavatory seats, had been priced below cost in an effort to sell it, but was widely reckoned to be cheap at half the price. In October, De Lorean was caught in possession of cocaine by the FBI; he was later acquitted on the grounds of 'entrapment'.

This is just an excuse to get rid of me and smear my reputation.

Joshua Nkomo, after he and two ZANU colleagues were dismissed from the cabinet of Robert Mugabe, Prime Minister of Zimbabwe, 17 February 1982. Large caches of arms had been discovered on farms owned by Nkomo.

The British are coming!

An exultant David Puttnam brandishes the Best Film Oscar he won for Chariots of Fire *on 29 March 1982.*

I am leaving this city, but my heart is here. I am leaving to continue the struggle, so that we can win the war.

Yasser Arafat, driven out of Beirut by the Israeli invasion of Lebanon, 31 August 1982. The Israelis began an aerial bombardment on 4 June, ostensibly in retaliation against the shooting of their Ambassador in London the day before, and mounted a full-scale invasion two days later. Arafat's Palestine Liberation Organisation was scattered to Syria, Jordan, North and South Yemen, Algeria, Iraq – and Tunisia, where Arafat himself was bound, his ambitions seemingly at an end. The following month, Lebanese Christian militias undertook the wholesale slaughter of hundreds of civilian Palestinian refugees in the Sabra and Chatila camps; Israel denied both complicity and knowledge. The killings followed the assassination by car bomb of the newly-elected Lebanese President, Bashir Gemayel; his elder brother then took over in the office. President Reagan ordered US Marines to resume their 'peace-keeping' functions in Beirut.

We cannot allow the enemy to impose on us the time and forms of the fighting.

Statement by the newly-banned Polish Solidarity movement, 8 October 1982.

It is a triumph for democracy; it is a triumph for the Spanish people.

The Socialists win a landslide victory in the Spanish elections on 28 October 1982, making their leader, 40-year-old Felipe Gonzalez, Europe's youngest Prime Minister.

The Falklands War

We got requests from people who wanted to sail with the task force from Dallas and San Francisco. I remember one man demanding to go who worked on the *Rocky Mountain News*.

After a night of unconfirmed rumours of an Argentinian invasion of the Falkland Islands, an unnamed public relations officer at the British Ministry of Defence fields enquiries as the world wakes up on 2 April 1982; but nobody in London was in a position to confirm or deny anything. All that was known for certain was that a group of Argentinian 'scrap metal dealers' had raised their country's flag on the island of South Georgia on 31 March. Quoted in Gotcha! The Media, the Government, and the Falklands Crisis, *Robert Harris (1983).*

The report on the tapes comes from an Argentine newspaper. We were in touch with the Governor half an hour ago and he said that no landing had taken place at that time.

Humphrey Atkins, Deputy Foreign Secretary, statement, House of Commons, 11 a.m. on 2 April 1982; the Foreign Secretary, Lord Carrington, was, of course, not a member of the elected Chamber. At 2.30 p.m. the same day, Leader of the House Francis Pym said that the situation was 'unchanged'. In fact, Argentinian forces had invaded the Falklands, where the Governor's Residence in Port Stanley was guarded by a small contingent of British troops, ten hours earlier. A fax reporting the invasion was sent from the Governor's Residence but, unaccountably, came through on the machine of a small South London plastic bag factory.

We have suffered the inevitable consequences of a combination of unpreparedness and feeble counsel.
The Conservative MP Julian Amery, speaking in an Emergency Commons debate on Saturday, 3 April 1982. On the initiative of Michael Foot, Leader of the Opposition, inter-party hostilities were effectively suspended for the duration of the crisis. It was widely accepted that the military regime in Argentina had been encouraged to invade the 'Malvinas' by the conciliatory noises being made by the UK Foreign Office during negotiations on sovereignty, and by the announcement that the Antarctic patrol vessel, HMS Endurance, was to be withdrawn from service. Lord Carrington, accepting full responsibility, resigned as Foreign Secretary on 5 April 1982, the day a British military Task Force began to set sail for the Falkland Islands, 8000 miles (12,875 km) away.

WE ARE ALL FALKLANDERS NOW [...] We are an island race, and the focus of attack is one of our islands, inhabited by our islanders. At this point of decision the words of John Donne could not be more appropriate for every man and woman anywhere in a world menaced by the forces of tyranny: 'No man is an island, entire of itself. Any man's death diminishes me, because I am involved in mankind; and therefore never send to know for whom the bell tolls; it tolls for thee.' It tolls for us; it tolls for them.
The peroration to 68 column inches of editorial prose: The Times, 5 April 1982. Even the Guardian, which was to prove a peacemonger later on, proclaimed that 'The cause this time is a just one.'

MIGHT ISN'T RIGHT [...] The main purpose of British policy now should be to get the best possible settlement for the islanders. ... The islands don't matter. The people do. We should offer each of them the chance to settle here or anywhere they choose and we should pay for it. ... The Argentine occupation has humiliated the Government. But military revenge is not the way to wipe it out.
Apart from the Communist Morning Star, the Daily Mirror, quoted above on the day the Task Force set sail, was the only national newspaper in Britain to maintain an anti-war line from the outset. Despite this (perhaps) it did not lose readers – as it had done during the Suez conflict of 1956, which it also opposed.

Failure? Do you remember what Queen Victoria once said? 'Failure? – the possiblities do not exist.'
Prime Minister Margaret Thatcher, TV interview, 5 April 1982.

The British won't fight.
General Galtieri, dictator of Argentina, gives his assessment of the situation to US Secretary of State Alexander Haig, who was conducting 'mediatory' talks, 10 April 1982. Britain secured the backing of the United Nations, which demanded the immediate withdrawal of Argentinian forces; only Panama, which put down a motion naming Britain as the aggressor, voted against it. On 10 April the EEC Commissioners agreed to ban Argentinian imports, and on 12 April Britain enforced a 200-mile (320-km) 'total exclusion zone' around the Falklands. On 19 April the British government formally rejected the Haig peace proposals; President Reagan pledged support for 'our oldest ally'.

Just rejoice at that news and congratulate our forces and the Marines. Good night, gentlemen. Rejoice. Rejoice!
Margaret Thatcher outside Number 10, after Defence Secretary John Nott had briefed reporters on the recapture of South

→

Georgia, 25 April 1982. (See 22 November 1990, p. 222.)

STICK IT UP YOUR JUNTA!

A headline in the Sun, *20 April 1982. Ten days later the paper offered STICK IT UP YOUR JUNTA T-shirts so that patriotic readers could 'give those damn Argies a whole lot of bargie'; and on 1 May it reported that it had 'sponsored' a missile, bearing the slogan 'Up Yours, Galtieri', on board HMS* Invincible. *The report drew protests from* Invincible's *crew.*

I'm not allowed to say how many planes joined the raid, but I counted them all out and I counted them all back.

Brian Hanrahan of the BBC, reporting from HMS Hermes *on a Harrier attack on Port Stanley airport, 1 May 1982. The BBC Director-General Alasdair Milne called this 'An elegant way of telling the truth without compromising the exigencies of military censorship.'*

GOTCHA!

Sun headline, first edition, 4 May 1982, reporting the sinking of the Argentine battle-cruiser General Belgrano *by a torpedo fired from the submarine HMS* Conqueror *on the night of 2 May; the paper was at the time being produced by its 13 editorial staff during a strike, and later headlines carried the 'more restrained' headline DID 1200 ARGIES DROWN? In fact, 362 Argentinian sailors lost their lives as the warship, outside the Total Exclusion Zone and apparently heading for its home port, was hit.*

In the course of its duties within the Total Exclusion Zone around the Falkland Islands, HMS *Sheffield*, a Type 42 destroyer, was attacked and hit late this afternoon by an Argentine missile. The ship caught fire which spread out of control [...] It is feared there have been a number of casualties, but we have no details of them yet.

Interrupting the BBC's Nine O'Clock News, which was enjoying a record audience of 12 million on the night of 4 May 1982, Ministry of Defence spokesman Ian MacDonald reports the first significant British casualty of the conflict, destroyed by an 'Exocet' missile fired from a plane 20 miles (32 km) away and below radar range. The loss of life was 21, less than originally feared. Other British naval losses included HMSs Coventry, Ardent *and* Antelope, *and the support ships* Atlantic Conveyor *(mistaken for HMS* Hermes *and, along with HMS* Invcincible, *regularly claimed by the Argentinians as a 'hit'),* Sir Galahad *and* Sir Tristan.

'The price of sovereignty has been increased by one penny' – official.

Caption to the Guardian's *reprinting of the 1942 Low cartoon in the* Daily Mirror. *The* Guardian *was criticized for 'disloyalty'.*

The widow of Portsmouth is no different from the widow of Buenos Aires. The BBC needs no lesson in patriotism.

Richard Francis, Director of BBC Radio, defends the Corporation at the International Press Institute; the BBC, and especially its News and Current Affairs staff, came under fire (not least from the Prime Minister) for not being sufficiently 'supportive' of British forces during the Falklands War.

We did not tell a lie – but we did not tell the whole truth.

Sir Frank Cooper, Permanent Under-Secretary at the Ministry of Defence, who briefed correspondents that there would be no 'D-Day style' invasion of the islands by British forces – which was, in fact, precisely what did happen on 21 May 1982 as 3000 troops went ashore in San Carlos Bay; one week later the settlement of Goose Green was retaken and its inhabitants released from detention in the Community Centre. Advancing on foot through difficult terrain in worsening winter weather, sometimes troops encountered fierce resistance.

They are reported to be flying white flags over Port Stanley.
Prime Minister Margaret Thatcher, to a jubilant House of Commons, 14 June 1982.

This is neither the time nor the place to murder Max Hastings.
After telexing the account of his entry into Port Stanley – 'with a civilian anorak and a walking stick' – where he chatted about surrender to an Argentinian colonel, the then correspondent of the Evening Standard *somehow failed to send his fellow-reporters' 'pooled' copy. In the Upland Goose pub the next day, 15 April, Ian Bruce of the* Glasgow Herald, *armed with a knife, took exception to this oversight and had to be restrained; quotation (David Hudson of the* Yorkshire Post*) from Robert Harris,* Gotcha!. *The landlord of the Upland Goose then banned the press corps from his pub, saying they were 'worse than the Argies'.*

We had to do what we had to do. Great Britain is great again.
Margaret Thatcher addresses crowds in Downing Street, 14 June 1982. A total of 255 Britons and 652 Argentinians are known to have died in the conflict. General Leopoldo Galtieri was ousted on 17 June; opposition politicians were later released from gaol, and elections were promised.

Now my charms are all o'erthrown And what strength I have's mine own, Which is most faint...
MoD spokesman Ian MacDonald, whose sepulchral monotone had made him a national celebrity, gives his last briefing on 18 June and quotes Prospero's farewell from Shakespeare's The Tempest.

The battle for women's rights has been largely won.
Margaret Thatcher, the Guardian, *1982.*

For the past few months she has been charging about like some bargain-basement Boadicea.
Denis Healey, Labour's Deputy Leader, on Margaret Thatcher; quoted in the Observer, *7 November 1982.*

He was a true continuer of Lenin's great cause and an ardent champion of peace and Communism. His name will live forever.
The official Kremlin obituary of Leonid Brezhnev, who died – or was finally pronounced dead – on 10 November 1982, at the age of 75. He was succeeded by the former KGB chief Yuri Andropov (61), who died 15 months later; he, in turn, was succeeded by Konstantin Chernenko, a 72-year-old emphysema sufferer.

Let no one expect us to disarm unilaterally. We are not a naive people.
President Yuri Andropov of the USSR, speech, Central Committee of the Soviet Communist Party, 22 November 1982. In Britain on 12 December, 20,000 women took part in a protest demonstration at the Greenham Common airbase, due to receive its first US-controlled Cruise missiles the following year. (See 8 March 1983, *p. 190.)*

Pennies do not come from heaven. They have to be earned here on earth.
Margaret Thatcher, Sunday Telegraph.

1983

Victorian values – those were the values when our country became great, not only internationally but at home.
UK Prime Minister Margaret Thatcher, interviewed on television on 17 January 1983 by former Labour MP Brian Walden, who had introduced the phrase.

A good man fallen among politicians.
Echoing Lenin on George Bernard Shaw, the Daily
Mirror, *28 February 1983, on Labour leader
Michael Foot.*

It is not what one would call a major
work, but it is a charming chamber symphony written with the boyish hand of a
great composer.
*Professor Jens Larsen of Copenhagen University
on the discovery in March 1983 of a minor
Mozart Symphony (in A Minor), written when the
composer was nine years old. On 27 June 1996,
a single page of a lost Mozart aria was sold at auc-
tion for £87,000.*

In my youth I imagined the universe as
an open book, printed in the language of
physical equations, whereas now it
appears to me as a text written in invisible ink, of which in our rare moments of
grace we are able to decipher a small
fragment.
Arthur Koestler, epilogue, Bricks to Babel
*(1970). On 3 March 1983 the philosopher,
essayist, novelist and Vice-President of the
Voluntary Euthanasia Society, who was suffering from leukaemia and Parkinson's disease,
committed suicide in a pact with his wife. He
was 77.*

In your discussions of the nuclear
freeze proposals, I urge you to beware
the temptation of pride – the temptation blithely to declare yourselves
above it all and label both sides equally
at fault, to ignore the facts of history
and the aggressive policies of an evil
empire.
*US President Ronald Reagan's first use of his
epithet for the Soviet Union, speech, Florida, 8
March 1983 in which he outlined proposals for
a 'Strategic Defense Initiative' involving the
deployment of ground- and satellite-guided
lasers to destroy incoming nuclear warheads
and so create a 'nuclear umbrella' over the con-*

• •

We are the true peace
movement.

Margaret Thatcher, The Times, *1983.*

• •

*tinental US. The scheme, which appeared to
require several gigantic mirrors, was dubbed
'Star Wars' by the media and received with
scepticism (or derision) by many scientists,
while the USSR denounced it as warmongering
and provocation. Later, Reagan invited the
USSR to join in the research.*

History buffs probably noted the reunion
at a Washington party a few weeks ago of
three ex-Presidents, Carter, Ford and
Nixon: See No Evil, Hear No Evil, and
Evil.
*Republican Senator Robert J. (Bob) Dole, speech
to the Washington Gridiron Club, 26 March
1983.*

It is one thing to forge a contemporary
document, in which only the hand-
writing and the content must be made
plausible, and another to manufacture
an ancient document, avoiding
the perils of anachronism not only
in writing and content but in paper
and ink.
A Hidden Life: The Enigma of Sir Edmund
Backhouse *(1976) by Hugh Trevor-Roper (Lord
Dacre), who was among the experts who authenti-
cated the 'Hitler Diaries', extracts from which
were published by* The Times *and* Stern *magazine
on 25 April 1983 in a deal reportedly worth £2.5
million. On 6 May they were declared to be a crude
forgery.*

One may be optimistic, but one can't
exactly be joyful at the prospect before
us.
Lord Clark (not, as Private Eye *dubbed him, 'of
Civilisation') who, as Sir Kenneth Clark, wrote
and presented the 1969 television series*
Civilisation, *of which the above quotation is (so
to speak) the end. He died on 21 May 1983, at
the age of 79.*

And what a prize we have to fight for: no
less than the chance to banish from our
land the dark divisive clouds of Marxist
socialism.
*Prime Minister Margaret Thatcher addresses the
Scottish Conservative conference in May.*

The longest suicide note in history.
*Labour MP Gerald Kaufman on his party's
manifesto for the general election of 9 June
1983; quoted in Denis Healey's* Time of My

Life. *The Conservatives were re-elected with 397 seats to Labour's 209; the Liberal–Social Democrat Alliance, with 25 per cent of the vote, won 25 seats; the leaders of both losing parties resigned. With other parties gaining 21 seats, the government's overall majority of 144 was the biggest since 1945. The following month the government announced an increased Defence budget, including £624 million for the Falkland Islands, while the new Chancellor, Nigel Lawson, cut domestic public expenditure by £500 million; Geoffrey Howe's March budget had cut income tax by £2000 million.*

This right is not given to us by the State. It is a right given by the Creator.

A welcome boost for Solidarity, though it raised some theological eyebrows: Pope John Paul II, addressing a congregation of some two million people in Katowice, Poland, 21 June 1983, on the right to join a free trade union. The following month, the Polish government lifted martial law – although many of its more draconian provisions had meanwhile been absorbed into the civilian legal code.

I no longer have the rights I thought I had to protect my own children.

Victoria Gillick, the mother of ten children, asked the High Court of England to rule that doctors were not permitted to supply contraceptive pills to children under 16 without their partents' knowledge or consent; it refused in July 1983 on the grounds that such action was necessary 'in exceptional circumstances'.

I have a face that is a cross between two pounds of halibut and an explosion in an old-clothes closet. If it isn't mobile, it's dead.

The debonair David Niven, who died on 30 July, at the age of 73.

Allah is great and it is sweet to die a martyr.

The chant of children sent by the Iranian commanders to clear minefields in the continuing war with Iran, in which the bitterest fighting occurred along the border between Iraqi Basra and Iranian Abadan in the summer of 1983; Iran launched ferocious counter-attacks during 1983, in which tens of thousands were sacrificed. Many of the 'boy soldiers' were the 'confiscated' children of executed opponents of the Khomeini regime.

What has happened to architecture since the Second World War that the only passers-by who can contemplate it without pain are those equipped with a white stick and a dog?

Bernard Levin, The Times, *1983.*

Of course, I can't protect everything. If they hit me in the head, I'm a goner.

The Philippine opposition leader, Benigno Aquino, returning on 21 August 1983 after three years of exile to contest elections against President Ferdinand Marcos, talks to reporters on his flight and shows them his body armour. He was arrested as he left the plane and, as he was being led into a van, shot in the head and killed; police then killed his assassin, whom they described as 'a lone gunman hired by Communists'. Aquino's widow Corazon addressed an audience of three million mourners at his funeral; Marcos subsequently banned those newspapers that suggested government complicity in the murder and, in October 1984, an independent commission ruled that the Philippine military was behind the killing. Marcos rejected this conclusion.

The Soviet government expresses regret over the death of innocent people and shares the sorrow of their bereaved relatives and friends. ... However, the entire responsiblity for this tragedy rests wholly and fully with the United States of America.

At an unprecedented military press conference on 6 September 1983, Soviet spokesman Nikolai Ogarkov explains the shooting-down, massively off-course over Sakhalin Island, Siberia, of South Korean Airlines flight 007, a Boeing 747 flying from New York to Seoul with 269 people on board; all were killed. The CIA denied any involvement with the flight; it subsequently emerged that it had been involved in a spying mission.

This so-called Solidarity lot aren't a trade union. They're an anti-Socialist organ who desire the overthrow of a Socialist state.

Arthur Scargill, President of the National Union

of Mineworkers, addresses the NUM conference in Blackpool, 7 September 1983. On 5 October, Solidarity leader Lech Walesa was awarded the Nobel Peace Prize.

I had to clip its wings, so I thought I ought to let it enjoy the sensation of flying.
Sir Ralph Richardson explains why he drives round Regent's Park on a motorbike with a parrot on his shoulder – a practice both enjoyed until shortly before his death on 10 October, aged 80.

It was carnage in there, just carnage. It was like Vietnam.
A survivor of the double suicide-bombing raid on the US-French headquarters of the peacekeeping mission to Beirut on 23 October 1983 in which 241 US Marines and 58 French paratroopers died. The bombers were members of the Iranian-sponsored Hizbollah ('Party of God') movement, who carried out similar attacks in the following weeks. Peacekeeping forces left Lebanon in the New Year.

What a foreign policy we have. Our house is on fire in the Mideast, so we go down the Caribbean block, sneak in the back door of another burning house, and kick Castro's dog. I can't say if dog kicking will endear us to Latin America, or stop houses from burning, but it seems to make Americans feel better.
Ian Shoales, Grenada, in I Gotta Go, November 1983. The USA invaded the Commonwealth island of Grenada, where Cuban troops were on exercise, in late October after the Prime Minister, Maurice Bishop, had been overthrown and imprisoned by the head of the Armed Forces, General Hudson Austin, with the support of the Deputy Prime Minister, Bernard Coard. Margaret Thatcher unsuccessfully asked President Reagan to call the invasion off, but the President, citing the threat of 'Marxism in America's back yard', refused. A total of 630 Cubans were taken prisoner in the fighting, and 16 US servicemen killed in a operation notable for the fact that the number of US combat medals awarded exceeded the number of US combatants. Grenadian casualties are not known, but 47 patients died in an accidental US air attack on their hospital. Maurice Bishop was murdered by his captors.

The armed struggle must go on until the last British soldier has left Ireland.
Gerry Adams MP, recently elected leader of Sinn Féin, the electoral wing of the IRA, 17 November 1983; on 20 November gunmen burst into a Presbyterian church, killing three worshippers and wounding seven, and on 22 November the Official Unionist party withdrew from the Northern Ireland Assembly.

We can all take pleasure in the restoration of democracy to Argentina, believing that it will bring freedom and justice to all your people. Today brings new hope to your country.
Prime Minister Margaret Thatcher, message to President Raúl Alfonsín, 10 December 1983. He announced that the country's former military rulers would be brought to justice to answer charges of causing 'terror, pain and death' and, in particular, for their policy of 'disappearing' all those suspected of dissent.

This is part of the long march to Jerusalem, capital of Palestine.
Once again, PLO leader Yasser Arafat feels betrayed by the Syrians, and once again he leaves Lebanon. On 20 December 1983 he led his beleagured force of 4000 from Tripoli, bound for Tunisia.

Down South where I come from you don't go roun' hittin' too many white keys.
The ragtime pianist and composer Eubie Blake (1883–1983) explains why his music contains so many sharps and flats.

This must be the first time a rat has come to the aid of a sinking ship.
An anonymous wag at the BBC on the misfortunes of its rival, TV-am. Launched with 'a mission to explain', it lost both viewers and presenters during 1983 and was rescued from extinction by Roland Rat, a puppet-with-attitude previously discarded by the BBC.

1984

I cast my bread on the waters long ago. Now it's time for you to send it back to me – toasted and buttered on both sides.
The Rev. Jesse Jackson, addressing black voters in election year, 30 January 1984.

There were so many candidates on the platform that there were not enough promises to go round.

President Reagan on the Democrat field in the New Hampshire primary, 6 February 1984.

In America, where the electoral process is drowning in commercial techniques of fund-raising and image-making, we may have completed a circle back to a selection process as unconcerned with qualifications as that which made Darius King of Persia.

Darius – as every schoolchild on both sides of the Atlantic was once presumed to know – was chosen as king because his horse was the first to neigh at sunrise. Barbara Tuchman surveys the 1984 primary elections in The March of Folly.

As far as I am concerned, I have the backing of my members.

In 1983 the National Union of Mineworkers, against the advice of its President, Arthur Scargill, held a strike ballot that decided against a strike: on 12 March 1984, he called one without benefit of ballot, having rejected a 5.2 per cent pay offer linked to agreement on a programme of pit closures.

Ian MacGregor, recently appointed as Chairman of the National Coal Board, warned that a prolonged strike would lead to more closures; Scargill maintained that the NCB already had a 'secret agenda' for closures, of which the published schedule was merely a foretaste. The government, caught on the hop with scant coal reserves early in its first term of office and forced to settle with the NUM in order to avoid shortages, had no intention of being caught twice. Coal reserves were high and plans had been laid to import cheap stocks from Eastern Europe. The NCB obtained a High Court injunction against 'secondary picketing' but on 15 March a 'flying picket' was killed at the Ollerton colliery, and the cause – on both sides – became a crusade.

On 5 April, miners in Nottinghamshire rejected NUM instructions not to cross picket lines; four days later, amid scenes of great violence, 100 'flying pickets' were arrested there, and in Derbyshire. On 12 April Scargill vetoed an NUM executive motion to hold a national strike ballot.

~

It's the sort of police state you might expect to see in Chile, but not here.

Miners' leader Arthur Scargill on South Yorkshire, after pitched battles between police and pickets outside the Orgreave coking plant left 41 police and 28 pickets injured. Coke continued to leave the Orgreave works as talks resumed – in vain, and in the absence of Scargill and MacGregor, who were not on speaking terms – on the NCB's plan to close 20 collieries and 'phase out' 20,000 jobs by voluntary redundancy. The two men did meet, unproductively, on 9 September in Wakefield; MacGregor wore a paper bag on his head as he arrived.

• •

Sex in the hands of public educators is not a pretty thing.

Fred Savage, The Wonder Years, *US television, 1984.*

• •

Advice to black immigrants – run fast and look pretty.

Graffito, Brixton, April 1984. Zola Budd, a 17-year-old white South African barefoot athlete, wished to register as a British citizen in order to further her career by competing in the Olympics, from which the world-wide anti-apartheid boycott of her country had barred her; the Daily Mail *ran a 'Zola for Britain' campaign, and her application was granted in a record 13 days.*

She duly competed as a member of the British team, tripped US golden girl Mary Decker in the 3000 metres final, and finished nowhere.

Yes, I haven't had enough sex.

John Betjeman, Poet Laureate, was asked in a 1983 television interview if he had any regrets: this was his reply. He died, aged 78, on 19 May 1984.

We had to fight the enemy without in the Falklands. We always have to be aware of the enemy within which is more difficult to fight and more dangerous to liberty.

Margaret Thatcher finds a new General Galtieri in Arthur Scargill, speech to the 1922 Committee of backbench Conservative MPs, 19 July 1984.

She's a woman, she's ethnic, she's a Catholic.
One of Walter Mondale's advisers explains why the Democrat hopeful has chosen Congresswoman Geraldine Ferraro as his Vice-Presidential running mate, 12 July 1984.

~

We must get the American public to look past the glitter, beyond the showmanship, to the reality, the hard substance of things. And we'll do it ... not so much with speeches that bring people to their feet as with speeches that bring people to their senses.
Mario Cuomo, Governor of New York, speech, Democrat National Convention, San Francisco, 16 July 1984. (See 8 April 1985)

~

My constituency is the desperate, the damned, the disinherited, the disrespected and the despised.
Rev. Jesse Jackson, speech, Democrat National Convention, 17 July 1984.

~

In the pageant of unity, one speaker after another recited a Whitmanesque litany of races and classes and minorities and interests and occupations – or unemployments. Some speakers, in fact, made the nation sound like an immense ingathering of victims – terrorized senior citizens, forsaken minorities, Dickensian children – warmed by the party's Frank Capra version of America: Say, it's a wonderful life!
Lance Morrow, All Right, What Kind of People Are We? in Time, 30 July 1984.

I have always been a grumbler. I am designed for the part – sagging face, weighty underlip, rumbling, resonant voice. Money couldn't buy a better grumbling outfit.
J. B. Priestley, quoted in the Guardian, 15 August 1984, the day of his death at the age of 89.

My fellow Americans: I am pleased to tell you today that I have signed legislation that will outlaw Russia forever. We begin bombing in five minutes.
President Reagan tests a microphone on 11 August 1984. Yup – it worked.

~

I will not make an issue of age in this campaign. I am not going to exploit for political purposes my opponent's youth and inexperience.
Ronald Reagan (73) in a television debate with Walter Mondale, 22 October 1984.

~

A shining city on a hill.
Ronald Reagan's campaigning image of America, used throughout the campaign.

~

This is not the end of anything, this is the beginning of everything.
Ronald Reagan's victory speech after re-election, 8 November 1984. He won 49 of the 50 States, taking 59 per cent of the poll.

In church on Sunday morning – it was a lovely morning and we haven't had many lovely days – the sun was coming through a stained-glass window and falling on some flowers, falling right across the church. It just occurred to me that this was the day I was meant not to see.
Margaret Thatcher, 14 October 1984. At 2.45 a.m. on 12 October she narrowly escaped death when a 20-lb IRA bomb, planted several months earlier, exploded under a bathroom she had just vacated, removing four floors of the Grand Hotel in Brighton, venue for the Conservatives' annual conference. Among the dead were MP Sir Anthony Berry and the wife of Chief Whip John Wakeham, who was himself seriously injured, as was Trade and Industry Secretary Norman Tebbit – a video of whose rescue he permitted to be used for Fire Brigade training.

~

Today we were unlucky, but remember – we have only to be lucky once.
IRA statement of responsibility for the Grand Hotel bomb.

I don't mind if my life goes in the service of the nation. If I die today, every drop of my blood will invigorate the nation.
Indian Prime Minister Indira Gandhi, speech, 30 October 1984. The following day she was assassinated by her Sikh bodyguards in revenge for the storming of the Golden Temple at Amritsar, which had been occupied by Sikh separatists. Rioting

swept India as the late Prime Minister's son Rajiv was sworn in as her successor.

I was cooking breakfast this morning for my kids, and I thought, 'He's just like a Teflon frying pan. Nothing sticks to him.'
Patricia Schroeder on Ronald Reagan, quoted by

Michael Kenney in the Boston Globe, *24 October 1984. The International Court of Justice ordered the US to stop aiding 'Contra' guerrillas fighting the Sandinista government in Nicaragua; the US ignored the ruling. On 5 November the Sandinista leader Daniel Ortega was elected President of Nicaragua.*

SLOGANS and CATCHPHRASES of THE EIGHTIES

Don't Blame Me, I Didn't Vote For Him/Her.
US/UK bumper sticker, referring to Reagan/Thatcher, c.1982.

Here we go, here we go, here we go. ...
... and so on. The English football chant, known and hated all over Europe from 1986.

Get the Government Off Our Backs.
Ronald Reagan's campaign slogan, 1980: adopted by Conservatives in Britain.

Go for gold.
Olympic slogan, 1980 and after: originally US.

Go for it!
The Yuppie Credo: adapted for aerobics by Jane Fonda as 'Go for it – go for the burn!'

[It's] Morning In America [Again]
Ronald Reagan, campaign slogan (in various forms), 1984.

Loadsamoney!
Catchphrase of the eponymous yob-yuppie character created by Harry Enfield, 1986.

One of us.
Somebody regarded as 'onside'; from Margaret Thatcher's alleged query of prospective political appointees, 'Is he one of us?'

On yer bike!
Derived from Norman Tebbit's 1981 Conservative conference speech on unemployment (see p. 185): meaning, roughly, 'Try your hard luck story on someone else.'

Tell Sid.
The catchphrase of the campaign to advertise the sale of shares in British Gas, 1986; it soon became extremely irritating, especially if your name was Sid.

Serious Money.
Generally reckoned to be anything in excess of a three-figure number followed by 'K'. The title of a 1987 play by Caryl Churchill.

Where's the beef?
Advertising slogan of Wendy Hamburgers, US, 1984: used by Walter Mondale to taunt presidential candidacy rival Gary Hart for his 'lack of substance on the issues'.

If we lack freedom, it is because we submit to falsehood; it's because we don't expose it every day.
Father Jerzy Popieluszko, the 'Solidarity priest' whose bound and beaten body was dragged from a reservoir on 30 October 1984, 11 days after his kidnap by three policemen.

The only way to get power to change laws and right injustice is for the people to win elections to that power.
Neil Kinnock MP, Labour Party leader, distances himself from Arthur Scargill on 6 November 1984, the day the High Court in Dublin sequestered the NUM's funds. Miners' leaders had moved the funds there from Britain, fearing sequestration in a British court for breaches of industrial relations legislation; £6 million of the £8.7 million had been moved out of Ireland before the Dublin ruling.

One nanny said, 'Feed a cold'; she was a neo-Keynsian. Another nanny said, 'Starve a cold'; she was a monetarist.
Harold Macmillan makes his maiden speeech as the Earl of Stockton in the House of Lords, 13 November 1984.

Here's a story for you: President Botha hears that I have committed suicide and he says, 'Oh, really? I didn't know he'd been arrested!'
Desmond Tutu, Bishop of Johannesburg, receives his Nobel Peace Prize in Oslo on, December 1984.

I like Mr Gorbachev, we can do business together.
Margaret Thatcher, 17 December 1984, on the man who led a 30-strong Soviet 'fact-finding mission' to Britain; following the death of Konstantin Chernenko, he became leader of the USSR on 11 March 1985.

Feed the World, Let them know it's Christmas.
Bob Geldof of the Boomtown Rats organizes

··

All politicians have vanity. Some wear it more gently than others.

David Steel, 1985.

··

'Band Aid', an all-star Rock'n'Roll fundraiser for the starving people of Ethiopia, and releases a Number One Christmas single. The appeal would have made another £500,000 if the government had waived VAT on the record – but it didn't.

1985

The petrol engine will be seen as a thing of the past by the end of the century.
On 10 January 1985, Sir Clive Sinclair, Mrs Thatcher's favourite inventor, goes for a spin on his battery assisted tricycle, the C5. It became a thing of the past rather sooner.

Thank God for the Church and Terry Waite. They showed they cared – unlike the Foreign Office.
Mrs Carol Russell, whose husband, along with three other Britons, was released on 5 February 1985 after negotiations between the Archbishop of Canterbury's 'special envoy' and the Libyan government, which had held them hostage for nine months. Britain broke off diplomatic relations with Libya after Police Constable Yvonne Fletcher was shot dead by a member of its 'People's Bureau' in London in April 1984.

———————————

I cannot and will not give you any undertaking at a time when I, and you, the people, are not free. Your freedom and mine cannot be separated.
Nelson Mandela, speech read by his daughter at a rally in Soweto on 10 February 1985, replying to a suggestion that he might be released from jail in return for a pledge to renounce violence on behalf of the ANC.

～

We don't want apartheid liberalized. We want it dismantled. You can't improve something that is intrinsically evil.
Bishop Desmond Tutu, speech, March 1985.

———————————

As far as I am concerned I have not been defeated and neither have the working class communities of Britain.
NUM President Arthur Scargill as, to shouts of 'scum, scabs, traitors' from demonstrators, the executive of the union votes by 98 to 91 to call off the year-long strike on 3 March 1985, after a

•••••••••••••••••••••••••••••••••••

Ya can't learn to be real. It's like learning to be a midget. It's not something you can learn.

Jeff Daniels, The Purple Rose of Cairo (1985).

•••••••••••••••••••••••••••••••••••

steady drift back to work of miners. The formation of a rival Democratic Union of Mineworkers was announced in October.

I have my veto pen drawn and ready for any tax increase that Congress might even think of sending up. And I have only one thing to say to the tax increasers: Go ahead – make my day!

A line first uttered by Clint Eastwood in Sudden Impact *in 1983; it subsequently appeared in 1984, in a parody issue of the* New York Post, *'reporting' a nuclear war begun by President Reagan issuing the challenge to the Kremlin. His use of it in real life was reported by* Time *magazine, 25 March 1985.*

A government is not legitimate merely because it exists.

Jeanne Kirkpatrick, recent defector from Democrats to Republicans, on the Sandinista government of Nicaragua, 17 June 1985.

We are not going to tolerate these attacks from outlaw states run by the strangest collection of misfits, Looney Tunes and squalid criminals since the advent of the Third Reich.

President Reagan, 8 July 1985. On 30 June, 39 Americans were released from captivity on board a TWA airliner at Beirut airport after being held for 16 days by Hizbollah militiamen who had murdered a US sailor during the hijacking; Israel simultaneously released the 700 Lebanese 'terrorist suspects' whose freedom the hijackers had demanded, but denied that any deal had been done. Reagan listed five countries – Iran, Libya, North Korea, Cuba and Nicaragua – as members of 'a confederation of terrorist states', although Shi'ite Hizbollah attacks in Lebanon – such as the recent massacres at PLO refugee camps – were known to be an instrument of Syrian policy, albeit abetted by Iranian sponsorship of Hizbollah training camps in the Bekaa Valley. On 23 June, all 325

people on board an Air India Boeing 747 flying from Canada to Ireland were killed when it exploded and plunged into the Irish Sea; Sikh separatists were suspected of the bombing, which was linked to an earlier explosion at Japan's Narita airport among baggage from a flight from Canada.

I don't think I am a genius. It came out of a lot of hard work.

Ruth Lawrence, aged 13, gained a first-class Honours degree in Mathematics from Oxford University on 4 July 1985, but had to wait another year before she could receive it as she had not satisfied the residential qualification: she had completed the course in two years, not three.

We must try to find ways to starve the terrorists of the oxygen of publicity on which they depend.

Prime Minister Margaret Thatcher addresses the American Bar Association in London, 7 July 1985; this was the reason given for the British government's subsequent ban on the broadcasting of the voices of Gerry Adams and other Sinn Féin spokespeople and IRA apologists. Broadcasting organizations hired actors to perform their words instead.

By signing the Anglo-Irish agreement with Irish Prime Minister Garret FitzGerald on 15 November, she paved the way for the Republic to become formally involved in the affairs of Northern Ireland – a concession which provoked the resignation of her friend and Treasury Minister, Ian Gow MP, a staunch Unionist. The IRA murdered him on 30 July 1990.

You should all stop being moaning minnies.

On a visit to the economic 'black spot' of Tyneside on 11 September 1985, Prime Minister Thatcher reacts to reporters' questions on unemployment, still running at over three million.

The grotesque chaos of a Labour Council – a *Labour* Council – hiring taxis to scuttle round a city handing out redundancy notices to its own workers.

Labour leader Neil Kinnock castigates the left-wing Liverpool City Council, which had failed to set a legal rate under new local government rules, September 1985; his speech at the Labour Party conference provoked a walkout of some delegates.

•••••••••••••••••••••••••••••••

You campaign in poetry. You govern in prose.

Mario Cuomo, New Republic, *1985.*

•••••••••••••••••••••••••••••••

I have the good fortune to be the first Liberal leader for over half a century who is able to say to you at the end of our annual assembly: Go back to your constituencies, and prepare for government!

Buoyed up by by-election success and a high opinion poll rating, Liberal leader David Steel MP addressed delegates, 18 September 1985.

I think, historically, the term 'Thatcherism' will be seen as a compliment.

Margaret Thatcher, interviewed after her party's autumn conference, 1985.

The subject no longer has to be mentioned by name. Someone is sick. Someone else is feeling better now. A friend has just gone back to hospital. Another has died. The unspoken name, of course, is AIDS.

David W. Dunlap, New York Times, *23 April 1985. On 2 October the disease claimed a headline victim whose identity brought AIDS to the forefront of 'Middle American consciousness': Rock Hudson died, aged 59.*

Move over, $7000 coffeepots! Stand aside, $400 hammers! We now have the $792 doormat!

William Proxmire, New York Times, *4 October 1985. A whiff of sleaze assailed the non-stick Presidency with revelations of some unfeasibly valuable (and wildly impractical) gifts to the First Family.*

There's one, there's a pig, get him, kill him now.

A cry from the mob on the Broadwater Farm Estate in Tottenham, North London, 7 October 1985; Police Constable Kenneth Blakelock was then hacked to death with machetes. Winston Silcott, gaoled for the murder, was subsequently cleared by the Court of Appeal, which found his conviction to be 'unsafe and unsatisfactory' but remained in prison, serving a life sentence for

another murder. The Broadwater riot began after a woman was shot during a police search of her flat on the estate; in January 1986 the policeman who fired the shot was cleared of criminal charges.

This is the biggest electric train set a boy ever had.

Orson Welles, on being let loose in a Hollywood studio at the age of 24; on 10 October 1985 he died, aged 70.

Very, very small. Tiny.

Holding forefinger and thumb a short centimetre apart, Prime Minister Thatcher indicates the amount to which she has restricted Commonwealth sanctions against South Africa on 10 October 1985. A delegation of South African businessmen broke the law that month by going to Zaire for talks with the banned and exiled African National Congress; when it returned with the announcement that it could work happily with an ANC government, President Botha placed new restrictions on the news media.

I am not prepared to lead white South Africans ... on a road to abdication and suicide.

South African President P. W. Botha rules out dialogue with the ANC, October 1985. His government did, however, lift the ban on 'mixed marriages' – without relaxing apartheid housing regulations.

I'm not interested in the bloody system! Why has he no food? Why is he starving to death?

Bob Geldof visits a refugee camp in Ethiopia in October 1985; his Band Aid concerts had raised over £40 million for famine relief.

I cannot claim we had a meeting of minds on such fundamentals as ideology or national purpose, but we understand each other better.

President Reagan reports on his 'fireside summit' with President Gorbachev in Geneva, 21 November 1985. The two leaders had spent six hours talking with no officials present.

Sexual intercourse began In nineteen sixty-three
(Which was rather late for me) –
Between the end of the *Chatterley* ban
And the Beatles' first LP.

Philip Larkin, Annus Mirabilis, *1974. He died on 2 December 1985, aged 63.*

The remarkable thing about Shakespeare is that he is really very good – in spite of all the people who say he is very good.

The poet, novelist and mythologist Robert Graves, quoted in the Observer, *6 December 1964; he died, aged 90, on 7 December 1985.*

1986

Oh! I have slipped the surly bonds of earth.... Put out my hand and touched the face of God.

President Reagan quotes the Second World War pilot-poet John Gillespie Magee in a moving tribute to the seven crew members on board the space shuttle Challenger, *who died when it exploded 72 seconds into its flight on 28 January 1986. One of the crew, schoolteacher Christa MacAuliffe, was the first 'ordinary American' chosen to fly on the Citizen in Space programme, designed to bring the work of NASA closer to the people whose tax dollars fund it.*

On 26 March, in an unprecedented gesture of goodwill, the USSR named seven asteroids after the Challenger *crew.*

~

A billion-dollar tragedy with a 50¢ cause.

A journalist's view of the Challenger *explosion. The report of the enquiry into the cause of the disaster, published on 9 June, found that the fault lay in the 'O-ring' seal on one of the solid fuel booster rockets; despite warnings that it was substandard, no steps had been taken to remedy the fault. The exceptionally cold pre-launch weather – the air temperature had fallen 8°F below freezing the night before, and ground crews had to chip icicles off the vehicle – had weakened the seal, which perished under the stress of launch, allowing hot gases to leak out and turning the vessel into a huge bomb.*

This operation has done an awful lot of good for Britain's reputation.

Rear Admiral John Garnier, master of the Royal Yacht HMS Britannia, *diverted en route to Australia in order to rescue over a thousand citizens of the UK, Bangladesh, East Germany and Japan who were stranded by civil war in the Port of Aden in January 1986. International co-operation was enhanced by the use of the* Soviet Embassy *as an emergency 'departure lounge'.*

A new life starts for our country – a life filled with hope and, I believe, a life that will be blessed with peace and progress.

Helping to make the Eighties a people's decade, and coining the term 'People Power': Corazon Aquino, widow of the murdered Philippine opposition leader, TV broadcast as President of the Philippines, 25 February 1985. Former President and virtual dictator, Ferdinand Marcos, had called a 'snap election' in the belief that Mrs Aquino would be unprepared; as the results stacked up against him he suspended the count, and election workers – many of them nuns – defended ballot boxes against the soldiery. Marcos ordered his own installation as Head of State for a further six years, but the ceremony was boycotted by his own Prime Minister and blacked out on television. Millions of people then took to the streets and, later that day, stormed the Presidential Palace; troops did not intervene, following the defection to the Aquino camp of the Defence Minister and the Army Chief of Staff. Ferdinand and Imelda Marcos then left the country by US military helicopter from the Palace roof, leaving the Filipino people to pick their way through the couple's huge and vulgar hoard of expensive chattels – and its government to pursue the recovery of tens of millions of dollars of national assets, siphoned off by the Marcoses and cached overseas.

(1) Democracy is the wholesome and pure air without which a socialist public organisation cannot live a full-blooded life.

(2) No party has a monopoly over what is right.

Two statements that really did change the world: (1) Mikhail Gorbachev addresses the 27th Congress of the Communist Party of the Soviet Union on 27 February 1986. At the beginning of the month he telegraphed his intentions by launching a withering attack on the 'years of stag-

• •

Preparing for suicide is not a very intelligent means of defence.

Mgr. Bruce Kent, Chairman of CND, 1986.

• •

nation' under Brezhnev and – in a phrase that might have been lifted from one of the plays of gaoled Czech writer Vaclav Havel – the 'armchair managers, hack workers, idlers and grabbers' who had prospered under them. (2) Gorbechev says what has been unthinkable in the USSR for 69 years, in a speech the following month. Two Russian words were now to dominate international affairs and the governance of the USSR and its satellite countries for the remainder of the decade: glasnost, meaning 'openness', and perestroika, meaning 'reconstruction'. It was Gorbachev's belief that some form of the Soviet model of state socialism could accommodate both.

No one can kill Americans and brag about it. No one.

President Reagan's immediate reaction to the bombing of a discotheque packed with GIs in West Berlin on 5 April 1986, presumed to be a retaliation for the US naval action against Libyan gunboats in the Gulf of Sirte the week before; the bombing of a TWA Boeing 727 en route from Rome to Athens, in which four people died, was ascribed to the same cause.

~

In the light of this reprehensible act of violence and clear evidence that Libya is planning future attacks, the US has chosen to exercise its rights of self-defence. ... Every effort was made to avoid civilian casualties.

The President's considered reaction to the Berlin disco bomb: White House spokesman Larry Speakes on the USAF bombing raid on Tripoli on 15 April 1986. There were civilian casualties as bombs fell on homes and hospitals as well as their intended military targets; one of President Gaddafi's homes was hit, and his infant daughter killed. In a reprisal for the USAF's use of bases in Britain, three British hostages held in Lebanon were murdered.

~

Everything was blamed on Castro. Mudslides in California. The fact that you can't buy a decent tomato anymore. Was there an exceptionally high pollen count in Massapequa, Long Island, one day? It was Castro, exporting sneezes.

A comment on the demonization of Muammar Gaddafi: Calvin Trillin, 'Castro Forgotten, Alas' in his King Features Syndicate column, 18 May 1986.

The Iran-Contra Scandal

They said that there is definitely a distinction between real life and the movies, despite the fact that President Reagan once mentioned as an example of inspiring patriotism a heroic act that turned out to have been from a World War II bomber movie starring Dana Andrews.

Calvin Trillin, 'The Gipper Still Lives', King Features Syndicate, 23 November 1986.

In early November of 1986 Dan Jacobson, an American held hostage in Lebanon for 18 months by Shi'ite militias, was released after negotiations with the Archbishop of Canterbury's 'special envoy', Terry Waite. What Waite did not appreciate was that one of his American acquaintances, Colonel Oliver North, was secretly negotiating arms sales to Iran – sponsors of Mr Jacobson's kidnapping – in return for his release, using Mr Waite as a sort of honest (albeit unknowing) broker for the deal. The money raised from this operation, some $30 million, was then channelled into the hands of the 'Contra' rebels fighting the elected left-wing government of Nicaragua; although President Reagan had identified Nicaragua (as, ironically, he had Iran) as a 'sponsor of terrorism', this action was illegal as Congress had voted to cut off funding for the Contras. Reagan, meanwhile, made no secret of his wish to see Daniel Ortega's Sandinista government overthrown.

We did not – repeat, did not – trade weapons or anything else for the hostages, nor will we.

A firm and unequivocal denial of the 'first leg' of the scandal from President Reagan, 13 November 1986.

I was not fully informed of one of the activities undertaken in connexion with this initiative.

On 30 November 1986, following the resignations of Admiral John Poindexter, the President's National Security Adviser, and his assistant, Colonel Oliver North, President Reagan leaves a little room for doubt as he announces a 'review' of the NSC's activities. It subsequently emerged that the President had personally sent Ayatollah Khomeini a birthday present of a cake and a Bible. It is unlikely that the gift was instrumental in the release of any American hostage.

I don't think there is another person in America that wants to tell this story as much as I do.
Testifying to the House Committee investigating the affair, Colonel North adopts a gung-ho attitude on 10 December 1986. He then fell silent on the advice of his lawyers.

My answer therefore and the simple truth is – I don't remember, period.
With a smile and a shrug, President Reagan plays up to his reputation for inattentiveness, 2 February 1987.

How much did the President forget, and when did he forget it?
During the Watergate hearings there was a much-quoted question: 'How much did the President know, and when did he know it?' Following Reagan's admission of forgetfulness, one anonymous wit adapted the question.

The review of the NSC, under ex-Senator John Tower, found fault with the President for not 'following up' on its work, and failing to monitor the operation to secure the release of hostages; it condemned the 'administrative chaos' under White House Chief-of-Staff Donald Regan, and criticized North for concealing information about the plan to trade arms for hostages and the proceeds for the overthrow of a foreign government.

It sort of settled down to trading arms for hostages.
President Reagan, 26 March 1987.

I didn't know how that money was to be used and I have no knowledge that there was ever any solicitation by our people with these people.
President Reagan denies knowledge of the 'second leg', 5 May 1987.

I'd say it was a neat idea.
Colonel North, Congressional hearings, 1987.

As a matter of fact, I was very definitely involved in the decisions about support to the freedom fighters. It was my idea to begin with.
On the other hand... President Reagan has his spin-doctors scrambling for 'clarifications' ten days later, 15 May 1987; they explained that 'support' in this context was not intended specifically to mean the profits of the Iranian arms deal – or anything else illegal.

I never said I had no idea about most of the things you said I had no idea about.
White House staffer Elliot Abrams gives evidence to the Iran-Contra hearings, 3 July 1987.

Sometimes you just have to go above the written law.
Colonel North's secretary Fawn Hall, dressed to charm for the Iran-Contra hearings, explains on 17 July why she willingly stayed up all night shredding documents for her boss; he was, she said, 'every secretary's dream of a boss'. 'God Bless Ollie North' T-shirts enjoyed booming sales in the Bible Belt.

I came here today to tell you the truth, the good, the bad, and the ugly.
Colonel North, granted limited immunity from prosecution, agrees to come back and testify to the Iran-Contra hearings in July 1987. He was subsequently indicted on serious counts of conspiracy; these were dropped in January 1989 and three lesser charges substituted, on which he was found guilty, fined, and released to earn the money back on the lecture circuit.

The Congressional Report, published in November 1987, laid responsibility for the whole affair at President Reagan's door; it did not conclude that he knew what was going on, but did point out that he ought to have known.

It's true, hard work never killed anyone, but I figure, why take the chance?
Still a non-stick President, Reagan, 27 March 1987.

Terry Waite – now identified in the minds of Shi'ite militants as a CIA stooge – became the one to suffer most from the fall-out of the Iran-Contra affair: on 21 January 1987 he was kidnapped in Beirut by a Hizbollah militia he had arranged to negotiate with.

If you haven't been happy very young, you can still be happy later on, but it's much harder. You need more luck.
Simone de Beauvoir, quoted in 1975; she died on 14 April 1986, at the age of 78.

Reactor Number Four at the Chernobyl power station in Ukraine has been damaged in an accident. Other reactors have been closed down and the authorities are dealing with the incident.
30 April 1986: a terse statement on Soviet television, four days after an explosion and fire, following reports of unusually high levels of radiation in the atmosphere over Sweden; shortly afterwards, however, President Gorbachev himself revealed the full extent of the calamity and appealed for international assistance. Slipshod construction, sloppy management and lax safety standards caused the top of the reactor to blow off, exposing the radioactive graphite core and leading to meltdown. The first crews to go in to the building wore no protective clothing; all have since developed cancer and most have died. The plant was subsequently buried beneath a mountain of sand and cement; recent reports say that this is cracking. A large area of the surrounding countryside was evacuated and much has been abandoned; cancer levels in the city of Kiev have since been consistently high. The ban on the movement of sheep remains in force in parts of western Britain at the time of writing. In large areas of the Scottish Highlands and Islands, where it rained heavily during the first week of May 1986, no testing of radiation levels in soil and grass was carried out; abnormally high 'cancer clusters' have recently come to light in the Hebrides.

Together, hand in hand, with our matches and our necklaces, we shall liberate this country.
Referring to 'necklace killings', in which a tyre

....

Should we force science down the throats of those that have no taste for it? Is it our duty to drag them kicking and screaming into the twenty-first century? I am afraid that it is.

Professor George Porter, 1986.

....

filled with petrol is hung around the victim's neck and then set alight, Winnie Mandela – a senior official of the ANC and wife of its gaoled leader – addresses her supporters; quoted in the Observer, *20 April 1986. She was subsequently to come under investigation for complicity in the murder of a 14-year-old boy beaten to death by her 'football team' of bodyguards.*

~

It seems that the British government sees black people as expendable.
Bishop Desmond Tutu, 12 June 1986, as President Botha of South Africa declares a State of Emergency to deal with 'ANC terrorism' and Prime Minister Thatcher refuses to countenance economic sanctions against the regime. Tutu was enthroned as the Anglican Archbishop of Cape Town in September.

The helicopter picked you up,
The pilot it was me.
The contribution of the new Poet Laureate, Ted Hughes, to the nuptial of HRH Prince Andrew and Sarah Ferguson on 23 July 1986.

We regard this as a gross breach of diplomatic civility.
US Diplomatic spokesman, 2 September 1986. At a meeting of representatives of 50 'non-aligned' nations in Zimbabwe, one of Mr Mugabe's ministers delivers a tirade against 'US imperialism' and former US President Jimmy Carter, present as an observer, walks out. The USA froze its $20 million aid budget to Zimbabwe as a result.
On 22 October, following a large majority vote for sanctions in the US Senate, four companies – General Motors, Honeywell, IBM and Warners – announced that were 'disinvesting' from South Africa; they were joined in November by Barclay's Bank – long the target of anti-apartheid campaigners in the UK – and in December by Exxon.

First of all the Georgian silver goes, and then all that nice furniture that used to be in the saloon. Then the Canalettos go.
Harold Macmillan (the Earl of Stockton) makes his maiden speech in the House of Lords on 8 November 1986, and takes as his theme the subject of 'privatization', the sale of State assets that was to be a feature of Eighties

Britain; at the time of this remark – frequently cited as 'selling off the family silver' – British Telecom had already been sold, and British Gas was about to be floated on the Stock Exchange the following month.

Greed is all right. Greed is healthy. You can be greedy and still feel good about yourself.

Ivan Boesky, Wall Street financier, who confessed (as part of a 'plea bargain') to illegal 'insider dealing' and other malefactions on 17 November 1986, causing shares to tumble on the world's exchanges. His evidence also led to the investigation of the successful takeover bid by Guinness plc for the Distillers' Co. and to the unearthing of unlawful 'share support' schemes; in January 1987, Gerald Ronson of the Heron Group repaid £5.8 million received as a 'thank you present' for one such operation. Guinness sacked its Chairman, Ernest Saunders, and he was indicted – along with Ronson, businessman-philanthropist Sir Jack Lyons, and merchant banker Roger Seelig – on criminal charges of theft and false accounting in May.

As one person said, it is perhaps being economical with the truth... It is not very original, I'm afraid.

Sir Robert Armstrong, British Cabinet Secretary, during cross-examination in the Supreme Court of New South Wales, 18 November 1986. When former MI5 man Peter Wright's book Spycatcher (1987) was banned in the UK by the High Court, its publisher, Heinemann, published in Australia; the British government sought to have it banned there, too. Armstrong's cross examination did not do the British government's case much good, and the book was published. Extracts were printed in the UK by The Sunday Times, which was prosecuted for Contempt of Court; meanwhile, the government appealed (unsuccessfully) against the Australian ruling. Proceedings against The Sunday Times – and, by then, three other British papers – went all the way to the Law Lords, who ruled that, since the book was already so widely available in the UK (it had by then been published worldwide, and imported) there would be no useful purpose in granting an injunction. Sir Robert's unfortunate phrase was first uttered by Samuel Pepys.

●●●●●●●●●●●●●●●●●●●●●●●●●●●●●●●●●

What sort of God are we portraying and believing in if we insist on what I will nickname the 'Divine laser beam' type of miracle as the heart and basis of the Incarnation and Resurrection?

David Jenkins, Bishop of Durham, 1986.

●●●●●●●●●●●●●●●●●●●●●●●●●●●●●●●●●

―――――――――

AIDS – DON'T DIE OF IGNORANCE

The slogan of the British government's £20 million education campaign, announced in November 1986, and of a leaflet printed for distribution to 23 million households through the Royal Mail.

~

Everywhere I go, I see increasing evidence of people swirling around in a human cesspit of their own making.

Sir James Anderton, Chief Constable of Greater Manchester, refers in a speech in Prestwick on 11 December 1986, to 'those most at risk of AIDS'. The following month, he told a BBC radio interviewer that he believed God might be using him as a prophet. (See December 1987, p. 206.)

~

If the AIDS antibody test becomes a requirement for passports or visas, millions of Americans can kiss their dream vacations goodbye.

The Boston Globe quotes 'a Gay Rights advocate' in January 1987.

~

If you turn your back on these people, you yourself are an animal. You may be a well-dressed animal, but you are nevertheless an animal.

New York Mayor Edward Koch on AIDS, State of the City address, 16 March 1987.

~

The most frightening fact about AIDS is that it can be spread by normal sex between men and women. This is still rare in Scotland.

With unintentional hilarity, the Scottish Sunday Mail in March 1987 tries to correct the misconception that AIDS is an exclusively 'Gay Plague'.

~

You can't prevent a sexually transmitted epidemic without talking about sex.

Sam Puckett, New York, 23 March 1987.

If freedom were not so economically efficient it certainly wouldn't stand a chance.

Milton Friedman, 1987.

1987

The gnomes were being very naughty.
In January 1987 the publishers of Enid Blyton's Noddy books deported all the golliwogs in Toytown and replaced them with gnomes (thereby, presumably, upsetting another, hitherto unknown minority). In the 1996 US edition of the Blyton canon, Big Ears became White Beard out of consideration for auricularly over-advantaged persons.

There is even a shortage of animals now.
A 12-year-old resident of the Bourj al Barajneh Palestinian refugee camp, where 30,000 people were reduced to hunting rats, cats and dogs; on 13 February 1987, Shi'te militiamen attacked two UN convoys bringing food and medicine, shooting out the tyres and killing one aid worker.

In the future everybody will be world-famous for fifteen minutes.
One quotation everbody thinks they know, Andy Warhol, 1964. He died on 23 February 1987, aged 58.

I am leaving port under full steam with my bow doors closed.
UK Environment Secretary Nicholas Ridley was obliged to apologize for this 'joke' at a press conference on 8 March 1987. Two days earlier, the car ferry Herald of Free Enterprise had keeled over and sunk a mile outside Zeebrugge harbour, drowning over 200 passengers. It had left port with its bows doors open, to save time and money – a practice that was widespread with 'ro-ro' ferries of this type.

Only socialism would put up with it for so long. Capitalism would have gone bankrupt years ago.
Mikhail Gorbachev, on sub-standard workmanship in the Soviet Union, television interview, 23 March 1987. In his book Perestroika *(1987) he commented adversely on the fact that Soviet technology could send spacecraft to Venus while many ordinary household appliances were either unavailable or else so badly made as to be useless.*

Soviet military technology was found wanting on 28 May when Mathias Rüst, a 19-year-old West German student with 24 hours' flying experience, evaded radar defences to land his Cessna plane in Red Square, where he signed autographs; he was imprisoned, then expelled.

The house is in order. There is no blood in Argentina.
President Alfonsín addresses 400,000 cheering people in the Plaza de Mayo on 19 April 1987 after personally facing down an armed revolt by senior Army officers at the Campo de Mayo military base.

People think we do not understand our black and coloured countrymen. But there is a special relationship between us.
Uttered without a trace of irony by Elize Botha, wife of the South African President, in May 1987; on 6 May Botha's National Party enjoyed its usual landslide win in the whites-only general election – but the far-right Conservative Party, campaigning on the platform that Botha was being 'soft on the blacks', won two seats and displaced the liberal Progressive Federal Party as the official Opposition.

She only went to Venice because somebody told her she could walk down the middle of the street.
Labour leader Neil Kinnock comments on the Prime Minister's departure for an EC Heads of government meeting shortly after she announced a general election for 11 June 1987.

~

He's a semi-detached member of the Cabinet.
Bernard Ingham, the Prime Minister's press secretary on Leader of the House John Biffen MP, who had ventured to suggest in early June that another landslide election victory would not be a good thing for parliamentary democracy; Ingham was, as usual, quoted by the media as 'a senior government source'. Biffen was sacked after the election.

~

I don't mind how much my ministers talk, as long as they do what I say.

Margaret Thatcher, in a Times *interview, on John Biffen and other 'Cabinet Wets'.*

~

Oh yes, I hope to go on and on.

Margaret Thatcher, asked by the BBC's John Cole whether she would seek a fourth term of office if she succeeded in winning a third, 11 May 1987.

    The Conservatives won the general election with an overall majority of 100 seats. The Liberal–SDP Alliance, which gained 22 seats for its 23 per cent of the poll, split up immediately, and Liberal leader David Steel called for a vote on merger.

    A week after the election, UK unemployment fell below three million.

I am not prepared to accept the economics of a housewife.

French Prime Minister Jacques Chirac combines Gallic hauteur with Anglo-Saxon sexism when referring to his EC colleague, Margaret Thatcher, July 1987.

A man in black has shot our Mummy.

No longer 'only in America': a pensioner walking in Savernake Woods, near Hungerford in Berkshire, on 20 August 1987 meets two toddlers who calmly tell of their mother's murder. Michael Ryan, a gun enthusiast, shot dead 14 people in the town, including his mother and himself, and wounded 15 others. The government subsequently banned automatic weapons of the type he used, and declared an arms amnesty in which 48,000 illegally held weapons were turned in.

You can rest assured there isn't going to be a hurricane.

But there was. BBC weatherman Michael Fish responds on 15 October 1987 to a viewer who phoned the Meteorological Office seeking confirmation of a rumour to that effect. England – a country where incorrect weather forecasts are as much a part of national life as traffic cones and the teapot – will never forget what happened next.

••••••••••••••••••••••••••••••••••••

The more you don't do it, the more it's fun to read about.

Caryl Churchill on sex in the age of AIDS,
Serious Money, *1987.*

••••••••••••••••••••••••••••••••••••

••••••••••••••••••••••••••••••••••••

The working classes are never embarrassed about money – only the absence of it.

Ken Livingstone MP, 1987.

••••••••••••••••••••••••••••••••••••

It caused 17 deaths and approximately £300 million damage, and left many parts of the south-east without electricity for several days. Hundreds of thousands of trees – including all seven oaks in Sevenoaks – were blown over.

This was a prudent yet restrained response.

President Reagan, 18 October 1987, after US warships blasted three Iranian oil platforms in the Persian Gulf. The US Navy patrolled Gulf waters to defend international shipping against Iranian attacks designed to cripple the economy of Iraq and deter other Gulf States from assisting its enemy in the continuing war; the oil platforms had been used as bases for Iranian 'Revolutionary Guards' to mount attacks, backed up by the firing of Chinese Silkworm missiles from the Iranian mainland. (See 3 July 1988, p.207.)

This is the nearest thing to a financial meltdown that I've ever come across.

John Phelan, chairman of the New York Stock Exchange, 19 October 1987. Five years of the Bull Market came to an end on Black Monday as share values in publicly quoted companies fell by 10 per cent in London and 22.5 per cent in New York – the biggest fall of the century. In London the plummet continued for several days, exacerbated by the government's ill-timed dumping of shares in British Petroleum. Apart from the usual 'cyclical factors' the big bust was caused by rising interest rates, the growing US trade and budget deficit, and the phenomenon of 'programme trading' brought about by computerized dealing: pension funds and investment trusts, designed to 'track' rises and falls in the index by automatically buying or selling, responded to the first falls by selling in ever-increasing quantities, thereby helping to set the trend they were designed to follow.

    A 23-year-old trainee accountant earning £6400 a year entered City folklore when it emerged that he was 'trapped in a position' that had turned him into a negative paper millionaire.

There is no such thing as Society. There are individual men and women, and there are families.
Margaret Thatcher, interviewed in Woman's Own, *31 October 1987. This was one of two remarks for which the Prime Minister is known to have later expressed regret: the other was made during a 1987 election phone-in, when she said that unemployed people should stop 'whingeing' about their plight.*

I bear no ill-will against those responsible for this. That sort of talk will not bring her back to life. I shall pray for those people tonight and every night. I know there has to be a plan even though we might not understand it. God is good and we shall meet again.
Gordon Wilson, Enniskillen, 8 November 1987: Remembrance Sunday, and as townsfolk assemble for the wreath-laying ceremony, a massive IRA bomb explodes in a disused school building adjacent to the Market Square, killing 11 people outright – including Mr Wilson's daughter – and injuring 63 others, some of whom died later. The IRA expressed 'regret at the loss of life' but blamed the British Army for triggering the bomb by using a high frequency scanning device to 'sweep' the area; it had, according to them, been intended to go off later.

A thing, I suppose a person, came stumbling down the stairs, his hair was all burnt off, his head was smoking and his skin blistering. He held his hands in front of him and there was smoke coming off them.
An anonymous survivor of the fire at King's Cross Underground station, in which 30 people died on 19 November 1987. The fire started underneath a wooden escalator, in a space clogged with decades of fluff and grease, and 'flashed over' to fill the ticket hall with smoke and searing heat; passengers disembarking from trains were thus 'evacuated' to the place of greatest danger. The cleaning service, recently privatized, had had its staff cut and an automatic sprinkler system, recommended after a safety inspection three years earlier, had not been installed. London Regional Transport responded to the disaster by banning smoking throughout the London Underground Network.

You have to give this much to the Luftwaffe – when it knocked down our buildings it didn't replace them with anything more offensive than rubble. We did that.
HRH the Prince of Wales continues to take a dim view of the 'monstrous carbuncles' of modern architecture: speech to the Corporation of London Planning and Communications Committee, 2 December 1987.

You say that every time we meet.
Soviet President Gorbachev responds to US President Reagan's 'Proverai no doverai' – 'Trust yet verify' – as the two leaders sign an agreement to reduce their medium-range nuclear arsenals: 8 December 1987. The treaty was ratified when Reagan visited Moscow the following May.

Every time you sleep with a boy you sleep with all his old girlfriends.
UK Department of Health AIDS awareness advertisement, 1987.

1988

Everything that is most beautiful in Britain has always been in private hands.
Malcolm Rifkind, Secretary of State for Scotland, promotes the policy of privatization; quoted in the Observer, *17 January 1988. Chancellor Nigel Lawson, in a speech the same month, said it was 'in harmony with the deepest instincts of the British people' and was helping to create 'one nation'.*

These demonstrations will continue to be met with might, power and beatings.
Israeli Defence Minister Yikzhak Rabin, 20 January 1988, on the intifada: *a co-ordinated campaign of protest by Palestinians in the occupied territories of the West Bank and Gaza. A shopkeepers'*

• •

Universities are the cathedrals of the modern age. They shouldn't have to justify their existence by utilitarian criteria.

David Lodge, professor and novelist, 1988.

• •

strike led to to food shortages but the Israeli author-
ities refused to allow relief supplies in, saying it
was a self-inflicted problem.

There is no such thing as collective guilt.
Kurt Waldheim, formerly Secretary-General of
the United Nations, now Chancellor of Austria.
On 11 February a panel of government-ap-
pointed historians found that he had 'let slip
parts of the past into oblivion and, if that was
not possible, made them appear harmless'.
Waldheim had served as an Intelligence Officer
with an SS unit in the Balkans during World
War Two, and was accused of complicity in the
deaths of thousand of Jews, Yugoslavs and
Italians. Opinion polls indicated that 70 per
cent of Austrians thought there was no reason
for him to resign.

Our parish is seen as dripping in the blood of murders.
Father Alec Reid, West Belfast, 19 March
1988. Three days earlier, a 'Loyalist' gunman
had opened fire and thrown grenades in
Milltown cemetery, during the burial service of
three IRA members shot by the SAS in Gibraltar
on 7 March; they had been carrying out a bomb-
ing mission there, but were unarmed at the
time. As the cortège for the three victims of the
Milltown attack was passing through the
streets of republican West Belfast, two British
soldiers unaccountably drove their car into the
crowd; they drew their pistols and tried to
escape but were overcome, bundled into a taxi-
cab, and driven to some nearby waste ground.
There they were stripped, beaten, and shot. Fr.
Reid administered the Last Rites.

The United States is the best and fairest and most decent nation on the face of the earth.
Vice-President George Bush, campaigning for
the Republican presidential nomination, May
1988.

You don't have power if you surrender all your principles – you have office.
British Trade Union leader Ron Todd, June 1988,
on moves to widen the electoral appeal of the
Labour Party. (See 27 May 1993, p.232.)

The United States will not be exempt from the consequences of this unpro-voked slaughter.
Iranian Prime Minister Mohammed Mousavi,

America is not a blanket woven from one thread, one colour, one cloth.
Rev. Jesse Jackson: speech at the Democrat
Convention, Atlanta, 1988.

3 July 1988, after the USS Vincennes, *on*
patrol in the Gulf, shot down an Iranian civilian
airliner: all 286 on board were killed. Ship's
captain Will Rogers said it had been mistaken
by the ship's tracking systems for an Iranian
F–14 Tomcat fighter. It subsequently emerged
that the civilian plane had been deliberately
routed to fly off-course and through a war zone
as an act of defiance of the US naval presence.
(See 22 December 1988, pp.208–9.)

The Soviet people want full-blooded and unconditional democracy.
Mikhail Gorbachev, July 1988; the previous year
he had said that democracy was 'just a slogan'. He
continued to rule out the possibility of any sort of
multi-party system, though in talks with West
German Chancellor Helmut Kohl he promised that
all political prisoners would be released by the end
of the year.

His foreparents came to America in immigrant ships. My foreparents came to America in slave ships. But what-ever the original ships, we are both in the same boat tonight. [...] Keep hope alive!
Speech and slogan: Rev. Jesse Jackson, at the
Democrat convention in Atlanta, Georgia, 21 July
1988, concedes the presidential nomination to
Governor Michael Dukakis.

~

The Congress will push me to raise taxes and I'll say no, and they'll push, and I'll say no, and they'll push me again. And I'll say to them: 'Read my lips: no new taxes.'
George Bush, speech accepting the presidential
nomination, Republican convention, New
Orleans, Louisiana, 19 August 1988. At this
stage in the campaign, Democrat Michael
Dukakis enjoyed an 18-point lead in the opin-
ion polls.

~

• •

Women who seek to be equal to men
lack ambition.

Bumper sticker, USA, 1988.

• •

I will keep America moving forward …
for a better America, for an endless
enduring dream and a thousand points of
light.
Coining a campaign slogan: George Bush, ibid.

~

We intend to have the best educated
Americans in the world.
*Described by George Bush as 'an inspiring young
leader': Vice-presidential candidate Dan Quayle,
41, a Senator from Indiana, outlines a policy after
his nomination, 19 August 1988.*

~

I served with Jack Kennedy. I knew Jack
Kennedy. Jack Kennedy was a friend
of mine. Senator, you're no Jack
Kennedy.
*Democrat Vice-presidential candidate Lloyd
Bentsen, in TV debate with his rival Dan Quayle,
6 October 1988; Quayle had evoked the name of
Kennedy in his own 'mission statement'.*

~

Would you vote for a man who turned a
killer loose?
*During a vicious presidential campaign, the Bush
team launched a series of TV advertisements
designed to undermine the 'character' of Dukakis;
this one referred to his decision, when Governor of
Massachusetts, to grant parole to Willie Horton, a
convicted killer who then killed again. In fact,
Dukakis had – as is usual – acted on the advice of
the State's parole board; the nicety was lost on
many voters, though the fact that Horton was
black was not. In the election of 8 November, Bush
was elected with 54 per cent of the vote and 40
States to Dukakis' 10.*

We have not successfully rolled back the
frontiers of the state in Britain, only to
see them reimposed at a European level,
with a European super-state exercising a
new dominance from Brussels.
*UK Prime Minister Margaret Thatcher addresses
her European partners at Bruges, 20 September
1988. The speech led to the foundation of the*

*'Bruges Group' of Euro-sceptic (or -phobic)
Conservatives.*

Our English countryside is one of the
most heavily man-made habitats in
Europe. To make it into a green
museum would be to belie its whole
history.
*Nicholas Ridley, UK Secretary of State for the
Environment, is critical of 'conservationists' in
November 1988; he went on to condemn the
'NIMBY' – Not In My Back Yard – mentality' of
people who rejected rural development simply
because they did not wish to live near it. The
remark rebounded on him when it emerged that
he had used his ministerial powers to veto a
housing development near his own country
residence.*

We have had twenty years of economic
stagnation, sterility and incalculable
moral loss.
*Former Czechoslovakian President Alexandr
Dubcek: published text of his speech on receipt of
an honorary degree from Bologna University on
13 November 1988. The speech he actually delivered contained no criticisms of anybody.*

Let us go forward towards a new world
order of peaceful international relations.
*Addressing the United Nations on 7 December
1988, President Mikhail Gorbechev announces
a cut of 500,000 (10 per cent) over two years
in Soviet military forces, and coins a phrase
that was to be associated later on with US
President George Bush. He also announced the
scrapping of 25 per cent of the Soviet Union's
tank and artillery forces, including 5000 tanks
based in East Germany, Hungary and
Czechoslovakia.*

We renounce, totally and absolutely, all
forms of terrorism, including individual,
group and state terrorism.
*Yasser Arafat, speaking on behalf of the PLO, 14
December 1988; he also accepted UN Resolutions
242 and 338, recognizing the State of Israel and
its right to exist with secure borders. The US
responded by promising 'substantive negotiations' with the PLO; Israel officially dismissed the
pledge as 'cheap words'.*

The whole sky lit up. It was raining fire.
Eyewitness Mike Carnahan, Lockerbie,

Dumfriesshire, 22 December 1988. After US Embassies worldwide receive warnings of an imminent terrorist attack on a Pan-American airlines plane in retaliation against the accidental shooting down of an Iranian airliner in July, Pan-Am flight 103 from Frankfurt to New York via Heathrow is blown apart at 31,000 ft (9450 m) at 7.19 p.m. on 21 December as it overflies the small Scottish market town of Lockerbie. All 259 people on board the plane were killed, and 11 residents of Sherwood Crescent in the town who died when part of the fuselage gouged a fiery trench through their homes. Conspiracy theories flew thick and fast as it emerged that the plane was carrying US Intelligence agents, and stories are told in Dumfriesshire of the unexplained disappearance of evidence found on the ground. The aircraft was painstakingly reassembled to determine the nature and location of the bomb; this was proved to be a barometric pressure device in a luggage hold, and a possible link was established with the Air India plane blown apart over the Irish Sea in June 1985. When a Shi'ite terrorist was arrested (and subsequently released) in Germany with the equipment to make an identical bomb, concealed in a cassette recorder, strong circumstantial evidence pointed to Iran and Syria as the 'enablers' of the outrage, but the blame was eventually fixed on Libya, which was then ostracized by Western countries.

I don't think a prostitute is more moral than a wife, but they are both doing the same thing.
Philip Mountbatten, wife of Queen Elizabeth II, speech, 6 December 1988.

1989

The author of the Satanic Verses book, which is against Islam, the Prophet and the Koran, and all those who were involved in its publication who were aware of its content, are sentenced to death. I ask all Muslims to execute them wherever they find them.
The fatwa, 14 February 1989. Ayatollah Ruhollah Khomeini puts a $2 million bounty on Salman Rushdie, British author of The Satanic Verses, *a multi-layered novel whose springboard is the suppressed (or 'satanic') verses of the Koran – the Islamic equivalent of the Gnostic*

gospels – which depict the prophet enjoying the company of houris. Rushdie immediately went into hiding, under the protection of the Special Branch of Scotland Yard, and remains in this condition, save for occasional appearances at literary occasions, at the time of writing (July 1996). The Ayatollah's 'sentence' has been carried out on translators and foreign publishers of the book, and bookshops have been firebombed. The Iranian government continues to insist that the fatwa cannot be 'repealed'.

~

I call upon the intellectual community in the country and abroad to stand up for freedom of the imagination, an issue much larger than my book or indeed my life.
Salman Rushdie, 14 February 1989. Some British Muslims in Bradford and elsewhere responded by burning the book and, in effigy, its author; Dr Khalim Siddiqi, who established an 'Islamic Parliament' in Britain, repeatedly called for the novelist's murder but was never prosecuted. Roy Hattersley, Labour's deputy leader and Home Affairs spokesman, himself a novelist (and, presumably, a member of the intellectual community) proposed a 'compromise' whereby the publishers, Viking Penguin, 'chose' not to publish a paperback edition. The book remains banned in India, Pakistan and Saudi Arabia – and in Iran, although extracts from it appeared in an Iranian literary magazine in 1988 and excited only literary interest. It became a bestseller – if not a best-read book – in Britain, Europe and the USA.

~

Life is a sexually transmitted disease.
Graffito, quoted in The Faber Book of Fevers and Frets *(1989).*

In America there are 30 channels, amazing documentaries, excellent serials. When I arrive here all I find late at night is snooker.

•••••••••••••••••••••••••••••••••••••

It's just called 'The Bible' now. We dropped the word 'Holy' to give it a more mass-market appeal.

Editorial spokesman, Hodder & Stoughton, quoted in the Sunday Telegraph, *1989.*

•••••••••••••••••••••••••••••••••••••

Sky satellite TV replaces snooker with American football – or would have done, if there had been dishes available to receive the signals. Rupert Murdoch launches the service, 5 February 1989.

We have become a grandmother.
Informing the press of a happy event in the family, Margaret Thatcher does Britain's satirists a good turn on 3 March 1989.

You have provided us with an occasion we shall never forget, and it is the start of something big.
Prime Minister Margaret Thatcher to President Mikhail Gorbachev at the end of his three-day visit to Britain on 7 April 1989, when he invited Queen Elizabeth II to visit Moscow; she accepted. The USSR withdrew its forces from Afghanistan in February, after a nine-year conflict in which at least 16,000 Soviet troops were killed, and 46,000 wounded. In March, the first quasi-democratic elections in the USSR saw a rout of Communist deputies in all but the 25 per cent of 'reserved' seats, and the election of Boris Yeltsin in Moscow with 90 per cent of the vote.

I think everyone knows there have been a few problems. Please try to be calm. We are doing our best for you.
Liverpool FC manager Kenny Dalglish appeals over the public address system at Hillsborough, Sheffield, as play is interrupted in the FA Cup semi-final match between Liverpool and Nottingham Forest on 15 April 1989. As play started, thousands of Liverpool fans were still outside the ground; police opened a gate to get them in quickly, by-passing the turnstiles, and with the sudden influx of people into an already crowded ground, 95 people were crushed to death against the fencing erected to keep hooligans off the pitch. Many of the dead were teenagers, and the youngest was ten years old – 170 people were injured.

~

SCUM
The headline in the Sun the following day, 16 April, over a 'report' alleging that the dead and injured were the authors of their own misfortune, being rowdy and drunk, and that Liverpool fans had spat and urinated over police and ambulance crews struggling to render assistance. The story was untrue, and led to a continuing boycott of the paper on Merseyside. The British tabloid press was generally reviled for

printing lurid colour photographs of the dead and dying. In August, an interim report into the Hillsborough disaster put the blame on the police decision to open the gates; a later report recommended sweeping changes to League football grounds, including the provision of exclusively seated accommodation and the removal of all barriers.

Success smells like Brighton.
Sir Laurence Olivier (Lord Olivier), quoted in the Peter Hall's Diaries (1983). He died on 11 July 1989 at the age of 82.

It was like a tank driving over a Mini.
A spokesman for Tidal Cruises, the owners of the pleasure boat Marchioness, *which was hit from behind by the 1,880-tonne dredger* Bowbelle *at 2 a.m. on the morning of 20 August 1989; of the 150 people celebrating a birthday on board the smaller boat, 60 died as it sank in a few seconds. In a macabre footnote to the tragedy, the coronor ordered that the hands be cut off the bodies of victims 'to assist identification.' The master of the* Bowbelle *was later convicted of being drunk on duty.*

Ah hauvnae pyed!
Slogan (translation: 'I have not paid') on badges worn in Scotland by 'Poll Tax' defaulters – 300,000 of them in Strathclyde alone, it was revealed in September 1989. The officially named and widely detested Community Charge, a replacement for the rates that was unrelated to the value of property or, for the most part, to the ability of people to pay it, was introduced in Scotland (where there was a large anti-government majority) a year earlier than the rest of the UK. An estimated one million British voters took themselves off the electoral register in the mistaken belief that this would enable them to evade the charge. In London 300,000 people marched on the eve of the introduction of the charge to England and Wales in March 1990; the demonstration ended in a riot.

Successful conduct of economic policy is possible only if there is full agreement between the Prime Minister and the Chancellor of the Exchequer.
The letter of resignation of UK Chancellor Nigel Lawson, 26 October 1989. The Prime Minister's 'economic adviser', Professor Sir Alan Walters, was against Britain's entry to the European Monetary System, seen as a precursor

China ~ Protest and Massacre

The age of the Emperor has ended.
Slogan on the wall of Peking University in early May 1989: precursor to extraordinary and tragic events.

We will enhance democracy, oppose corruption and expand openness.
Chinese Communist Party chairman Zhao Ziyang, 16 May 1989 as, during a historic visit by Mikhail Gorbechev to Peking, students with tents and blankets occupy Tiananmen Square, erect a replica of the Statue of Liberty, and demand democratic freedoms. Martial law was declared after the Soviet leader's departure, as it became clear that the students enjoyed widespread support among ordinary citizens and even the police. On 3 June the army was ordered to put the protest down; several thousand troops – brought in from other provinces because local soldiers were considered unreliable – advanced with tanks and armoured personnel carriers through the streets of the capital, where they were met with opposition; petrol bombs were thrown, and 26 people are known to have died. One frail demonstrator held up a column of four tanks by standing in front of them, his arms at his sides. The armoured columns then smashed through a barricade of buses into the square, where they opened fire indiscriminately and drove over any students who got in their way; hundreds died and thousands were injured. Unknown thousands, including anyone known to have given succour to wounded demonstrators, were later executed in 'People's Courts'. On 25 June Prime Minister Li Peng announced that Zhao Ziyang and other 'revisionists' had been stripped of their posts. The aged President Deng Xiaoping was produced to give his blessing to the massacres.

Truthfulness means precisely upholding the party's ideological line.
Jiang Zemin, newly installed as Party chairman, June 1989.

'Salute the People's Liberation Army of China,' reads the banner on the Peking Hotel, from whose balcony I last week watched 30 or more people mowed down in a single volley of gunfire. 'Salute the public security forces, salute the police, salute the armed militias.'
Andrew Higgins, the Independent, *13 June 1989.*

They presented food and official reports as usual and issued imperial commands from the covered litter. It was summer and the litter began to smell. To disguise the stench the escort was told to load a cart with salted fish.
The classic Chinese chronicle The Historical Records *narrates how elaborate steps were taken to conceal the fact that the Great Emperor Ch'in Shih-huang – who only murdered 46 scholars – had died on a tour of his Empire: quoted in the* Independent, *27 December 1989.*

There was no tragedy in Tiananmen; there was no bloodbath. There is no change in China's basic policy. The open door remains open.
Prime Minister Li Peng, June 1989, seeks to allay fears over Britain's handover of Hong Kong to China, due in July 1997.

to full monetary union; Lawson favoured it. John Major, appointed only weeks before to replace the dissenting Sir Geoffrey Howe at the Foreign Office, became Chancellor; Douglas Hurd became Foreign Secretary. Howe was appointed Deputy Prime Minister – a post Mrs Thatcher was at pains to make clearly devoid of useful function. In a contested election for the Conservative leadership on 5 December – triggered by the token candidacy of backbench MP

Sir Anthony Meyer – 60 MPs did not support their Prime Minister. Britain joined the system a year later, with sterling fixed at a higher rate of exchange with the Deutschmark than many thought sustainable.

It could be that they will have a long-term resident on their hands.
US Defence Secretary Dick Cheney, 28 December 1989, after President Noriega, wanted for multi-million dollar drug trafficking, took refuge in the Vatican Embassy in Panama City following a US

military invasion of his country. American 'psy-ops' experts recommended the deposed dictator be regaled with loud round-the-clock Heavy Metal music to persuade him to leave. After a few days it worked, and Noriega was flown to Miami to face charges.

One moment more. One last. Grace to breathe that void. Know happiness.
Samuel Beckett, Ill Seen Ill Said (1982) The author, dramatist and Nobel Prizewinner died in Paris on 22 December 1989, aged 83.

THE WALLS COME TUMBLING DOWN

As Mikhail Gorbechev tried, with increasing desperation, to reconcile the concepts of state socialism and democracy and to hold the USSR together as a single political entity, he sent an implicit message to the regimes of its one-party satellite states in Eastern Europe: 'Your life support machine has been switched off.' By the end of 1989, all were extinct.

The Solution
After the uprising of the 17th June
The Secretary of the Writers' Union
Had leaflets distributed in the Stalinallee
Stating that the people
Had forfeited the confidence of the
    government
And could win it back only
By redoubled efforts. Would it not be
    easier
In that case for the government
To dissolve the people
And elect another?
Bertolt Brecht's poem, written after the suppression of the East German workers' uprising in 1953, perfectly expresses the arrogance of the rulers of Europe's post-war 'People's Republics' whose demise is chronicled below.

POLAND – A Ten Year Haul

The birth of the Solidarity movement – and the election, from a strongly if mutedly Roman Catholic populace, of a Polish Pope – paved the way for a decade of change; as already recorded, Poland inched its way towards a dissolution of the one-party state. On 17 April the Polish government lifted the ban on Solidarity, which on 4 June was permitted to contest one-third of the seats in an election for the lower house of Parliament.

The Winter is yours – the Spring will be ours.
Warsaw graffito, Christmas 1981, as martial law is imposed; seven years later, the prophecy came true. After months of strikes, the government began 'round table' negotiations with Solidarity in January 1989.

With us – you can be more sure of things.
An ironic double-entendre: slogan on a government poster in June. The ruling Communist Party campaigned anonymously, under such abstractions as 'moderation', 'good sense', and 'stability'; Solidarity candidates plastered their posters with the familiar splashy red logo.

Many voters simply put a huge X through the entire list; vote-tellers later confirmed that in many cases the X simply did not reach to the bottom of the page.
Steve Crawshaw of the Independent *on the Polish parliamentary election of 4 June 1989. There were two ballot sheets, one for contested seats, and one, containing 35 names, for 'protected' members of the ruling regime; by leaving this latter list blank, an elector was deemed to have voted for all 35. Adam Zielinski, alphabetically situated at the foot of the list, was one of only two to escape the voters' contemptuous crossing-out.*

In elections to a newly-established Senate (upper house) two weeks later, Solidarity candidates won 99 of the 100 seats.

Hopes are turning in the direction of a man who has devoted all his life to the struggle for Poland.

Solidarity leader Lech Walesa on his colleague Tadeusz Mazowiecki, elected as Poland's first post-war non-Communist Prime Minister on 24 August 1989. He had spent a year in prison under martial law, for editing the Solidarity weekly newspaper. After a spell of uneasy 'power-sharing' in the weeks following the June elections, Lech Walesa had invited elected members of the People's and the Peasants' parties – for 40 years the puppets of the Communist Party – to join a Solidarity-led coalition government. They accepted with alacrity.

HUNGARY – THANK YOU

Headline in the Solidarity daily, Warsaw, 11 September 1989 (see below).

HUNGARY – An Equable Surrender

May God spare me the punishment of being rehabilitated by my own murderers.

Imre Nagy, Prime Minister of Hungary in 1956, executed for treason in 1958. Thirty years later, on the anniversary of the uprising (23 October 1988) the crowd who assembled in Budapest to bear witness to it did so, for the most part, in uneasy silence.

Pluralism within a one-party setting.

A 'buzz-word' after November 1988, when the Hungarian Communist Party, essaying its own version of perestroika, announced a move towards a sort of democracy; alone among the East European states, Hungary had not experienced mass protest, but the economic outlook was grim, and Moscow had provided what appeared to be a safe escape route.

After me, Comrade Deluge.

New Year's Day, 1988: in a satirical cabaret on Hungarian radio, a soundalike for János Kádár, Party boss for 32 years, makes an entirely accurate prophecy: Kadar was ousted in May 1988.

I could quite happily see an elective dictatorship – such as you have in Britain.

An off-the-record briefing from 'a close aide' of

Karoly Grosz, newly installed as Party leader; quoted by Steve Crawshaw in the Independent.

I do not know what motivated Imre Pozsgay to highlight this single element in a work spanning four decades.

Imre Pozsgay, a flamboyant member of the new ruling class, awarded himself the job of launching the publication of an official history of Hungary's post-war Communist Party. While his leader was out of the country on 29 January 1989, he gave prominence to a section declaring the events of 1956 to have been a 'popular uprising' and Imre Nagy an 'outstanding statesman'. Grosz, quoted above, was rather nettled, but the genie was out of the bottle.

This is what you could call Designer Communism.

Anonymous observer at the official unveiling of the renovated Budapest Cemetery where Plot 301, formerly strewn with deliberately dumped rubbish and overgrown with weeds and bushes was now, with its Heroes' Memorial, mosaic paths and neatly-planted borders, the official resting place of the leaders of the 1956 uprising.

I believe that the political testament of Imre Nagy was resurrected today.

Sandor Kopacsi, commander of the Budapest police in 1956, attends the delayed funeral of Prime Minister Imre Nagy, 17 June 1989.

Will they never leave us alone?

A shout from the crowd as the cortege of Nagy and the other rehabilitated leaders arrives at the cemetery, led by a police Mercedes with flashing light. God did not spare him his final punishment.

During the summer of 1989, Budapest had several times its usual quota of East German holidaymakers; Hungary was one of the few countries East Europeans were permitted to visit, and these visitors seemed in no hurry to go home. Hungary had taken down the watchtowers and barbed wire on its border with Austria in May, and turned a blind – or blindish – eye to East Germans passing through to Austria and then West Germany, where they were automatically entitled to citizenship. The thousands gathering in Budapest camps hoped a deal could be done to travel directly to West Germany; at 7 p.m.on 10 September 1989, to the fury of the East German regime, Hungary opened its borders. Within 72 hours, 12,000 East Germans rushed through, making a total of around 100,000 in all; then East Germany banned its citizens from travelling to Hungary. Hundreds of East Germans then occupied the West German Embassy in Prague, seeking asylum.

On 7 October, Hungary's Communist leadership voted to have themselves called Social Democrats.

EAST GERMANY –
Voting With One's Feet

We want to stay! We are the People!
The slogans of Leipzig, September 1989, as thousands took to the streets demanding reform in their own country. The Protestant churches of the city were the nucleus of opposition organization; seemingly within days, an alternative government – the New Forum – was preparing itself for office, despite the mass beatings and arrests of its supporters.

We must heed the impulses of the times. Those who delay are punished by life itself.
Mikhail Gorbachev, visiting East Germany to celebrate its 40th anniversary as a sovereign state on 8 October 1989, has words of advice for Erich Honecker, the man who built the Berlin Wall. By ignoring them, Honecker turned them into prophecy: on 9 October he ordered the Militia to fire live ammunition at demonstrators in Leipzig. The order was disobeyed, and on 18 October Honecker was ousted, after 18 years in power, by Egon Krenz. Events now moved with dizzying swiftness. Half a million people demonstrated in Leipzig on 31 October; the following day, the border with Czechoslovakia was reopened, and tens of thousands poured through, all heading for the West German Embassy in Prague. On 3 November, Krenz announced that East Germans were free to travel, via the small triangle of Czechoslovak territory between the two countries, to West Germany. On 4 November, a million people took to the streets in East Berlin; three days later, the entire Cabinet resigned and Hans Modrow, a liberal who had argued for the legalization of New Forum, became Prime Minister and appointed a new Politburo.

Also it is announced that citizens of the German Democratic Republic will be able to travel across all East German border checkpoints. Visas will be required and
all applications will be handled without delay.
A throwaway announcement at the end of a routine press conference on 9 November 1989, Information Minister Günther Schabowski.

Desperately, with deadlines looming, I wrote: 'East Germany last night decided to throw open the Berlin Wall and its heavily fortified 'Iron Curtain' border and let its unhappy people go.' I prayed to God I was right.
Reporter Patricia Clough, writing in the Independent, *29 December 1989.*

I am taking my orders from television.
East German guard on the Berlin Wall, 9/10 November 1989. Tens of thousands of East Berliners poured through the Wall, without benefit of visa; thousands more sat on it, playing instruments, singing, and letting off fireworks. Quite a lot of them had hammers.

So ein Tag, so Wunderschön!
'What a day, what a wonderful day... ': the Song of the Wall, 9/10 November 1989.

Our interest must be that East Germans stay at home.
West German Chancellor Helmut Kohl, visiting Poland, 9 November 1989; one of his Interior Ministry officials had already told the television from which the border guards took their orders: 'No-one will be turned back,' West Germany's population had already increased by over half a million: 225,000 East Germans, and 300,000 ethnic Germans from Poland and the USSR.

Now that people can go, there is not the same urge to leave for good.
An anonymous young man, quoted by Patricia Clough in the Independent, *11 November 1989.*

I'm elated; I'm just not an emotional kind of guy.
US President Bush, quoted in the Independent, *11 November 1989.*

My boss came in this morning, slapped the newspapers on my desk, and said: 'Today is holiday. Go off and see West Berlin. But make sure you're back on Monday.'
Wolfgang, an electrician from East Berlin enjoying the Kurfürstendamm on 10 November 1989;

quoted by Adrian Bridge in the following day's Independent.

CZECHOSLOVAKIA –
Chimes of Freedom

The huge influx of East Germans passing through Czechoslovakia on their way to the West acted like a spark on touchpaper; yet it was, at first, a slow kindling – slow, at any rate, in comparison with the breakneck speed of events in East Germany. But the mass demonstration of 17 November 1989 – and, crucially, the brutality with which it was met – set the wheels of revolution in unstoppable motion.

Why is it that we are such cattle?
An anonymous woman speaks to an Independent *reporter on 29 October 1989; the previous night had seen a sparsely-attended student demonstration demanding democracy – yet, as Steve Crawshaw observed on 29 December – she herself had not taken part.*

I laboured under a burden of guilt for twelve years because I didn't sign Charter 77. On 17 November, as I lay on the ground and the police beat me – I felt free!
Simon, a telephone engineer; quoted by Edward Lucas in the Independent, *29 December 1989. A large crowd, predominantly comoposed of students, held a peaceful demonstration in Wenceslas Square on 17 November; candles were lit and national songs of Bohemia and Slovakia sung. The people were then attacked by police and armed anti-terrorist units; hundreds of students were clubbed and beaten, and reports at first said that two had died. The response seemed to bring fresh hope and purpose to the demonstrators; the national mood changed overnight.*

Concerts postponed until the time of freedom.
Posters for the Czech Philharmonic Orchestra, which appeared all over Prague in November 1989.

If these are all students, then the whole nation is a university faculty.
A construction worker, Prague: night after night, bigger and bigger crowds assembled, of all ages, all occupations, all backgrounds.

The last in Europe.
The slogan on handbills in shop windows after 17

November 1989; *the symbol of the revolution became a drawing of a clock, its hands pointing to 11.55.*

The bell is ringing. The story is over.
The closing words of a traditional Czech fairy-tale, and an astonishing phenomenon: half a million people bedecked with ribbons of red, white and blue are gathered in silence in Wenceslas Square, where the clocks are all stopped at five to midnight; nobody chants, nobody sings; the only sound is the jangling of half a million bunches of keys in the still winter air of Thursday 23 November 1989.

There are Soviet troops in Czechoslovakia, but that does not mean they are there to solve the country's internal problems.
Soviet Defence Minister Dimitri Yazov, visiting Vienna, destroys any hope the regime might have had of another 'friendly intervention', 23 November 1989.

Socialism with a human face must function again for a new generation. We have been too long in the darkness. Once already we have been in the light – and we want it again.
Spring in winter: Alexandr Dubcek addresses the vast crowd in Wenceslas Square on 24 November 1989; he had made the same speech the day before, in his home city of Bratislava, Slovakia. In Hradcany Castle, President Milos Jakes and the Politburo of the Czechoslovak Socialist Republic were preparing a statement of resignation. Vaclav Havel – co-founder of Charter 77, banned as a playwright, imprisoned from 1979–83 and the leader of Civic Forum, the government-in-waiting – delivered a letter to the Soviet Embassy that evening demanding an acknowledgment that the Soviet 'intervention' of 1968 was a criminal act, and an apology for it; it was received with 'much pleasure' and telexed to Moscow. Both were duly given.

Weapons are powerful. More powerful is the law. Most powerful is a word of truth.
Banner, Wenceslas Square, 24 November 1989.

STRACH On 17 November 1989. Our beloved son, father, brother, and comrade: Died, aged 21, after a long and serious illness. There are and will be no funeral rites. This announcement is in the name of all surviving family: the

Secret Police and the Special Riot Control Regiment; his children, Truncheons and Persecution; his brother, Silence, and sister, Despair; and his colleagues, Milos Jakes and Miroslav Stepan.

This black-edged poster appeared in Wenceslas Square after the Communist Party of Czechoslovakia renounced its 'leading role' and invited Civic Forum to take over in government on 29 November 1989. Strach is the Czech word for fear.

BULGARIA – One Little Push

In some ways the least likely candidate for revolution, with a tiny opposition of intellectuals, no free trade union movement, and a long unbroken history of remote and autocratic rule, Bulgaria shrugged off its one-party rule with apparent ease. A campaign to force the country's large ethnic Turkish population to 'Bulgarianize' itself led to a mass exodus in July: a quarter of a million people left the country and the position of the President, Todor Zhivkov, was weakened within the Politburo. Small demonstrations against the envirnomental damage caused by the country's backward industries, and calling for 'Eco-Glasnost', went unchecked.

Our beloved leader Comrade Zhivkov has asked to be relieved of his duties on grounds of health. The people thank him for his long selfless service to the Party and the people.

Statement released by the Bulgarian news agency on 9 November 1989 – the day the Berlin Wall was opened. The palace coup that replaced him, after 35 years in power, with Petar Mladenov was triggered by a demonstration of 10,000 people in Sofia.

Communism cannot be reformed, it can only be dismantled.

One of the slogans shouted by a larger crowd – perhaps 40,000 – on 18 November 1989. On 1 December, after another demonstration, Mladenov renounced the party's 'leading role' and promised free elections in the New Year.

ROMANIA – Blood And Vengeance

Romania had perhaps the most autocratic and certainly the most cruelly capricious regime of all Eastern Europe: Nicolae Ceausescu and his wife Elena regarded the country as their personal fief-

dom, and nowhere was worship of the 'cult of personality' so savagely pursued.

A good lunch and a fine car isn't everything. Where is the rest? Where is the feeling of ideological happiness?

Ilie Ceausescu (relation), Deputy Defence Minister, on life in the West.

Ceausescu is a madman. His wife, thirsty for power, is also mad, and his son is an idiot. And it's these three people who are being allowed to freely torture 23 million people.

Eugene Ionesco, Romanian-born playwright, 17 December 1989: the morning after the massacre of Timisoara. Laszlo Tokes, an ethnic Hungarian priest who had long been outspokenly critical of the regime, faced eviction from his apartment: a crowd gathered to support him, and soon became the focus for a larger demonstration in the town, formerly part of Hungary. Protestors expected a violent reaction, but perhaps not the tanks and machine-guns that were turned on the crowd. An unknown number died; a week later, a crew from Hungarian television was shown a mass grave containing 4630 bodies. The horror of Timisoara united Hungarian and Romanian peoples, and disturbances spread through the Transylvanian region – but not at once to Bucharest. Ceausescu flew to Tehran for a comradely meeting with Ayatollah Khomeini.

A massacre is taking place. Tanks are crushing students in the street and the police are firing on everyone who's moving.

Yugoslav news agency report on the night of 21 December 1989. On his return from Tehran, Ceasescu organized a mass rally in his own support in Bucharest. It went horribly wrong: the crowd began to boo, slow-handclap and heckle. Nothing like it had happened before. Ceasescu became incoherent with rage; he spluttered and squawked and gesticulated wildly; the crowd responded – and it was shown live on Romanian television, which faded out seconds later. A huge demonstration followed – and scenes like the one reported above. Civil war broke out between people and police, and among pro- and anti-Ceausescu troops.

This was the revolution of the children and youth. The dictator has been overthrown, the country is free. … Our brothers: be free and happy as we are. Keep calm. We must now rebuild the country and not destroy it. We want to be a clean, honest and frank nation. We shall be the most correct in the world. Let us have peace in our country, too.

Bucharest radio, 23 December 1989. Ceausescu and his wife disappeared after being helicoptered from the roof of the burning Central Committee building; some sort of order seemed to be emerging, and celebrations had begun after the Army decided to abandon all support for the deposed dictator. But the secret police, the Securitate, loyal to Ceausescu as the SS had been to Hitler, hit back; battles raged all over Christmas on and under the streets, as the city's warren of sewers became a hidden war zone. Thousands, possibly tens of thousands, died in Bucharest and other cities and towns; Nicu Ceausescu, the dictator's son, was arrested in the northern town of Sibiu, where he had been commanding his own battalion of Securitate in acts of mass murder among civilians.

We believe we were in a situation which did not allow us to wait.

Prime Minister Petre Roman of the hastily-formed National Salvation Front (already under fire from the Democratic Party for alleged totalitarian ambitions) explains the execution by firing squad of Nicolae and Elena Ceausescu on Christmas Day.

Sporadic fighting continued into the New Year, and conditions of anarchy prevailed in many areas.

We are witnessing sad things in other socialist countries.

Fidel Castro, President of Cuba, quoted in the Independent, 11 November 1989.

The New Uncertainty
1990~1996

It Could Be You.

~ Britain's National Lottery slogan,
introduced in November 1994

After the momentous events of 1989, the countries of the former Soviet bloc were faced with the problem of adjusting to their new circumstances. Freedom brought its own perils and uncertainties and, for many, the rapid transition to the 'market economy' exacted a heavy toll. In the USSR itself, an attempted coup by hard-line Communists, in which President Gorbachev was abducted, was faced down and defeated, and the Soviet Union was effectively dissolved in favour of a vaguely defined and short-lived 'Commonwealth of Independent States'. Boris Yeltsin, who became President of Russia, then called on the military to defeat a rebellion by members of the elected Parliament and, in the name of democracy began to rule largely by decree. Although his position was afterwards weakened by an ineffectual campaign against separatists in Chechenya, the rise of Mafia-style crime, and his own ill-health and rumoured drinking problems, he secured re-election in 1996 despite a strong showing by the Communist Party candidate. As Yugoslavia disintegrated with the passing of Communist rule, the new state of Serbia began a military campaign of conquest with the aim of assimilating Serbians in the neighbouring states of Croatia and Bosnia and reviving the old dream of a 'Greater Serbia'; the principal victims were the Muslim people of Bosnia against whom was waged, sometimes with Croatian support, a vicious campaign of blitzkrieg, siege and genocide; after countless UN-brokered 'cease-fires' and 'settlements' came to nothing, a NATO air campaign led to the signing of the 'Dayton Accord' in 1995, under which Bosnia was dismembered and parcelled out between Serbia, Croatia and its own Muslim-led but still multi-ethnic former government; a process of 'population redistribution' then began. The leaders of the Bosnian Serbs were indicted for trial as war criminals as evidence emerged of the horrific consequences of 'ethnic cleansing', predominantly in former Serb-held areas.

In 1990 the Iraqi President Saddam Hussein ordered the invasion of the neighbouring oil-rich state of Kuwait and the United Nations sanctioned military action, led by the NATO allies and effectively controlled by the US, to eject the occupying army. An air campaign was followed by a brief and devastating ground war in February 1991, and the Kuwaiti regime was restored. Iraq's oppression of its own people, particularly the Kurds, continued unabated as the UN ensured the destruction of Iraq's nuclear and chemical warfare capability.

In the Middle East, a breakthrough in negotiations between the Israeli government and the Palestine Liberation Organisation led to the creation of autonomous Palestinian areas within the state of Israel. Israeli Prime Minister Yitzak Rabin attracted the odium of his country's Zionist organizations, and those Israelis who had been previously encouraged to settle in occupied areas now scheduled for return to the Palestinians. In November 1995 he was assassinated by a gunman whose actions had been blessed by Rabbis of an extreme right-wing religious group. Israel's new leader, Benjamin Netanyahu, elected the following year, had campaigned on a 'tough' policy towards the PLO but continued discussions with its leaders after taking office.

In August 1994 the IRA declared an indefinite ceasefire and a 'peace process' began, with the intention of agreeing a form of government for Northern Ireland that would prove, if not acceptable, then at least not impossibly unacceptable to all parties. The process foundered eventually on three issues: the British government's insistence on the 'decommissioning' of the IRA's arms stockpile as a precondition to its admission to the 'process'; the IRA's unshakable aim to bring about, by any means, the unification of North and South with no British presence; and the refusal of 'hard-line' Unionists to share power with anybody. The IRA, which had continued its operations throughout the ceasefire, resumed bombing in the City of London in February 1996, and in the 'marching season' of July that year, sectarian violence in parts of the province was as ugly as it had ever been. Dropping its previous demand for 'decommissioning', the British government set the reimposition of a ceasefire as precondition for the admission of elected Sinn Fein members to 'peace-process' talks in the new Assembly - but it seemed doubtful if there was in fact any sort of 'process' to pursue.

[Note: Recent events have a habit of turning out to be a lot less important in the long run than they seem at the time, or even within their own decade. Quotations in this section have therefore been confined – with some deliberate exceptions – to what seem likely to be regarded in the cold light of the 21st century as significant events

1990

The bonfire of the certainties.
A senior NATO official's assessment of the revolutionary changes in Eastern Europe: from the Tom Wolfe novel, The Bonfire of the Vanities.

I greet you all in the name of peace, democracy and freedom for all. I stand here before you not as a prophet, but as a humble servant of you, the people.
Nelson Mandela, freed after more than a quarter of a century of imprisonment on 11 February 1990, addresses a huge and ecstatic rally in Cape Town.

~

Nelson always insisted on the island that we had to forget all our factionalism. It didn't matter whether we were ANC, or PAC, or Black Consciousness, or Communist Party, or UDF, or whatever. We had a common enemy, the white prison authorities, who bundled us all together in the hope that we would disgaree and divide. But we didn't.
'George', who spent 18 years on Robben Island with Nelson Mandela, interviewed in the Independent, *12 November 1990.*

~

The AWB will never allow the ANC and the South African Communist Party to open their offices here.
Condemning (among others) President F. W. de Klerk, Jesse Jackson and Margaret Thatcher –and, for good measure, burning the Star of David – Eugene Terre Blanche addresses a rally of 1000 members of his AWB 'Afrikaner Resistance' Party in Pretoria, 11 November 1990. As he spoke, several times that number of teenagers and students

219

• •

History gets thicker as it approaches recent times.

A. J. P. Taylor, English History 1914–1945, (1965); died on 7 September 1990, aged 84.

• •

paraded through the streets in support of the University of Pretoria Rag Week. President de Klerk had announced the 'unbanning' of the ANC and SACP on 2 February.

~

This is a very bad day for South Africa. Where can the white people go? There is only the sea.

A liquor store owner in Paarl, location of the Victor Verster prison where Mandela served the last years of his sentence, quoted by Gavin Bell, The Times, 12 November 1990. 'What you have in London are educated blacks,' his wife added. 'The ones here don't know what hygiene is.'

Mandela's release is no victory for us. The leftists among his own people are going to hunt him down. ... This is not empty rhetoric, the threat is real. I won't be the one to pull the trigger, but I won't be sorry when it happens.

'Faried', a spokesman for AZAPO (the Azanian People's Movement, affiliated to the Black Consciousness Movement), speaks to Gavin Bell, The Times, 12 November 1990.

~

In conclusion I wish to go to my own words during my trial in 1964. They are as true today as they were then. I quote: 'I have fought against white domination and I have fought against black domination. I have cherished the ideal of a democratic and free society in which all persons live together in harmony and with equal opportunity. It is an ideal which I hope to live for and to achieve. But if needs be, it is an ideal for which I am prepared to die.' Amandla!

Nelson Mandela: closing words of his speech, Cape Town, 11 November 1990.

———————

The way is now clear for the reunification of the two German states. Peace must come from German soil. That is the way for the future.

West German Chancellor Helmut Kohl, returning from talks in Moscow with Soviet President Mikhail Gorbachev, 11 February 1990.

~

We can accept a European Germany, but not a German Europe.

Alexander Yakovlev, USSR Politburo member, 11 November 1990.

~

We agreed [at Helsinki in 1977] that no boundaries would be changed except by agreement. If they are to be changed, this would require massive consultation.

UK Prime Minister Margaret Thatcher, 11 November 1990.

~

This is a day of jubilation, a day of remembrance and gratitude. Our common task now is to establish a new European order.

Helmut Kohl, 9 September 1990, after reaching agreement on German reunification.

~

The Gulf War – Desert Shield

I can't remember a time when the world was so strongly together against an action as it is now.

Margaret Thatcher, 7 August 1990. On 2 August, Saddam Hussein, military dictator of Iraq, ordered the invasion of the neighbouring state of Kuwait, whose Emir fled to Saudi Arabia as tanks and aircraft crushed what scant resistance was offered. On 8 August, Saddam announced that Kuwait had been annexed 'for eternity' and called on other Gulf Arabs to 'liberate Mecca from the spears of the Americans and Zionists'. He seized several hundred British and American civilians and held them hostage in Baghdad, saying they would come to no harm so long as the West took no military action. The Arab League, meeting in Cairo on 10 August, condemned his actions.

The highlights and shadows of our history give us cause to reflect in these days, to reflect on that which was done in the name of Germany. That will not repeat itself.
Hans-Dietrich Genscher, West German Foreign Minister, 4 October 1990. East and West Germany were reunited on 3 October 1990; on 2 December, Helmut Kohl was elected Chancellor of Germany.

What is there left to believe in?
Diane Garvey, estate agent, Manhattan.

~

An entire class of people have just had their weekend ruined.
John Buckley, Republican Party consultant.

~

Personally, I am not going to be satisfied until thousands of rats have consumed millions of bottles and survived.
Senator Al Gore, Democrat presidential contender and future US Vice-President. A tiny cloud forms on the Yuppie horizon as Perrier water is withdrawn from the market after the

discovery of trace elements of benzine on 9 February 1990.

Economic and political union ... is the next step toward a United States of Europe.
Helmut Kohl, West German Chancellor, on the 'Delors Plan' for a single currency and a central European bank, Dublin, 26 June 1990.

~

We can always rely on the British Prime Minister to ensure that the debates are long and that the decisions taken are always retaken.
President Mitterrand of France, Dublin, 26 June 1990. Britain, in the person of Margaret Thatcher, was isolated in opposition to plans for an Exchange Rate Mechanism within a European Monetary System.

~

A German racket to take over the whole of Europe ... you might just as well give it to Adolf Hitler.
Thoughts on European currency union from Her Majesty's Secretary of State for Trade and

Are you getting your milk? Are you getting your cornflakes, mmm?
Saddam stages a photo-opportunity by playing Father Christmas with British hostage children in front of TV cameras on 23 August 1990. Six-year-old Stuart Lockwood, arms folded and face composed in silent contempt, spoiled his show by ducking away as the dictator tried to ruffle his hair. He freed all the women and children four days later; by mid-December he appeared to have abandoned his plan to use the remainder as a 'human shield'; most were freed.

I will draw a line in the sand.
President George Bush on the defence of Saudi Arabia against threatened Iraqi attack; a multi-national force began to assemble for Operation 'Desert Shield' at the beginning of September 1990. Troops and marines from the US were the first, followed by France and the 'Desert Rats' from Britain; the USSR offered direct assistance, and Turkey turned off the Iraqi oil pipeline across its territory. Diplomatic relations between Europe and Iraq were severed on 25 September; two days

later, relations between Britain and Iran were restored; Syria followed on 28 November.

Our fingers are touching the trigger. We will shoot the minute Iraq suffers aggression.
George Habash, leader of the Popular Front for the Liberation of Palestine, 18 September 1990. Yasser Arafat's PLO also gave Iraq enthusiastic support.

They will drown in their own blood.
Saddam Hussein, on the growing forces assembling against him in Saudi Arabia in September 1990.

If Kuwait and Saudi Arabia sold bananas or oranges, the Americans would not go there. They are there because Kuwait is an oil monarchy.
President Julius Nyerere of Tanzania, 28 September 1990; possibly the first of many to make a pointed distinction between oil and various fruits and vegetables.

Industry, Nicholas Ridley, interviewed in The Spectator, *13 July 1990. He resigned.*

~

Britain does not want to be ruled by a conglomerate in Europe which includes Third World nations such as Greeks and Irish, nor for that matter the Italians and French, whose standards of political morality are not ours, and never will be.

Alfred Sherman, UK journalist and Conservative aide, the Independent, *10 August 1990. Margaret Thatcher had reacted in the Commons to proposals for European Union with, 'No, No, No!'*

~

You can call an ecu a pound in Britain. A single currency does not need a single name, but it does need a single value.

Michael Heseltine, the former UK Defence Secretary and leadership contender, 18 November 1990. Britain had joined the Exchange Rate Mechanism – at a rate against the Deutschmark many thought alarmingly high – on 5 October.

Hostage is a crucifying aloneness... It is a silent, screaming slide into the bowels of ultimate despair. ... I want to drink all the drink in the world and make love to all the women.

Brian Keenan, released on 23 August 1990 after 1597 days' captivity in the hands of the Hizbollah. There was still no word of journalist John McCarthy or Anglican envoy Terry Waite.

It is rather like sending your opening batsmen to the crease, only for them to find that their bats have been broken before the game by the team captain.

Labour statesman Denis Healey once compared being attacked by Sir Geoffrey Howe with 'being savaged by a dead sheep'. On 13 November 1990, two weeks after his resignation from the Cabinet, the former Deputy Prime Minister fatally wounded his leader in the Commons; ministerial resignation statements are, by tradition, heard in uninterrupted silence. Margaret Thatcher had frequently spoken of 'batting for Britain' as 'captain of the team'.

~

I am now persuaded that I would have a better prospect than Mrs Thatcher of leading the Conservatives to a fourth electoral victory and preventing the ultimate calamity of a Labour government.

Michael Heseltine, the celebrated non-candidate, finally comes out on 14 November 1990.

~

I fight on. I fight to win.

In Paris for EC talks on 20 November 1990, Margaret Thatcher learns that she has emerged from the first round of balloting among her parliamentary colleagues with four votes more than her combined opposition. On her return, a large majority of her Cabinet colleagues advised her that it was time to go.

~

It's a funny old world.

Margaret Thatcher formally informs her Cabinet colleagues of her decision not to contest a second leadership ballot, 22 November 1990.

~

Rejoice! Rejoice!

A long-harboured grudge puts to sea under full sail with pennants unfurled: ex-Premier Edward Heath telephones his friend Madron Seligman with the news of the usurper's fall, 22 November 1990.

~

I'm enjoying this!

Hitting her best form, Margaret Thatcher leads the attack for the last time, against an Opposition motion of No Confidence on the afternoon of 22 November 1990. She won.

~

My aim is to create a nation at ease with itself.

After only three years in government – as Treasury Secretary, Foreign Secretary and Chancellor of the Exchequer – John Major secures victory in a fresh ballot and becomes Conservative leader and, at 47, the youngest Prime Minister of the century on 27 November 1990. He won 185 votes to Michael Heseltine's 131 and Douglas Hurd's 56; it was not an outright win, but his opponents immediately withdrew.

~

John Major will, I predict, turn out to be one of the great political figures of our time.

John Hunt MP talks his way into becoming Welsh Secretary in the new Major Cabinet.

The Gulf War - Desert Storm

The Air Attack

The mother of battles will be our battle of victory and martyrdom.
Saddam Hussein, 13 January 1991: the date set as a deadline for the withdrawal of Iraq from Kuwait. A 28-nation contingent with a combined force of 700,000 personnel – 420,000 from the US, 25,000 from Britain – and 2730 aircraft waited for orders to enforce the UN resolution for the restoration of Kuwaiti sovereignty. Iraq had a million men under arms.

Just two hours ago, allied air forces began an attack on military targets in Iraq and Kuwait. These attacks continue as I speak. ... We are determined to knock out Saddam Hussein's nuclear bomb potential... his chemical weapons facilities. ... Some may ask, why act now? Why not wait? The answer is clear: The world could wait no longer. ... While the world waited, Saddam Hussein systematically raped, pillaged and plundered a tiny nation, no threat to his own... While Saddam stalled, more damage was being done to the fragile economies of the Third World, the emerging democracies of Eastern Europe, to the entire world including our own economy. ... This is an historic moment. We have, in this past year, made great progress in ending the long era of conflict and Cold War. We have before us the opportunity to forge, for ourselves and for future generations, a new world order – a world where the rule of law, not the law of the jungle, governs the conduct of nations. ... Our goal is not the conquest of Iraq – it is the liberation of Kuwait.
At 7 p.m. EST (midnight GMT) on 16 January 1991, President George Bush announces the beginning of Operation 'Desert Storm'; at this stage, no ground forces among the 28-nation coalition were involved. The air attack was led by the USAF with support from the RAF. A total of 1300 sorties were flown against 300 'high-value' targets in the first 24 hours. The Iraqi telecommunications centre was destroyed by a 2000-lb 'smart' bomb; Tomahawk Cruise missiles with map-reading software were launched against government and military buildings in Baghdad. It was reported that 24 days after the offensive began, more than 44,000 sorties had been flown.

If a bomb falls in the desert and audio doesn't pick it up, does it still make a sound?
Daniel Golden, Boston Globe, 20 January 1991. Allied Commander Norman Schwarzkopf hosted 'video shows' of bombing missions on bridges and buildings, filmed from the attacking aircraft.

Going up in front of you is just a mass of fire. If it doesn't hit you, you can breathe again.
RAF Tornado pilot, 24 January 1991. Not all air attacks involved long-range technology. In a strategy regarded, with some justification, as suicidal by USAF crews, Tornadoes bombed and mined Iraqi airstrips from a height of 100 ft (30 m). Five aircraft were lost; some crew were captured, tortured and beaten, and exhibited on Iraqi TV.

It will be the darndest search-and-destroy operation the world has ever seen.
President Bush promises to deal with the threat from 'Scud' missiles – the primitive rocket bombs Iraq used against targets in Saudi Arabia and, indiscriminately and in the hope of provoking a military response and ending Arab league support for the Allies, against Israel. Although US 'Patriot' missiles dealt effectively with the missiles themselves, the operation against the launchers proved, as an Israeli spokesman said, 'less than completely effective'. In fact, not a single launcher was destroyed; Israel, however, did not retaliate.

The days of delusion are dead in Baghdad. The city has finally discovered the obvious: a contest between a Third World semi-power fighting World War II and a First World superpower fighting World War III is no contest at all.
Michael Kelly, New Republic, 11 February 1991.

All wars begin in an atmosphere of innocence and optimism, and this one started with ... techno-innocence, techno-optimism. ... The networks, with their repulsive computer-generated graphics, their self-important promo-spots, their maestro anchormen orchestrating live theatrical reports from around the globe, have

➤

been covering this conflict as though it were a mini-series. Order a pizza and watch a building disappear.

Philip Caputo, 'War Torn', in the New York Times Magazine, *24 February 1991. While many strategic targets were destroyed, Iraq's nuclear, chemical and biological warfare facilities emerged relatively unscathed. In an air-raid bunker on 13 February 400 Iraqi civilians died.*

The Land War

We're Going To War To Defend People Who Won't Let Women Drive?
US lapel badge, January 1991.

Our strategy for dealing with this army is very simple: first we are going to cut it off, then we are going to kill it.
General Colin Powell, Chairman of the US Joint Chiefs of Staff, 25 January 1991. The following day, the first of over 130 Iraqi pilots flew their planes to Iran, where they remained. On 28 January, Allied commanders reported that air supremacy had been achieved, and on 1 February a 10-mile (16-km) column of Iraqi tanks was attacked from the air as it attempted to advance towards the border with Saudi Arabia. As Saddam Hussein – who on 11 February informed his people that the war had already been won – announced changing and often contradictory plans for a conditional cease-fire, President Bush set noon (EST) on 23 February (7 a.m. GMT) as the dealine for compliance with UN Resolution 660. It passed without sign or notification of a withdrawal from Kuwait.

The liberation of Kuwait has now entered a final phase.
President George Bush announces the commencement of the ground war, 23 February 1991.

We're going around, over, through, on top, underneath.
US General Norman Schwarzkopf answers a journalist's question about Allied ground war tactics, 24 February 1991.

Oh great Iraqi people, oh brave men of our heroic armed forces, oh faithful and noble people. ... From the beginning, the evil ones worked on this path, the path of hostility and evil, in order to

harm the Iraqi people and smother the shining candles of their hearts. ... Fight them, oh brave, splendid men. Oh men of the mother of battles. ... As men collide with each other, the weapons of supremacy will disappear and the only thing that remains to decide the final result will be the bravery of believers. Fight them, and show no mercy to them, for this is how God wishes the faithful to fight the infidel.
Saddam Hussein, radio address to Iraq, 24 February 1991.

They looked like ghostly sheep, flushed from a pen... One by one, they were cut down by attackers they couldn't see or understand. Some were literally blown to bits by bursts of exploding 30 mm exploding cannon shells. ... The Iraqi soldiers, big as football players on the TV screen, ran with nowhere to hide. These are not bridges exploding or airplane hangars. They are men.
John Balzar of the Los Angeles Times *watches a US military video of a helicopter gunship attack: pooled report for Reuter, 25 February 1991. On the first day of fighting 10,000 Iraqi troops were taken prisoner.*

I find this all a bit unreal. We dare not assume that it's going to be like this all the way.
Lieutenant-Colonel Peter Marwood of the British First Armoured Division, Kuwait, finds his units advancing almost too rapidly; quoted in the Independent, *26 February 1991. Approximately 50,000 Iraqi troops had already surrendered.*

If you come to Kuwait you will say this is not Kuwait at all. Kuwait, it's not Kuwait any more.
A woman in Kuwait City speaks to CBS reporter Bob McKeown, who 'did a Max Hastings' on 26 February 1991; after the Saudi unit he was with stopped advancing, he borrowed a jeep and drove 45 miles (75 km) to the capital, finding most of it deserted, vandalized and – as in the case of the museum, parliament building and library – burned. Most of the animals in the city zoo had been slaughtered; some had been eaten.

Stories abounded of rape, torture and murder; departing Iraqi troops had plundered the city of all its consumer, and consumable, goods. While pockets of resistance remained to be overcome in Kuwait, most Iraqi forces had withdrawn across the northern border – setting fire to over 500 oil wells as they went.

In the mother of battles we have succeeded in harvesting what we have sown. ... How sweet victory is.
Saddam Hussein, ordering the withdrawal from Kuwait sometime after the event, 26 February 1991.

This is it, we have them checkmated. If they go back to Basra, the airforce will kill them. If they try for the other side of the Tigris, the bridges are down. If they flee north to Baghdad they will run into the US Army, and if they move south they run into coalition forces.
Pentagon spokesman, 26 February 1991, referring to the double encirclement of the Iraqi republican Guard, the élite of Saddam's army. It was crushed in the ensuing tank battle, the biggest since World War II. A huge column of Iraqi troops returning to Basra with loot from Kuwait was attacked from the air, and annihilated.

As far as Saddam Hussein being a great military strategist, he is neither a strategist nor is he schooled in the operational art nor is he a tactician nor is he a general nor is he a soldier. Other than that, he's a great military man. I want you to know that.
General Norman Scwarzkopf, press conference, Ryadh, 27 February 1991.

Kuwait is liberated. Iraq's army is defeated. I am pleased to announce that at midnight tonight, exactly 100 hours after ground operations commenced and six weeks since the start of Operation Desert Storm, all United States and coalition forces will suspend offensive combat operations.
President Bush proclaims victory on 27 February 1991. American commentators had expressed disquiet at the 'turkey shoot' of Iraqi forces on the road to Basra, and he did not wish to become involved in anything that might

resemble Vietnam or dissolve the Western–Arab coalition – but many, including senior military staff, regretted the lost opportunity to remove Saddam and disable his army – much of which remained intact to persecute his own people, particularly the Kurds in the north and the Shi'ite Marsh Arabs in the southeast. A blockade of all supplies except essential foods and medicines was enforced, and an embargo imposed on oil exports which was only lifted in June 1996.

At least 50,000 Iraqi troops died in the six weeks of the war. There were 172 Allied fatalities; of 148 Americans killed, 35 fell to accidental 'friendly fire', which was also the cause of nine of the 16 British deaths. Compensation claims remain in dispute for 'Gulf War Syndrome' – a combination of lassitude, nausea and paralysis blamed by many on the cocktail of antidote injections against chemical and biological weapons, which in the event were not used. Veterans in the US and UK claim many ex-comabatants are affected, and some of their children, conceived since the conflict.

The Kurds have no friends except the mountains.
Kurdish proverb. The Kurds – 'the world's largest nation without a county' – inhabit the upland territories on the borders of Iraq, Iran, Turkey, Syria and the former USSR. Persecuted throughout this century, they were used by Saddam Hussein for chemical weapons practice in the run-up to the Gulf War, nearly all 5000 inhabitants of the town of Halabja being killed by poison gas. As the war ended the Kurds, along with Iraqi Shi'ites, were urged to rise up against Saddam; many responded, unsuccessfully. UK Prime Minister John Major then proposed a UN-policed 'safe haven' for the Kurds in northern Iraq, and for a while this was provided, with a 'no-fly zone' imposed against Iraqi helicopters. The policy was quietly abandoned on 15 July 1991. The persecution of the Kurds continues, not only in Iraq.

The war wasn't fought about democracy in Kuwait.
President Bush responds to criticism that the restored al-Sabah regime in Kuwait is behaving even more repressively than it did before the Iraqi invasion: quoted in the Observer, 14 July 1991.

1991

I think we had better start again some-where else.

John Major, as the IRA launch three mortar bombs at Number 10 Downing Street from the back of a van in Whitehall on the morning of 7 February 1991; one found its target, next to a room in which the Prime Minister was holding a meeting with ministers. On 18 February one person was killed and 43 injured when the IRA bombed Victoria Station.

The judge at the original trial, Lord Bridge, said that if the defendants were telling the truth then the greatest con-spiracy in the annals of criminal history had occurred. Those words will have to be remembered.

Labour MP Chris Mullin, a leading campaigner for the release of the 'Birmingham Six' gaoled for the 1974 Birmingham pub bombings.

Money can't make up for all those years. I do not think about it and never have done. I just did not doubt that the truth would come out.

Hugh Callaghan, one of the 'Birmingham Six'. On 14 March 1991 the Court of Appeal declared their sentence to be 'unsafe and unsatisfactory', upholding their claim that police had falsified and fabricated crucial evidence at their trial; a sugges-tion that Lord Denning once said would open up 'appalling vistas'. West Midlands police responded by saying that they would continue to regard the case as closed.

It was the wrong sort of snow.

British Rail manager Terry Worrall explains the conspicuous failure of anti-snow measures on Southern Region, which slithered to a halt as a result; quoted in the Observer, *17 February 1991.*

•••••••••••••••••••••••••••••••••••

A writer's imagination, like the body, fights against all reason against death.

Graham Green, Ways of Escape, (1980); died on 3 April 1991, aged 86.

•••••••••••••••••••••••••••••••••••

If we had spent £167 million on con-doms we wouldn't have these problems in the first place.

Nicholas Fairbairn MP, former Solicitor-General for Scotland, on British food aid for Sudan, where seven million people faced death by starvation after drought.

It's easy to say with hindsight that we were wrong to put all our eggs in one basket.

Donald MacLeod, Director of Finance, Comhairle nan Eilean (the Western Isles Council), which lost £23 million – including £1.3 million deposited 15 minutes before the Bank of England closed it down on 20 July 1991 – in the Bank of Credit and Commerce International. The Bank of England was later criticized for delaying its deci-sion, and for continuing to list BCCI as 'respectable' when it had ample grounds – includ-ing BCCI's 1990 conviction in a Florida court for laundering $32m of drug money – for knowing otherwise.

Rising unemployment and the recession have been the price we've had to pay to get inflation down: that is a price well worth paying.

Norman Lamont, Chancellor of the Exchequer, as Britain's recession – the existence of which had previously been denied by government ministers – bit into 'white collar' employment, May 1991

Sitcoms.

The situation quite a lot of 1980s 'dinkies' found themselves in when the party was over: Single Income, Two Children on a Mortgage. Base inter-est rate remained in double figures through 1991, and unemployment rose above 2.5 million at the end of the year.

————————

Maastricht is dead. Historians will proba-bly see the Treaty as a bit of a fossil.

Norman Lamont, part of John Major's negotiating team at Maastricht, 10 December 1991.

~

It's game, set and match for Britain.

Prime Minister John Major, 11 December 1991, after signing the Maastricht Treaty, which set 1999 as the deadline for a Single European Currency, introduced majority voting on EC foreign policy, extended the executive power of the European Commission, and included a Social Chapter governing working hours and conditions, and a minimum wage. Major 'opted Britain out' of the Social Chapter in the expectation that foreign companies would be keen to invest in an economy with 'competitive' wage levels, and negotiated a 'separate entry' for Britain into the single currency; meanwhile, Britain remained a member of the ERM. On its enactment in March 1992, the people of all EC countries automatically acquired common citizenship.

~

Robert Maxwell's premature death is a great loss to the world of business and publishing. He was the one man you could rely on in times of trouble.
Lord Stevens of Ludgate, proprietor of the Daily Express, *pays tribute to his fellow tycoon and publisher, drowned after a fall from his yacht on 5 November 1991.*

~

It's been an awful week, the worst I can remember, and I need someone to talk to. ... Now I think I'll go home and have a good bath.
Joe Haines, Daily Mirror, *6 December 1991 – the*

day the newspaper Maxwell bought in 1984 carried the headline: MAXWELL: £526 MILLION IS MISSING FROM HIS FIRMS. *The Maxwell empire passed into the hands of administrators as it was revealed that Maxwell –given a hero's funeral on the Mount of Olives – had stolen more than £400 million from his employees' pension funds.*

———

I thought, my word Bunyan, you're a lucky fellow. You've got a window out of which I can look, see the sky, and here am I in a dark room ... I've got nothing, and you've got your own clothes and a table and chair.
Three months after the release of John McCarthy, Terry Waite is freed by his Hizbollah captors after spending nearly five years chained to a wall in a dark room; he arrived in Britain on 19 November 1991. A few months earlier he had been given a postcard sent from an anonymous well-wisher: it was of a stained glass window depicting John Bunyan in Bedford Jail.

RUSSIA – COUP AND COUNTER-COUP

This is a historic moment. Russia has entered the family of civilized nations.
Gavril Popov, who became the first elected Mayor of Moscow on 16 June 1991. Three days earlier, also in the first free elections in Russia's history, Boris Yeltsin – who had resigned from the Communist Party a year earlier, and had recently denounced Mikhail Gorbachev for being 'dictatorial' – was elected President of Russia. Another Yeltsin supporter was elected Mayor of Leningrad – which then voted in referendum to revert to its Tsarist name, St Petersburg.
The elections came at a time of tension in the USSR, which seemed to many to be on the brink of fragmentation. Independence movements in the Baltic republics of Lithuania, Latvia and Estonia had been repressed with most un-perestroika-like brutality; as it was later to appear, these tactics were part of the preparation for a military-KGB coup.

Gorbachev's an idiot. He should never have gone on holiday. They've done him, just like Krushchev.
Anonymous Moscow voice, quoted by Sian Thomas in the Independent, *20 August 1991, after an 'old guard' Communist junta comprising Gennady Yanayev, Gorbachev's Vice-President, KGB chief Vladimir Kryuchkov, Prime Minister Valentin Pavlov, Defence Minister Dmitri Yazov, Interior Minister Boris Pugo and senior apparatchik Oleg Baklanov, had seized power, claiming that Gorbachev, then on holiday in the Crimea, was 'tired and ill' and 'needed a good rest'; they purported to be acting with his approval and set about making arrests.*

Only yesterday, the Soviet person abroad

felt himself to be a worthy citizen of an influential and respected state. Now he is often a second-class foreigner, treated with disdain or pity. The pride and honour of the Soviet person must be fully restored.
Statement issued on behalf of 'The Committee for the State of Emergency', 19 August 1991.

We won't fire. We haven't even got any bullets – but we wouldn't fire on our own people.
A soldier on the streets of Moscow reassures the crowd; observed by Sian Thomas, the Independent, *20 August.*

We call on workers, peasants, the labour intelligentsia and all Soviet people to

restore labour discipline and order in the shortest period of time, raise the level of production and consequently move forward decisively.
Lest the government lose confidence in the people. ... Coup statement, 19 August 1991.

– Either we must fight or flee the country.
– I don't believe this, I must be dreaming.
– Yes, I have heard. Ants are crawling all over me, as we say in Russian.
Anonymous voices, on hearing of the coup, quoted by Helen Womack, the Independent, *20 August 1991.*

You can make a throne from bayonets, but you can't sit on it for long.
Boris Yeltsin, standing on the turret of a tank outside the White House – the Russian Parliament building – on the morning of 19 August 1991 – and quoting Dean Inge.

Soldiers, officers and generals, the clouds of terror and dictatorship are gathering over the whole country. They must not be allowed to bring eternal night. ... In this tragic moment for Russia I appeal to you: do not allow yourself to be ensnared in a net of lies and promises and demagogic calls to 'military duty'.
Boris Yeltsin, President of Russia, 19 August 1991: in the afternoon he addressed 5000 people from the White House balcony. He had become the focus of resistance to the coup as a general strike, called by him, began to take effect.

We will hold out here as long as we must to remove this junta from power and bring it to justice.
Boris Yeltsin addresses cheering crowds from the White House balcony; 20 August 1991. He issued a radio appeal to Muscovites to man barricades round the building.

We have won already. They should have got him in the first few hours. Now they are doomed to fail. They are just grey puppets and we are not afraid of them.
Mikhail Polykov, academic-turned-street-warrior, interviewed on a barricade by Helen Womack, the Independent, *21 August 1991. Several hundred thousand people answered Yeltsin's call for a mass display of 'people power'; most expected a Tiananmen-style military attack.*

Could it happen in any civilized country that the army seizes power and all the people get is *Swan Lake* repeated four times on the television?
Lieutenant Alexandr Ivanov, a defector to the resistance the day after the coup; quoted in the Independent, *24 August 1991.*

I'm sorry comrades, but I'm very excited!
A grinning-weeping Valery Mironov, newscaster on state-run television, 3 p.m. on 21 August 1991. The tanks did move against the White House on the night of 20–21 August, and three people died as a tank tried to smash through a barricade of trolleybuses; there were also reports of fighting in passages beneath the Parliament building itself. But senior military and KGB figures decided to throw in their lot with Yeltsin, and the coup began to crumble; Yeltsin rejected an offer to fly him to the Crimea to meet Gorbachev, suspecting a trap. At some time in the early morning of the 21st, the coup leaders abandoned their offices; later, they flew to the Crimea, where they were arrested. The Defence Ministry ordered all troops to withdraw to their barracks outside Moscow and, amid scenes of wild jubilation – with many soldiers joining in – the coup was over.

We wanted to wait until we could call a plenum of the central committee, but the critical emergency of the last few days prevented us from holding one, so here we are.
Alexander Zakhoshlov, accompanied by fellow members of the Politburo, explains why the ruling body of the Communist Party remained silent for a day and a half while its leader was under arrest. They had decided to support Gorbachev, he said, because reforms were a 'historical necessity'.

Gorbachev was overthrown by the people he had hand-picked. Can we really afford to be ruled by someone who is obviously so out of touch?
Engineer Georg Astafyev, quoted in the Independent, *22 August 1991.*

If one speaks in general about the Party as a reactionary force, I must disagree.
Mikhail Gorbachev, restored to Moscow and to an utterly changed situation, 22 August 1991. Boris Yeltsin had issued a decree appointing him-

self head of the Soviet armed forces, and more republics had proclaimed their own independence. A session of the Russian Parliament, to be addressed by Yeltsin, its saviour, and Gorbachev, the opponent he had rescued, was convened for the next day.

Take that bloody criminal out of the mausoleum!
Anonymous passer-by of Lenin's tomb, quoted in the Independent, 23 August 1991.

If there is no space, then there are some people there we can dig out.
Eduard Shevardnadze, formerly Gorbachev's foreign minister, proposes that the three Muscovites who died on the barricades be interred as heroes in the Kremlin Wall.

All right, all right, I'll read it, but you must know that I haven't read it myself yet.
After many interruptions to his prepared speech, and at the finger-wagging insistence of Boris Yeltsin, Mikhail Gorbachev reads aloud the full list of coup conspirators to the Russian Parliament; it included many of his own close colleagues, and the Soviet leader was clearly rattled as Yeltsin loomed at his side on 23 August 1991.

On a lighter note, let us turn to the suspension of the Communist Party.
Boris Yeltsin records a faint echo of the words of

V. I. Lenin in 1917, and raises a laugh from the Parliament – but he was in earnest. As a first move, he banned the Party newspaper, Pravda ('truth') and raised the old tricolour flag on all Russian state buildings. All over the USSR, people began pulling down statues of Lenin.

I don't think it is possible to carry out the functions as General Secretary of the Communist Party of the Soviet Union, and I am relinquishing those powers.
By continuing in office as President of the USSR, Mikhail Gorbachev effectively ended 73 years of Communist rule on 24 August 1991; he also called for the dissolution of the Party's Central Committee.

Communist rule began in 1917: Gorbachev ended it yesterday.
Headline, the Independent on Sunday, 25 August 1991.

This is a ridiculous country. It can't do anything properly, not even carry out a coup.
Igor Zakharov, Russian journalist; quoted in the Observer, 'Sayings of the Week', 25 August 1991.

The old system fell apart before the new one began to work.
Mikhail Gorbachev resigns as President of the now practically non-existent Union of Soviet Socialist Republics on Christmas Day 1991.

1992

I can't hide the emotion I felt when he telephoned me during some of the most difficult hours in Russia since the Second World War.
An emotional (but not tired) Boris Yeltsin embraces John Major on 30 January 1992, after signing a defence co-operation agreement. Britain undertook to assist with the decommissioning of Russia's nuclear weapons; Russia, in return, undertook in the meantime not to point any of them at Britain.

Today we have closed the book on apartheid.
South African President F. W. de Klerk, 18 March

1992. In a referendum turnout of 85.7%, white South Africans had voted by 68.7 to 31.3 per cent in favour of full legal equality for all other citizens.

Hubble's observations suggested that there was a time, called the big bang, when the universe was infinitesimally small and infinitely dense. Under such conditions all the laws of science, and therefore all ability to predict the future, would break down. ... If we do discover a complete theory... we would know the mind of God.
Stephen Hawking, A Brief History of Time, 1988. Humankind inched closer to the Grand Unifying Theory in April 1992, when NASA's Cosmic Background Explorer (COBE) sent back

data from some wispy, cloud-like formations at the very edge of the Universe – hence, from the very edge of time itself. The data appeared to confirm the hypothesis of the 'big bang': the creation of time and space in a single cataclysmic moment some 15,500,000,000 years ago; also the expansion of the Universe, like a design on the surface of an inflating balloon, since that point – and, perhaps, the eventual recollapse of everything in a 'big crunch' that will lead in turn to another big bang... and so on. While subsequent data appears to show that some of the observable stars in the Universe are older than the Universe itself (which is, so far as can be known, impossible), the theory remains the most likely explanation for the way things are – and, arguably, the most convincing proof of the argument that Science – like Art – demands to be pursued for its own sake, God or no God.

That's only fair – it is, after all, their turn.

Paddy Ashdown, leader of the Liberal Democrat Party, reacts to the news that David Owen (Lord Owen) – former Labour Foreign Secretary, Social Democrat Party leader, Liberal–Social Democrat Alliance co-leader, and Social Democrat leader (again) – has announced his support for the Conservative Party at the forthcoming general election: March 1992.

~

I think Essex Man will vote for a Conservative government.

A remark interpreted as support for her successor: Baroness Thatcher's prediction for the outcome of the election, 1 April 1992. 'Essex Man' is 'admass' shorthand for the 'Social Class C' citizen, or upwardly-aspiring non-professional, materially-oriented voter.

~

I'm feeling lucky.

With all the opinion polls predicting a more or less comfortable Labour victory at the end of a lacklustre Conservative campaign, John Major is quietly confident, 8 April 1992.

~

IF LABOUR WINS TODAY, WILL THE LAST PERSON TO LEAVE BRITAIN PLEASE PUT THE LIGHTS OUT.

The Sun's front page, 9 April 1992, polling day. Labour leader Neil Kinnock's head was portrayed as a light bulb.

~

IT WAS THE SUN WOT WON IT!

On 10 April 1992, Rupert Murdoch's tabloid daily claims credit for the fact that the Conservatives won the general election with an overall majority of 21. By July 1996 a succession of by-election defeats and backbench defections had reduced this to just one.

On the night of 10 April the IRA exploded a huge bomb in the Baltic Exchange, in London; three people were killed and hundreds of millions of pounds' worth of damage was sustained.

They are smashing us to pieces and starving us to death, and the world does nothing.

Anonymous citizen of Dubrovnik, 'Pearl of the Adriatic', blockaded and bombarded in October-December 1991 by 'federal Yugoslavian' – in reality, Serbian – forces. Thwarted in their attempt to extend 'Greater Serbia' into newly-independent Slovenia, the Serbs, with the bulk of the armaments of the former Yugoslav Republic, began a conquest of 'ethnic Serbian' territory in Croatia; the Croatian town of Vukovar fell in December, with at least 5000 civilian deaths. Other towns and villages were utterly destroyed.

The region is undergoing ethnic cleansing.

Serbian Radio news broadcast, reported on 21 May 1992. The people of Bosnia-Herzegovina - an ethnic mix of Muslim, Roman Catholic Croatian and Orthodox Serbian – voted by a clear majority for independence and a power-sharing government. Serbian President Slobodan Milosevic then sent troops in to occupy the country, and set about a policy of 'ethnic cleansing' – doing to the non-Serbian populace (and Muslims in particular) what Hitler did to Europe's Jews. Four years of hideous conflict – more or less feebly 'mediated' by international organizations – ensued, during which ordinary people who had lived peaceably together in towns and villages turned on each other to rape, loot, burn and murder. While it is undeniable that atrocities were and continue to be committed on all sides, it is also clear that the guilt for most of them lies at the door of the Serbians and, in particular, on the heads of the Bosnian Serb leader, Radovan Karadzic, and his army commander, General Ratko Mladic, both of whom have been listed by the United Nations as indicted War Criminals, personally and knowingly responsible for the murder of tens of thousands of Bosnian Muslim civilians. After four years of ineffectual involvement, during which innumerable cease-fires were violated, countless agreements were reneged upon, a 'no-fly-zone' was flagrantly violated, the city of Sarajevo was beseiged and substantially reduced to rubble by encircling Serb artillery, and one 'safe haven' after another was overrun and annihilated, the UN gave NATO authority to intervene with direct military action against the Serbian warlords: this was executed in 1995 with an efficiency and completeness reminiscent of Operation Desert Storm in the Gulf. At Dayton, Ohio, an agreement was then forced on the Bosnian Serb commanders – who had by then been abandoned by Serbia itself after the imposition of UN sanctions – by which Bosnia was administratively divided between its various peoples and a UN peacekeeping force sent in with power to implement the agreement by force. At the time of writing, a sort of peace prevails and a sort of reconstruction has been begun, while mass graves of slaughtered Bosnians continue to be discovered.

Warring factions.
The term used throughout the Bosnian war by the 'international community' to denote not only the Serb and Croat militias fighting the multi-ethnic Bosnian army (and, at times, each other), but also the elected government of Bosnia itself.

You can't expect the Rapid Reaction Force to be ready immediately.
British military spokesman, interviewed on BBC Radio 4 Today programme: the formation of force was announced as Serb forces took over 350 UN 'peacekeepers' hostage in May 1995, including the tiny contingent guarding the 'safe haven' of Goradze, which was then abandoned; thousands of its Muslim populace were slaughtered, as was also the case in Srebrenica. NATO ground troops subsequently arrived to impose the terms of the Dayton Agreement.

I would compare the future of the Serbs to the life of Israelis in their state. They are doing their business with a rifle always at their side. That is our destiny.
Ms Bijana Plavsic, who took over the leadership of the Bosnian Serbs from indicted War Criminal Radovan Karadzic at the end of June

1996; quoted in the Los Angeles Times, 5 July 1996.

She is a simple, loyal soldier. You are looking for a person where there is no person. She does what Karadzic tells her.
Bosnian Vice-President Ejup Ganic, who served with Ms Plavsic in the period of 'collective presidency' before the war, on Karadzic's nominated successor, currently accepted by the UN and its peacekeepers as a representative of post-Dayton Bosnia; quoted in the Los Angeles Times, 5 July 1996.

Who am I? Why am I here?
US Vice-Admiral James Stockdale sounds more plaintive then rhetorical as he debates with other vice-presidential candidates on US television in October 1992, during the presidential campaign. Stockdale was the running-mate of H. Ross Perot, who entered the contest as an Independent.

~

My dog Millie knows more about foreign policy than these two bozos.
President George Bush on the qualifications of his Democrat rival, Governor Bill Clinton of Arkansas, and his running-mate, Senator Al Gore, October 1992.

~

It must have been Millie that taught him to roll over and play dead.
Al Gore bites back.

~

Bimbo eruptions.
Shorthand term among Clinton's campaign staff for the unwelcome tendency of their candidate's sexual past to catch up with him during the campaign. Gennifer Flowers, a night-club singer, claimed he had had a long-term extra-marital affair with her; Clinton confessed to a past indiscretion and received the public support of his wife, Hillary.

~

If you'll be my voice today, I'll be yours for the next four years.
Bill Clinton makes his last campaign speech, inhibited by laryngitis, on polling day, 3 November 1992. He won 43 per cent of the popular vote to 38 per cent for George Bush and 19 per cent for Ross Perot.

~

I have nothing else to say. We, we did, if, the, I, I, the stories are just as they have been said. They're outrageous and they're not so.

President Clinton's verbatim reaction, in December 1992, to another Bimbo Eruption: this time, a former secretary, Paula Jones, given leave to sue him over 'lewd and humiliting' sexual services she alleged he made her perform for him while he was Governor of Arkansas; claiming immunity on the grounds of military service as Commander-in-Chief of the Armed Forces, he has so far succeeded in postponing a court hearing until such time as he ceases to be President of the USA. In the meantime, attempts by his political opponents to turn some apparently dubious (and financially unsuccessful) land dealings in Arkansas into another 'Watergate' have, to date, failed to bear fruit.

Reforms mean you can have a big car if you're in the mafia. Reforms mean hard-currency shops for a handful of people who have it. I'm a factory worker. I'll never have a big car or dollars, so reform for me will be when the milk isn't sour, that's all.

Anonymous Russian woman, queueing for food: quoted in The Times, *25 November 1992. The year began with Operation 'Provide Hope', a limited US airlift of medicines and surplus Gulf War food rations to Moscow; as it proceeded, the Rouble became virtually worthless and the mass of the Russian people experienced conspicuous deprivation as the economic reforms, demanded by the International Monetary Fund and the 'Group of Seven' as a prerequisite for Russia's aceptance as a financial and trading partner, took their toll on Russia's exhausted and largely obsolete industrial infrastructure; it seemed that only the organized criminal gangs were able to function efficiently and profitably. In December, President Yeltsin came under pressure from former Communist 'hard-liners' to halt the process, and he was forced to sack his ally and Prime Minister, Victor Gaidar, and replace him with Viktor Chernomyrdin. Ten months later, in September 1993, faced with what looked like an attempted coup d'état by pro-Communist deputies in the Russian Parliament, Yeltsin proclaimed a government by decree and sent the army to shell the building he himself had defended only two years before. Vice-President Aleksandr Rutskoi and Speaker Ruslan Khasbulatov were arrested when the deputies surrendered on 4 October.*

Let the great Russian empire extend once again to its former glory, and let the Russian Army wash its feet in the Indian Ocean.

12 December 1992 Vladimir Zhirinovsky, the fervently nationalistic leader of the inaptly named Liberal Democratic Party, emerges with the largest number of seats in parliamentary elections; a coalition of otherwise less than compatible political groupings was hastily assembled to deny him office.

Membership of the ERM remains at the heart of the Government's economic policy.

Chancellor of the Exchequer Norman Lamont attempts to calm the foreign exchange markets as the UK Treasury spends £15 billion of the nation's currency reserves to buy sterling and maintain it at its ERM entry level; interest rates galloped up to 16 per cent before it was decided, on 16 September 1992 (known afterwards to Europhobic politicans as 'White Wednesday') to 'suspend' Britain's membership of the Exchange Rate Mechanism. The pound was immediately devalued by 30 per cent against the German mark.

~

You can't buck the markets.

A favourite saying of Margaret – now Baroness – Thatcher, much rehearsed during the sterling crisis of September 1992.

~

We give the appearance of being in office but not in power.

Union leader Ron Todd's 1988 aphorism is given new life in Norman Lamont's 'resignation statement': he was sacked as Chancellor on 27 May 1993.

Of course I was economical with the *actualité*.

Former Trade and Defence Minister Alan Clark gives evidence at the 'Matrix Churchill trial' in November 1992. Three directors of Matrix Churchill plc – an Iraqi-owned British company – were accused of breaking Britain's arms embargo on Iraq by exporting machine tools with a dedicated armaments manufacturing capability; the case arose after the 'Supergun Affair' in which UK Customs and Excise prosecuted a British firm for exporting as a piece of oil pipeline part of a huge piece of artillery for

Saddam's arsenal; it turned out the deal had been done with the government's knowledge and tacit approval. The Matrix Churchill defendants' case was potentially damaged when Cabinet ministers, acting on the instructions of the Attorney-General, signed 'Public Interest Immunity Certificates' with the intention of suppressing evidence that the shipment had government approval – indeed, one of the defendants had been working for the British Intelligence Service. The judge overruled the Certificates, and Clarke was called as a witness. He cheerfully admitted that government guidelines had been secretly amended, and that he'd had full knowledge of the whole transaction. The case collapsed, and the Prime Minster ordered an inquiry under the chairmanship of Lord Justice Scott.

I get bit confused when morality is invoked.
Sir Stephen Egerton, Assistant Secretary (Middle East) at the Foreign Office, gives evidence on day 11 of the Scott Inquiry.

I have no knowledge of this at all ... I couldn't read everything that crossed my desk.
Former Prime Minister Baroness Thatcher gives evidence on day 48 of the Scott Inquiry.

One of the charges at the time of course was that in some way I must have known because I had been the Chancellor, because I had been the Foreign Secretary, because I had been the Prime Minister and therefore I must have known what was going on. ... Something that I was not aware that happened suddenly turned out not to have happened.
John Major gives evidence on day 55 of the Scott Inquiry. (See 15 February 1996.)

1992 is not a year I shall look back on with undiluted pleasure. In the words of one of my more sympathetic correspondents, it has turned out to be an 'annus horribilis'.
Her Majesty Queen Elizabeth II, in a speech at the Guildhall on 24 November 1992, looks back on a year that included the divorce of her daughter, the Princess Royal, the formal separation of the Prince and Princess of Wales, the publication of Andrew Morton's book Diana:

Her True Story *with its tales of husbandly neglect and adultery, and wifely attacks of bulimic self-destruction, and a devastating fire at Windsor Castle. It was later announced that Buckingham Palace would be opened to the public in order to raise funds for the castle's restoration, and in February 1993 the Queen offered to start paying Income Tax; her own Inland Revenue accepted.*

A Season of Embarrassment in British Government

There has been a barrage of stories about me in tabloid newspapers ... The stuff about the Chelsea strip is nonsense.
Heritage Secretary David Mellor (dubbed the 'Minister of Fun') resigned on 24 September 1992 after it was revealed that he and his family had holidayed at the expense of Monica Bauwens, the daughter of an official in the Palestine Liberation Organisation; Mellor had previously been a Foreign Office minister with responsiblity for Middle East affairs. In July it had emerged that he had had an affair with Antonia de Sancha, an actress who was quoted as saying he liked to wear the replica kit of Chelsea Football Club in bed.

~

I misjudged. I didn't make a judgement. It was all done third hand.
Conservative Party Chairman Lord MacAlpine reacts to press reports that he accepted donations totalling £440,000 for party funds from Asil Nadir, Chairman of the spectacularly bankrupt Polly Peck International. In May 1993 Nadir, on £3.5 million bail for fraud charges, fled the country from the Compton Abbas airfield in North Dorset; he turned up later in the extradition-free zone of North Cyprus.

~

Don't let the buggers get you down.
Inscription on a watch given to Asil Nadir by Michael Mates MP, junior Northern Ireland minister and confidant of the fugitive entrepreneur. Mates resigned on 24 June 1994.

~

I am absolutely confident that I won't have to resign.
Tim Yeo MP, junior minister at the Department of Environment, 4 January 1994; it was revealed that he had fathered two illegitimate children by different women. The revelation came at a time when the government was running a 'Back to

Basics' campaign concerning, among other things, questions of national 'morality' and the supposedly demoralizing effect on society as a whole of single mothers. He resigned the following day. On 8 February the Tory MP Stephen Milligan suffocated himself during a bizarre auto-erotic act.

~

If any of you have got an A-level, it is because you have worked to get it. Go to any other country and when you have got an A-level, you have bought it.
Michael Portillo MP, Chief Secretary to the Treasury, addresses students at Southampton University on 4 February 1994 and makes a remark later described as having been taken out of context. He went on to become Secretary of State for Defence.

~

The French are a nation of collaborators... Germany's unique contribution to Europe has been to plunge it into two World Wars... The purpose of the government's European policy is to avoid being thrown into some bastardised, federalised, European destiny, actively and fawningly crawling to France and Germany as the lesser countries insult us to the tune of their begging bowls.
Patrick Nicholls MP, Deputy Chairman of the Conservative Party, publishes an article in the Western Morning News, 23 November 1994. He resigned that evening.

~

The Conservative Party has let voters down, been in Government too long, is complacent and has lost its sense of direction. We fail to fulfil promises, are clumsy at implementing policies, and shoot ourselves in the foot.
John Maples, newly-appointed Deputy Chairman of the Conservative Party, writes a memo in November 1994. It was leaked.

~

They're all the same. They're short, they're fat, they're slimy and they're fundamentally corrupt.
Rod Richards MP, junior Welsh Office minister, airs his views on Labour councillors in December 1994. In June 1996, in the midst of his constituency campaign for 'family values' it was revealed that he had had a long-running affair. He resigned.

Northern Ireland – Days of Hope and Despair

The wickedness of this act defies belief.
John Major, 21 March 1993: two children are killed and 50 people injured as two IRA bombs explode in a shopping centre in Warrington, Cheshire: an IRA statement said that it regretted the 'tragic consequences' of its bombs, and blamed the police for not evacuating the area quickly enough. A huge IRA bomb in the City of London the following month killed one person and caused £1 billion damage. On 23 October that year the IRA bombed a fish-and-chip shop in the Shankill Road, Belfast – nine people, including two young girls and one of the bombers, were killed. Two days later, 'Loyalist' terrorists sprayed a pub in Greysteel with bullets, killing seven people. In December, after it was revealed that the government had held secret meetings with senior officials in Sinn Féin, Irish Prime Minister Albert Reynolds joined John Major to issue the 'Downing Street Declaration': an all-party forum was to be established to discuss the constitutional future of Northern Ireland, and Sinn Féin would be welcome to attend if it renounced violence, forever. The first response of the IRA was to carry out three mortar attacks on Heathrow Airport in March 1994.

TIME FOR PEACE – TIME TO GO
Slogan on a wall in Londonderry as the IRA announces a 'complete cessation of military operations' after 25 years of bombings and shootings in which thousands have died, 31 August 1994.
   The British government responded by ceasing armed patrols on the streets of Northern Ireland, and implementing troop reductions, and the broadcasting ban on Gerry Adams and other Sinn Féin spokesmen was lifted. The Irish government began a phased release of IRA prisoners.

We have taken a great step by removing the gun from Irish politics.

Gerry Adams, President of Sinn Féin, 31 August 1994. Repeatedly pressed to confirm that the IRA cease-fire was to be permanent, he would say only that it was 'complete'.

We are beyond the beginning, but we are not yet in sight of the end.

John Major, 31 August 1994. He then raised the issue of 'decommissioning' – the demand that the IRA begin to hand over its arms and explosives, as a sign of good faith. This subsequently became the British government's precondition for admitting Sinn Féin to all-party talks.

We are at the beginning of a new era – all totally and absolutely committed to democratic and peaceful methods of resolving our political problems. That's a very clear, unequivocal statement from Sinn Féin.

Irish Prime Minister Albert Reynolds, September 1994. Visiting the USA that month, Adams was greeted at Boston Airport by Senator Edward Kennedy, who hailed him as a 'courageous leader'. On a visit to the UK on 23 October, Sinn Féin deputy leader Martin McGuinness warned that IRA violence would resume if the 'peace process' did not have a 'satisfactory outcome'.

Another very important part of the jigsaw has fallen into place.

John Major, 13 October, as the three 'Loyalist' terrorist groups, responsible during 25 years for over 900 deaths, announce their own ceasefire to run 'parallel' to that of the IRA.

He had a leadership role. He performed it. And I think the whole of Ireland and the whole of these islands, and I think arguably the whole of the world, is grateful to him for having done it.

Former UK Northern Ireland Secretary Peter Brooke MP, on Gerry Adams: Panorama, BBC TV, January 1995.

I urge Unionists to study it, talk about it, and think of the prize at the end.

John Major recommends the Anglo-Irish peace plan to disaffected Unionist politicians in Northern Ireland, 22 February 1995. Under its terms, the Dublin government would be represented in a Northern Irish legislative assembly; in return, it renounced its constitutional claim to the province. British ministers entered talks with Sinn Féin in May.

I've always been conscious of being Irish. I mean, I sort of – I look Irish. I am Irish.

President Bill Clinton, who invited Gerry Adams to the White House in May 1995 and urged him to 'begin to discuss the decommissioning of weapons' and 'abandon guns for good'. Adams was granted permission to raise funds for Sinn Féin in the USA, amid reports that the IRA was using its ceasefire to plan future terrorist operations.

Your day is over.

Visiting Northern Ireland at the end of November 1995, President Clinton was hosted through the streets of Belfast by Gerry Adams and issued this message to terrorists of all persuasions. US Senator George Mitchell – a Roman Catholic distrusted instinctively by Unionists – chaired discussions in December and recommended the destruction of terrorist weapons as a prelude to all-party talks. Throughout 1995 the IRA carried out 'punishment beatings', ostensibly of alleged drug dealers, as part of its self-appointed role as the 'effective policing authority' in Nationalist areas of Northen Ireland. In January 1996, John Major announced elections for a Northern Ireland Assembly; the beginning of IRA 'decommissioning' was to be the condition of which any elected Sinn Féin members would take their seats.

As far as we're concerned the ceasefires are solid, are holding and will continue to hold.

Dick Spring, Irish Foreign Minister, addresses a news conference in Washington, DC, after talks with President Clinton on 9 February. Sinn Féin had urged him to act on their behalf in

➤

➔

Dayton-style 'proximity talks', since they were prevented, on the 'decommissioning issue' from taking part in direct negotiations with the British and Irish governments.

It is with great reluctance that the leadership of Oglaigh na hEireann announces that the complete cessation of military operations will end at 6 p.m. on February 9, this evening. ... Instead of embracing the peace process the British Government has acted in bad faith, with Mr Major and the Unionist leadership squandering this unprecedented opportunity to resolve the conflict. ... The blame for the failure thus far of the Irish peace process lies squarely with John Major and his Government.

Statement received and broadcast by Radio Telefís Eirann, the Irish broadcasting service. Sixty-one minutes after the stated end of the ceasefire, the IRA carried out a 'military operation' in London's Docklands: a semtex-assisted fertilizer bomb caused millions of pounds worth of damage and killed two men in a newsagent's shop. Further attacks in Britain included a huge bomb under Hammersmith Bridge, which failed to explode, and the bombing of the Arndale Shopping Centre in Manchester during the Euro 96 football championships in June; in early July it carried out an abortive rocket attack on a British Army base in Germany. At the time of writing (July 1996) there have been no IRA bombings in Northern Ireland since the cease-fire ended, though IRA gunmen murdered a policeman in the Republic in June.

My message to the Loyalist paramilitaries at this moment is for heaven's sake, and for the sake of the people of the whole of Northern Ireland, hold anything that you may anticipate doing until such times as the situation becomes clear. I am down on my knees begging.

'Gusty' Spence, who announced the 'Loyalist' ceasefire in October 1994, issues an appeal, 9 February 1996.

GIVE US BACK OUR PEACE
Banner borne at a mass demonstration in Belfast, 25 February 1996.

Several Sinn Féin delegates were elected to the all-party Assembly in May 1996 but have been prevented from taking their seats pending a reinstatement of the IRA ceasefire. Members of the Rev. Ian Paisley's Democratic Unionist Party have disrupted its proceedings in protest at the involvement of Senator Mitchell.

It is not easy for a government by a single act to abdicate its own moral authority, undermine confidence in the police, insult church leaders of the four principal faiths, and boost the aceptability of a terrorist organisation. But last Thursday, a British government managed at one fell swoop to do all four. ... When a government abandons the rule of law in favour of the rule of the mob, one must be very fearful of the long-term consequences.

Former Irish Prime Minister Dr Garret Fitzgerald, writing in the Independent, 13 July 1996. The RUC, enforcing government policy, had prevented members of the Protestant Orange Order from marching with their banners, Lambeg drums and sectarian songs through Nationalist areas in the town of Drumcree and elsewhere. The marchers refused to move from a police barricade and a 'Loyalist' mob then proceeded to attack and firebomb the houses of Roman Catholics, many of whom were rendered homeless. Protestants were driven out of their homes in retaliatory rioting in Londonderry. On 11 July the march was allowed to proceed, a decision which unleashed a wave of rioting and brought more troops to the Province. A bomb destroyed a hotel in the largely Protestant town of Enniskillen; the IRA denied responsibility, but the 'peace process' was reckoned to be at an end and the British government widely discredited as exchanges between it and the government of the Irish Republic were described in Dublin as 'difficult and frank'. On 22 July it was reported that Prime Minister John Major was to hold talks with leaders of the 'Loyalist' paramilitary groups, whose cease-fire was assumed to be still in force.

1993

Shalom, salaam, peace.
President Clinton addresses Israeli Prime Minister Yitzhak Rabin and PLO Chairman Yasser Arafat on 13 September 1993 as the three leaders sign an agreement on the establishment of autonomous Palestinian authorites in Gaza, Jericho and parts of the West Bank; Arafat returned in July 1994 after a 27-year exile. Palestinian police afterwards co-operated with Israeli security forces after a wave of Iranian-inspired bombings carried out by the 'Hamas' terrorist group; in one of the worst attacks, 21 people were killed by a suicide bomber in Tel Aviv on 19 October 1994.

~

There are enemies of the peace process, and they try to hurt us. But violence undermines democracy and must be denounced.
November, 1995: after two years of enduring increasingly vitriolic attacks from extreme right-wing and Zionist opponents for his policy of pursuing peaceful co-existence with his country's Palestinians, Israeli Prime Minister addresses a 100,000-strong peace rally in Tel Aviv's Kings of Israel Square.

~

Don't you think your husband should be wearing a flak jacket at a time like this? – Shh, don't say such things. I don't believe anyone is capable of doing anything like that.
Conversation between Meir Doron and Leah Rabin, the Prime Minister's wife, as the rally comes to an end. (Quoted in Time *magazine.) Rabin had received death threats from Israeli settlers in the occupied territories, accusing him of treachery and apostasy. After the rally, the Prime Minister left by a rear staircase; as he was about to get into his car, a 25-year-old militant*

• •

I know how Liberals love to have meetings, so I'll leave you to it.

Jo Grimond, at the special Liberal Assembly in 1976 to debate the leadership election; died on 24 October 1993, aged 80.

• •

student, Yigal Amir, ducked under a railing and, at point-blank range, killed him with two hollow-pointed bullets from a .22 pistol.

~

Shir Ha-Shalom: 'The Song of Peace'.
Rabin had been singing it minutes earlier, and the bloodstained songsheet was found in his breast pocket.

~

We must vomit from among us those who do not abide by one of the basic rules of society: Thou shalt not kill.
Benjamin Netanyahu, leader of the right-wing opposition Likud Party, condemns the killing: but his party's supporters had been among the most extreme of Rabin's critics. Rabin's deputy, Shimon Peres, took over as Prime Minister, and announced that the government would run its full term until elections fell due at the end of May 1996.

~

I am sorry that citizens of Lebanon were killed. ... The right to defend ourselves is not dependent on anyone's permission.
Israeli Prime Minister Shimon Peres, TV broadcast, 18 April 1996. In retaliation against Hizbollah rocket attacks on northern Israel – and, cynics suggested, with an eye to 'hanging tough' in the election campaign – Peres ordered Operation 'Grapes of Wrath', a week-long bombardment of Lebanon, ostensibly 'targeting guerrilla bases' with the object of ending terrorist harassment from across the Israel-Lebanon border. One thousand air raids were launched, 15,000 artillery shells were fired, and 400,000 Lebanese civilians fled their homes and headed for refugee camps. On 18 April the Qana camp suffered a direct bombardment: over 100 refugees, the majority women, children and old men, were blown to pieces. The operation was a disaster, both in terms of international opinion and on a purely practical level: the rocket attacks did not cease.

~

It's amazing: for decades, each Israeli Prime Minister was as bad for us as every other. But this time our whole future is on the line.
Nabil Shaath, Palestinian Authority Minister for International Relations, May 1996: the Labour Party of Shimon Peres was running neck-and-neck with Netanyahu's Likud in campaign opinion polls.

~

I am looking at where I keep my suitcases, and I feel like packing my bags as

quickly as possible and flying away from here.
Leah Rabin, as Benjamin Netanyahu wins the election with a majority over Peres of 29,507 out of 3.1 million votes cast. He has promised to give Israeli security forces 'complete freedom of action' in Gaza and the West Bank: this would violate the 1993 Agreement.

1994

Let there be justice for all. Let there be peace for all. Let there be work, bread and salt for all. The time for the healing of the wounds has come.
Nelson Mandela, installed as President of South Africa on 10 May 1994 after the African National Congress gained an overwhelming victory in the country's first ever one-person-one-vote elections.

He displayed unswerving loyalty to his party and a deep concern with the welfare of his country. ... I will miss him not only as a formidable opponent but also as a man whom I liked and respected.
Prime Minister John Major's tribute to John Smith, Leader of the Opposition, who died of a heart attack at his London home on 14 May 1994, at the age of 55. He was succeeded, after an election, by fellow-Scotsman Tony Blair.

I am not in favour of minor changes: it serves no purpose.
Bangladeshi author Taslima Nasrin, raised as a Muslim, renounces her faith and calls for a 'revised standard edition' of the Koran: on 4 June a warrant was issued for her arrest as fundamentalists called for her death, and she went into hiding. Sweden granted her political asylum in August.

• •

When the President does it, that means it is not illegal.

Richard Nixon, interviewed by David Frost (1977); died on 22 April 1994, aged 81.

• •

I feel it in my fingers, I feel it in my toes, Love is all around me, and so the feeling grows.
Reg Presley/Troggs – Wet Wet Wet: re-released as the theme song of Four Weddings and a Funeral, the film hit of 1994.

1995-1996

Forceful intervention in Chechenya is unacceptable. If we violate this principle, the Caucasus will rise up. There will be so much terror and blood that afterward no one will forgive us.
Russian President Boris Yeltsin rules out the use of force against the rebel Republic of Chechenya, in August 1994; it appeared that he came under irresistible pressure from his Army chiefs to salvage their 'honour' in the face of the rebellion.

~

The military phase of the Chechen campaign is now effectively over.
Boris Yeltsin, 19 January 1995, after Russian troops destroyed the Parliament building and presidential palace in the capital, Grozny, along with most of the city itself. Yeltsin's announcement was to prove premature.

~

TEN DAYS OF PAIN, IMPOTENCE AND SHAME
The headline in Izvestia after the Russian assault, in January 1996, of the Caucasus hamlet of Pervomaiskoye (pop. 870) where a band of 320 Chechen guerrillas had taken 110 people hostage against their safe passage. The Russian army pounded the hamlet with helicopter gunships and lethal – and crudely indiscriminate – Grad ground-to-ground missiles. After ten days, there was very little of the village left; the government reported 18 hostages missing presumed dead (the true figure was at least twice this), 26 Russian soldiers dead, and 161 rebels dead – the rest escaped.

~

We will see how things turn out. If this accord is violated, we know where to find each other.
As Presidential elections loom, Boris Yeltsin negotiates a truce with Chechen leader Zelinkhan Yandarbiyev, 6 June 1996.

~

I will fight to the bitter end, even if you crucify me. ... I am reminded of Jesus Christ on the way to Golgotha, how he walked through the streets and people spat at him.

Mikhail Gorbachev campaigns in Russia's presidential election, June 1996; he received a little less than 1 per cent of the vote in the first round.

~

I am proud of you, and proud of Russia.

Boris Yeltsin, 4 July 1996: in the second ballot, he won 54 per cent of the vote to 40 per cent for his Communist opponent, Gennady Zyuganov. Yeltsin reappointed his reforming Prime Minister, Viktor Chernomyrdin, and offered Cabinet posts to some of his Communist opponents, who had campaigned in an uneasy alliance with extreme nationalists and religious parties.

———————————

We hate and despise the people who did it. But we're a strong and simple folk. We'll rebuild and roll with this thing.

Oklahoma District Judge Fred Daugherty, 21 April 1995. A 5000 lb fertilizer bomb exploded in a truck parked outside the Alfred P. Murrah federal office building in the state capital, Oklahoma City: 169 people were killed, including 19 children in the employees' day-care nursery, and over 400 were injured. At first it was suspected that the bombing was the work of Muslim terrorists; then followed the arrest of former soldiers Timothy MacVeigh and Terry Nichols, both of whom had links with one of America's many 'freedom militias' – heavily armed groups of right-wing 'survivalists' who reject all Federal government authority and attempt to use the US Constitution to justify their refusal to obey federal laws, particularly those relating to taxation, gun control and racial integration. Another such group is suspected to be behind the derailment of the 'Sunset Limited' Florida–Los Angeles express train on 9 October, in which one person died and 100 were injured.

~

In order to get our message before the public with some chance of making a lasting impression, we've had to kill people. ... Through our bombings we hope to promote social instability in industrial society... and give encouragement to those who hate the industrial system.

A message from the 'Unabomber', behind the intricately-wrought postal-packet bombs that, between 1978 and 1995, killed two people and

injured 22 working in universities, airlines and federal offices. A 'manifesto' was sent by the 'group' to the New York Times in May, with a letter saying that the bombings might cease if it were published; in September, the Times and the Washington Post duly published the 35,000-word mixture of Thoreau-esque musings and apocalyptic ecobabble. In April 1996, the mother and brother of 53-year-old genius and Harvard drop-out Ted Kaczynski cleared out papers in the family home and recognized his style from the printed manifesto; when FBI agents visited his remote cabin in Montana they found a bomb-making factory and a typical 'Unabomber' device nearing completion.

~

If anyone thought the NRA's intention was to paint all federal law-enforcement officials with the same broad brush, I'm sorry.

Wayne LaPierre, Executive Vice President of the National Rifle Association, June 1995, responds to former President George Bush, who resigned his life membership after it issued a fundraising letter describing FBI agents as 'jack-booted thugs... wearing Nazi bucket helmets and black storm-trooper uniforms'. Bush pointed out that a former presidential personal security officer had been killed in the Oklahoma bombing – allegedly carried out by neo-Nazis. The NRA continues to campaign against the recent Federal ban of assault weapons.

~

I wish they'd go in there and shoot them all. It would save the taxpayers a lot of money.

Montana ranch-hand Terry Kastner, 1 April 1996, on an FBI siege of heavily-armed 'Freemen' on a farm called 'Justus Township'; in the event, the affair ended peacefully amidst congratulations from all sides (including those arrested) for its conduct.

Militias were suspected of the bombing at the Olympic Games in Atlanta at the end of July 1996.

———————————

This result puts to rest any question or speculation about the leadership of the Conservative Party.

On 22 June 1995 John Major resigned the job and offered himself for re-election; on 4 July, 218 of his 327 colleagues supported him; 89 voted for the right-wing John Redwood.

~

Today a New Labour Party is being born. Our task now is nothing less than the rebirth of our nation.
Labour leader Tony Blair, 29 April 1996, after winning the support of his party to scrap Clause Four of its Constitution, calling for the 'common ownership of the means of production, distribution and exchange'.

Sure, he did it – but the cops framed him anyway. We all know why, for sure.
Anonymous black American in Pasadena, California, October 1995, in conversation with the author, as the trial of football star and film actor Orenthal James Simpson ('O.J.') for murder of his wife Nicole and her lover Ron Goldman entered its final stages. Simpson had been arrested after a bizarre slow car chase through the Los Angles freeway system, watched by millions live on TV in June 1994.

~

Listen, if I see a nigger in a car with a white woman, I'm gonna pull 'em over and make sure I find something wrong, every time.
The rabid racial prejudice of chief prosecution witness, Los Angeles policeman Lt Mark Fuhrman, did not help the prosecution's case. He had given lengthy interviews to a would-be screenwriter in which he freely expressed his desire to 'beat up all the fucking niggers I can lay hands on' and boasted that he had done so many times in the course of his duties. His words evoked memories of the 1992 Los Angeles riots, triggered by the acquittal – by an all-white jury – of Los Angeles policemen for beating a black drink-driving suspect.

~

If it doesn't fit, you must acquit!
Defence Attorney Johnnie Cochran, in his summing-up to the jury, on the infamous 'bloody glove', allegedly found by Lt Fuhrman in the garden of Simpson's house; the accused had tried it on during the trial and, in a classic coup de theatre, had found it too small. The trial exposed grotesque

• •

I forgive you all.

Harold Wilson's farewell to journalists, (1976); died on 24 May 1995, aged 79.

• •

shortcomings in the procedures of LAPD's under-funded forensic science department; it also emerged that a policeman had carried round a blood sample taken from the murder site for several hours before handing it in for analysis; in that time, it had mysteriously reduced in quantity. The jury took less than four hours to reach its verdict, which the judge, Lance Ito, ruled should be held over to the following day. At 10 a.m. (Pacific Time) on 3 October 1995 O. J. Simpson was pronounced not guilty on both charges. He vowed to 'provide whatever it takes to find the real killers' but, to date, LAPD has not taken him up on his offer.

~

We not only played the race card, we dealt it from the bottom of the deck.
Defence Attorney Robert Shapiro, speaking after the verdict.

~

We chose to call it the credibility card.
Defence Attorney Johnnie Cochran, speaking after Mr Shapiro.

~

If we had God booked and O.J. was available, we'd move God.
TV interviewer Larry King, after the verdict – but public protests, particularly from Women's Groups, kept O.J. off the nation's screens.

What Would Nicole Say?
*Placard carried by a protestor outside Simpson's mansion in June 1996 as the confessed wife-beater hosted a fundraising party for 'spousal abuse awareness'. *

Look, half the time when I see the evening news, I wouldn't be for me, either. [Bill] Sometimes I read stories and hear things about me, and I go, 'Ugh, I wouldn't like her either' [Hillary].
President and Mrs Clinton's way of dealing with record low 'approval ratings' in the wake of Republican victories in both Houses of Congress in 1995. The 'Contract With America' written by Senator Newt Gingrich remains unfulfilled, and the President entered his 1996 re-election campaign with what appeared to be, at the beginning of July 1996, a comfortable lead over Republican rival, Bob Dole.

There were three of us in the marriage, so it got a bit crowded.
The Princess of Wales, interviewed by Martin

Bashir on BBC TV's Panorama *in November 1995, on her estranged husband's relationship with Mrs Camilla Parker-Bowles. She agreed that she had committed adultery with Major James Hewitt.*

~

I think every strong woman in history has had to walk down a similar path, and it's the strength that causes the confusion and the fear. Why is she strong? Where does she get it from? Where is she taking it?
Elsewhere in her Panorama *interview, the Princess echoes the teachings of her psychotherapy counsellor, Susie Orbach.*

~

It cultivates the image of a strong woman, and wanting to be in control of the messages.
The Princess's public relations assistant, Jane Atkinson, explains why her employer leaked details – contended by Buckingham Palace – of her proposed divorce settlement, 29 February 1996.

~

I want to be the queen of people's hearts.
The Princess maps out her future role in the Panorama *interview. In April 1996 she arranged for a TV crew to film her watching a child's open-heart surgery.*

The approach ought to have been to consider what documents the defence might reasonably need and then to consider whether there was any good reason why the defence should not have them. The actual approach, in respect of all documents, seems to have been to seek some means by which refusal to disclose could be justified.
Lord Justice Scott's report into the 'Arms-to-Iraq Affair', published on 15 February 1996, is critical of the 'culture of secrecy' in government; it singled out minister William Waldegrave for criticism for making statements to MPs that he knew to be untrue, and Attorney-General Nicholas Lyall for not knowing the law; however, the overall conclusion of its five thick volumes – in which the 'double negative' was deployed as never before in the English language – seems to have been that, while government ministers knowingly made statements which were untrue and duplicitous,

• •

It's not dying about which I have any great worry, it's not living any more.

François Mitterrand, after chemotherapy treatment (1994); died on 8 January 1996.

• •

they did not knowingly and duplicitously make untrue statements. The Prime Minister welcomed the report as an exoneration of all concerned; nobody resigned, and the government won the vote when the matter was debated in the Commons. The inquiry cost around £5 million.

———————————

Ici pas d'abats Anglais. Mangez Francais.
Sign in a French butcher's shop window, reported in the Daily Telegraph, *21 March 1996: 'Here there is no English offal. Eat French.' The EC banned worldwide exports of British beef after Douglas Hogg, Secretary of State for Agriculture, announced in the Commons that the possibility of a link between BSE, the degenerative brain disease of cattle, and CJD, the degenerative brain disease of humans, 'could not be ruled out'. BSE was first identified in 1988, when the most likely cause was diagnosed as the feeding of sheep-offal to cattle; sheep have suffered a similar disease, called 'scrapie', for at least 200 years.*

~

The problem is not only about contaminated beef but a contaminated Government and their legacy of lies and mistrust. People are not prepared to put their faith in the Government any more.
Harriet Harman MP, Opposition spokesperson on Health, House of Commons, 25 March 1996. The government responded to the EC export ban by using its 'wrecking veto' whenever possible in EC Ministerial Committees. By the end of May, British consumption of domestic beef was at 80 per cent of pre-scare levels.

~

We have interfered with the whole process of nature and what is now happening is one of our worst nightmares.
Professor Tim Lang of Thames Valley University, 22 March 1996.
(The government has announced a slaughter

·····································

Why shouldn't I play God? Anything I do at my age is a miracle.

George Burns, on portraying the Supreme Being in Oh, God; *died on 9 March 1996, aged 100.*

·····································

plan for all cattle over 30 months old; at the time of writing, it has yet to be completed.)

~

The risk of BSE from eating beef [is] infinitesimal *based on the the available data.* Unfortunately, the latter phrase, though scientifically accurate, can be reworked by any journalist to mean almost anything. ... So believe the scientist before you believe the journalist – and, of course, before you believe the politician.

Dr Richard Sharpe of the MRC Reproductive Biology Unit, Edinburgh, Daily Telegraph, *5 June 1996.*

~

She has BSE-pattern Creutzfeld-Jacob disease picked up through hamburgers. Her parents told me she had a penchant for them.

Professor Peter Behan, consultant neurologist, Southern General Infirmary, Glasgow, on a dying 15-year-old patient; quoted in the Daily Telegraph, *27 April 1996.*

~

Fear From The Madding Cow.

Photo caption, Time, *April 1996. The USA banned British beef imports in 1988.*

————————

Evil visited us yesterday. We don't know why, we don't understand it, and I guess we never will.

Ron Taylor, Headmaster of Dunblane Primary School, Perthshire, 14 March 1996: the day after Thomas Hamilton, 43, a failed and locally distrusted leader of 'boys' clubs', walked into the school and fired four handguns into a class of Primary One children in the gymnasium. Sixteen children and their teacher were killed before he killed himself. In evidence given to the subsequent enquiry it became clear that he had intended to open fire while classes 1,2,3 and 4 were in asssembly; he had earlier asked a child when assembly was held, and been given the wrong time.

~

How many parents last night will have clutched their own children to them, looking at them differently and imagining the pain which, for others, is all too real? Politics is silent today. We grieve.

Labour leader Tony Blair speaks for all sides in the House of Commons on 14 March 1996. Dunblane forms part of the constituency of Scottish Secretary Michael Forsyth; Opposition Scottish spokesman George Robertson, who lives in the town, had withdrawn his own son from one of Hamilton's 'clubs'.

————————

Ever since I came back from gaol, not once has she entered my bedroom when I was awake. ... I was the loneliest man during the period I stayed with her.

Nelson Mandela, granted a divorce from his wife Winnie, the self-styled 'Mother of the Nation', on 18 March 1996.

We in Westminster are trying to gentrify the City. We must protect our electoral position which is being seriously eroded by the number of homeless that we have been forced to house. I am afraid that unless something can be done, it will be very difficult for us to keep Westminster Conservative.

Letter from Dame Shirley Porter, then leader of Westminster City Council, to Prime Minister Margaret Thatcher, 1987. On 4 May 1996 the report of the District Auditor, John Magill, found Dame Shirley and five of her former colleagues guilty of gerrymandering in what came to be known as the 'Homes-for-Votes Scandal'; £31.6 million of public money had been used to move likely Labour-voting tenants out of council property, and sell it to likely Tory-voting homeowners. The six were odered to repay the sum involved; Dame Shirley, heir to the Tesco Stores fortune, called the report 'blatantly unfair' and announced that she was taking the case to the High Court.

We have carried out our election in the face of threats and intimidation. We have answered the call of destiny and opened the great door of democracy in Taiwan.

President Lee Teng-hui, re-elected with 54 per cent of the vote in Taiwan's elections on 24 March

1996. He had campaigned on a platform of complete independence for the island; China undertook 'naval exercises' during the campaign, firing dummy missiles over coastal areas.

If you're part of a movement for democracy in Burma, imprisonment is simply an occupational hazard.
Aung San Suu Kyi, 1991 Nobel Peace laureate, released from 5 years' house arrest in July 1995, began hosting 'democracy parties' in her garden in June 1996; the SLORC government arrested people it suspected might be going to them.

It is a long way from the country village in which I was born and brought up but fortunately I will be in the company of a very gracious lady. ... I am sure she is the type of lady who will put any country boy at rest.
Nelson Mandela, Breakfast with Frost, BBC TV, 7 July 1996, looks forward to meeting Queen Elizabeth II during his visit to Britain.

I like it. We won, the end. Leadership. America. Good over evil.
Presidential candidate Bob Dole, quoted in the Independent, 3 August 1996, on the premiere of the film Independence Day.
~

All over the world, men and women come and go, but their organisations remain. There have been many great leaders. I don't expect any change when I go.
President Nelson Mandela of South Africa, June 1996.

Let me be the bridge to a time of tranquility, faith and confidence in action. And to those who say it was never so, that America has not been better, I say, you're wrong, and I know, because I was there. I have seen it. I remember.
Bob Dole accepts the Republican nomination for the presidency, San Diego, California, 15 August 1996.

There will never again be an official salad cream of the Olympic Games.
Michael Payne, marketing director of the International Olympic Committee, quoted in the Daily Telegraph, 5 August 1996. The 1996 Olympiad was noted for its 'fringe festival' of commercial exploitation.

Index of Names

Key: **Bold** numbers indicate that the person is the source of a quotation. Roman numbers indicate that the person is mentioned in a quotation. *Italic* numbers indicate that the person is mentioned in the source notes. <u>Underlined</u> numbers are for mentions in the narrative text.

Index of Events and Themes

Key: Roman numbers are for events/themes mentioned in the quotation or its source. Underlined numbers are for events/themes mentioned in the narrative text.